Let's Talk...

A Pocket Rhetoric

W. W. NORTON & COMPANY

Let's Talk…

A Pocket Rhetoric

SECOND EDITION

Andrea Lunsford
Stanford University

W. W. NORTON & COMPANY has been independent since its founding in 1923, when William Warder Norton and Mary D. Herter Norton first published lectures delivered at the People's Institute, the adult education division of New York City's Cooper Union. The firm soon expanded its program beyond the Institute, publishing books by celebrated academics from America and abroad. By midcentury, the two major pillars of Norton's publishing program—trade books and college texts—were firmly established. In the 1950s, the Norton family transferred control of the company to its employees, and today—with a staff of five hundred and hundreds of trade, college, and professional titles published each year—W. W. Norton & Company stands as the largest and oldest publishing house owned wholly by its employees.

Editor: Marilyn Moller
Project Editor: Christine D'Antonio
Associate Editor: Caroline Fairey Meese
Editorial Assistant: Anthony Cardellini
Managing Editors, College: Kim Yi and Carla Talmadge
Production Manager: Jane Searle
Media Editor: Joy Cranshaw
Media Editorial Assistant: Felicia Jarrin
Media Producer: Lindsey Heale
Ebook Producer: Sophia Purut
Marketing Research and Strategy Director, Composition: Michele Dobbins
Design Director: Rubina Yeh
Design and Illustrations: Doyle Partners
Director of College Permissions: Megan Schindel
College Permissions Specialist: Josh Garvin
Photo Editor: Melinda Patelli
Composition: Brad Walrod/Kenoza Type, Inc.
Manufacturing: Transcontinental—Beauceville

Permission to use copyrighted material is included in the Credits section, which begins on page 595.

ISBN 978-1-324-07075-7

W. W. Norton & Company, Inc., 500 Fifth Avenue, New York, NY 10110
www.norton.com

W. W. Norton & Company Ltd., 15 Carlisle Street, London W1D 3BS
1 2 3 4 5 6 7 8 9 0

As we live, we can learn.
It is important to listen.

RUTH BADER GINSBURG
(1933–2020)

Preface

As I write this preface, we are deep into September—my favorite time of year. Back to school time. Time to welcome new first-year students to our campuses, to our classrooms, and into our hearts. Time to listen to their hopes and dreams and aspirations.

And yet. Increasingly, floods, hurricanes, and wildfires threaten communities across the land. On some of our campuses, concerns about food insecurity and adequate housing loom large. And the deep divisions throughout our society continue to affect the way we regard and care for one another. So listening to our students also means engaging with their genuine fears and anxieties. As they gather to begin a new year, many of them are struggling—feeling fearful about the future, having trouble engaging with their classes or completing their assignments, "doing school" with much enthusiasm or hope.

And yet. It is still the beginning of a new school year. And we go on. As teachers everywhere, and especially teachers of writing, we go on as we always have—making connections with our students by listening, really listening.

Making and sustaining connections has been at the heart of my efforts over the years to meet all students where they are, to stretch out a hand, to listen and to learn, and to provide help where I can. And I've tried to do so not only with my own students, but in the work I do on textbooks—and now in this second edition of *Let's Talk*.

When I first imagined this book, I aimed to provide a short, sweet, and inexpensive little rhetoric that would provide just the guidance today's students need to succeed in writing. But as I dug in, I saw that students didn't just need help with writing: they needed help with engaging in classroom discussions, with listening to and understanding people whose beliefs differed from theirs, with having their say without silencing others. Hence the title, *Let's Talk*, with chapters on **Listening** and **Engaging Respectfully with Others**—

and essays, examples, and epigraphs from over 200 people, making it a book of many diverse voices, some I agree with and some I definitely do not!

And yet. Times change, and the last few years have brought new challenges. Who could have anticipated the advent of generative AI, or the sheer intensity of campus protests that pit student against student? What in this environment could *Let's Talk* do to help? For a start, might it help encourage students to stop shouting and start talking to one another, to get out of their polarized stances and into some real conversation?

That's a goal that led to a new part, on **Speaking with Others**, which includes three new chapters. First comes a chapter on **The Need for Conversation**, which aims to help move students beyond the agonistic debate that's so prevalent today and into open and productive conversation—talking *with* rather than *at* one another. This chapter provides guidelines for conversations across a range of situations, including those that are difficult and contentious, and for letting others speak rather than shouting down people whose ideas they dislike or even loathe.

Then comes another new chapter, **Let's Chat: Using AI Carefully & Ethically**, which aims to guide students as they learn to negotiate the new AI terrain, using it as a tool that can *help* them write rather than as something that writes *for* them, and recognizing what it can and cannot do. Finally comes **Presentations & Podcasts**, which covers kinds of speaking that students are often assigned to do, and that they listen to and do themselves.

And that's not all. We've also added two other new chapters. **The Role of Argument in Our Lives** shows students that argument is central to almost all writing. So this is a go-to chapter that will support them in the many kinds of writing they do, from a personal narrative in sociology to an analysis in history or a lab report in engineering. And a new chapter on **Reviewing** covers a genre many instructors have asked for, and one that provides yet another opportunity for students to grapple with complex ideas and to consider many points of view, with examples from *Gilmore*

Girls to *Killers of the Flower Moon* that we hope will resonate with our students.

And several chapters have been revised. The reporting chapter has been expanded to cover both **Synthesizing & Reporting**, making it one that could serve as a framework for developing a research project. And the chapter on mixing languages and dialects has been broadened to focus on **Using Languages & Dialects Rhetorically**, a chapter that will prompt students to think about their use of language in any (and every!) situation.

You'll also hear many new voices in this book, from Jay-Z to Ethan Mollick, Robin Kimmerer to Dawn Staley, Tommy Orange to Jimmy Santiago Baca—to name only a few. In short, I hope there'll be a lot for you and your students to talk *about* and to talk *with* in this new edition—to talk as a means of connecting and understanding, as a way of sharing, as conversations that will lead to and embody learning.

I'm excited about this book, and about the important new material we've added. And yet. I know that this book will come alive only in the hands of you and your students, and in conversations that will have at least a chance of changing them, and maybe the world they inhabit, for the better.

Acknowledgments

One set of voices echoing in the pages of this book is those of the many friends, colleagues, and reviewers who have prodded, questioned, sometimes heckled, and ultimately inspired me to think harder and more deeply, to identify weak spots (and to improve them), to meet students where they are and to recognize and honor the wisdom and strengths they bring with them into our classrooms. In fact, one hallmark of this book is its multivocality, its inclusion of and attention to a wide range of diverse and lively voices. Among these is my editor, the inimitable Marilyn Moller; for almost forty years (and counting!), Marilyn's ingenuity, tough-mindedness, and sheer brilliance have challenged and inspired me to reach beyond my grasp, to try and try—and then try again. We often joke that we are "two women with one brain," meaning that our partnership has enriched my thinking and my life, every day. One of Marilyn's many strokes of genius led us to the world-renowned graphic designer Stephen Doyle, whom she somehow convinced to design *Let's Talk*. His consummate artistry and razor-sharp wit are on display in the cover designs and throughout the book, and we are profoundly grateful for his contributions to this project.

We are also fortunate to have the support of a magnificent team at Norton, starting with Christine D'Antonio, who consistently goes above and beyond, and has skillfully guided this book from manuscript to final pages, improving it immensely along the way. Next comes Jane Searle, who has produced the book beautifully and, miraculously, on time—and contributed both her words and image to the book as well.

And very special thanks to Debra Morton Hoyt, Rubina Yeh, and Michael Wood for overseeing the entire design of this book, and to Tyson Cantrell for the whimsical interior design, one that has made this book easy to use.

Many others have given their time and talent to this project. Special thanks to Melinda Patelli and Josh Garvin for securing permission for the many images and texts. And we owe an especially big thank-you to Claire Wallace for her excellent work on *InQuizitive for Writers* and *Let's Teach*—and for truly heroic work on the MLA and APA chapters. Big thanks as well to Caroline Fairey Meese for her help finding (and editing) good examples and images, and to Anthony Cardellini, for assistance on so many things both large and small.

We're similarly grateful to Joy Cranshaw and Lindsey Heale for all they've done for media, to Sophia Purut for all she's done for the ebook, and especially to Kim Yi for making sure everything ran smoothly. Thanks also go to Jodi Beder for her very careful copy-editing, Mary Kanable for proofreading, and Eric Chernov for his work updating the index.

Thanks as well to Michele Dobbins, Elizabeth Pieslor, Heidi Balas, Sarah Purnell, Ryan Schwab, and Emily Frankenberger for all they've done and will be doing to introduce *Let's Talk* to teachers across the country—and as always to Erik Fahlgren and the fabled Norton travelers: they rock!

As always we are grateful to Ann Shin, Mike Wright, and Julia Reidhead for their unwavering and enthusiastic support for this book.

And I am especially grateful to the many colleagues who reviewed *Let's Talk* for their generous and astute comments and suggestions:

Vanita Adams, Northwest Mississippi Community College; Whitney Jordan Adams, Trident Tech; Amand Anderson, West Kentucky Community and Technical College; Dustin Atkinson, California Lutheran University; Cynthia Bailin, College of Southern Nevada; Iva Balic, Harrisburg Community College; Jessica Lynn Bannon, University of Indianapolis; Marc Barrington, Green River College; Ben Batzer, Truman State; Larry Beason, University of South Alabama; Greg Belliveau, Capital University; Alice Bendinelli, Southwestern College; Kris Bigalk, Normandale Community College; Kristie Boston, Lone Star College; Janice Brantley, University of Arkansas at Pine Bluff; Martin Brick, Ohio Dominican University; April Bristow-Smith, Nash Community College; Deborah Brothers, Lincoln Land Community College; Camy Brunson, South Plains College; Kendra Bryant, NC A&T State; Elizabeth Buchanan, Porterville College; Adam Burgess, College of Southern Nevada; Ginny Callahan, Northeast Community College; Catherine Childress, Lees-McRae College; Scott Chiu, California Lutheran University; Billy Clem, Waubonsee Community College; Janet Cobb, Austin Community College; Daniel Compton, Midlands Tech; Ginny Crisco, Cal State Fresno; Bruce Crissinger, University of Akron; Kimberly Crowley, Bismarck State College; Heather Dail, University of South Alabama; Debra Danielsen, Cal State Fullerton; Jill Darley-Vanis, Clark College; Yvette de la Vega, Cal State Northridge; Sarah de Villiers, Austin Community College; Amy Dennis, Collin College–Wylie; Jane Dougherty, Southern Illinois University; Sarah Duerden, Arizona State; Shanna Early, Pepperdine University; Fay Ellwood,

Hope International University; Gregory Emilio, Kennesaw State; Kevin Ferns, Woodland Community College; Ginger Fray, Lone Star College; Elizabeth Gaffney, Westchester Community College; Dane Galloway, Ozarks Technical Community College; Mallory Garcia Grismer, Hope International University; Joseph Gaudiana, SUNY–New Paltz; Melissa Goldthwaite, Saint Joseph's University; Pamela Haji, Bergen Community College; Andrew Hamilton, College of Southern Idaho; Amara Hand, Norfolk State; Brian Harrell, University of Akron and University of Wisconsin–Green Bay; Alexis Hart, Allegheny College; Heather Hill, Northwest Missouri State; Brigitte Hoarau, Georgia Gwinnett College; Max Hohner, Eastern Washington University; Corrina Honeycutt, Trident Tech; Christy Jickling, Trident Tech; J. Angie Johnson, Bethany Lutheran College; Margaret Johnson, Idaho State; Nicole Kenley, Baylor University; Vincent Kmetz, Western Connecticut State; Kim Lacey, Saginaw Valley State; Cheri Larsen Hoeckley, Westmont College; Kimberly Lewis, Moorpark College; Santiago Longoria, University of Texas at San Antonio; Travis Matteson, Alfred State; Kate McCahill, Santa Fe Community College; Jolivette Mecenas, California Lutheran University; L. Adam Mekler, Morgan State; Annie Mendenhall, Georgia Southern University; Trevor Meyer, Northwest Missouri State; Anna Mills, City College of San Francisco; Rebecca Mitchell, Northwest Mississippi Community College; RJ Murphy, Washington State–Pullman; Ryan Naughton, Arizona State; Silvia Neves, Moorpark College; Matt Norman, Vincennes University; Amy Novak, Cal State Fullerton; Olesya Ostapenko, University of Wisconsin–Whitewater; Shelley Palmer, Catawba College; Lynn Pattnosh, College of Southern Idaho; Elisabeth Pitts, Coastal Carolina Community College; Richard Potsubay, Green River College; Lynne Purtle, Western Connecticut State; Teresa Purvis, Lansing Community College; Rhea Ramey, University of Tampa; Anne Rennick, Santa Fe Community College; Elizabeth Rhoades, University of Akron; Jennifer Riske, Northeast Lakeview College; Tim Roberts, University of Louisville; Lisa Roddy, University of South Alabama; Melissa Rohrer, Kansas Wesleyan University; Kim Russell, West Kentucky Community and Technical College; Cheryl Saba, Cape Fear Community College; Anthony Sams,

Ivy Tech Community College; Scott Sandler, Gavilan College; Sherri Sawicki, Cal State Fullerton; Renee Scariano Willers, Oxnard College; Hogan Schaak, Idaho State; David Seelow, College of Saint Rose; Denise Sharrock-Mueller, Saint Mary's University of Minnesota; Dixie Shaw-Tillman, University of Texas at San Antonio; Danielle Shorr, Chapman University; Marcia Smith, Salt Lake Community College; Nicole Solis, Cal State Northridge; Claudia Springer, Framingham State; Ellen Stenstrom, Indiana University–Bloomington; Rachel Stroup, Capital University; Ashley Supinski, Penn State–Lehigh Valley; Margaret Teichman, Trident Tech; Melissa Toomey, Temple University; Chad Walden, Montcalm Community College; Hope Walker, Kennesaw State; Rob Watkins, Idaho State; Suzanne Webb, Southwestern College; Amy Whitson, Ozarks Technical Community College; Leigh Ann Williams, Georgia Southern University; Angela Williamson-Emmert, University of Wisconsin–Oshkosh; Paul Wise, University of Toledo; Martha Witt, William Paterson University; Shane Wood, University of Central Florida; Myndalynn Word, Pellissippi State; Christivel Zulu, Southern Illinois University.

And my deepest thanks to the many students whose writing animates this book. Their voices bring fresh, diverse, and provocative perspectives, and it has been my great pleasure to listen to—and to learn from—them. I thank Audrey Ashdown, Appalachian State; Yazmin Carbajal, Sonoma State; Wesley Cohen and Stephanie Pomales, both of UC Davis; Trey Connelly, Jackson Parell, and Lauren Rose Reyes, all of Stanford; Colin Flanagan, Brandon Hernandez, and Jack Long, all of Ohio State; Sam Forman, Grinnell; X González, Marjory Stoneman Douglas High School; Melissa Hicks, Lane Community College; Julia Johnson and Taylor Jordan, both of North Carolina A&T; Gabriela Moro, Notre Dame; Olivia Steely, University of Missouri–St. Louis; and Eli Vale, Texas A&M–San Antonio.

Finally, I want to offer thanks to those whose scholarship and leadership I deeply admire and from whom I have learned so much over the years: friends and colleagues Samy Alim, Kendra Bryant,

Jennifer Cognard-Black, the late beloved Lisa Ede, Cheryl Glenn, Melissa Goldthwaite, Shirley Brice Heath, Susan Jarratt, Jamila Kareem, Shirley Logan, Karen Lunsford, Aja Martinez, Jaime Mejia, Beverly Moss, Roxanne Mountford, Krista Ratcliffe, Jackie Royster, and Geneva Smitherman. Beloved partners at Stanford Adam Banks, Marvin Diogenes, and Christine Alfano. The Next/Gen and Bread Loaf Teacher Network group and La Casa Roja, inspired and led by Dixie Goswami, Lou Bernieri, Tom McKenna, Ceci Lewis, and Rex Lee Jim. Khirsten Scott, whose work to establish and maintain the DBLAC (Digital Black Lit and Composition) group continues to inspire me. And so many brilliant writers and thinkers whose work continues to challenge me in all the best ways: April Baker-Bell, Lorena German, Susan Jarratt, Carmen Kynard, Lou Maraj, Alexis McGee, Gwendolyn Pugh, Shauna Shapiro, Susan Thomas, and David Wandera. Because of you, I am learning still.

Andrea Lunsford

Resources

Like the book itself, the resources that accompany *Let's Talk* provide just enough detail, for instructors and students alike, while remaining brief and to the point.

THE LETSTALKLIBRARY offers a wealth of online readings, sortable by theme, genre, and medium. Each reading is accompanied by a headnote and prompts that guide students to analyze, to discuss, to reflect, and to respond to in writing. The *LetsTalkLibrary* offers readings in a variety of media, with new, up-to-the-minute selections posted twice per year.

THE EBOOK allows highlighting and note-taking to help students understand, engage with, and respond to what they read, and instructors can share their own models of engaged reading with students using the instructor annotation tool. Short animations and new author videos are now embedded within the ebook to reinforce the guidance provided in the text with additional examples, contexts, and real world applications. Norton ebooks can be viewed on all devices and are born-accessible, with content and features designed from the start for all learners. Ebook access comes with all new print copies of this book or can be purchased directly from digital.wwnorton.com/letstalk2.

INQUIZITIVE FOR WRITERS allows students to practice writing skills in a low-stakes, feedback-driven environment. Interactive questions help students to explore writing processes and genres, practice sentence editing, and apply good research habits, building their confidence at all stages of the writing process. The activities are adaptive, so students receive additional practice in the areas where they need more help; and explanatory feedback and direct links to relevant sections in the *Little Seagull Handbook* offer advice precisely when it's needed. Access to *InQuizitive for Writers* and the *Little Seagull Handbook* is included with all new copies of *Let's Talk* and can be integrated directly into most campus learning management systems.

 **THE LITTLE SEAGULL HANDBOOK.** Access to the *Little Seagull* ebook is included with all new copies of *Let's Talk*—or the print book can be packaged with *Let's Talk* for a discount, providing the help all students need on punctuating and editing what they write—and the help L2 students need on using articles, prepositions, phrasal verbs, and idioms. Whether they need help analyzing a text, creating a works-cited list, or knowing where to put a comma, these two little paperbacks will be there to help.

 VIDEOS. A new collection of author videos, along with Norton's animated composition videos, are embedded in the Second Edition ebook with short contextualizing introductions. Informed by feedback from hundreds of composition instructors, topics include writing processes, rhetorical situations, specific kinds of writing, the importance of listening, lateral reading strategies, and more.

A PLAGIARISM TUTORIAL, now with coverage of generative AI, explains why plagiarism matters, what counts as plagiarism, and how to avoid plagiarism—and concludes with a short quiz to assess what students have learned.

 **LET'S TEACH!** Available in both print and PDF formats, with teaching advice for each chapter and reading in the text. Brief like the student book, this guide includes: classroom activities and sample writing assignments for every chapter in the rhetoric. Written by Andrea Lunsford herself, this little book is full of stories, suggestions, and advice from her own 50 years in the classroom.

 THE NORTON TEACHING TOOLS SITE offers a comprehensive collection of materials for teaching first-year writing with downloadable and customizable sample assignments, peer-review templates, rubrics, model student essays, and more. Practical guidance from instructors across the country gives suggestions for everything from developing a syllabus to responding to student writing to embracing equity-minded teaching. The Norton Teaching Tools site searchable and can be filtered by chapter or by resource type, making it easy to find exactly what you need..

All resources can be found at **digital.wwnorton.com/letstalk2**.

Contents

Synthesizing & Reporting   205

5 LANGUAGE & STYLE / Get Attention

How to Use This Book

You could look it up.

—JAMES THURBER

Many people attribute the above statement to Casey Stengel, the late great manager of the New York Yankees. But if in fact you do look it up, you'll find that it comes from the title of a short story written by James Thurber. Whoever said it first, it works for this book. Whether you're trying to figure out how to conclude an essay, fact-check an outlandish statement, or come up with a good title, *Let's Talk* is here to help. And whatever the advice or help you're looking for, here are various ways you can look it up.

Brief menu. If you're looking for a specific chapter, check the Brief Menu on the inside front cover. If you're looking for a specific section of a chapter, look in the Contents on pages xvii–xxix.

Glossary/index. The fastest way to find something in any book is with the index, and this book combines the glossary and the index where you'll find both the definitions of key terms and concepts and the pages where you'll find more detail. Words highlighted in RED are all defined there, and many of the definitions include enough detail that you'll find all you need there.

Color-coded organization. The various parts of this book are color-coded for easy reference: green for the INTRODUCTION, turquoise for the RHETORIC chapters, orange for the WRITING chapters, gold for the READING chapters, blue for the RESEARCH chapters, pink for MLA, light blue for APA, blue-green for LANGUAGE & STYLE, tan for DESIGN, purple for MEDIA, and red for the GLOSSARY/INDEX.

Writing guides. Chapters 9 to 15 cover eight kinds of writing that college students are often assigned to do, along with essays written by students demonstrating each kind of writing.

Index of common kinds of writing. Whatever kind of writing you are assigned or simply decide to do, you'll find guidance in this book. Inside the front cover flap, you'll see a list of commonly assigned kinds of writing and where you'll find help in this book.

A roadmap for doing research on the back flap refers you to pages in the book you'll want to consult when doing research.

MLA and APA guidelines. If you need to document sources, turn to Chapters 22 for MLA style and 23 for APA. Each chapter provides color-coded templates that show what information to include, along with documentation maps showing where to find that information. Directories in the back of the book will lead you to the specific examples you need. You'll also find a full MLA-style research essay on page 420 and an APA-style essay on page 462.

The LetsTalkLibrary. Here you'll find an online collection of essays, articles, op-eds, videos, speeches, and more—all searchable by theme, genre, and medium. Check it out at **letstalklibrary.com**.

Editing what you write. This book comes with digital access to both *The Little Seagull Handbook* and *InQuizitive for Writers*. You'll find help with sentence-level editing in the *Little Seagull* and game-like practice editing common errors and working with sources in *InQuizitive*. Access is free with all new print copies and can be activated on the registration card included in the book. You can also purchase access at **digital.wwnorton.com/letstalk2**.

Introduction: Stop! Look! Listen! and Write!

Caitlin Clark and Angel Reese Deserve Better
—*THE NEW YORK TIMES*

Fans Booing McDonald's Halloween Boo Baskets
—*THE COLUMBUS DISPATCH*

Wildfires Raging in California and Colorado
—*NPR*

Headlines like these jostle with hundreds of others vying for our attention, all too often leaving us out of breath just trying to keep up with "breaking news." And while these three headlines report actual, factual information, much of the "news" that reaches us is based on misinformation and oddball conspiracy theories that aim at nothing so much as creating divisiveness, stoking fears, and inciting distrust. It's enough to make us want to throw up our hands and just tune out. But I say: resist that urge!

If we have ever needed to put our critical thinking caps on, to take a deep breath, to *stop, look,* and *listen,* this is it. For all the junk that clogs our news feeds and inboxes, there's much of real importance to think about, to read about, to talk about—and yes, to write about. And that's what this book will help you do. To talk about these and other important issues with others, including those whose views differ from yours—and to listen to what they say, respectfully and with an open mind. To research topics and issues you care about as a matter of inquiry, searching for multiple perspectives rather than just for data to support what you already believe. And of course to write—as a way to explore ideas, to respond to something you've read or heard, to report on a topic you've researched or argue a position you want others to think about. In fact, thinking and writing almost always go hand in hand: as one of my students put it, "I really can't think without a pen in my hand—or a mouse." This book is here to help you do all that.

Stop!

In the face of so many urgent issues, it seems especially important to hit the pause button long enough to look very closely at these issues in all their immediate complexity. In other words, to resist the urge to rush from one tweet to another, one headline to the next. Instead, we need to slow down to a crawl, and then to a halt: close observation and real understanding take time and patience—they can't be done on the fly. So turn off your devices, put distractions aside, and practice being still and open to what is happening around you.

Look!

We all have ways of seeing the world, some of which are so deeply ingrained that we're not even aware of them. So it's especially important to understand them, to look at where they come from, and to ask if they really reflect values we want to embrace. *We need to look at ourselves* as clearly as possible—our age, race, ethnicity, religion, gender identity, sexual orientation, political affiliation; where we live, where we work and play, where we go to school, what interests we pursue—and ask how these factors lead us to see and understand the world from a certain position, and how that position keeps us from seeing the world as others from different backgrounds see it. This kind of up close and personal looking at ourselves is not easy. But it is necessary if we are to recognize and understand—and acknowledge—the role we may be playing in going along with the status quo, and even in perpetuating unjust systems.

> Your assumptions are your windows on the world. Scrub them off every once in a while, or the light won't come in.
>
> ALAN ALDA

Consider the coronavirus, for instance. How do we understand competing beliefs about protecting people's health and respecting the rights of those who want to make their own decisions about their health, about whether or not to vaccinate, about something as simple as whether or not to wear a mask? The covid pandemic may now seem to be in the distant pass, but as new variants continue to emerge, what are our responsibilities—to ourselves, our families, and our fellow citizens? And what can we actually do, what actions can we take?

Such choices, though often unconscious, reveal what we pay attention to and how they affect and limit what we see—and also what we read. So as a reader, you first need to be aware of how your preferences and ways of seeing the world lead you to value (and trust) some things and not others, and to think critically about what that means for what you know—and what you don't know. Second, you need to learn to pay close attention to what you read, especially when the stakes are high. Most of all, you need to read with an open mind, saying "maybe" to ideas you're not sure about and attempting to understand them before saying "no" or rejecting them. It means looking closely at texts you might once have rejected, giving them a chance to make their points to you, and being open to the idea that they just might be right. When you read in this way, you are actively reading to understand, to learn, and to respond thoughtfully to what someone else thinks.

Listen!

Where do you get most of your news? *Facebook*? *TikTok*? Take some time to switch gears and listen for half an hour or so to a news source you don't normally pay attention to—or even resist listening to (MSNBC, say, or Fox News). *Pay attention to* how *you are listening*: With sources you like, do you accept what you hear without questioning or even thinking about what they say? And with sources you don't like, are you listening with a chip on your shoulder, looking for ways they're wrong? All of us have such patterns of listening, so it's important to get a sense of where your listening biases lie and to keep them from clouding your good judgment.

In addition, we all need to listen consciously and critically, doing the kind of listening that rhetoric professor Krista Ratcliffe calls "rhetorical listening." This kind of listening means opening yourself up to the views of others, even those with whom you disagree, and really hearing what they have to say. It means taking their views seriously, listening to really understand what they're saying.

> We have to listen to other people, so that *we* and *they* may lay *our* stories alongside one another's.
>
> KRISTA RATCLIFFE

This is the kind of listening that one student did when he read a series of *Facebook* posts attacking a politician in his Navajo community who "proudly supports" Donald Trump. Rather than joining them and screaming out "hate speech," he responded to those posts with a call for listening and understanding. As he listened more carefully to this politician, he said:

> I began to understand more about why she supports what we don't like. In her positions, I have to applaud her for having a clear and civil stance. She doesn't come off to me as aggressive like the comments have labeled her. We need to remember that she is also a loving mother, aunt, and relative in the community. Creating memes to "Put her in her own casket" is taking it too far! You don't understand what this kind of a violent witch hunt can do to a person. I am certain she means good.
>
> Furthermore, social media has its good and bad sides, and learning more about an issue before posting that next hate speech is the

best method for starting a proper conversation. I know that discussing politics is not all rainbows and butterflies. I get it. She is controversial. But taking time to at least know where she's coming from may help you understand her politics (even if, like me, you disagree). After understanding her stance, you can proceed to make a critique that's not violent or threatening.

—KYLE WHITE

This post is a product of sound rhetorical listening, of listening as a way of coming to understand another person. So the next time you're talking with someone with whom you deeply disagree, take a tip from Kyle White: don't attack, don't insult, don't hate. It's always better to stop and listen.

Think!

The listening and reading this book advocates, and the writing that grows out of them, go hand in hand with *thinking*—not just skimming over words and passages, but putting your mind to it and asking questions at every turn. But what does that really mean? It means paying very close attention and then asking serious and often detailed questions about what you are hearing or reading. In other words, it means not just agreeing or going along with it, but challenging it to convince you.

> I don't write to make readers think like me. I write to make them think.
>
> ANNA QUINDLEN

One student who was taking a course examining cultural stereotypes started wondering where his own largely negative impressions of Iran as a country of religious zealots came from. Since he was reading Marjane Satrapi's *Persepolis* for another course, he decided to make some notes about how Satrapi represents Iran, her home country—and he quickly saw that her perceptions of Iran differed from those he held. This careful reading led him to dig further, looking back to the time of the 1979 Iranian revolution, which overthrew the US-backed regime of the shah. Carefully and methodically, he read coverage of Iran in national newspapers and found that

> *New York Times* reporting from 1979 reveals a narrative emphasizing a solidly unified, radical religious movement that brought the Islamic Republic into reality. Such a narrative laid the foundation for characterizations of Iran by future leaders, whether by President Bush in his famous claim that Iran was part of an "axis of evil" or by Iranian Mahmoud Ahmadinejad when he spoke of Holocaust denial in the name of Iran.
>
> —DREW AGUILAR

This analysis led to further reading on Iranian history and especially on the diversity within Iran, a diversity that contradicted the monolithic stereotype he saw reflected in the *Times* coverage. At the end of his investigation, this student had not only learned a great deal about Iran; he had also thought about how narratives about entire countries can build up in our minds almost without our even noticing—and he was able to bring this new understanding to his reading of Satrapi's famous graphic novel as well. Best of all, he was well prepared to write essays in both of his classes that drew on the knowledge he had gained and on his growing understanding of how cultural stereotypes get established and reinforced.

Act!

Taking time to stop, look, listen, think, and write can bring us only so far. Sooner or later we need to roll up our sleeves and do something—to take some kind of action. When 17-year-old Trayvon Brown, who had organized a protest following the death of George Floyd, found a burning cross propped up on the lawn of his home in Monroe, Virginia, he was so shocked and taken aback that the event stopped him in his tracks. What deeply held beliefs could have propelled such a hateful and violent attack? As he looked at the situation in his community and listened to those on both sides of the debate surrounding police violence, Brown came to the conclusion that he had to do something—to lead a second protest. Here's what he said to those who joined him as the protest began:

Stand up, speak up, and speak out!
JOHN LEWIS

> This is your chance, young people. Y'all complain about the laws? Go change those laws. You don't have to destroy anything. You don't have to tear down statues.
>
> —TRAYVON BROWN

As news of that second protest march had spread, counterprotesters were there as well, some waving Confederate flags, some armed. Law enforcement officials gathered to try to keep the two sides apart, as those on both sides began shouting angrily at each other. With tensions at a boiling point, Brown took another action: he knelt, raised his arm, and began shouting "I love you" to those on the other side. He was soon joined by the rest of the protesters, who did the same—thus defusing the situation and leading to a peaceful conclusion to the march.

Remember the Golden Rule

Trayvon Brown's actions call to mind the Golden Rule, of "doing unto others as you would have them do unto you." Showing respect and concern for others and for their views will encourage them to reciprocate, and in so doing will pave the way for establishing common ground that can move a conversation forward. And doing so is pretty simple, even if sometimes challenging: you demonstrate concern when you take other people's feelings and thoughts and needs seriously, and respect when you acknowledge them as equals in conversation, when you listen to what they say carefully and with an open mind, and when you are truthful.

Such concern is especially necessary now, as raging wildfires and hurricanes have destroyed thousands of homes and flattened or flooded whole towns, and as the effects of climate change are more visible and frightening than ever. Such times call for us to think beyond our individual selves, to recognize that we are all in this together, and to take action not just for ourselves but for the greater good of all. In short, we need to focus less on "I" and more on "we," knowing that in helping—and respecting—others we will in the long run be helping everyone.

When "I" is replaced with "we," even illness becomes wellness.
MALCOLM X

This kind of thinking is the very opposite of the kind of trolling, cyberbullying, and harassment that often takes place online—actions that seek to disrupt, to attack, to sow discontent and distrust and even fear. This is not to say you cannot disagree with someone; just keep in mind that you can disagree without being disagreeable, much less frightening or disruptive.

We all need, then, to stop, look, and listen—to step back and think hard about how we communicate with others, about how respectfully we listen and how we show that we have their best interests at heart. But we can't stop there. Eventually, we will need to engage with the issues most important to us and to other people, including those who do not share our views as well as those who do.

Write!

This kind of engagement will often involve writing. Taking notes and trying to capture in words what you've heard someone say, for example, is a very good way to help understand it better, and to remember it. And just think of the role that writing plays in the courses you're taking, from preparing reports to analyzing issues, summarizing and synthesizing information drawn from many sources, developing a script to use in an important oral presentation, and reflecting on the ideas and perspectives of others—all writing. And don't be surprised if you find that as you write, your thinking gets sharper, your ideas more focused, your message more clear: you are, in fact, writing yourself into the role of a college student. Then, as you move toward your major, absorbing its vocabulary and methods and style, you are writing yourself into that discipline, becoming a member of its intellectual community.

> How can I know what I think till I see what I say?
> E. M. FORSTER

And then there's the role that writing plays well beyond the classroom. Think about posters and signs proclaiming No Justice, No Peace! Make America Great Again! I Can't Breathe! Vote!—these are all words, yes, but they are actions as well. Think about the writing you do on social media—*Instagram*, *Facebook*, and *X* all connect you to friends and family as well as to people you might never otherwise know. Podcasts and *YouTube* videos—these allow you to put the power of your spoken voice and your personality to work in getting your messages across.

No matter what kinds of writing you do, you'll be aiming to reach particular audiences in particular contexts and for particular reasons. That means you'll be listening and thinking hard about what others say. Thus moving purposely from listening to thinking, and from thinking to writing, is a kind of dance that good communication calls for—and the more we practice that dance, the better we will get.

Stopping, looking, listening, thinking, taking action. None of the steps in this dance are easy or simple, especially in times as contentious as those we face today. But we need to try—and to recognize that our differences are some of our most valuable assets. We won't know about those differences, however, without being open to them, without opening ourselves to the thoughts and ideas and beliefs of others. This book is one attempt to begin and sustain such conversations. So—let's talk!

REFLECT! Fox News host **Laura Ingraham** once famously criticized **LeBron James** for commenting on political issues, saying that he should "shut up and dribble." Her comment got instant blowback from many, including James and other athletes, who posted on social media with the hashtag #wewillnotshutupanddribble. Ingraham and James are coming from completely different places in terms of their personal beliefs and ideologies, but how might this exchange have gone differently had they at least attempted a face-to-face conversation—and first taken time to stop, look, listen, and think?

Let's Talk...

A Pocket Rhetoric

1 Listening

Listening to others, especially those with whom
we disagree, tests our own ideas and beliefs.
It forces us to recognize, with humility,
that we don't have a monopoly on the truth.

—JANET YELLEN

If you want to be listened to, you should put in time listening.

—MARGE PIERCY

hy would a book titled *Let's Talk*
begin with a chapter on listening?
That's a good question, and it has an
important answer. Talking is (at least) a two-way
street: when you talk, you're talking *to* someone,
and you want that someone to listen, to hear what
you're saying, whether you're calling a clinic to
make a doctor's appointment or talking confidentially
with your best friend about whether to break off a
relationship. You want—and sometimes need—
to be listened to. You can probably think of times
when you've felt like you weren't being listened to,
or when the person you were talking with was only
halfway listening.

Elizabeth MacGregor certainly has such memories. As the first person in her family—and one of only two students in her high school graduating class—to go to college, she remembers feeling insecure when she first arrived at college. "Do I really belong here?" she wondered. Faced with some daunting assignments in the first weeks of fall term, she asked for advice from an older student in her dorm. That person was sympathetic, but he was checking email and was somewhat distracted, responding, "Don't worry; you'll be fine." She also went to her history instructor's office hours, hoping to get some guidance for doing the first assignment. He merely encouraged her to "start on the assignment early" and wished her luck; he didn't seem to hear what she was really asking for, which was concrete advice on how to address the assignment. Reflecting on these experiences two years later, MacGregor said, "They were well meaning, but they just weren't listening to me."

Or you may be part of a group that feels ignored or not listened to. That was certainly the case for more than two hundred women gymnasts who, for decades, had been reporting sexual abuse by Larry Nassar, doctor for the US gymnastics team. Their reports were ignored: very few people with the power to stop Nassar's abuse were willing to listen, much less to speak up on their behalf. But as the #MeToo movement gained momentum in 2016, hundreds of gymnasts, including gold medalist Simone Biles, raised their collective voices to speak out about his crimes. Coaches and USA Gymnastics officials began to listen, and Nassar was fired, charged, and convicted. This series of events led to a shift in the culture of gymnastics as coaches began to listen to their athletes. So in 2021, when Biles told her coach she could not continue in the Tokyo Olympics, the coach listened, and had Biles's back when many commentators and fans attacked her decision to withdraw as cowardly—and much worse. At this point, Biles needed to listen to her own inner voice and *not* to the yammering critics. In short, there are times to listen—and times not to.

Many of us, however, need to listen more, not less. NBA star Draymond Green admits that he sure does. During the 2019 NBA

> Listening is the ultimate sign of respect. What you say when you listen says more than any words.
>
> THOMAS FRIEDMAN

finals, Green—known for his constant chatter on and off the court—decided he'd been doing too much talking and not enough listening. In particular, he decided to listen to his mother and his fiancée, both of whom told him he needed to learn some self-discipline and especially to stop screaming at the referees. As Green put it:

> Sometimes I'm not mindful, and I'll get a tech and that will just kill the energy of our team. I've really been focused and locked in on that, and I realized I got to a point where I was doing more crying than playing. I'm sure it was disgusting to watch, because I felt disgusting playing that way.
>
> —DRAYMOND GREEN

Sometimes we all need to take a good look at our behavior to see if we are doing more talking than listening.

Think of the times when you have most needed someone to listen—openly and carefully and intently—to something you needed to say: when you were talking through a serious conflict with a family member, for instance, or when you were trying to

Draymond Green, frustrated by getting a tech for yelling.

explain to a professor something you didn't understand about a complex topic. On occasions like these, you want the person you're addressing to really listen—to look up from what they're doing and pay attention to what you're saying. And in return, you'll want to reciprocate, listening—*really listening*—to what others are saying. At times you may be tempted to jump into a conversation—but think again: it's often much more effective to find out what others think before doing so.

Listening with an open mind

Careful listening has been in short supply in the last few years, as the divisions in our society have grown deeper and more entrenched and as many people have retreated into their own bubbles or echo chambers where they hear only those they already agree with—and have stopped listening to anyone else. Yet if we don't learn to listen openly and carefully to others, including those whose views differ from our own, we can't hope to gain understanding and insight into their motivations, hopes, and goals. So that's why this book opens with a chapter calling on you to start by listening and calling on all of us to pay attention to the words of others—and to be willing to hear what they say.

> We have two ears and one mouth so we can listen twice as much as we speak.
> EPICTETUS

Whether you're writing an essay or participating in a face-to-face discussion, you'll need to engage with other people's views. In order to do so, you'll need to listen to what they say—and even to repeat back to them what they say as a way of making sure you've understood before responding with what *you* want to say. This kind of listening is what rhetorician Krista Ratcliffe dubs RHETORICAL LISTENING—opening yourself to the thoughts of others and making the effort not only to hear their words but to take those words in and fully understand them. It means paying attention to what others say as a way of establishing goodwill and acknowledging the importance of their views. And yes, it means taking seriously and engaging with views that differ, sometimes radically, from your own.

See p. 31 for advice on getting to know people different from you.

Rhetorical listening is what middle school teacher Julia Blount asked for in a *Facebook* post following riots in Baltimore after the death of Freddie Gray, who suffered fatal spinal injuries while in police custody:

> Every comment or post I have read today voicing some version of disdain for the people of Baltimore—"I can't understand" or "they're destroying their own community"—tells me that many of you are not listening. I am not asking you to condone or agree with violence. I just need you to listen. . . .
>
> —JULIA BLOUNT, "Dear White *Facebook* Friends:
> I Need You to Respect What Black America Is Feeling Right Now."

Blount went on to call for her friends to expose themselves to unfamiliar perspectives, and to engage in conversation—in other words, to listen rhetorically. Learning to listen this way takes time and attention and practice, but it is a skill you can develop and one that will pay off in better and more effective communication. There isn't any magic potion for becoming a good listener, but here are some tips that should put you on your way to achieving that goal.

Advice to listen and really hear what others are saying was much needed during the 2023 Israel-Hamas war. This issue led to intense, sometimes even violent, confrontations between pro-Israeli and pro-Palestinian supporters who were unwilling to listen to or talk with one another—and equally unwilling to think outside the narrow boundaries of their own beliefs, or to think about where those beliefs came from. This dispute erupted on many college campuses, where hate speech, both antisemitic and Islamophobic, left little or no room for listening. These incidents demonstrate how hard it can be in times of such intense disagreements to stop shouting, step back, and at least try to begin listening to what others are thinking and feeling.

But listen we must. Shouting and violence too often lead to more shouting and violence—and rarely if ever lead to resolution. So why not at least give listening a try?

Tips for listening respectfully and with an open mind

- *Give the gift of your full attention*; it is a precious one that you hope will be reciprocated. Turn off your phone, and don't allow yourself to be distracted by texts, emails, or social media.

- *Listen with an open mind* and without an agenda. Listen to learn, and with the goal of understanding.

- *Let others speak* before stating your own opinion or asking questions. Even if you disagree with what someone says, don't shout them down; everyone deserves to be listened to.

- *Listen with empathy* to try to see things from the other person's point of view. Make it a goal to understand their perspective, where they're coming from. Be on the lookout for COMMON GROUND, things you can agree on: "I can see where you're coming from."

- *Summarize* what the other person says to be sure you understand what they're saying.

- *Offer affirmation* when you can: "Good point; I hadn't thought of that."

- *Don't interrupt,* and don't be thinking about what you're going to say in response.

- *Be sure that any questions you ask are respectful,* not judgmental. Ask questions that are open-ended ("What do you think we should do?") or that clarify, not challenge ("Are you saying—?" rather than "Don't you think—?").

- *Pay attention to body language* and TONE of voice, yours and theirs. These can give you insight into the message the other person is trying to send. And maintain a respectful tone and posture yourself: lean in, nod your head.

Listening to understand complex issues

There are likely to be opportunities at your school to learn about **PERSPECTIVES** that differ from your own: courses on topics you've never before studied, guest lectures on issues that are being debated, and more. When protests broke out about the Israel-Hamas war, for example, many colleges offered courses on the history of Israel and Palestine and forums designed to foster thoughtful discussion about the conflict. These are all opportunities to learn about and listen to multiple perspectives on complex issues.

Beyond campus, there are a number of organizations that provide guidance for listening with an open mind, along with opportunities to meet up with people who think differently than you do.

One such organization is the *Listen First Project*, founded by Pearce Godwin with the goal of "mend[ing] the frayed fabric of America by bridging divides one conversation at a time." In 2019, *Listen First* launched the *National Conversation Project*, which helps people start new conversations, ones dedicated to moving "from *us vs. them* to *me and you*." By 2023, over 500 schools, libraries, and other groups hosted *Listen First* conversations. Go to listenfirstproject.org or conversation.us if you're interested in joining or hosting such a conversation.

> When you look at election results, the color red doesn't necessarily mean white power. It can also mean there are people who want the world to pay attention to them.
>
> TREVOR NOAH

We hope you'll take the advice in this chapter to heart, seeking to understand those with whom you may disagree, and learning to become a better listener as you do.

What's listening got to do with writing?

Here's what: whatever you're writing, you need to start by doing your homework: reading up on your topic, doing research, maybe conducting some interviews. That means listening.

Writing doesn't begin when you sit down to write. It's a way of being in the world, and its essence is paying attention.
JULIA ALVAREZ

And whatever your topic, it's unlikely that you'll be the first to write about it. In fact, when it comes to academic writing, what you write will usually respond to something that others have already said about your topic: they say this, you think that. So after introducing your topic, one effective way to proceed is to **QUOTE**, **PARAPHRASE**, or **SUMMARIZE** what others have said about it and presenting your ideas as a response. And that means listening carefully to what's already been said, not just launching into what you have to say.

So writing is actually a way of participating in a larger conversation, of engaging with the ideas of others. When you quote, paraphrase, or summarize sources, you're weaving their words or ideas in with yours—and hopefully responding to them in some way. You can't do that unless you've listened closely to those words and ideas.

Like writing, reading demands listening, really hearing what an author has to say. And if you read rhetorically, not just to absorb information but also to question and respond to the text, you enter into a dialogue with the author. That too starts with listening.

REFLECT! Think of a time when you were in a conversation with someone whose views you strongly disagreed with. How did the topic on which you disagreed come up? How carefully were you listening to the other point of view—and how well were you being listened to? Write a paragraph describing the incident, and how you think you handled it. Was the disagreement resolved—and if so, how? What might you have done differently, and why? What lessons can you take from the experience about interacting with people you don't agree with?

② Thinking Rhetorically

The only real alternative to war is rhetoric.

—WAYNE BOOTH

We didn't burn down any buildings....
You can do a lot with a pen and pad.

—ICE CUBE

Wayne Booth made the above statement at a conference of writing teachers held only months after 9/11 and quickly drew a range of responses. Just what did Booth mean by this stark statement? How could rhetoric—usually thought of as the art, theory, and practice of persuasion—act as a counter to war?

A noted critic and scholar, Booth explored these questions throughout his long career, identifying rhetoric as an ethical art that begins with intense listening and that searches for mutual understanding and common ground as alternatives to violence and war. Put another way, two of the most potent tools we have for persuasion are language and violence: when words fail us, violence often wins the day. Booth saw the careful and ethical use of language as our best approach to keeping violence and war at bay.

In the years since 9/11, Booth's words have echoed again and again as warfare has continued to rage in Israel, Gaza, Ukraine, Iraq, Afghanistan, and elsewhere. And in the United States, many thousands of people die from gun violence every year. In 2023 alone, there were eighty-two school shootings, thirty of them on college campuses. Michigan State. Morgan State. UC Santa Barbara. Umpqua Community College. Virginia Tech. The list goes on and on. Groups such as Students Demand Action, Everytown for Gun Safety, and March for Our Lives have taken to the streets and to social media demanding changes in gun safety laws, using dramatic and memorable statements as rhetorical strategies to capture and hold the attention of people around the world.

Students at Portsmouth High School in New Hampshire calling for protection from gun violence.

Rhetoric as an ethical art

Note that while Booth speaks of rhetoric as an "ethical" art (based on good intentions), rhetoric can also be used for unethical purposes (with bad or evil intent)—as Hitler and other dictators have done. In fact, rhetoric used in unethical ways can itself lead to violence. That's why the ancient Greek philosopher Aristotle cautioned that we need to understand rhetoric both to communicate our own ethical messages *and* to be able to recognize and resist unethical messages that others attempt to use against us. That's also why this book defines rhetoric as the practice of ETHICAL communication.

So how can you go about developing your own careful, ethical use of language? One short answer: by developing habits of mind that begin with listening and searching for understanding before deciding what you yourself think, and by thinking hard about your own beliefs before trying to persuade others to listen to and act on what you say. In other words, by learning to THINK RHETORICALLY.

Learning to think rhetorically can serve you well—at school, at work, even at home. After all, you'll need to communicate successfully with others in order to get things done in a responsible and ethical way. On the job, you and your coworkers might do this kind of thinking to revise a shift schedule so that every worker is treated fairly and no one is required to work double shifts. Or in your college courses, you'll surely encounter class discussions that call for rhetorical thinking—for listening closely and really thinking about what others say before saying what you think.

When a group of college students became aware of how little the temporary workers on their campus were paid, for example, they met with the workers and listened hard, gathering information about the situation. They then mounted a campaign using flyers, social media, speeches, and sit-ins—in other words, using the available means of persuasion—to win attention and convince the administration to raise the workers' pay. These students were thinking and acting rhetorically—and doing so responsibly. Note that the students worked together, both with the workers and with one another. After all, none of us can manage such actions all by ourselves; we need to engage in conversation with others and listen hard to what they say. Perhaps that's what philosopher Kenneth Burke had in mind when he created his famous "parlor" metaphor:

> Imagine that you enter a parlor. You come late. When you arrive, others have long preceded you, and they are engaged in a heated discussion, a discussion too heated for them to pause and tell you exactly what it is about…. You listen for a while, until you decide that you have caught the tenor of the argument; then you put in your oar.
>
> —KENNETH BURKE

In this parable, each of us is the person arriving late to a room full of animated conversation; we don't understand what's going on. Yet instead of butting in or trying too quickly to get in on the conversation, we listen closely until we catch on to what people are saying. And *then* we join in, using language and rhetoric carefully to engage with others as we add our own voices to the conversation.

This book aims to teach you to think rhetorically

- To listen to others carefully and respectfully
- To try to understand what they think, and why— and then to think hard about your own beliefs and where they come from
- To do these things *before* deciding what you yourself think and trying to persuade others to listen to what you say

Pay attention to what others are saying— and think about why

Thinking rhetorically begins with a willingness to hear the words of others with an open mind. It means paying attention to what others say before and even *as a way* of making your own contributions to a conversation. More than that, it means being open to the thoughts of others and making the effort not only to hear their words but also to take those words in and fully understand what they are saying. It means paying attention to what others say as a way of establishing

To pay attention, that is our endless and proper work.
MARY OLIVER

good will and acknowledging the importance of their views. And most of all, it means engaging with views that differ from your own—and being open to what they say.

When you enter any conversation, whether at school, at work, or with friends, take the time to understand what's being said rather than rushing to a conclusion or a judgment. Listen carefully to what others are saying, and think about what motivates them: Where are they coming from?

Developing such habits of mind will be useful to you almost every day, whether you're participating in a class discussion, negotiating with friends over what movie to see, or thinking about a local ballot issue to decide how you'll vote. In each case, thinking rhetorically means being flexible, and determined to seek out varying—and sometimes conflicting—points of view.

In ancient Rome, the great statesman and orator Cicero argued that considering alternative **POINTS OF VIEW** and **COUNTER-ARGUMENTS** was key to making a successful argument, and it is just as important today, maybe even more! Even when you disagree with a point of view—perhaps especially when you disagree with it—make the effort to see the issue from the viewpoint of its advocates before you reject their positions. Say, for example, you're skeptical that hydrogen fuel will be the solution to climate change: don't reject the idea until you've thought hard about what those in favor of it say and carefully considered other possible solutions.

REFLECT! Blogger **Sean Blanda** warns that many of us gravitate on social media to those who think like we do, which often leads to the belief that we are right and that those with other worldviews are "dumb." He argues that we need to "make an honest effort to understand those who are not like us" and to remember that "we might be wrong." Look at some of the posts you have "liked," as well as those you've written. How many different perspectives do you see represented? What might you do to think—and listen—more rhetorically, or to seek out a wider variety of viewpoints?

Consider the larger context

Thinking hard about the views of others also means considering the larger CONTEXT and how it shapes what they're saying. When you think rhetorically, you may need to do some research, to investigate whether there are any historical, political, or cultural factors that might account for where someone's beliefs are "coming from."

If you were analyzing the Land Back movement, in which tribal nations are reclaiming ancestral lands, for instance, you would look at the issue in a larger context by researching the history of how those lands came to be taken away, learning about the political agendas of those advocating for land return as well as those opposed to it, and thinking about the economic ramifications. In short, you would try to see the issue from many different perspectives before even thinking about what you think and why. And in writing about this issue, you would draw from all those perspectives.

What do you think, and why?

Examining all points of view on any issue will involve some tough thinking about your own STANCE—your attitude toward the issue and why you think as you do. Such thinking can help you define your stance or perhaps even lead you to change your mind; in either case, you stand to gain. Just as you need to think hard about the motivations of others, it's important to examine what's motivating you, asking yourself what influences in your life lead you to think as you do or to take certain positions.

Ibram X. Kendi offers an example. When a student from Ghana gave a "monologue" in class detailing negative and racist ideas about Black Americans, Professor Kendi provided data to counter his views, to no avail. After class, however, the discussion continued, with Kendi asking the student if he could name "some racist ideas the British say about Ghanaians." The student hesitated, but then came up with a list of such ideas, which he vehemently agreed were not true. Then Kendi returned to the student's earlier statements about Black Americans, asking him where he got those ideas. On reflection, the student said he got them from his family, friends, and his own observations. And where did he think those people get their ideas about Black Americans? "Probably American Whites," the student said.

> His mind seemed open, so I jumped on in. "So if African Americans went to Ghana, consumed British racist ideas about Ghanaians, and started expressing those ideas to Ghanaians . . . What would you think about that?"
>
> He smiled, surprising me. "I got it," he said, turning to walk out of the classroom.
>
> "Are you sure?" I said. He turned back to me. "Yes, sir. Thanks, Prof."
>
> —IBRAM X. KENDI, *How to Be an Antiracist*

Examining your own stance and motivation is equally important outside the classroom. Suppose you're urging members of a campus group to lobby for a rigorous set of procedures to deal with accusations of sexual assault. You've been alarmed by the statistics showing a steep increase in cases of rape on college campuses, and the number of incidents that go unreported. But then you read an account in your school newspaper of a case where an accusation of sexual assault proved to be untrue, and you begin to consider the experience of those who stand accused. This information leads you to realize that the issue of sexual harassment on campus is more complex than you thought. Your commitment to reduce sexual violence still holds, but thinking rhetorically has led you to a more nuanced understanding of what it means to have fairness and justice for all.

Find out what's been said about your topic

Rhetorical thinking calls on you to do some homework, to find out everything you can about what's been said about your topic, to **ANALYZE** what you find, and then to use that information to inform your own ideas. In other words, you want your own thinking to be well informed and to reflect more than just your own opinion.

To take an everyday example, you should do some pretty serious thinking when deciding on a major purchase, such as a new laptop. You'll want to begin by considering the purchase in the larger context of your life. Why do you need a new laptop right now? If you're considering buying the newest model, is it for practical reasons or just because it seems likely to be the best? If you're concerned about the environment, how will you dispose of your current laptop? Analyzing your specific motivations and purposes this way can guide you in drawing up a list of laptops to consider.

Then you'll need to do some RESEARCH, checking out product reports and reviews. Don't just trust the information provided by the company that manufactures and sells the laptops you're considering. Instead, you should consult multiple sources and check them against one another. This is a stage when AI can be helpful, perhaps in summarizing reviews of the laptop you're considering or suggesting additional sources you might check out. (Remember, though, that you'll need to double-check any information provided by AI for accuracy.)

See Ch. 30 for tips on checking anything from AI.

You'll also want to consider your findings in light of your priorities. Cost, for instance, may be a greater priority to consider than brand loyalty. Such careful thinking will help you come to a sound decision, and then explain it to others. If your parents are helping you buy the laptop, you'll want to consider what they might think, and to anticipate questions they may ask.

You'll also need to recognize and analyze how various rhetorical strategies work to persuade you. You may have been won over by a funny Apple commercial you saw on Super Bowl Sunday. But what made that ad so memorable? To answer that question, you'll need to study it closely, determining just what qualities—a clever script? memorable music? celebrity actors? cute animals? a provocative message?—made the ad so persuasive. Once you've determined that, you'll want to consider whether the laptop will actually live up to the advertiser's promises. This is the kind of research and analysis you will do when you engage in rhetorical thinking.

Give credit

Part of engaging with what others have thought and said is to give credit where credit is due. Acknowledging the work of others will show that you've done your homework and that you want to credit those who have influenced you. The great physicist Isaac Newton famously and graciously gave credit when he wrote to his rival Robert Hooke in 1676, saying:

> You have added much in several ways.... If I have seen a little further it is by standing on the shoulders of giants.
>
> —ISAAC NEWTON

In this letter, Newton acknowledges the work of Hooke before saying, with a fair amount of modesty, that his own contributions were made possible by Hooke and others. In doing so, he is thinking—and acting—rhetorically. In your own work, you will want to acknowledge any help from others: friends, a peer reviewer, or AI!

You can give such credit informally, as Newton does in his letter, or you can do so formally with a full CITATION and DOCUMENTATION. Which method you choose will depend on your purpose, genre, and the rest of your RHETORICAL SITUATION. Academic writing, for instance, usually requires documentation, but if you're writing for a personal blog, you might embed a link that connects to a work you've cited—or simply give an informal shout-out to a friend who contributed to your thinking. In each case, you'll want to be specific about what words or ideas you've drawn from others, and to make clear what they say and what you're saying. Such care in crediting your sources contributes to your credibility—and is an important part of ethical, rhetorical thinking.

Be imaginative

Remember that intuition and imagination can often lead to great insights. While you want to think carefully and analytically, don't be afraid to take chances. A little imagination can lead you to new ideas about a topic you're studying and about how to approach it in a way that will interest others. Such insights can often pay off big-time. One student athlete found himself searching for a research topic that he could really get into. At the time, he was interested in how mass media covered the Olympics, and he began his research by looking at the coverage in *Sports Illustrated* over the years. So far, so good: he found plenty of information for an essay showing that the magazine had been a major promoter of the Olympics.

While looking through old issues of *Sports Illustrated*, however, he kept feeling that something he was seeing in the early issues was different from more recent issues . . . though he couldn't quite put his finger on just what that was. This hunch led him to make an imaginative leap, to study this difference even though it was beyond the topic he had set out to examine. On closer inspection, he found that over the decades *Sports Illustrated* had slowly but surely moved from focusing on teams to depicting only individual stars.

This discovery led him to make an argument he would never have made had he not followed his hunch—that the evolution of sports from a focus on the team to a focus on individual stars is reflected in the pages of *Sports Illustrated*. It also helped him write a much more interesting—and more persuasive—essay, one that captured the attention not only of his instructor and classmates but also of a local magazine, which reprinted his essay. Like this student, you can benefit by using your imagination and listening to your intuition. You just might stumble on something exciting.

A hunch is creativity trying to tell you something.
FRANK CAPRA

REFLECT! Think about a topic you'd like to explore or a question you'd like to answer. You could do some research . . . or you could begin by thinking outside the box. Draw a picture that captures your topic, or compose a brief rap, or create a meme. If you made a movie about your topic, what would the title be—and who would star in it? In other words, use your imagination!

Put in your oar

So rhetorical thinking offers a toolkit of strategies for entering a conversation, strategies that will help you understand the situation, "put in your oar," and make your voice count. Whatever you say, give some thought to how you want to present yourself and how you can best appeal to your audience:

- How do you want to come across—as thoughtful? serious? curious? skeptical? something else?
- What can you do to represent yourself as knowledgeable and CREDIBLE?
- What can you do to show respect for your AUDIENCE?
- How can you show that you have your audience's best interests at heart?

Imagine you want to create a campus food pantry and are preparing a presentation for your meeting with the dean and the director of food services. You'll want to come across as knowledgeable and well informed, to show them that you've done your homework. You'll need to present evidence of food insecurity on your campus and of what other colleges have done—statistics about how many students often go hungry, anecdotes about students you know, examples of food pantries at similar schools, and so on. (You might ask AI to provide information about food pantries on other campuses to widen your point of view.) You may want to put this information on a slide to reinforce the points you are making.

You'll also want to demonstrate respect for your audience. That means thanking them for meeting with you, being well prepared, and keeping to the time allotted for the meeting. And you'll want to show that you're aware of the stakes involved and to acknowledge that they have other issues to deal with. Finally, you'll want to listen carefully to what they say, and with an open mind.

In other words, you'll want to think and act rhetorically—and to use language that shows you have the best interests of the college and its students in mind. You might say you "wish to suggest" that "opening a food pantry is one way to help students who are food insecure"—rather than expecting your audience to come up with a solution and insisting that something "needs to be done right now." This is not to say that you should underestimate the problem; but better to focus on your proposed solution, on how the college can help students who are food insecure.

This kind of rhetorical thinking will go a long way toward making sure you will be listened to and taken seriously.

As the examples in this chapter illustrate, rhetorical thinking involves certain habits of mind that can and should lead to something—often to an action, to making something happen. And then, those who think rhetorically are in a very strong position. They have listened attentively, engaged with the words and ideas of others, viewed their topic from many alternative perspectives, and done their homework. This kind of rhetorical thinking will set you up to contribute your own ideas—and will increase the likelihood that your ideas will be heard and will inspire real action.

Indeed, the ability to think rhetorically is of great importance in today's global world, as professors Gerald Graff and Cathy Birkenstein explain:

> The ability to enter complex, many-sided conversations has taken on a special urgency in today's diverse, post-9/11 world, where the future for all of us may depend on our ability to put ourselves in the shoes of those who think very differently from us. Listening carefully to others, including those who disagree with us, and then engaging with them thoughtfully and respectfully . . . can help us see beyond our own pet beliefs, which may not be shared by everyone. The mere act of acknowledging that someone might disagree with us may not seem like a way to change the world; but it does have the potential to jog us out of our comfort zones, to get us thinking critically about our own beliefs, and perhaps even to change our minds.
>
> —GERALD GRAFF and CATHY BIRKENSTEIN,
> *"They Say / I Say": The Moves That Matter in Academic Writing*

In the long run, if enough of us learn to think rhetorically, we just might achieve Wayne Booth's goal—to use words in thoughtful and constructive ways as an alternative to violence and war.

REFLECT! Spend a half hour or so looking back over the above advice for thinking rhetorically, and then make some notes about how many of those tips you currently follow—and to what effect.

THINK ABOUT YOUR OWN RHETORICAL SITUATION

Whatever you're writing—a text to a friend, a job application, an essay exam, a script for a presentation—will call for you to consider your rhetorical situation: your *purpose* for writing, your *stance* toward your topic, the *audience* you want to reach, the *genre* and *medium*, and the *language* you will use. In addition, you'll want to consider the larger *context*, about both the topic and what you'll need to know to write well about it. These are all things to think about early in the process of writing. The following questions will help guide your thinking.

What is your purpose for writing, and what motivates you to do so?

What drives you to write? In college, it may be an assignment. Even then, it's likely that you'll write about something that matters to you, that grabs your attention. But beyond an explicit assignment, what gives you the itch to write? Most likely it will be some issue you're passionate about, and that inspires you to speak up, to add your voice to the conversation. It's worth taking time to explore your purposes for writing: Do you want to explain a topic? To persuade someone to agree with your position on an issue? To fulfill an assignment? To entertain, or bring a smile to those who read what you write? Whatever your purpose, it affects your choice of genre, medium, language, and design: the material needed to entertain is not the same as that needed to explain a theory or to persuade an audience to support a certain cause. So your purpose becomes your guiding light, one that helps you stay on track.

What audience do you want to reach?

Before starting to write, take some time to think about your potential audiences. Today, that audience might be as narrow as your instructor or as wide as anyone with access to the internet; but the more you can know about who you're writing to, the better chance you have of connecting with them. If your audience is an instructor, for instance, you know that they value clarity, so you should choose your words carefully and make sure that your points are clear. If you're posting for friends, however, you can probably assume that they want information about you and your thoughts—and that they won't hold you to a high standard in terms of precision. Here are some questions for thinking about your audience:

- What do you and your audience have in common? In what ways do you differ?
- What values do they hold, and what kinds of **EVIDENCE** will they accept? How can you build on any **COMMON GROUND** you share with them and appeal to their values?
- What do they know about your topic, and how much background information will they need? Can you assume they'll be interested in what you say—and if not, how can you get them interested?
- What do you want your audience to think or do in response to what you say—take your ideas seriously? Take some kind of action?

If your audience is largely unknown, be careful not to assume that they think as you do, value what you value, or have the same cultural and linguistic background as you do. Instead, it's best to take a calm and respectful stance, hoping that they will respond to you in the same way.

What is your stance on your topic, and what do you want to say about it?

Think of stance as your attitude toward the topic. If your topic is one about which you have some depth of knowledge, you may take an authoritative stance: you've done your homework and know what you're talking about. Or you might take a reporter's stance, laying out information you've researched so that others can understand it. Or your stance may be that of a critic who analyzes a text and raises questions about it. On other occasions, you may take up the stance of an advocate, a skeptic, even a cheerleader for an issue you're passionate about. In each case, your stance will guide the TONE you adopt in your writing: whether passionate, objective, curious, outraged, or something else; you'll want to make sure that it reflects your stance and is appropriate to your AUDIENCE and PURPOSE.

What genre(s) will you use?

Academic genres include many of the assignments you regularly receive: ARGUMENTS, ANALYSES, REPORTS, REVIEWS, and ANNO-TATED BIBLIOGRAPHIES. All genres. In some cases, you may be assigned to write in a specific genre ("Write an argument related to the maker movement"). But if not, you'll need to decide which genre best matches your purpose, audience, and stance. Then you'll have to make sure that you understand the characteristic features of your chosen genre, including format.

What media will you use, and how will you design what you write?

Closely aligned to the genre you choose are questions of MEDIA and DESIGN. Do your purpose, stance, and audience call for a written print text, perhaps with illustrations? a website? an oral presentation with slides? Whether your medium is oral, print, or digital, you'll need to consider questions of design: what you want the look of your text to be—informal or formal, serious or humorous, and so on. What headings, fonts, color, or white space will help achieve your purpose? What VISUALS or audio might enhance your text?

Think about your use of language

What kind of language will best suit your purpose and be most appropriate to your audience and genre? If you're writing a text to a friend or classmate, you'll probably use informal language and a friendly, casual tone. If you're writing a project proposal to an instructor, on the other hand, you will want to choose more formal language. In fact, what language(s) should you choose for any particular rhetorical situation—English? Spanish? Urdu? Navajo?—and what would this choice accomplish in terms of your audience and purpose? And if you are writing or speaking in English, what dialect(s) should you choose—standardized English? Black English? Appalachian English? Something else? And what would these choices accomplish in terms of your audience and purpose?

See Ch. 26 on using language rhetorically.

Consider context: What do you need to know?

Answering this question calls for taking an inventory of what you know about your topic. For an assignment that asks you to ANALYZE a text or image, you'll need the ability (and the time) to do a detailed close reading. For an ARGUMENT on films based on Marvel comics, you might need to research the history of the genre, its ups and downs in popularity, and what's already been said about it. For a presentation on the need for more lighting on campus to make it a safer place, you might conduct a survey of students, carry out observations on poorly lit areas of campus, or interview campus officials. In all these instances, you would also need to decide whether you need illustrations. Consider your answer to this question in context:

How much time do you have to complete the project, and what sources will you need and find available in that time frame?

If you've thought about the questions in this chapter for considering your own rhetorical situation, you should have a pretty good grasp of the circumstances within which you write. It's important to recognize that your writing doesn't come out of nowhere but rather occurs in a particular time and place, in response to particular things others have thought and said, and in relation to those who will be receiving your message.

It's also important to recognize that the advice offered here is itself part of a particular context—of college writing in English-speaking countries. But writing and rhetoric differ across contexts and cultures. That's one more reason to analyze the contexts you're working in as well as the audience you're trying to reach. Wherever you are, think of yourself as being at the center of an ongoing conversation, one in which what you have to say matters. Then start to write!

REFLECT! Look over something you've written, and think about the rhetorical situation in which you wrote it—your intended audience and purpose, the genre and medium, language choices, and so on. Choose one of those elements, and think about how well you addressed it. Then think about what you would have done differently if your rhetorical situation had been different—for example, if you'd written in a different genre or medium—and write a paragraph or two about how your writing would have been different, and why.

3

Engaging Respectfully with Others

Let us talk with—not at—each other—
in our homes, schools, workplaces,
and places of worship.

—CONDOLEEZZA RICE

Where something stands,
something else stands beside it.

—IGBO PROVERB

In the late spring of 2017, Oprah Winfrey stood before a cheering crowd of graduating students at Agnes Scott College, urging them to learn to engage respectfully with others. She told the assembled crowd about how she'd once invited a group of women voters—half on the right and half on the left, politically—to join her at a diner for breakfast. Nobody wanted to come, but she insisted, saying "it's gonna be so great . . . croissants, we're gonna have some nice jams, ladies." They came in "all tight and hardened," saying they'd "never sat this close" to someone from the other side and didn't want to be around them. But as she went on to say in her speech, it worked.

29

After two and a half hours, I had those women . . . eating croissants, sitting around the table listening to each other's stories, hearing both sides, and by the end they were holding hands, exchanging emails and phone numbers, and singing "Reach Out and Touch." . . . Which means it's possible; it can happen. So I want you to work in your own way to change the world in respectful conversations with others. . . . And I want you to enter every situation aware of its context, open to hear the truths of others and most important, open to letting the process of changing the world change you.

—OPRAH WINFREY, Agnes Scott College commencement address

Watch Oprah's speech at letstalklibrary.com.

You have probably encountered views that differ a great deal from your own in your college classes: after all, that's one good reason for going to college—to learn about people and cultures and places other than those you call home. And some of your instructors may have focused on how to engage in critical conversations without being belligerent or disrespectful. But consider this incident that took place some years ago in one writing class at Ohio State.

Students who were serving as peer reviewers were reading a narrative essay called "The Little Squirrel" in which the author described finding a "small, helpless squirrel" caught in a trap on his family farm. His descriptions of the squirrel were empathetic and emotional as he contemplated his choices: "What should I do now?" he asked. The peer reviewers, expecting him to free the little squirrel, were quite startled when he continued the essay by saying that with only a few seconds' hesitation, he pulled out his gun and killed the squirrel. "How could you do that to a little squirrel?" two students demanded, one coming just short of calling him a murderer.

The author responded defensively and said he thought they were being "wimps." At this point, they weren't even talking about the essay anymore, until another student who'd been quietly observing the scene said, "Hold on now! This isn't getting us anywhere. We need to step back and give each other a little space—and a little respect." This intervention allowed the writer to say he thought he had made the ethical decision because the squirrel had a broken leg and wasn't going to survive. In his view, he had done the right thing. Giving him their attention enabled the group to understand his motives better. In addition, they noted that if the author had explained his rationale in the narrative, rather than arousing their empathy for the little squirrel, they might still disagree with his decision but wouldn't have been so horrified and antagonistic to him. In this case, paying respectful attention didn't lead to unanimous agreement, but it did lead to defusing a very contentious situation and to learning about differing views of responsibility and action.

The goal of this chapter is to encourage and guide you as you engage with others: respectfully listening to their stories, their truths—and contributing to a process that may, indeed, change the world. Here are some steps you can take to realize this goal.

Get to know people different from you

It's a commonplace today to point out that we often live in silos, places where we encounter only people who think like we do, who hold the same values we do. Even though the internet has made the whole world available to us, we increasingly choose to inter-act only with like-minded people—online and in person. We operate in what some call echo chambers, where we hear our views echoed back to us from every direction. It can be easy, and comforting, to think this is the real world—but it's not! Beyond your own bubble of posts and conversations lie countless others with different views and values.

So one big challenge we face today is finding ways to get out of our echo chambers and make an effort to know people who take different positions, hold different values. But simply encountering people who think differently is just the start. Breaking out of our bubbles calls for making the effort to understand those different perspectives, to listen with empathy and an open mind, and to understand where others are coming from. As we see in the story Oprah Winfrey tells in her commencement address, even the first step is hard: she had to convince the women to just meet one another, and then she had to persuade them to listen, as she says, with respect. Once they did, things changed: they realized that it's not as easy to dislike or dismiss someone when you're sitting face-to-face.

To make sense of the world, look to those who see it differently.
THE ATLANTIC

That's certainly what one Canadian student found when she spent a semester in Washington, DC. She had expected the highlights of her semester to be visiting places like the Smithsonian museums or the Library of Congress, but her greatest experience, as she describes it in a blog post, turned out to be an "unexpected gift: while in DC, I became close, close friends with people I disagree with on almost everything." As she got to know these people, she found that they were

> funny, smart, and kind. We all really liked music.... We even lived together. We ate dinner together, every single night. So I couldn't look down on them. I couldn't even consider it. And when you can't look down on someone who fundamentally disagrees with you, when you're busy breaking bread, sharing your days, laughing about the weather ... well.
>
> —SHAUNA VERT, "Making Friends Who Disagree with You (Is the Healthiest Thing in the World)"

During a conversation with one of her housemates, a deeply conservative Christian from Mississippi, Vert mentioned that she was "pro-choice," realizing as she did so that this was "dangerous territory." To her surprise, she met not resistance or rebuke but curiosity:

She wanted to know more. Her curiosity fueled my curiosity, and we talked. We didn't argue—we debated gently, very gently. . . . We laughed at nuance, we self-deprecated, we trusted each other. And we liked each other. Before the conversation, and after the conversation. To recap: Left-wing Canadian meets Bible Belt Republican. Discusses controversial political issues for over an hour. Walks away with a new friend.

Read Shauna Vert's full blog post at letstalklibrary.com.

This kind of careful, respectful exchange seems particularly hard in today's highly polarized society, where anger and hate are fueled by incendiary messages coming from social media and highly partisan news organizations, messages that became increasingly fever-pitched following the Supreme Court's decision to overturn *Roe v. Wade*. With such issues, disagreement runs deep, and it can be harder than ever for people whose beliefs differ to communicate at all, let alone with open minds. But, like Vert, some people have taken up the challenge and acted to find ways to bring people with different views together.

One group dedicated to helping people listen and talk across differences is *Living Room Conversations*, which provides guidelines for building connections through conversations, aiming to "increase understanding, reveal common ground, and discuss possible solutions."

North Carolina State's *Campus Conversations Project* has a similar goal, aiming to cultivate an environment of respectful conversation across campus with virtual discussions and events on topics like "Mending the Social Fabric" and "More Curious, Less Furious." Co-director Lily Morrell says she's seen students "cry, laugh, express anger . . . and make new relationships," based not only on shared experiences, but newfound respect.

Chances are there's a group like these on your campus—or perhaps you could start one: visit livingroomconversations.org to find resources for starting a living room conversation yourself.

The point is that you should make an effort to find and engage with those who have different ideas and values than you do. And you should become familiar with the sources they read too. Sites like allsides.com that present views from left, right, and center can help. Try to get out of your comfort zone, look beyond the sources you know and trust, and check out what "the other sides" are reading. You just might find something you like—or even agree with!

Practice empathy

Many of the examples above suggest the power of EMPATHY, the ability to share someone else's feelings. Dylan Marron is someone who directly addresses empathy and shows how it works. As the creator and host of several popular video series on controversial social issues, Marron has attracted quite a bit of attention and, he says, drawn "a lot of hate." Early on, he tried to ignore hateful comments, but then he started to get interested and began visiting commenter profiles to learn about the people writing them. Doing so, he said, led him to realize "there was a human on the other side of the screen"—and prompted him to call some of these people and talk with them on the phone. He shares these conversations on his podcast *Conversations with People Who Hate Me*.

Dylan Marron, host of a podcast of conversations among people who disagree.

In one of these talks, Marron learned that Josh, who had called Marron a "moron" in an online comment and said that being gay was a sin, had recently graduated from high school, so Marron asked him, "How was high school for you?" Josh replied that "it was hell" and elaborated by saying that he'd been bullied by kids who made fun of him for being "bigger." Marron went on to share his own experiences of being bullied, and as the conversation progressed, empathy laid the groundwork that helped them relate to each other.

At the end of another conversation, a man who had called Marron a "talentless hack" reflected on the ubiquitous Comment fields where such statements often appear, saying that "the Comment sections are really a way to get your anger at the world out on random strangers"—an insight that made him "rethink the way I interact with people online." Marron's work shows that Comment sections are sometimes used to release anger—and often hate, the very opposite of the kind of empathy that can bring people together. More than that, his work demonstrates the power of practicing empathy and how it can help us to see one another as human, even in the most negative and nasty contexts.

In his 2018 TED Talk, Marron stresses the importance of empathy, noting, however, that "empathy is not endorsement" and doesn't require us to compromise our deeply held values but, rather, to acknowledge the views of "someone raised to think very differently" than we do. That's the power and the promise of practicing empathy.

Watch Dylan Marron's TED Talk and listen to his podcast at letstalklibrary.com.

Demonstrate respect

If you've never heard Aretha Franklin belt out the lyrics to "Respect," take time to look it up on *YouTube*. Franklin added two now-famous lines along with a chorus to Otis Redding's original song, transforming it into an anthem for all those who demand R-E-S-P-E-C-T.

Franklin's message is still a timely one today, when *dis*respect seems so common, especially among those who don't agree. If we want others to respect us, then we also need to respect them. In other words, respect is a two-way street: it needs to be reciprocal.

Respect is like air. As long as it's present, nobody thinks about it. But if you take it away, it's all that people think about.

JOSEPH RENNY

Aretha Franklin onstage in 1968.

At the same time, it's important to note that those in subordinate or marginalized positions sometimes feel as if they're expected to show respect without feeling respected themselves. In short, we need to remember that *everyone* wants to be respected. Easy to say, but sometimes hard to do. So just how can you go about demonstrating respect?

Tips for demonstrating respect

- Come into conversations with *a desire to understand, and listen*—with genuine interest and an open mind, and without interrupting or making snap judgments.
- *Be helpful* and cooperative.
- *Try to build bridges* and to find common ground.
- *Represent other people's views fairly* and generously, and acknowledge their accomplishments whenever you can.
- *If you disagree,* focus on what was said rather than criticizing who said it.
- *Ask questions* rather than issuing orders or challenges.
- *Apologize* if you say something you regret. We all make mistakes!

- *Be sincere,* and remember to say "thank you."
- *Be on time:* even that is a sign of respect.
- *Do what you say you'll do.* Keep your promises.

This advice largely holds for writing as well as speaking. Whether online or in print, our written words will usually be more effective if they come across as sincere, cooperative, and fair—and if we consider viewpoints other than our own and acknowledge them evenhandedly. These acts help build bridges in our writing, connecting us to members of our audience, including those who may not agree with us on all things.

If you respect others in these ways, in both writing and speaking, it's more likely that you'll earn their respect in return. Remember that respect can engender respect in return and thus lead to common ground, compromise, and understanding. This is not to say that you should not stand up for your own carefully considered beliefs, but that you should be careful not to demonize those whose beliefs differ from yours.

Search for common ground

Even children learn pretty early on that digging into opposing positions doesn't usually get very far: "No you can't!" "Yes I can!" can go on forever, without getting anywhere. Rhetoricians in the ancient world understood this very well and thus argued that for conversations to progress, it's necessary to look for and establish some **COMMON GROUND**, no matter how small. If "No you can't!" moves on to "Well, you can't do that in this particular situation," then maybe the conversation can continue.

> You like dogs? So do I.
> TRISH HALL,
> *How to Persuade*

After the October 7, 2023 Hamas attack on Israel left 1,200 dead, and Israel's counterattack on Gaza in the subsequent weeks killed more than 15,000 people, divisions between Israelis and Palestinians seemed unbridgeable. Yet amid unspeakable desperation and fear, many insisted on searching for ways to reach across enmity, hatred, and vast differences.

One such organization is *Parents Circle–Families Forum*, a Palestinian-Israeli group for people who have lost family members. One Israeli member recalls "looking into the eyes of the Palestinian mothers and recognizing that we shared the same pain."

Standing Together is another group refusing to give in to hopelessness and despair. When Sally Abed, a Palestinian citizen of Israel, and Alon-Lee Green, a Jewish Israeli, came to the United States in November 2023 to talk about how Jews and Palestinians can and must work together, they faced a toxic atmosphere. But as they met with groups and tried to explain their own experiences, they were often surprised to find that they were being listened to. The only way forward, they argued, could not be reduced to a slogan or a hashtag. Their vision is one in which millions of Palestinians and Israelis would stay, together, on the land they both call home.

To their surprise, it's a message that's been met with interest and often a sense of relief, perhaps because it holds out some hope. As the moderator of one of their events said,

Sally Abed and Alon-Lee Green of *Standing Together*.

This isn't "Kumbaya, let's all hold hands and love each other." It's "There's actually no way that one side is going to win. Our futures are intertwined and the only way that we can keep ourselves alive is by keeping each other alive."

—LIBBY LENKINSKI

In short, this is all about Palestinians and Israelis finding common ground: something they can all agree on—and something they can literally stand on.

Groups like *Standing Together* and the *Parents Circle* continue to work together and to hope, but they are very cautious in their optimism. They know that the deep chasms that divide Palestinians and Israelis will not be easily bridged. Yet as they face the inevitable obstacles ahead, they continue to try.

As these examples demonstrate, sometimes the stakes in trying to bridge differences can be very high, and potentially dangerous. That was the case when Daryl Davis, a Black blues musician, decided to do some research on the Ku Klux Klan, a white supremacist group that has terrorized Black people in the past. Davis's research led him to try to meet with some Klansmen, and to listen to them and try to engage with what they said. Davis has written widely about these experiences (which eventually led over 200 members to leave the Klan), about the importance of finding common ground, and how the rest of us can go about doing so:

> We're in this boat together. We sink or swim together. And when there's a leak in the boat and people are at risk, it puts all of us at risk.
> SUSAN RICE

Look for commonalities. You can find something in five minutes, even with your worst enemy. And build on those. Say I don't like you because you're white and I'm black. . . . And so our contention is based upon our races. But if you say "how do you feel about all these drugs on the street" and I say "I think the law needs to crack down on things that people can get addicted to very easily." . . . and you say "Well, yeah I agree with that." You might even tell me your son started dabbling in drugs. So now I see that you want what I want, that drugs are affecting your family the same way they affect my family. So now we're in agreement. Let's focus on that. And as we focus more and more and find more things in common, things we have in contrast, such as skin color, matter less and less.

—DARYL DAVIS, "How to Argue"

Tolerance shares DNA with respect. It recognizes that other people have rights even if we disagree with them.

FRANK BRUNI

Davis reports that he was not always successful—there were some people he met with whom it was impossible to find common ground. Yet he urges us whenever possible to seek out areas of agreement and compromise, and to listen carefully and respectfully to one another. And he reminds us that argument doesn't need to be insulting or condescending—**TONES** that usually make things worse. But he notes as well that looking for areas of compromise doesn't mean giving in to ideas you know are not right. As Davis says, "You're going to hear things that you know are absolutely wrong. You will also hear opinions put out as facts." In such cases, he suggests offering facts or other **EVIDENCE** that disprove the opinion being put forward. Then, if the person still holds to the opinion, try saying something like "I believe you are wrong, but if you think you're right, then bring me the data."

Such a response invites the other person to bring information that may carry the conversation forward. So when you hear things you believe to be wrong, be careful to respond in a civil way, showing data that refutes what they say, or asking them to show you evidence that *you* are wrong—with the hope of continuing the conversation based on data and evidence rather than mere opinion.

What if you sense danger? It's important to remember that some situations may not allow for you to engage with those who disagree vehemently with you—or who perhaps even threaten you. Some social media threads are so hateful and toxic that you'd be wise *not* to engage in the discussion. Remember as well that in the case of clearly dangerous exchanges, simply not engaging isn't enough, especially if the discussion is one that could lead to violence. In such cases, you must remove yourself from the situation as quickly as possible, and then call for help.

Souad Kirama, who is Muslim, described being confronted by teenage girls in New York who screamed curses and charges of "terrorist" at her, clearly targeting and endangering her. Such a situation allows for little or no possibility for discussion. Kirama had very little choice then but to get to safety, and quickly. And at Tulane University, pro-Palestinian protesters attacked Dylan Mann, a Jewish student, leaving him bleeding profusely. Alas, a surge of antisemitic and Islamophobic incidents on US campuses in late 2023 often involved violence.

If you encounter such a dangerous situation in which all the empathy and efforts to find common ground you can think of fail to work, remember: your own physical safety is paramount.

REFLECT! Some would say it's pointless or even wrong to try to find common ground with people whose views they find hateful or dangerous. **Daryl Davis** would probably disagree. Based on your own experiences, what do you think—and why?

Invite response

Note that all the examples in this chapter feature dialogue and conversation; the road to understanding is never a one-way street. That's why long harangues or speeches—monologues—often have little effect on anyone who doesn't already agree with you. But tuning out is a lot harder in "live" conversations—face-to-face or on the phone. So if you want to engage successfully with people who think differently from you, then inviting them to respond, to join the conversation, is a good way forward. To invite response, you have to make time for it, and make a space for them to chime in: pause, make eye contact, even ask for response directly—"So how do you feel about what I've just said?"

You can invite response to your writing as well. Online, you can turn on Commenting features and ask explicitly for responses to your posts—and then respond to those who leave comments for you. In doing so, you show that you value what others think and that you really want to hear and understand their views.

Join the conversation: collaborate! engage! participate!

Especially in times of such deep societal divisions, it may be tempting to retreat, to put our heads in the sand and hope that somehow things will get better. But don't give in to that temptation. Your voice is important, your thoughts are important, and you can best make them heard if you engage with other people. That may mean working with groups of people to speak out about important social issues. That kind of civic engagement and participation is important in a democracy.

> The simple act of paying attention can take you a long way.
> KEANU REEVES

But there are smaller ways to engage as well, like seeking out those who think differently than you do, collaborating with them, paying attention to what they say, understanding their reasons for thinking as they do—and then finding a shared goal you can work toward together. As a country, as a world, we have a lot riding on being able to reach across barriers and work together for the common good. And as writers, we all have much to offer in this endeavor. So let's get going!

REFLECT! "Throughout history, generalizations have been made about 'other people,' but the only true generalization you can say about other people is that they are not you. They have done different things than you have. They were raised differently, maybe, or they have seen or heard things, perhaps, about which you don't know. They have different thoughts. Listen to them, and you may find out what everyone is arguing about." That's what **Lemony Snicket** has to say about "other people." Think about your own experiences interacting with people who think differently from you. How much listening have you done, and how much talking? Have you been satisfied with the results? What might you try to do differently next time?

4 The Role of Argument in Our Lives

The other night I ate at a real nice family restaurant.
Every table had an argument going on.

—GEORGE CARLIN

From the sweet nothings you whisper to someone you love, to conversations with friends and colleagues, to *Instagram* posts that go out to your followers, most of what you say contains arguments. No matter what medium (oral, print, digital) or genre (report, narrative, review) you choose, you are making a point of some kind—and that means you are arguing something. And *that* means you are doing so with others, in class, on the bus, at dinner. Arguments are all around us, like the air we breathe—which means you need to pay very close attention to what they say. When so many others (humans,

43

and now machines) are trying to sell you everything from new running shoes to entire worldviews, it's time to wake up, listen up, and think—first to understand what others are saying and why, and then to reflect on what *you* think, and why. This chapter provides practical advice that will help you recognize and think about arguments: those you read, see, and hear—and those you write or speak yourself.

Why do we argue, anyway?

A baby crying makes an argument; so does a two-year-old who has just learned the power of "NO!" A smile makes a powerful argument—as does a scowl or a grimace. But why—and what for? Here's a list of five reasons people argue:

- *To explore.* We are a curious bunch, and arguing—with things we hear or read, with other people, or with ourselves— is one way to explore the world of ideas we live in.

- *To understand.* Being curious means we don't want simply to hear or read something: we want to *understand* it and think about its significance. Careful, persistent argument can often lead to understanding.

- *To make decisions.* There's no better way to come to a decision than to argue the choices from all sides, considering every possible consequence along with any pros and cons.

- *To seek consensus.* While each of us is a unique individual, we long for connection with others. Arguing is one way that we can find and explore common ground and ways to come together.

- *To convince.* We often want or need to convince someone to think about or do something that we think matters. Arguing is one way to convince them.

REFLECT! Choose one of these five reasons for arguing—and think of a time when it led you to an encounter with someone else. What were you trying to accomplish, and how did it turn out? Write a paragraph describing that situation and what you learned from it.

Arguments are always part of larger conversations

Ever since the US Supreme Court issued the decision that overturned *Roe v. Wade* and the right to abortion, rallies both for and against the decision have been ongoing across the United States. The first image below shows anti-abortion proponents celebrating the "death" of *Roe* and claiming that the future is "anti-abortion," while the second image shows protesters challenging the decision, refusing to accept it, and arguing that the future must once again be pro-choice.

Both of these images raise complex questions that call on us to read the images carefully. They also demonstrate a basic truth about arguments: they always stand in response to other arguments and are embedded in particular contexts that we need to explore and understand. We can read the two images as part of a much larger **CONVERSATION**, a give-and-take of ideas and beliefs. Our job in

The signs in these two photos make decidedly different arguments.

reading these arguments is to consider them in as full a context as possible, to think about where they're coming from and what they're responding to—before deciding what we ourselves think and want to say.

Where's the argument coming from?

Thinking about an argument in its full context calls on you to look closely at what it says and to think about where it's coming from. Consider what Golden State Warriors star Steph Curry wrote in an *Instagram* post in the summer of 2023 about his former teammate Jordan Poole:

> Yo—so, now that the trade is actually final, I felt like I needed to come on here and just say—JP, how much I appreciated the four years brother. You're a champion. You grew up right in front of everybody's face in terms of, you know, that first year where it was rough—a lot of injuries, just trying to find your way . . . and coming back and helping us finish 15–5 down the stretch of your second year to us winning a championship your third year . . . and fighting till the end this past year.
>
> I can't wait to see you blossom, big fella. I can't wait to see you shine in your own situation. Just looking forward to competing, obviously with being a fan of everything you become. Good luck to you.
>
> —STEPH CURRY, *Instagram*

What are Curry's arguments here, and what are his REASONS for making them? To answer those questions, we need to fill in the CONTEXT: Who is JP? Jordan Poole. What is the "trade"? Poole from the Warriors to the Wizards. What details surround the events Curry describes during Poole's four-year tenure with the Warriors? Poole had his ups and downs during those four years, helping them win a championship but also having a serious altercation with a teammate. What can all that context do to help us understand the argument Curry is making here, first to Poole but then to all those who follow Curry on *Instagram*? That Poole has Curry's respect and

Steph Curry #30 and Jordan Poole #3 celebrate a Warriors victory in 2022.

best wishes—and has a great future ahead. Finally, what does it tell us about Curry's attitude toward those he competes against and about what he values? That Curry, himself a superstar, is generous in praising others and in creating good will. Speaking informally and seemingly straight from the heart, Curry enacts the culture of respect, collaboration, and support he has helped to create for the Warriors. Answering these questions helped us explore the context of his argument and see more clearly just where it's coming from.

As a writer, you need to think hard about where you are coming from in the arguments you make. What's your **STANCE**, and why? How can you convey it? Through your words, of course—both *what* you say and *how* you say it. What's your **PURPOSE**, and how do you want your **AUDIENCE** to perceive you?

What's the claim?

If you look and listen closely, you'll find claims all around you, in essays and op-eds, on *Instagram* and *TikTok*, on t-shirts and even on Girl Scout cookies, emojis, and works of art.

The cookie here claims (or proclaims!) that Girl Scouts are go-getters. What about the emojis? These are a signal (or a claim) that there's something to laugh about. And the "Think" flag by American painter William Copley? Does it claim that we need to do more than simply "pledge allegiance" to the flag? That we need to *think* about what it means? Or something else? As these examples show, some claims are very explicit, but some are less so. The arguments you read and write in college often begin with a claim, but then there are those like Copley's flag that hold off on telling us explicitly what they are claiming.

Sometimes writers open with an explicit thesis, but often they'll start with a few sentences that provide some kind of context before stating their claim. In an article about the huge popularity of the Sunfish sailboat, journalist Bruce Burdett opens with some history of the little boat, telling readers that only a few things have changed during its sixty-year run and that its simplicity of design and ease of use keep factories "churning them out." This information then lead up to his thesis:

> Quick to rig and figure out, it is the boat that has launched more people into the sport of sailing than any other, the one that has flipped more people into the drink, and the one dragged up onto more beaches.
>
> —BRUCE BURDETT,
> "Sunfish at Sixty: Most Popular Boat Ever
> Still Keeps Them Busy at Portsmouth Plant"

A Sunfish sailboat.

In the rest of the article, Burdett goes on to provide additional reasons and plenty of evidence to support that claim.

As Burdett's example shows, some claims are not stated right up front. Consider the following paragraph from a journal article by civil rights activist W. E. B. Du Bois in 1922.

> Abraham Lincoln was a Southern poor white, . . . poorly educated and unusually ugly, awkward, ill-dressed. He liked smutty stories and was a politician down to his toes. Aristocrats—Jeff Davis, Seward and their ilk—despised him, and indeed he had little outwardly that compelled respect. But in that curious human way he was big inside. He had reserves and depths and when habit and convention were torn away there was something left to Lincoln—nothing to most of his contemners. There was something left, so that at the crisis he was big enough to be inconsistent—cruel, merciful; peace-loving, a fighter; despising Negroes and letting them fight and vote; protecting slavery and freeing slaves. He was a man—a big, inconsistent, brave man.
>
> —W. E. B. DU BOIS, "Abraham Lincoln"

Here the claim is withheld until the last sentence, which tells us in an explicit thesis that the contradictions Du Bois has been describing are part of what made Lincoln "big" and "brave."

In most of the writing you do in college, you'll be expected to state your claim explicitly as a THESIS, a statement that identifies your topic and the point you want to make about it. You may need to QUALIFY your thesis in some way, including words like *often*, *sometimes*, or *might* to limit your claim to one you can support.

DEVELOPING AND ORGANIZING AN ARGUMENT

What's at stake in your argument? How can you come up with evidence to support what you say? And how can you organize all that? Following are some questions and strategies that will guide you.

What's at stake?

One way to examine a claim and the thesis it is embedded in is to answer the question of what is at stake in the claim. Rhetoricians and orators in ancient Rome developed stasis theory, a simple system of four questions that can help identify the crux of an argument:

1. *What happened? What are the facts?* Take climate change as an example. It's now clear that global temperatures are increasing: July 4, 2023, was the hottest day in recorded history, and 2023 turned out to be the warmest recorded year ever.

2. *How can the issue be defined?* Some people still define climate change as a natural occurrence, saying it has happened before and will happen again. But many scientists believe that changes in our climate are primarily the result of human activity.

3. *How much does the issue matter, and why?* Different sources will answer this question in different ways: some fossil fuel advocates play down the significance of global warming; most scientists and government officials agree that the fate of the world depends on how quickly and effectively we can act to slow climate change. This question leads us to ask whom this issue affects the most, and why: Who stands to lose, and who if anyone stands to gain?

4. ***What actions should be taken as a result?*** If global warming is just a natural event, is any action required? On the other hand, if it is caused primarily by humans, then many actions can and should occur. If you study proposals for such actions, you can assess their feasibility as well as what will be required to make them successful.

These questions can help you understand what's at stake in an argument—to figure out and assess the arguments put forth by others and identify what is at the heart of an argument. As a writer, these questions can help you examine a topic from a number of different perspectives, identify the main point you want to argue, and even decide the GENRE you want to write: a question of fact might lead you to write a NARRATIVE, telling about what happened, or a question about what action should be taken could lead to a PROPOSAL.

Developing evidence

Any claim you make calls on you to provide good, reliable evidence to support what you say. Here are some familiar strategies that can help you both find and present evidence for what you claim.

Cause and effect. When we analyze causes, we're trying to understand and explain why something happened: Why have there been so many devastating wildfires in recent years? What has caused the recent surge in interest in the WNBA? And when we consider effects, we're thinking about what might happen: How will the use of self-driving cars affect public transportation? Will the growing interest in pro women's basketball lead to higher salaries for the players?

Arguing about causes or effects can be tricky, since it's often hard to link a specific cause to a specific effect. Consider what we know (and don't know) about the causes of long COVID, or the long-term effects of that disease: in this case there are many possible causes and effects. When you write about causes and effects, then, you may need to **QUALIFY** your claim, arguing that they are *possible* or *probable*—or using words like *might* or *could* to limit what you claim.

Classification. When we classify things, we group them into categories. Books, for example, can be classified as fiction, nonfiction, fantasy, picture books, and so on. As a writer, you might use classification as a way to organize a text or to elaborate on a topic. If you are arguing that big-budget films have relied on only three plotlines in the last fifty years, you might organize your evidence by classifying the films as comedies, thrillers, musicals, romance, and so on, and then discussing them genre by genre.

Comparison and contrast. When we compare things, we focus on their similarities, while when we contrast them, we focus on their differences. These strategies can help support what you say, explaining one thing by comparing (or contrasting) it with something else. An article about "The Amazon That Customers Don't See" contrasts how well the JFK8 Amazon warehouse did during the 2020 pandemic at serving its customers with how badly it did at managing its employees.

> Driven by a new sense of mission to serve customers afraid to shop in person, JFK8 helped Amazon smash shipping records, reach stratospheric sales and book the equivalent of the previous three years' profits rolled into one. That success, speed and agility were possible because Amazon and its founder, Jeff Bezos, had pioneered new ways of mass-managing people through technology, relying on a maze of systems that minimized human contact to grow unconstrained.
>
> But the company was faltering in ways outsiders could not see. . . . In contrast to its precise, sophisticated processing of packages, Amazon's model for managing people—heavily reliant on metrics, apps and chatbots—was uneven and strained even before the coronavirus arrived, with employees often having to act as their own

caseworkers, interviews and records show. Amid the pandemic, Amazon's system burned through workers, resulted in inadvertent firings and stalled benefits, and impeded communication, casting a shadow over a business success story for the ages.

—JODI KANTOR, KAREN WEISE, and GRACE ASHFORD, "The Amazon That Customers Don't See"

As a student, you'll often be assigned to compare or contrast things: the music of Philip Glass and Steve Reich, the political philosophies of John Locke and Thomas Hobbes, Keynesian economics and Reaganomics. You can structure comparisons two ways: the *block* method, in which you discuss first one item and then the other (as is done in the Amazon example); or the *point-by-point* method, in which you discuss one point for both items, then go on to the next, and so on.

Definition. A definition says what something is—and what it is not. As a writer, you'll often need to define words that your audience may not understand. And you may need to provide definitions for words that are key to your argument: if you're arguing that *Barbie* is a feminist film, the way you define "feminist" will be crucial to your success. Definitions can play an especially important role when you're writing about controversial topics. If you define abortion as killing an unborn child but your readers define it as a right for women to have control over their own bodies, they are unlikely to agree with any arguments you make.

In an article in *Teen Vogue* about how social media affects our mental health, the author quotes a scientist who argues that dopamine is partly to blame. Here's how she defines "dopamine":

Dopamine is a naturally-occurring "feel-good" chemical that triggers our inner rewards system (it's released when we eat delicious food, have sex, and—crucially—when we take addictive drugs). Social media mimics human connection, prompting dopamine release when we get likes and comments. According to Anna Lembke, Chief of the Addiction Medicine Clinic at Stanford University, the "bottomless bowl" of social media, where we see flashing lights, rankings, and beautiful images of other people all with minimal effort makes the brain release more dopamine than it would with a typical real-life interaction. That, she says, is why it has the potential to be like a drug, explaining that "things that are addictive release a lot more dopamine in the brain."

—BRITTNEY McNAMARA, "The Science behind Social Media's Hold on Our Mental Health"

The effects of dopamine are a major part of the argument, so the definition of dopamine is central to that argument. The author defines it here because she could not assume that the readers of *Teen Vogue* would know what it is.

Description. When you describe something, you say what it looks like, or how it sounds, smells, feels, or tastes. Good descriptions provide concrete details that create some kind of **DOMINANT IMPRESSION** that helps readers imagine what you're describing, and engages their interest as well. See how Maya Angelou describes a group of people in a store to listen to a prize fight on the radio:

Women sat on kitchen chairs, dining-room chairs, stools, and upturned wooden boxes. Small children and babies perched on every lap available and men leaned on the shelves or on each other.

—MAYA ANGELOU, "Champion of the World"

She could have simply said "the room was full of women, children, babies, and men"—but her vivid descriptive writing brings the scene to life, helping us to picture who was in the room. You'll have reason to use description in almost all the writing you do.

In an article **REVIEWING** a new bakery in town, for example, you might want to describe its beautiful cookies. And while you could surely do that with words, you might want to include an image so your readers can actually see what they look like, as we've done here with a photo of a delicious sugar cookie from Shugga Sweets bakery in Decatur, Georgia.

Examples. Good examples bring a subject to life, making abstract ideas more concrete and easier to understand—and providing specific instances to support a point. Here's Jose Antonio Vargas, someone who's won the Pulitzer Prize and "lived the American Dream," writing about the fact that he is still undocumented:

> But I am still an undocumented immigrant. And that means living a different kind of reality. It means going about my day in fear of being found out. It means rarely trusting people, even those closest to me, with who I really am. It means keeping my family photos in a shoebox rather than displaying them on shelves in my home, so friends don't ask about them. . . .
>
> —JOSE ANTONIO VARGAS,
> "My Life as an Undocumented Immigrant"

With one example after another, he helps us understand what it means to live in the United States as an undocumented immigrant.

Examples can often be presented visually as well. Say you're writing about the environmental impact of discarded plastic. You could present facts and figures about plastic bottles, straws, grocery bags, and more. But you could also include a visual, which might get your audience's attention in a way that words alone may not. See how a work by Brooklyn artist Duke Riley consisting of fishing lures made entirely out of plastic found in New York waterways provides powerful evidence of the pollution that plastic causes.

"Monument to Five Thousand Years of Temptation and Deception (1)," by Duke Riley.

Narrative. Using narrative means telling a story. And as *Game of Thrones'* Tyrion Lannister puts it, "There's nothing in the world more powerful than a good story." Exactly! A good story well told can engage your audience and provide memorable support for an argument. In an article about the controversy over legacy admissions to some universities, Daniel Gross begins with a story about one student's experience:

> When Andrea Bian applied to college last year, she made a difficult decision: she chose not to talk about her race, fearing that it would hurt her chances of admission. Bian is of Chinese descent, and she knew that at many US colleges, Asian-American applicants are accepted at lower rates than others with the same grades and test scores.
>
> —DANIEL GROSS, "How Elite US Schools Give Preference to Wealthy and White Legacy Applicants"

Gross goes on to assess the effects legacy admissions have had on enrollment at elite colleges and the fact that legacy students tend to be white. You can use narratives to good effect in your writing as well—in an essay ARGUING for universal early child education, you might include a brief narrative about your own childhood experience in preschool. Be sure, however, that any story you tell supports your point, and that it is not the only evidence you offer.

Narrative sequencing is a rhetorical strategy often used by African American writers to support a point, linking stories or parts of stories to make abstract points more concrete and memorable as narratives. In her address to the 2016 Democratic National Convention, Michelle Obama used this strategy with stories from her own experience in arguing that her husband would make a good president.

She began with a story about her anxiety watching their young daughters set off for their first day of school in a big SUV "with all those big men with guns" and then used this story to launch a discussion of what her husband had done to protect not only his own children but *all* children. Then later in the speech she turned to a story about her ancestors, who had endured slavery and servitude and segregation:

> but who kept on striving and hoping and doing what needed to be done so that today I wake up . . . in a house that was built by slaves. And I watch my daughters . . . playing with their dogs on the White House lawn.

See how narrative sequencing is used in this speech at letstalklibrary.com.

This use of narrative sequencing makes Obama's argument personal, and also one that might appeal to everyone who has hopes and dreams for their children.

Reiteration. A form of repetition, reiteration helps support an argument through emphasis: like a drumbeat, repeating a key word, phrase, or image can drive home your point in a memorable way. Here's Gloria Anzaldúa, on how the languages she speaks are central to her identity:

> So, if you really want to hurt me, talk badly about my language. Ethnic identity is twin skin to linguistic identity—I am my language. Until I can take pride in my language, I cannot take pride in myself. Until I can accept as legitimate Chicano Spanish, Tex-Mex, and all the other languages I speak, I cannot accept the legitimacy of myself. Until I am free to write bilingually and to switch codes without having always to translate . . . my tongue will be illegitimate.
>
> —GLORIA ANZALDÚA, "How to Tame a Wild Tongue"

This is a famous passage, memorable both for what it says and for the way it's said. Try reading it aloud, and listen for how the reiteration of "until" and the parallel clauses establish a rhythm that drives the argument.

Reiteration works in visual texts as well and is a hallmark of graphic novelist Marjane Satrapi's *Persepolis*. Arguing implicitly that repressive regimes squelch individuality, the panel above shows a class of female students, using reiteration to emphasize her point.

Means of persuasion

Whether it's a *TikTok* video, a newspaper op-ed, or Beyoncé's latest hit song, you can be sure that it is drawing on some time-tested appeals—to our emotions, to our sense of ethics, or to our minds. Recognizing these appeals will take you a long way toward understanding how a video, op-ed, and Beyoncé are trying to appeal to you—and using them in arguments of your own will help you connect with those you want to reach.

Emotional appeals (pathos)

It's probably no surprise that arguments that touch our hearts are especially effective. Take a look back at the Steph Curry *Instagram* post on page 46 and you'll see Curry appealing to emotion when he speaks directly to Jordan Poole, recounting the challenges Poole faced, and overcame, during his four years with the Warriors—and then looking to the future, saying, "I can't wait to see you blossom, big fella." Curry pulls on the heartstrings again later in the post when he addresses Chris Paul, his former opponent, saying, "I can't wait to rock with you. Let's get it!" Such appeals help support

Curry's argument: that both players are champions, no matter what team they play for. In essence, Curry is creating a little narrative here, one that has happy endings all the way around—and who doesn't love a happy ending?

Sometimes it helps to appeal to an audience's emotions. Keep in mind, however, that you'll want to think hard about how such an appeal would support your argument, and how it would (or would not) suit your audience and purpose. Would Steph Curry have tugged on our heartstrings quite so hard if he'd been writing a report for his composition class?

Ethical appeals (ethos)

You will find ethical appeals—those aimed at establishing the credibility and good will of a writer or speaker—in almost every argument. When Ukrainian president Volodymyr Zelenskyy addressed the 2023 graduating class of Johns Hopkins University, he argued that they should be very careful about how they use time, never taking it for granted. In reflecting on a recent visit to the front lines of the war, Zelenskyy remarks on how many of the people he saw fighting fiercely there were in many ways the same as the graduates he was addressing:

> They and you have similar hopes for life, similar expectations from life. But there is a fundamental difference that comes down to the question of time. The time of your life is under your control. The time of life of our folks on the front line . . . unfortunately, is subject to many factors that are not all in their control.
>
> —VOLODYMYR ZELENSKYY,
> Johns Hopkins University commencement address

President Zelenskyy wants to convince these college grads to think about how they decide to use their time, to make certain that their time counts and that what they spend their time on reflects and supports their most strongly held values (such as the struggle for democracy and freedom that college grads in his country are

President Zelenskyy speaking with a soldier on the front lines.

devoting their time to). He establishes his credibility for making such an argument right away, when he points out that he has recently been with his fellow Ukrainians on the front lines. His presence on the front lines provides a dramatic demonstration of how he chooses to use his time in support of those things he holds most dear. Later in the address, Zelenskyy offers one piece of advice: "You have to know exactly why you need today and how you want your tomorrows to look." Again, he establishes his authority to offer this advice both by showing that he knows what he's talking about and that he has his audience's best interests in mind.

You too need to establish your own authority with your audience. You can do this by citing trustworthy sources to show that you know what you're talking about, and by representing other positions evenhandedly and accurately to demonstrate that you're fair.

Logical appeals (logos)

Logical appeals play an important role in making a persuasive argument, especially in US academic contexts. That means you need to provide evidence to support your claims—and to look for **EVIDENCE** in any arguments that you encounter. Following are some kinds of evidence that you'll likely encounter or use yourself.

Facts and statistics. Facts are claims that are proven to be true, while statistics are research-based numerical data. Both can serve as powerful sources of evidence. Note how this argument that the United States needs more EV charging stations provides numerical data as evidence.

> Using the US Department of Energy's alternative fuel locator, we can see that the US has [as this book goes to press]:
>
> - 129,598 publicly available EV charging ports spread over 50,401 public charging stations.
>
> - 14,673 private charging ports over 3,743 private charging stations. (These do not include residential charging stations.)
>
> - 290 planned public EV charging ports over an additional 76 planned public charging stations.
>
> - 361 additional planned private EV charging ports over an additional 79 planned private EV charging stations.
>
> Even with all these currently available and planned public and private EV charging stations, it will leave a significant shortfall for the millions of cars charging within the next decade.
>
> —BLINKCHARGING.COM, "The US Needs Twenty Times More EV Charging Stations by 2030 . . . or Else"

Surveys and questionnaires. How many times have you been asked to "take just a few minutes" to respond to a "short" survey? Probably more than you'd like to remember! But gathering information in this way can provide good evidence in support of arguments, including ones you may want to make. One person we know surveyed colleagues at the company where they worked in order to find out which of the many meetings they were required to attend were useful (or not!)—and cited her findings as support for a **PROPOSAL** to management that they eliminate several of the meetings.

If you cite survey results in something you write, you'll need to provide some context: How many people were surveyed, and how were they chosen? What was the response rate? Who conducted the survey, and why? Finally, you'll need to explain what the findings show or suggest—and how they support your argument.

Observations. Sometimes direct observations can help you make a point. Here's how an article in *Discover* magazine uses direct observation to support an argument that whale communication is similar in some way to human communication:

> A man peers over the edge of a boat at a white beluga whale just inches away . . . and plays a harmonica in three tones, over and over. Just like a scene from *Free Willy,* the whale appears to respond. The creature floats close to the boat, head bobbing, looking almost expectantly at the man and circling back. It's a response that can only be described as listening.
>
> —SOPHIE PUTKA, "Understanding How Whales Communicate"

Interviews and conversations. Sometimes you will have the opportunity to interview someone with expertise in a topic you're writing about; or you may find published interviews with information that can provide evidence for a point you're trying to make. Quoting from those interviews can add both authenticity and credibility to your writing. It's also a way to incorporate other voices—which can help to engage your audience.

You may also gather useful information through informal conversations—and that may be what you need to do in communities where formal, scripted interviews might not be welcomed. When two Navajo students wanted to learn about how elders in their community managed to cope in the COVID-19 pandemic, they visited several elders at home and spoke with them about their lives during the pandemic, listening respectfully to what they said.

Expert testimony. Most of us turn to testimony from reliable sources to help us accept or reject arguments: a respected friend tells us that the TV show *American Born Chinese* is a "beautiful story with a shocker ending that really grabs your attention," and we will probably watch at least one episode. Testimony provides an especially strong support for an argument when it comes from trusted experts and authorities on a topic. And citing such authorities to support something you say will also add to your credibility on the topic, letting readers know you have done your homework. Remember too that you can find authorities all around you: your grandmother, for example, may be an expert on herbal remedies—and your local mechanic could be an authority on antique cars.

See how one student cited the work of an expert in a research-based argument for an education course on the influence of culture on literacy practices. Arguing that reading is in some communities deeply collaborative—and should not be taught as a solitary activity—the student cited the work of MacArthur Fellow Shirley Brice Heath, an anthropological linguist whose ground-breaking ethnographic study, *Ways with Words: Language, Life, and Work in Communities and Classrooms*, focuses on the literacy practices in three communities in South Carolina:

> As Heath (1983) demonstrated in *Ways with Words*:
>
>> Reading was a public group affair for almost all members of Trackton, from the youngest to the oldest. Miss Lula sometimes read her Bible alone and Annie Mae would sometimes quietly read magazines she brought home, but to read alone was frowned upon, and individuals who did so were accused of being antisocial. . . . In general, reading alone, unless one is very old and religious, marks an individual as someone who cannot make it socially. (p. 191)
>
> In short, students who grow up in communities where reading is a group activity may struggle if they are required to read entirely on their own—and challenge us to think hard about the way we will one day be teaching reading.

Note how the student did not identify Heath or describe her expertise, assuming that her audience, all students of literacy, would be well acquainted with Heath's work, and very likely with *Ways with Words* in particular. Citing Heath added powerful support to the student's argument—and also to her own CREDIBILITY, showing that she'd done her homework and was aware of some of the research on her topic. Her essay is in APA style, the documentation style used in education.

Experiments. Experiments provide information that's particularly important to the sciences and social sciences, where data is highly valued as support for a claim. One student writing about how multitasking affects attention span cited an experiment that tracked attention in which participants looked at images on a screen and then were shown other images and asked to say which ones they had seen before and which ones were new. Studying brain and eye response, researchers could identify lapses in their attention, and then compare these findings to answers the participants gave about their own attention, mind wandering, and media multitasking. The results? Those participants who reported more media multitasking correlated with more lapses in attention.

While this experiment reinforced earlier research on memory and media multitasking, the writer was careful to point out that its findings only show a *correlation* between the two: they do not tell us if media multitasking *causes* memory lapses. In using data drawn from experiments, you will want to be equally cautious in the claims you make based on it.

Charts, images, and other visuals. Sometimes you'll have evidence that is best presented visually, as a table, pie chart, bar graph, or some other visual. The pie chart on the next page shows what literary genres students in one college dorm are reading. It would be possible to convey the same information in a paragraph, but the pie chart makes it easier to see and understand the information—and with more impact. Were you surprised to see that almost half of

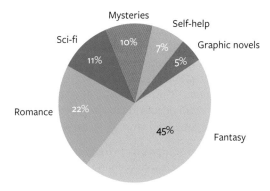

What Genres Are Students Reading

the students favor fantasy? Remember, though, that visual evidence often needs to be explained: photos require captions, and any visuals you don't create yourself need to be acknowledged and documented.

Personal experience. Your own experiences may provide powerful support for an argument. After all, you've "lived it," and thus can provide a firsthand account that supports what you say—and, by the way, you can also build your credibility with your audience. One college student based her proposal for more campus support for students with eating disorders on her own experience with anorexia. Augmenting a searing NARRATIVE of her personal struggle with this disease with data drawn from research and interviews with campus medical professionals, she wrote a PROPOSAL arguing for changes in campus policies.

Are there any problems with the reasoning?

Some appeals use reasoning that is misleading, unfair, or simply lazy. Such appeals are called FALLACIES, and because they can often be very powerful and persuasive, you may not recognize them as problems at all. Therefore, it's important to keep an eye out for them in arguments you read as well as in those that you yourself write. Here are some of the most common fallacies.

Ad hominem (Latin for "to the man") arguments make personal attacks on those who support an opposing position, rather than addressing the position itself. "Of course school board member Etione doesn't want to build a new elementary school: she doesn't even have any children." The board member's lack of children may have nothing to do with opposition to a new school, nor does the attack provide an argument in favor of the school.

Bandwagon appeals just urge others to go along with the crowd. "Join the millions of people who've found pain relief with Mybest Remedy." Such an appeal aims to make us believe that if "millions" have benefited from this remedy, we will too. But where's the proof?

Begging the question just restates a question in other words. "We must reduce the national debt because the government owes too much money" begs the question by essentially saying the same thing twice.

Either/or arguments pose a false dilemma by arguing that only two alternatives are possible in a situation that is actually more complex. "I will not allow the United States to become a weak, defenseless nation: with my leadership, it will remain the world's greatest superpower" ignores all other possibilities between these two extremes.

Faulty analogies are comparisons that don't hold up under scrutiny. "Credit card companies are just like vultures: they take advantage of their victims at their weakest moments" ignores the fact that vultures prey on other birds for their own survival, while credit card companies do it for profit or the bottom line.

False cause arguments assume that because one event happened after another, the first event *caused* the second. Arguing that unemployment is down this year because government reduced the tax on gasoline assumes a causal connection that may not be there.

Hasty generalization leads to sweeping conclusions on the basis of too little evidence. "The Lyft driver I had today was a jerk, so I'll never take another Lyft." Many such generalizations come from stereotypes about groups of people. It's difficult to make arguments without generalizing at all, but be sure that any generalizations you use are based on sufficient evidence and carefully qualified with words like *most, usually, sometimes,* and so on.

Paralipsis (from Greek for "omissions") arguments provide information after saying that such information will not be included, as Robert Downey Jr. does in *Iron Man* when he says, "I'm not saying I'm responsible for this country's longest run of uninterrupted peace in thirty-five years."

Slippery slope arguments contend that if a certain event occurs, it will or at least might set a chain of events in motion that will end in disaster. Opponents of physician-assisted suicide sometimes warn that making it legal for doctors to help people end their lives would ultimately lead to an increase in suicide or even to murders disguised to look like suicide. Slippery slope arguments are not always wrong, but keep in mind that the greater the difference between the initial event and the predicted outcome, the more evidence is needed to claim the situation will actually play out as predicted.

Straw man appeals misrepresent an opposing argument in order to attack it more easily. Some critics of the Affordable Care Act attacked it as a "federal takeover of health care" when in reality the legislation increased the government's role in health care but left the primarily private systems of insurance intact.

Considering multiple perspectives

You've likely seen a lot of ads for Bitcoin, Ethereum, and other crypto currencies, ads promising huge returns on investment. Or rave endorsements by celebrities—Reese Witherspoon! Tom Brady!

Matt Damon! Naomi Osaka! These ads and endorsements are typically 100 percent positive: they focus on convincing us to invest in a digital currency.

Such ads seldom if ever consider alternative viewpoints. That means that as careful consumers, we need to seek out other perspectives on our own. In the case of digital currencies, you might turn to an article in *Forbes*, a magazine devoted to finance and investing, to check out Nikita Tambe and Aashika Jain's article on the "Advantages and Disadvantages of Cryptocurrency." In their analysis, Tambe and Jain point out what they see as advantages crypto offers—speed and ease of use, accessibility, and transparency—but go on to note that problems associated with blockchains, a lack of clear policies on cancellations or refunds, and extreme volatility could be serious disadvantages. Rather than arguing that readers should or should not invest in cryptocurrencies, their argument is, "Buyer beware."

These examples represent two different genres and purposes: advertisements exist to sell something, whereas *Forbes* is a magazine that includes articles and opinion pieces for those who follow or work in finance.

Whenever you read something that makes an argument, ask yourself whether it considers any COUNTERARGUMENTS or differing views. And that goes for texts that are not necessarily making an argument, such as reports or profiles; they too are making some kind of point. In short, you should question any texts that present only one point of view. And even when more than one point of view is acknowledged, you need to see how the author responds to views that differ from their own: that they show evidence refuting those views, acknowledge that some other views might be valid, or qualify what they say.

In a newspaper profile of Adam Sandler, see how the author acknowledges that not everyone agrees with those of us who love *Big Daddy* and his many other zany comedies—and admits that such criticism is "sometimes" fair:

> Critics, as a group, hate Sandler comedies, sometimes fairly, but just as often because the movies undermine the project of close reading

Cole Sprouse and Adam Sandler in *Big Daddy*.

altogether. If you don't think a Sandler comedy is funny, no amount of thinking on the page is ever going to convince you otherwise. It either tickles your funny bone or it doesn't.

—JAMIE LAUREN KEILES, "Adam Sandler's Everlasting Shtick"

In the same way, you need to consider multiple viewpoints in what you write. It's not enough to simply state your position in an argument or to make a point of some kind in a report or synthesis; you need to acknowledge what others say fairly and respectfully—and to address any views that differ from what you say.

REFLECT! Look back at two or three pieces of writing you have done recently. In what way might you describe these pieces as *arguments*? What claim, either direct or indirect, have you made? Then skim through this chapter again, and think about what kinds of evidence you used. Do you seem to favor statistics, or perhaps testimony, or personal experience—or something else? If so, why do you think that is? What emotional, ethical, or logical appeals have you used? In retrospect, how might you revise one of these pieces of writing to make use of one or more strategies discussed in this chapter?

5 Developing Academic Habits of Mind

College inspired me to think differently.
It's like no other time in your life.

—LARISA OLEYNIK

You can't be afraid to fail.
It's the only way you succeed—
and you're not going to succeed all the time.

—LeBRON JAMES

Have you given some thought to what exactly you want to accomplish in college? What do you want to learn, but more than that: What do you hope to gain from your time in college? Larisa Oleynik said that college inspired her to "think differently," that it was like "no other time" in her life. And here's what Michelle Obama said, to a group of students at Howard University: "College did everything for me." She then offered some advice, noting that going to college "opens up a world of opportunity" and urging them to try new things—and "step out of [their] comfort zone and soar!" That's pretty darned good advice. And a nationwide group of group of writing teachers have figured out some additional advice, identifying several habits of mind that are important for achieving that kind of success in college. This chapter provides guidelines for developing ten habits of mind as you travel the path toward being a curious and engaged reader, writer, and thinker.

Be curious

Inquire, investigate, ask questions. Poke and pry until you find answers. Explore the college catalog, looking for courses you *want* to take, even if they're not required. If you're assigned to do research, don't think of it just as an assignment you've got to "get done." Take it as an opportunity to learn something that you don't already know. And do the same with any writing assignments. Whatever position you take in an essay, find out about other POSITIONS—and take them seriously. Be curious about what others think: they just might change your mind. You can practice curiosity by asking questions: What? What *if*? Why? Why *not*? Who? How? Where? When?

Let's not forget that exploration is the catalyst of learning.
TIM DONAHUE

Two students at Ohio State were tired of walking fifteen minutes through rain and snow from the parking lot to class and wondered why student parking was outdoors rather than in a garage. And why was it so far from the classrooms? Could it be located any closer, and in a garage? They were curious about who makes such decisions and whether students are ever consulted—and so they drafted an OP-ED for the student newspaper raising their concerns.

Be open to new ideas

You're sure to encounter all kinds of new ideas in college, and new perspectives. In class or elsewhere, you'll have occasion to discuss ideas with others, including people whose views may differ from yours. Make it a goal to listen carefully until you understand their views, to try to see the world from their perspective. Ask questions, and be interested in what they say. Resist the temptation to respond too quickly with your own opinions. Remember that they just might be right. And even if they aren't, they'll get you thinking. New ideas do that!

The writing and research you'll do will be all about ideas. Here too you'll need to start by seeking out multiple positions on your topic—and to do so before even thinking about where you stand. What you don't want to do is to start with an idea you already have and simply look for sources that support that idea; you'll never learn anything new if you do that.

Seek out ideas and viewpoints that differ from yours. In a campus discussion about anti-racism, for example, be sure to examine your own assumptions and biases and try to put yourself in the position of people with different perspectives—a student from Kenya or India, a descendant of Japanese grandparents who were incarcerated during World War II, a victim of police violence. And remember that new ideas can also come from friends and family: your great uncle who served in the Vietnam War, for instance, may have ideas about American foreign policy that will be completely new to you. You're looking for a wide range of different viewpoints, ones that should be part of your thinking about the topic.

Engage

Grapple with ideas: focus. To really focus on something—reading, writing, listening to a lecture, whatever—you need to clear your mind of everything else and pay attention to what you're doing, 100 percent. Let the phone ring; resist the temptation to check email or *Instagram*. **ANNOTATING** as you read can help you engage with the text: underline key points, scribble questions in the margins. **SUMMARIZING** can help you understand and remember a difficult or complex text.

If you're in a class that doesn't engage your interest, look for an angle that does. That's what one student did in an economics course. She found econ difficult and abstract—and boring. Then one day her instructor mentioned the role of the exchange economy in *Animal Crossing*. That was her favorite video game, and the concepts of scarcity and utility became much less abstract when she could think of them in terms of paying Tom Nook (pictured here) with Bells. Soon she was trading like a tycoon—and finally enjoying her econ class.

Be creative

Explore new ideas, try out new methods, experiment with new approaches. Play around with ideas, and see where they take you. Try BRAINSTORMING and FREEWRITING. If you're struggling to write an essay, for instance, try expressing your ideas in a different MEDIUM. One student who was taking a course on ancient religious texts, primarily to fulfill a requirement, and when he was assigned to read the Samson and Delilah story in different religious traditions—and then he used his keen interest in comics to create a graphic narrative of his favorite version. His creative approach to the assignment made it one that he was excited about—and that earned high praise from the instructor!

If you think about your most successful school endeavors, you'll probably find that creativity played an important role: the science project you created and presented that was unlike anything anyone else imagined; those hip-hop lyrics you wrote to illustrate a point in a history presentation; the marathon that you managed to finish, which led to a fascination with effective training processes—and a senior thesis in human biology.

> Creativity is intelligence having fun.
> ALBERT EINSTEIN

Be flexible

Whether you're at a small college or a large university, there will be much more work than you've had before now, and a lot to deal with—labs and lab reports in science classes, reading lists and essays in English, large textbooks and online homework in physics. Maybe you have a part-time job, or a young child. Or maybe you're caring for an elderly parent. It's a lot to juggle. This means you need to develop strategies for managing your time, planning for due dates, and keeping yourself on task—and that you need to be flexible.

Perhaps you prefer to do your serious reading early in the morning, but one term you have early classes every day. Rather than getting up earlier and earlier, try to stay flexible and find a time later in the day you can devote to your reading assignments. One student was so determined to write a summary of an assigned article that she told herself she couldn't get up from her desk until it was done. Hours later, she was still sitting there, praying for inspiration that just wouldn't come. A little flexibility—getting up and taking a walk, doing another task that she could accomplish easily, or just taking a brief break—would probably have helped her make a fresh start. If ever you're feeling stuck, a CONVERSATION with a friend or roommate—or AI—might help you get unstuck—and can even be a turning point.

Be persistent

Keep at it. Follow through. Take advantage of opportunities to revise and improve. Keep track of what's challenging or hard for you—and look for ways to overcome those obstacles. You've probably already seen the positive effects of persistence in your life, and these effects will double (or triple) in college: successful students don't give up but keep on keeping on.

One student who was searching for information on a distant relative who had played a role in the civil rights movement kept coming up empty-handed and was about to give up on the project. But she decided to try one last lead through ancestry.com—and discovered a crucial piece of information that led to a big breakthrough and a sense of personal satisfaction. Her persistence paid off, and it eventually led her to write a profile of her relative introducing that person to the rest of her large extended family.

You just can't beat the person who never gives up.
BABE RUTH

Take responsibility

The work you do in college will call on you to take responsibility for what you say and write and do. You'll need to take charge of your learning and make the most of your education. While you may use AI to help you find alternative points of view on a topic, you're the author and you must take responsibility for any information you get from AI—and acknowledge your use of it. That means not just being engaged with the topics you're researching, but owning what you say about them, standing behind your words. And that also means being able to vouch for the sources you use.

One student who was interested in the right-to-die movement in his state began researching arguments on all sides of this debate. Coming to the conclusion that those in favor of the movement were persuasive, he began incorporating some of their arguments into an essay. But something began nagging at him when he realized that several of his sources said almost exactly the same thing. He traced these sources back to one single source: a website owned by the Euthanasia Society, a group dedicated to assisted suicide. That discovery led him to do additional research, including sources by groups that oppose assisted suicide. This additional research then led him to qualify his conclusions—and to present a more balanced argument about this volatile issue. In short, he took responsibility for what he wrote—and for the sources he used.

Ch. 17 provides tips for determining if a source is reliable.

Collaborate

Work with others! When it comes to solving problems or coming up with ideas, two heads are better than one—and more than two are often better still. Lots of your college work will call for collaboration, from conducting an experiment with a lab partner to working with a team to present a report. As a writer you're in constant collaboration with those who read and respond to your ideas. Then there's all you might do online—on *Zoom* or *TikTok*—or in conversation with AI. All COLLABORATION. And all important: learning to work well with others is as important as anything else you learn in college.

Talk to the person next to you, make a network, have an open mind, and don't be ashamed to ask for help.
GAIL MELLOW

Reflect

Think about how you learn, and make it a habit of thinking about that often. *Where* do you do most of your learning—in class? at the library? at home? *How* does your learning take place—from lectures? textbooks? browsing online? doing research? talking to others? writing? *Who* takes charge of this learning—instructors?

your mom? you? Research has identified this kind of purposeful reflection as instrumental to becoming well educated. And many students find that keeping an informal journal to write about what they're learning, how they're learning it, and how they're learning to overcome obstacles leads to better comprehension and better success. Some students we know use *Discord* to share and chat about what they're learning, saying that doing so helps them "learn it better."

Don't be afraid to fail!

You may remember your grandmother or some other wise person saying "Nothing ventured, nothing gained." They were right! After all, we all learn from our mistakes, from doing something wrong and then keeping at it until we get it right. The first time I tried to ride a bike, I promptly fell off. But with encouragement and a little instruction from my dad, I got back on and kept trying until I was zooming around the neighborhood like an ace.

When former Philadelphia Eagles quarterback Nick Foles was asked about his amazing career, from barely a starter to a backup, and then, in 2018, to Superbowl MVP, here's what he said:

> I think the big thing is, don't be afraid to fail. In our society today—*Instagram, Twitter* [now *X*]—it's a highlight reel. It's all the good things. And then . . . when you have a rough day . . . you think you're failing. Failure is a part of life . . . a part of building character and growing. . . . I wouldn't be up here if I hadn't fallen thousands of times. Made mistakes. [So] if something's going on in your life and you're struggling? Embrace it. Because you're growing.
>
> —NICK FOLES, Super Bowl LII press conference

It's no coincidence that all these habits of mind go along with what it means to think and act rhetorically. The same practices that make us careful, ethical, and effective communicators (listen, search for understanding, put in your oar) also lead to success in college—or

Nick Foles scoring on fourth-down-and-goal in Super Bowl LII, the first player in Super Bowl history to throw and catch a touchdown.

in the Super Bowl. You'll have plenty of opportunities to practice and develop these habits in the writing and reading and speaking and listening you'll do in college. I bet you'll enjoy the ride—and if, like Michelle Obama, you work at it, you too can soar!

REFLECT! What new things have you tried so far in college? And what other new things do you hope to try? Make a bucket list of all that you hope to experience and accomplish before you graduate. Then get started—and remember: don't be afraid to make mistakes. That's just part of trying new things!

PALAMEDE, REMIGIA ED IO   61

iva per suo conto. Ero lì lì su quel-
limite: v'ero giunto senza saperlo,
dall'incalzare dell'angoscia: se l'ol-
vo, senza averne coscienza, ero un
un uomo libero finalmente le cui scia-
n hanno più senso. Invece, al varco
io, la coscienza m'avvertiva ch'io
pazzo... ed era finita! Ritorna
librio di macigno: mi sentiva

con le scarp Ma
bisbiglio de sacerd
lamede, ch
l'altare
ne

PROVENCE TED

6 Reading to Understand, Engage & Respond

The words on the page are only half the story. The rest is what you bring to the party.

—TONI MORRISON

Chances are, you read more than you think you do. You read print texts, of course, but you're probably reading even more on a phone, a tablet, a computer, or other devices. Reading is now, as perhaps never before, a basic necessity. In fact, if you think that reading is something you learned once and for all in the first or second grade, think again. Today, reading calls for strategic effort. As media critic Howard Rheingold sees it, literacy today involves at least five interlocking abilities: attention, participation, collaboration, network awareness, and critical consumption. Of these, attention is first and foremost. In short, you need to work at paying attention to what you read. In *The Economics of Attention*, rhetorician Richard Lanham explains: "We're drowning in information. What we lack is the human attention needed to make sense of it all."

When so many texts are vying for our attention, which ones do we choose to read? In order to decide what to read, what to pay attention to, we need to practice what Rheingold calls "infotention," a word he coined to describe a "mind-machine combination of brain-powered attention skills and computer-powered information filters." Put simply, infotention helps us to focus. And while some of us can multitask (fighter pilots are one example Rheingold gives of those whose jobs demand it), most of us aren't good at it and must learn to focus our attention when we read.

READING TO UNDERSTAND

Your first job as a reader is to make sure you understand what you are reading, and why you're reading it.

Start by previewing

Reading experts tell us that it's best to begin not by plunging right into a text but by previewing it to get a sense of what it's about.

- ***Look at the title*** and any subtitle, the first paragraph, and any headings to get a sense of what the text covers.

- ***What do you know*** (and think) about the topic? What do you want to learn about it?

- ***Who are the authors***, and what's their expertise? Where do you think they're coming from? Might they have an agenda?

- *Who's the publisher* or sponsor, and what does that tell you about the text's intended audience and purpose?
- *Consider any sources* that are cited. Are they credible?
- *Look at any visuals*—photos or drawings, charts, graphs. What information do they contribute?
- *Consider the design.* How does it affect the way you understand the text? What do the fonts and any use of color suggest about the text's TONE? Are there any sidebars or other features that highlight parts of the text?
- *What's your first impression* of the text, and what interests you the most?

Think about your rhetorical situation

Once you have a sense of what the text is about, think about why you're reading it and the rest of your rhetorical situation.

- What's your PURPOSE for reading? To learn something new? To fulfill an assignment? To prepare for a test? Something else?
- Who's the intended AUDIENCE for the text? What words or images in the text make you think so? Are you a member of this group? If not, there may be unfamiliar terms or references that you'll need to look up.
- What's the GENRE? An argument? A report? A narrative? An annotated bibliography? Knowing the genre will tell you something about what to expect.
- How do the MEDIUM and LANGUAGE affect the way you read the text? Is it a written print text? a podcast? a visual or MULTIMODAL text, such as an infographic?
- Think about the larger CONTEXT. What do you know about the topic and what others say about it? What do you need to find out?
- What's your own STANCE on the topic? Are you an advocate? a critic? an impartial observer?

Read difficult texts strategically

You'll surely encounter texts and subject matter that are hard to understand. Most often these will be ones you're reading not for pleasure but to learn something. You'll want to slow down with such texts, to stop and think—and you might find this easier to do with print texts, where paragraphs and headings and highlighted information help you see the various parts and find key information. Here are some other tips for making your way through difficult texts:

Reading is an active, imaginative act; it takes work.

KHALED HOSSEINI

- Read first for what you can understand, and simply mark places that are confusing, things you don't understand, words or concepts you'll need to look up.

- Then choose a chapter, or part of a chapter, and try to identify its main points—look at headings, and any THESIS and TOPIC SENTENCES.

- Check to see if there's a SUMMARY at the beginning or end of the text. If so, read it very carefully.

- Reread the hard parts. Slow down, and focus.

- Try to make sense of the parts: this part offers evidence; that paragraph summarizes an alternative view; here's a signal about what's coming next.

- If the text includes VISUALS, what data or other information do they contribute to the message?

- Resist highlighting: it's better to take notes in the margins or on digital sticky notes.

- Read together with a classmate, talking through anything you find difficult. Or just try talking about what you've read. No telling where that might lead. . . .

- If AI is permitted, paste the text into a chatbot and ask it to give a brief recap of what the text says and to highlight the key points. Keep in mind that AI cannot summarize a text accurately because it does not really understand what it says.

ENGAGING WITH WHAT YOU READ

Reading can take you places you have never been before.
OHRAN PAMIK

Engagement is one of the habits of mind that are crucial to success in college and to the reading you do there. You're "engaged" as a reader when you approach a text with an open mind, ready to listen to what it has to say. This kind of engagement may come naturally when you're reading something you want to read. But what about texts you're assigned to read, ones you wouldn't read otherwise? How do you engage productively with them? There's no magic wand you can wave to make this happen, but here's a little advice, based on what students have told us about how they can get "into" an assigned text.

First, find your comfort zone, a place where you can concentrate. A comfy lounge chair? A chair with good back support? Starbucks? Wherever it is, getting up to stretch every half hour or so will help you maintain focus.

Then choose the medium or device that helps you focus. Some readers like print text best for taking notes. Others prefer ebooks, which can be read on a Kindle or similar device to avoid the distractions phones and computers have.

And consider reading with classmates. Particularly with difficult texts, two heads are usually better than one—and discussing a text with others will help you all to engage with it. Try to explain something in the text to a friend: if you can get the major points across, you've understood it!

Annotate as you read

Annotating enables you to note the key points in the text. Do what literary critic Anatole Broyard once recommended: "Stomp around in it . . . underlining passages, scribbling in the margins, leaving [your] mark." Broyard's point echoes what reading experts say: the more you "stomp around" in a text, the better you'll understand it and engage with what it says. On the next page is a list of things to consider as you read and annotate.

- What CLAIMS does the text make? Note any THESIS statement.
- What REASONS and EVIDENCE are offered to support any claims—examples, DEFINITIONS, and so on?
- Identify any key terms (and look them up if necessary).
- Note places in the text where the author demonstrates AUTHORITY to write on the topic.
- What is the author's STANCE toward the topic—passionate? skeptical? neutral? something else? Note any words that reflect the author's stance.
- How would you describe the author's STYLE and TONE— formal? conversational? skeptical? something else? Mark words that establish that, and think about how they affect the way you react to the text.
- Mark any COUNTERARGUMENTS or other perspectives. How fairly are those views described, and how does the author respond to them? Are there any perspectives that the author neglects to mention?
- Consider any sources cited in the text and think about whether you can trust them. If you have any doubts, FACT-CHECK.
- Pay attention to the DESIGN and any VISUALS, and think about how they affect the message.
- Underline any points that are unclear or confusing, and jot down your questions in the margins.

Note anything that you find surprising, that seems questionable, or that you disagree with. But keep an open mind—and remember that some views that differ from yours just might be right.

A sample annotated text

On the following page is the opening of an essay about minority student clubs on college campuses written by Gabriela Moro, a student at the University of Notre Dame. See how one reader has annotated her text—and how it helped that reader engage with her argument. You can read Moro's full essay on page 147.

Minority representation on US college campuses has increased significantly in recent years, and many schools have made it a priority to increase diversity on their campuses in order to prepare students for a culturally diverse US democratic society (Hurtado and Ruiz 3–4). To complement this increase, many schools have implemented minority student clubs to provide safe and comfortable environments where minority students can thrive academically and socially with peers from similar backgrounds. However, do these minority groups amplify students' tendency to interact only with those who are similar to themselves? Put another way, do these groups inhibit students from engaging in diverse relationships?

Good question! What's the answer?

Is this her thesis?

She's going to consider more views. Good!

Many view such programs to be positive and integral to minority students' college experience; some, however, feel that these clubs are not productive for promoting cross-cultural interaction. While minority clubs have proven to be beneficial to minority students in some cases, particularly on campuses that are not very diverse, my research suggests that colleges would enrich the educational experience for all students by introducing multicultural clubs as well.

I need to check out this source—are these real students or just stereotypes?

Who are these students and how did she find them? What's she mean by "minority" students?

To frame my discussion, I will use an article from *College Student Journal* that distinguishes between two types of students: one who believes minority clubs are essential for helping minority students stay connected with their cultures, and another who believes these clubs isolate minorities and work against diverse interaction among students. To pursue the question of whether or not such groups segregate minorities from the rest of the student body and even discourage cultural awareness, I will use perspectives from minority students at Notre Dame to show that these programs are especially helpful for first-year students. I will also use other student testimonials to show that when taken too far, minority groups can lead to self-segregation and defy what most universities claim to be their diversity goals.

Findings from research will contribute to a better understanding of the role minority clubs play on college campuses and offer a complete answer to my question about the importance of minority programs.

—GABRIELA MORO,
"Minority Student Clubs: Integration or Segregation?"

Looks like her stance will be to take the middle ground in this debate. Let's see if this holds true.

Consider the larger context

All texts are part of some larger conversation, and one reason academic writers document their sources is to acknowledge an awareness of that conversation. Considering that larger context will help you understand the text and shed light on issues that you may not have known about.

When, in 2017, Secretary of Education Betsy DeVos said that Historically Black Colleges and Universities (HBCUs) stand tall as "pioneers of school choice," her words sounded like a compliment. But putting that claim into context helps to assess—or reassess— what she said. After all, HBCUs arose in response to Jim Crow segregation at many colleges and universities, from which Black students were excluded. Putting DeVos's statement in context, then, calls it into question, revealing that in fact students of color had very few choices in terms of higher education.

Here are some tips to help you consider the larger context of texts you read:

- What else has been said about this topic? What's the larger conversation surrounding it, and how does this text fit into that conversation?

- Is the author responding to what someone else has said— and if so, what?

- Is their point confirmed (or challenged) by what else has been said?

- Who's cited, and what does that tell you about the author's **STANCE**?
- Does the text consider **COUNTERARGUMENTS** and multiple **PERSPECTIVES** on the topic fairly and respectfully?
- Who cares about this topic, and why does this topic matter in the first place?
- How does the larger context inform your thinking about the topic?

REFLECT! The next time you read a text online, pay attention to your process. Do you go straight through, or do you stop often? Do you take notes? Do you turn away from what you're reading to look at or attend to something else? What do you do if you don't understand a passage? How long can you read at a stretch and maintain full concentration? Then answer the same questions the next time you read a print text. What differences do you notice in the way you read each kind of text? What conclusions can you draw about how to be a more effective reader, both on- and off-screen?

RESPONDING TO WHAT YOU READ

Whenever you actively engage with a text, annotating and "stomping around" in it, you are already responding, talking back to it, questioning it, assessing its claims, and coming to conclusions about whether or not you accept them. There are many ways to respond more explicitly—from jotting a quick reply to a blog post, to writing in the comment space following a news article, to writing a full-blown review. Following are three kinds of writing you may be assigned to do when responding to something you've read: to summarize what it says, to respond to what it says, and to analyze the way it's written.

Summarize

Summarizing something you've read in your own words can help you understand and remember its main points. Following are some tips for doing so:

- Keep your summary short and sweet, capturing the text's main ideas but leaving out its supporting information.

- Take care that your summary is fair and accurate—and uses neutral, nonjudgmental language.

- Use your own words and sentence structure; if you do QUOTE any words from the original text, be sure to enclose them in quotation marks.

- DOCUMENT any texts you summarize in academic writing of your own.

Here's a summary of Gabriela Moro's essay:

> In a time of increasing diversity on US college campuses, Gabriela Moro asks whether minority student clubs and programs help minority students succeed and have a good "college experience," or whether they result in separation and even segregation. Moro considers the pros and cons of each position and concludes that while these clubs and programs are "especially helpful for first-year students," they can work against college goals for inclusiveness.

See Moro's full essay on p. 147.

If you're assigned to write a SUMMARY/RESPONSE essay, there are various ways to respond. Two ways that are often assigned are by responding to what the text says and by analyzing the way it says it.

Respond to what the text says

Agree or disagree—or even agree with some parts and disagree with others. However you respond, you'll be making an ARGUMENT for what you say. Some tips to help you do so are on the next page.

See an essay that responds to an op-ed on p. 199.

- What does the text CLAIM, and is it stated explicitly in a THESIS? Does the claim need to be QUALIFIED—or stated more strongly?

- What REASONS and EVIDENCE does the author provide? Are they sufficient?

- Does the author acknowledge any COUNTERARGUMENTS or other positions? If not, what other views should be addressed?

- Has the author cited any sources—and if so, how trustworthy are they?

- Do you agree with the author's position? disagree? both agree and disagree? Why?

Analyze the way the text is written

See an essay that analyzes a magazine on p. 175.

How does the text work? What makes it tick? ANALYZING how a text is written can help you to understand what it's saying. Here are some questions to consider:

- What interests you in the text you're analyzing? What are you trying to understand by analyzing it?

- What kind of analysis will you conduct—RHETORICAL ANALYSIS? CAUSAL ANALYSIS? DATA ANALYSIS? Something else?

- What does the text CLAIM, and is it stated explicitly in a THESIS? What EVIDENCE is provided to support that claim? SUMMARIZE what it says for your readers.

- Think about the text's RHETORICAL SITUATION—its purpose, audience, and so on—and how that affects the way you understand its message.

- How does the text work? Is it all paragraphs, or does it include lists, charts, equations, or other kinds of text? Are there headings? How about photos or other images? How do these things affect what the text says?

- How is the text organized, and how does that affect the way you understand it?
- Look for patterns—repeated words, structures, or themes—and think about what they reveal about the author's STANCE.
- What insight does your analysis lead to? How does the way the text is written affect the way you understand it? This will be the point of your analysis—*your claim*, which you'll then need to support with evidence.

READING ON-SCREEN AND OFF

Once upon a time "reading" meant attending to words on paper. But today we often encounter texts that convey information in images and in sound as well—and they may be on- or off-screen. Whatever texts you're reading, be sure to think carefully about how the medium may affect your understanding, engagement, and response.

Researchers have found that we often take shortcuts when we read online, searching and scanning and jumping around in a text or leaping from link to link. This kind of reading is very helpful for finding answers and information quickly, but it can blur your focus and make it difficult to attend to the text carefully and purposefully. Here are a few tips to help you when reading on a screen:

- Be clear about your PURPOSE for reading. If you need to remember the text, remind yourself to read very carefully and to avoid skimming or skipping around.
- Close *Facebook* or any other pages that may distract you.
- Try taking notes on PDFs or *Word* documents so that you can jot down questions and comments as you read. Alternatively, print out the text and take notes on paper.
- Look up unfamiliar terms as you read, making a note of definitions you may need later.

The pervasiveness of reading on-screen may suggest that many readers prefer to read that way. But current research suggests that most students still prefer to read print, especially if the reading is important and needs to be internalized and remembered. Print texts, it's worth remembering, are easy to navigate—you can tell at a glance how much you've read and how much you still have to go, and you can move back and forth in the text to find something important.

In addition, researchers have found that students who read on-screen are less likely to reflect on what they read or to make connections in ways that bind learning to memory. It's important to note, however, that studies like these almost always end with a caveat: reading practices are changing, and technology is making it easier to read on-screen.

It's also important to note that online texts often blend written words with audio, video, links, charts and graphs, and other elements that can be attended to in any order you choose. In reading such texts, you'll need to make decisions carefully. When exactly should you click on a link, for example? The first moment it comes up? Or should you make a note to check it out later, since doing so now may break your concentration—and you might not be able to get back easily to what you were reading? Links can be a good thing in that they lead to more information, but following them can interrupt your train of thought. In addition, scrolling seems to encourage skimming and to make us read more rapidly. In short, it can be harder to stay on task. So you may well need to make a special effort with digital texts—to read them attentively, and to pay close attention to what you're reading.

We are clearly in a time of flux where reading is concerned, so the best advice is to think very carefully about *why* you're reading. If you want to find some information quickly, to follow a conversation on social media, or to look for online sources on a topic you're researching, reading on-screen is the way to go. But if you need to fully comprehend and retain the information, you may want to stick with print.

READING VISUALS

Visual texts present their own opportunities and challenges. As new technologies bring images of all kinds into our phones and lives on a minute-by-minute basis, visual texts have become so familiar and pervasive that it may seem that "reading" them is just natural. But reading visual texts with a critical eye takes time and patience—and attention.

Take a look at the advertisement for a Shinola watch on the next page. You may know that Shinola is a Detroit-based watchmaker proud that its watches are "built in America"; if not, a quick look at Shinola.com will fill in this part of the ad's CONTEXT. But there's a lot more going on in terms of its particular rhetorical situation. The ad first ran in 2015, when it was clearly responding to smart watches in general and to the launch of the Apple Watch in particular, with its full panoply of futuristic bells and whistles. "Hey," the Shinola ad writers seemed to be saying, "our watch is just smart enough."

Thinking through the rhetorical situation tells us something about the ad's purpose and audience. Of course its major PURPOSE is to sell watches; but one other goal seems to be to poke a little fun at all the high-tech, super-smart watches on the market. And what about its AUDIENCE—who do you think the ad addresses most directly? Perhaps Americans who think of themselves as solid "no frills" folks?

Reading a visual begins, then, with studying its purpose, audience, message, and context. But there's a lot more you can do to understand a visual. You can look closely, for instance, at its DESIGN. In the Shinola ad, the stark, high-contrast image takes center stage, drawing our eyes to it and its accompanying captions. There are no other distracting elements, no bright colors, no glitz. The simplicity gives the watch a retro look, which is emphasized by its sturdy straps, open face, and clear numerals, its old-fashioned wind-up button and second hand.

A WATCH SO SMART
THAT IT CAN TELL YOU THE TIME
JUST BY LOOKING AT IT.

THE RUNWELL. IT'S JUST SMART ENOUGH.™

SMART ENOUGH THAT YOU DON'T NEED TO CHARGE IT AT NIGHT. SMART ENOUGH THAT IT WILL NEVER NEED
A SOFTWARE UPGRADE. SMART ENOUGH THAT VERSION 1.0 WON'T NEED TO BE REPLACED NEXT YEAR,
OR IN THE MANY DECADES THAT FOLLOW. BUILT BY THE WATCHMAKERS OF DETROIT TO LAST
A LIFETIME OR LONGER UNDER THE TERMS AND CONDITIONS OF THE SHINOLA GUARANTEE.

SHINOLA
DETROIT

Where American is made.

NEW YORK 177 FRANKLIN ST.
DETROIT • MINNEAPOLIS • CHICAGO • WASHINGTON DC • LOS ANGELES • LONDON

SHINOLA.COM

You'll also want to take a close look at any words. In this case, the Shinola ad includes a large headline right above the image, three lines of all-caps, sans serif type that match the simplicity of the image itself. And it's hard to miss the mocking TONE: "A WATCH SO SMART THAT IT CAN TELL YOU THE TIME JUST BY LOOKING AT IT." The small caption below the image underscores this message: "THE RUNWELL. IT'S JUST SMART ENOUGH." Take that, Apple!

READING ACROSS ACADEMIC DISCIPLINES

Differences in disciplines can make for some challenging reading tasks, as you encounter texts that seem almost to be written in foreign languages. As with most new things, however, new disciplines and their texts will become familiar to you the more you work with them. So don't be put off if texts in fields like psychology or physics seem hard to read: the more you read such texts, the more familiar they'll become until, eventually, you'll be able to "talk the talk" of that discipline yourself.

Pay attention to terminology

It's especially important to read carefully when encountering texts in different academic fields. Take the word *analysis*, for instance. That little word has a wide range of definitions as it moves from one field to another. In *philosophy*, analysis has traditionally meant breaking down a topic into its constituent parts in order to understand them—and the whole text—more completely. In the *sciences*, analysis often involves the scientific method of observing a phenomenon, formulating a hypothesis about it, and experimenting to see whether the hypothesis holds up. In *business*, analysis often refers to assessing needs and finding ways to meet them. And in *literary studies*, analysis usually calls for close reading in order to interpret a passage of text. When you're assigned to carry out an analysis, then, it's important to know what the particular field of study expects you to do and to ask your instructors if you aren't sure.

Know what counts as evidence

Beyond knowing what particular words mean from field to field, you should note that what counts as EVIDENCE can differ across academic disciplines. In literature and other fields in the *humanities*, textual evidence is often the most important: your job as a reader is to focus on the text itself. For the *sciences*, you'll most often focus on evidence gathered through experimentation, on facts and figures. Some of the *social sciences* also favor the use of "hard" evidence or data, while others are more likely to use evidence drawn from interviews, oral histories, or even anecdotes. As a reader, you'll need to be aware of what counts as credible evidence in the fields you study.

Be aware of how information is presented

Finally, pay attention to the way various disciplines format and present their information. You'll probably find that articles and books in *literature* and *history* present their information in paragraphs, sometimes with illustrations. *Physics* texts present much important information in equations, while those in *psychology* and *political science* rely on charts, graphs, and other visual representations of quantitative data. In *art history*, you can expect to see extensive use of images, while much of the work in *music* will rely on notation and sound.

So reading calls for some real effort. Whether you're reading words or images or bar graphs, literary analysis or musical notation, in a print book or on a screen, you need to read attentively and intentionally and with an open mind. On top of all that, you need to be an active participant with what you read. As Toni Morrison says: "The words on the page are only half the story. The rest is what you bring to the party."

REFLECT! Take a tip from novelist **Francine Prose**, and try *reading as a writer*, paying attention to how a piece of writing you really admire is written. Look closely at the choices the writer made that resulted in such memorable writing: specific words, sentences, figures of speech like analogies or metaphors, repetition to make a point. Then think about how the writing made you feel, and look for specific places in the text that you think sparked those feelings: What did the writer do to affect you in that way? Finally, write a note to yourself about what you've learned about writing by reading as a writer: What strategies might you try out in your own writing?

7 Recognizing Facts, Misinformation & Lies

Facts are facts and will not disappear
on account of your likes.

—JAWAHARLAL NEHRU

You know where I'm coming from,
but you can fact-check anything I say.

—RACHEL MADDOW

Self-driving Cars Organize Traffic Jam Protest." "Pope Francis: God Has Instructed Me to Revise the Ten Commandments." "Miami-Dade to Create Freeway Texting Lane with Bumpers." Really? Well, no. While these are in fact actual headlines, none is anywhere near the truth. But being false hasn't kept them from being widely shared—and not as jokes, but as facts. With so many people spreading misinformation, unsubstantiated claims, and even outright lies today, it can be hard to know who and what to trust, or whether to trust anything at all. The good news, however, is that you don't have to be taken in by such claims. This chapter provides strategies for navigating today's choppy waters of news and information so that you can make confident decisions about what to trust—and what not to.

Facts, misinformation, fake news, and lies

Some say we're living in a "post-truth" era, that the loudest voices take up so much airtime that they can sometimes be seen as telling the "truth" no matter what they say. A 2018 study by MIT scholars examined tweets about 126,000 major news stories in English and came to the conclusion that "the truth simply can't compete with hoax and rumor." In fact, the study says, "fake news and false rumors reach more people, penetrate deeper into the social network, and spread much faster than accurate stories."

It's worth asking why misinformation and even lies outperform real news. While it is notoriously difficult to establish an airtight cause-and-effect relationship, these researchers suspect that several reasons account for their "success." First, they're often outlandish and novel in a way that attracts attention. Second, the content of such stories is often negative and tends to arouse very strong emotions. Third, they use language that evokes surprise or disgust, and seems to lead to the information going viral. Accurate tweets, the researchers found, use words associated with trust or sadness rather than surprise or disgust—and as they note, "the truth simply does not compete."

Lies and misinformation are nothing new. What's new is that anyone with an internet connection can post whatever they think (or want others to think) online, where it can easily reach a wide audience. And unlike mainstream newspapers and other such publications, online postings go out without being vetted by editors or fact-checkers.

Perhaps it's time to step back, take a deep breath, and attend to some basic definitions. Just what is a fact? What's fake news? And what about misinformation and lies? Both misinformation and lies give false or inaccurate information. The difference is that

A lie can travel halfway around the world while the truth is putting on its shoes.
MARK TWAIN

misinformation is not necessarily intended to deceive, whereas *lies* are always told deliberately, for the purpose of giving false information. *Fake news* stories are fabricated and false articles are made to look authentic. Often they're used to spread conspiracy theories or deliberate hoaxes—the more bizarre, the better. In addition, many people simply dismiss anything they don't like or agree with as fake news. *Facts*, on the other hand, can be verified and backed up by reliable evidence—that the Vegas Golden Knights won the 2023 Stanley Cup, for example, or that the consumption of soft drinks in the United States has declined in the last five years. Unlike claims about what God has instructed Pope Francis to do, these statements can be checked and verified; we can then trust them.

Think about your own beliefs

It's one thing to be able to spot misinformation, unsubstantiated claims, and exaggerations in the words of others, but it's another thing entirely to spot them in our own thinking and writing. So we need to take a good look at our own assumptions and biases. We all have them!

Attribution bias is the tendency to think that our motives for believing, say, that the Environmental Protection Agency (EPA) is crucially important for keeping our air and water clean are objective or good, while the motives of those who believe the EPA is unnecessary are dubious or suspect. We all have this kind of bias naturally, tending to believe that what we think must be right. When you're thinking about an argument you strongly disagree with, then, it's a good idea to ask yourself *why* you disagree—and why you believe you're right. What is that belief based on? Have you considered that your own bias may be keeping you from seeing some sides of the issue fairly, or at all?

Confirmation bias is the tendency to favor and seek out information that confirms what we already believe and to reject and ignore information that contradicts those beliefs. Many studies have documented this phenomenon, including a university experiment with student participants, half of whom favored capital punishment and thought it was a deterrent to crime and half of whom thought just the opposite. Researchers then asked the students to respond to two studies: one provided data that supported capital punishment as a deterrent to crime; the other provided data that called this conclusion into question. And sure enough, the students who were pro capital punishment rated the study showing evidence that it was a deterrent as "more highly credible," while the students who were against capital punishment rated the study showing evidence that it didn't deter crime as "more highly credible"—in spite of the fact that both studies had been made up by the researchers and were equally compelling in terms of their evidence. Moreover, by the end of the experiment, each side had doubled down on its original beliefs.

> Don't believe everything you think.
> JOSEPH NGUYEN

That's confirmation bias at work, and it works on all of us. It affects the way we search for information and what we pay attention to, how we interpret it, and even what we remember. That's all to say you shouldn't assume a news story is trustworthy just because it confirms what you already think. Ask yourself if you're seeing what you want to see. And look for confirmation bias in your sources; do they acknowledge viewpoints other than their own?

REFLECT! Where do you get the news? Whatever your sources, what do you pay attention to, and why? What are you most likely to click on? What, on the other hand, are you likely to skip, or ignore? Can you see confirmation bias at work in the choices you make?

Read defensively

Well over 2,000 years ago, the philosopher Aristotle said that one reason people need rhetoric is for self-defense, for making sure we aren't being manipulated or lied to. Today, the need for such caution may be more important than ever—especially in social media and elsewhere online, where false stories may look authentic and appear right next to accurate, factual information. These times call, then, for *defensive reading*—that is, the kind of reading that doesn't take things at face value, that questions underlying assumptions, that scrutinizes claims carefully, and that doesn't rush to judgment.

This is the kind of reading that media and technology critic Howard Rheingold calls "crap detection." Crap, he says sardonically, is a "technical term" he uses to describe information "tainted by ignorance or deliberate deception." He warns us not to give in to such misinformation. As Rheingold and many others note, there is no single foolproof way to identify lies and misinformation. But the following discussion offers some specific strategies for determining whether or not a source can be trusted.

Triangulate—and use your judgment

If you have any doubts, find three different ways to check on whether a story can be trusted. Google the author or the sponsor. Consult fact-checking sites such as *Snopes* or *FactCheck.org*. Look for other sources that are reporting the same story, especially if you first saw it on social media. If it's true and important, you should find a number of other reputable sources reporting on it. But however carefully you check, and whatever facts and evidence you uncover, it's up to you to sort the accurate information from the misinformation—and often as not that will call on you to use your own judgment to do so.

See p. 337 for more tips on triangulating.

Before reading an unfamiliar source, determine whether it can be trusted

Take a tip from professional fact-checkers, who don't even start to read an unfamiliar website until they've determined that it's a trustworthy site. If you have any doubts, here are some ways to proceed:

Do a search about the author or sponsor. If there's an author, what's their expertise? Do they belong to any organizations you don't know or trust? Be wary if there's no author. And do a search about the site's sponsor. If it's run by an organization you've never heard of, find out what it is—and whether it actually exists. What do reliable sources say about it? Read the site's About page, but check up on what it says.

If an organization can game what they are, they can certainly game their About page!
SAM WINEBURG

Check any links to see who sponsors them and whether they are trustworthy sources. Do the same for works cited in print sources.

Be careful of over-the-top headlines, which often serve as CLICKBAIT to draw you in. Check to see that the story and the headline actually match. Question words like *amazing*, *epic*, *incredible*, or *unbelievable*. (In general, don't believe anything that's said to be "unbelievable!")

Pay attention to design. Be wary if it looks amateurish, but don't assume that a professional-looking design means the source is accurate or trustworthy. Those who create fake news sites are careful to make them to look like authentic news sites.

Recognize satire. Remember that some authors make a living by writing satirical news stories. Here's one: "China Slaps Two-Thousand-Per-Cent Tariff on Tanning Beds." This comes from Andy Borowitz, who writes political satire in the *New Yorker*. Their website tips us off not to take it seriously by tagging it as "humor." The *Onion* is another source that pokes fun at gullible readers. Try this: "Genealogists Find 99% of People Are Not Related to Anyone Cool." This one's silly enough that it can't possibly be true. But if you're not sure, better check.

Ask questions, check evidence

Double-check things that too neatly support what you yourself think, or that seem too good to be true.

***What's the* CLAIM**, and what EVIDENCE is provided? What motivated the author to write, and what's their PURPOSE? To provide information? Make you laugh? Convince you of something?

Check facts and claims using nonpartisan sites that confirm truths and identify lies. *FactCheck.org*, *Snopes*, and *AllSides* are three such sites. Copy and paste the basics of the statement into the search field; if it's information the site has in its database, you'll find out whether it's a confirmed fact or a lie. If you use *Google* to check on a stated fact, keep in mind that you'll need to check on any sources it turns up—and that even if the statement brings up many hits, that doesn't make it accurate.

See p. 334 for more on fact-checking sites.

If you think a story is too good to be true, you're probably right to be skeptical. And don't assume that it must be true because no one could make up such a story. They can. Check out stories that are so outrageous that you don't believe them; if they're true, they'll likely be widely reported in credible sources. That said, double-check stories that confirm your own beliefs as well; that might be confirmation bias at work.

Check anything from AI, keeping in mind that it sometimes makes up facts and even cites sources that don't actually exist.

Look up any research that's cited. You may find that it has been taken out of context or misquoted—or that it doesn't even exist. Is the research itself reliable? Pay close attention to QUOTATIONS:

Who said it, and when? Is it believable? If not, copy and paste the quotation into *Google* or check *FactCheck.org* to verify that it's real.

Check any comments. If several say the article sounds fake, it may well be. But remember that given the presence of BOTS and TROLLS— and people with malicious intent—comments, too, may be fake.

Fact-check photos and videos

Is a picture really worth a thousand words? In some cases, yes—but only if the picture is an accurate depiction. Today, it's never been easier to falsify photographs. Take the often-repeated, reposted, and repurposed story of a shark swimming down a highway whenever a hurricane strikes or some other natural disaster causes flooding. Some years ago, someone tweeted: "Believe it or not, this is a shark on the freeway in New Burn, North Carolina. #Hurricane Florence"—a message that was retweeted 88,000 times. But the same shark popped up on *Twitter* swimming down a road in Houston, Texas, and in many other cities. Easily done with *Photoshop*.

Home-grown Cheez Doodles, as seen on *Instagram*. Better fact-check!

Go to letstalklibrary.com to see LeBron in pink.

And have you seen the photo of LeBron James dressed in pink, perhaps on the way to see *Barbie*, which went viral in 2023? A little investigation, however, showed that the photo had been created by AI; he wasn't actually wearing pink shorts *or* carrying a pink purse.

Again, there are no simple, foolproof ways to identify doctored photos, but here are various steps we can take:

- ***Do a reverse image search*** using *Google Images* or *TinEye* to see if an image has been recirculated or repurposed from another website. Both sites allow you to drag an image or paste a link to an image into a search bar to learn more about its source and see where it appears online.
- *Check* **Snopes,** where altered images can be identified by typing a brief description of the image into the site's search box.
- *Check* **AI or Not** to determine whether an image has been generated by artificial intelligence.
- *Check Amnesty International's* **Evidence Lab** to see whether videos and other images that you find on social media have been doctored or manipulated in other ways.

Sometimes the best defense against fabricated photos and videos is to stop and think about whether you can trust the source—especially before you share them on social media. After a shooter killed seventeen people at a Florida school in 2018, an altered photo of X González, one of the students who protested the mass shooting, went viral, showing them tearing up a page of the US Constitution. In fact, they were actually tearing up a shooting target as part of their advocacy for gun control; the Constitution had been photoshopped in.

The same advice holds true for video, which is all too easy to falsify. Videos that flicker constantly or that consist of just one short clip are often questionable, as are videos of famous people doing things that are highly suspicious. How likely was it that Kobe Bryant could jump over a speeding Aston Martin? Not very—but a lot of us were fooled by a fake video made for Nike.

Such fabricated videos proliferate daily, especially on *YouTube*, now an extremely popular source of news. As *YouTube* has found in trying to control or ban fake videos, those who make them are getting more and more sophisticated. As the *Guardian* reports, artificial intelligence and computer graphics now make it possible to create "realistic looking footage of public figures appearing to say, well, anything."

Thanks to the internet, there's a lot of misinformation and fake news out there. But the fact-finding and defensive-reading strategies described in this chapter will help you sort out fiction from fact, falsehood from truth—and determine with confidence who and what you can trust. You may have to dig a little, but truth and the "good stuff" are out there. Take it from Elvis Presley: "Truth is like the sun. You can shut it out for a time, but it ain't goin' away."

REFLECT! Look for something that has been sent to you on social media—forwarded, "liked," whatever. Then take the time to check out its source, using the help provided in this chapter. After checking, do you find that the information in the source holds up as credible and trustworthy? Why—or why not?

WRITING

MAKE YOUR POINT

8 # Writing Processes

The function of writing is to do more than tell it like it is—
it is to imagine what is possible.

—BELL HOOKS

If you've got a process . . . you have a list of things
to do to get to your goal.

—NIPSEY HUSSLE

Do you knit? play video games? do yoga?
If so, you're probably accustomed
to following a process of some kind,
whether it's for making socks, playing *Fortnite*, or
doing a downward-dog yoga pose. The same goes
for writing: whether it's a thank-you letter after
a job interview, an email to a teacher, or an essay
for a class, you follow some kind of process. This
chapter will help you make your way through the
process of writing, from a blank page to a finished
text. Think of it as a GPS that will help you navigate
the many choices you have along the way—and
direct you to places in the book with additional
detail if you need it.

Start with questions

Whatever your topic or purpose, start out by asking questions. Even if your purpose is to solve some kind of problem, don't just go looking for answers. Whatever the task, approach it with an open mind. If you already have some ideas about your topic, expect to find new ideas. Be curious: inquire! explore!

Ideas come from curiosity.
WALT DISNEY

If you already know something about your topic, what do you think about it, and why? What more do you want to find out? Be aware of CONFIRMATION BIAS, which can make you too quick to accept ideas that confirm what you already believe.

Keep an open mind, ready to be challenged. You're sure to encounter views that differ from yours. If you don't, seek them out—and then take them seriously and be open to the possibility that they might be right. Even if that's not the case, they'll get you thinking!

Ask questions: What? Who? How? Where? When? Why? Why *not*?

What are others saying about your topic, and why? What else might be said? What do you want to say?

Think about your rhetorical situation

Whether you're writing a text or a post, an essay or a speech, you have a RHETORICAL SITUATION that you need to consider:

- A PURPOSE—what you're trying to accomplish by writing.
- An AUDIENCE—those who will be reading or seeing or listening to what you say.
- Your own STANCE, or attitude about the topic, which you convey in the TONE of your writing.
- A larger CONTEXT. What else has been said about your topic? If you're writing for an assignment, what are its requirements—and what can you accomplish in the time you have?

- One or more **GENRES**. You may be **ARGUING** a position, **REPORTING** information, **SUMMARIZING** a text, or something else. Whatever it is, your genre will determine the way you approach your topic.

- One or more **MEDIA**—print, oral, digital, and social. If you have a choice, choose the one(s) that best suit your purpose and audience.

- **LANGUAGE.** Does your rhetorical situation call for a certain kind of language? Informal language may be appropriate for a personal narrative, but a lab report might call for some kind of technical language. Standardized English may be expected in a history essay, but if you're writing an essay for a class where you've been learning about using various languages and dialects in your writing, you may be expected to do that yourself.

- **DESIGN.** What fonts serve your purpose? Do you need headings? images? charts or graphs?

Chapter 2 provides detailed guidelines for thinking about each element of a rhetorical situation, but you'll want to keep your audience and purpose in mind from start to finish of whatever you're writing.

If you're permitted to use AI, it might be helpful at several points throughout the writing process—for generating ideas, getting started on research, getting response to a draft, and more. Check with your instructor to find out how you should (or should not) use it, and refer to Chapter 30 for guidelines on how to use AI carefully and ethically.

I had an old typewriter and a big idea.

J. K. ROWLING

Generate ideas

Once you have a topic, it's time to learn what you can about it—to *think* about it and start writing about it. Here are several techniques that can help you think about the topic and generate ideas.

Freewriting is a technique for exploring a topic through writing. Start by writing quickly, without stopping. Some writers find it useful to freewrite for five or ten minutes; others find it works better if they write until they fill a screen or a certain number of pages. Don't worry about your spelling or grammar; just write! Your goal is to come up with ideas, and the more the merrier!

Brainstorming is a process for generating as many ideas as you can, quickly. And don't worry about whether they're right or wrong, smart or silly. You can brainstorm on your own by simply writing down all the ideas you have, or you can work with a group, with everyone suggesting whatever ideas they have, as many as possible. The more brains the better—and the greater the likelihood that you'll discover a range of viewpoints. Alone or with others (or with AI, if that's permitted), the goal is to explore an idea and to be open to whatever it turns up.

Questioning is a good way to explore a topic and to get beyond what you already know or think about it. And it's easy: just ask *what, who, where, when, how,* and *why.* What happened (or happens)? Who's involved? Where and when did (or does) it take place? How does it happen? And why: What caused (or causes) it to happen?

Do some research

Unless your topic is a personal one, you'll probably need to do some research. *Wikipedia* can be a good starting point, likely to provide an overview of the topic, to give a sense of the various perspectives that exist on it, and to list sources you can check out. If you're writing about a current issue, you may want to check news articles or periodicals or do a KEYWORD search. If you're writing about a topic from the distant past, you'll need to look for older sources, but you may also need to see if there's any recent scholarship on the topic. And if you're writing about a local issue, you may want to interview experts or do some other kind of FIELD RESEARCH. If you're permitted to use AI, it too can be a good starting point; see Chapter 30 about ways it can help,

Start by thinking about what you already know about the topic. What do you need or want to learn? What questions do you have?

What have others written about the topic? What are the various issues, and the different PERSPECTIVES and viewpoints? Be sure to seek out a variety of opinions, and read them all with an open mind.

***Check* FACTS *and* CLAIMS.** If something seems questionable, check it out. If you see a claim that sounds too good to be true, chances are it's not true. Search the web to see if anyone else is saying the same thing; if not, it may not be true. Or maybe you find several sources that say exactly the same thing; check them out—are they all sponsored by a single organization? Even if sources *look* real, don't assume they are; fake sources are usually designed to look legitimate. See Chapter 17 for more on FACT-CHECKING.

Come up with a working thesis

At this point, you should be ready to write out a thesis, a sentence that identifies your topic and the point you want to make about it. Rarely if ever will you have a final thesis when you start drafting, but establishing a tentative one will help focus your thinking and any research you may yet do. Here are some prompts to get you started:

- ***Write out the point you want to make***: "In this essay, I will present reasons to quit social media."

- ***Plot out a working thesis in two parts,*** first stating your topic and then making a claim about the topic:

TOPIC	CLAIM

Quitting social media will improve your ability to focus, eliminate stress, and make you happier.

- ***Be sure your*** CLAIM ***is debatable—and that it matters.***
  There's no point in arguing for a claim that is a fact or that no one would disagree with—or that no one would even care about.

- ***Do you need to narrow or*** QUALIFY ***your thesis?*** You don't want to overstate your case, or make a claim that you'll have trouble supporting. Adding words like *generally* or *sometimes*, or saying *might* or *could* rather than *will*, can make your thesis easier to support: "Quitting social media *could* help you sleep better, *might* make you more productive, and *may* even make you happier."

- ***Does the thesis tell readers what's coming?*** Will it help keep you and your readers focused on your message? Will it interest your readers?

At this point in your process, this is a tentative thesis, one that could change as you continue to do research, write, and revise. Continue exploring your topic, and don't stop until you feel you understand it well. But once you're confident that your thesis makes a claim that you can support and that will interest your audience, gather up the notes from your research. This is the information you'll draw from as support for your thesis.

Write out a draft

Once you have a working thesis, you will need to organize the evidence that supports what you're claiming and to start drafting. If you're writing a narrative, you might tell the story in CHRONOLOGICAL ORDER. If you're making an argument, you might present your evidence in order of importance, starting with the information that's the most important, followed by the less important information. And if you're describing something, you might organize your description SPATIALLY, from left to right or top to bottom.

The difference between screwing around and science is writing it down.
ADAM SAVAGE

Ways of beginning

The way you begin a text can grab an audience's attention, or not. Here are some ways of making your readers interested in what you've got to say—and want to read on:

- By QUOTING or SUMMARIZING something others have said about your topic
- By telling an ANECDOTE that will get your audience's attention
- By posing a provocative question
- By stating your THESIS
- By using a startling fact or statistic

Chapters 8 and 24 have more tips on powerful OPENING sentences.

Ways of organizing your evidence

Whatever your thesis, you need to provide solid, reliable EVIDENCE to support what you say. The good news is that the ancient Greek philosopher Aristotle long ago developed strategies for providing such support, ones that will serve you well both for finding evidence and for organizing it into paragraphs in the body of your text. And most of these strategies are ones that you're already familiar with, and probably use every day: COMPARISONS. DEFINITIONS. DESCRIPTIONS. EXAMPLES. NARRATIVES. CAUSES AND EFFECTS.

No matter what you're writing or speaking about, or what GENRES you're using, you'll have occasion to describe something or someone, compare one thing to another, argue about causes and effects. And whatever you want to say—whatever!—these basic strategies will help you make your case. You'll find details and examples about how to use them effectively in your own writing on pages 51–58 and 133–37.

Consider counterarguments and other perspectives

Unless you're the first to write about your topic, many others will have opinions about it as well—and some of them will have ideas that differ from yours. If you've done your homework, you'll be aware of what else has been said and will have thought about it. You need to acknowledge other perspectives, and to do so respectfully and accurately.

And you need to respond to any COUNTERARGUMENTS, objections that others may have to your position. Whether you provide evidence refuting ideas you take issue with, admit that some other position just might be right, or QUALIFY what you yourself say, acknowledging other perspectives demonstrates that you've done your homework and that you've considered opinions other than your own carefully. See Chapter 3 and pages 141–43 for more guidance on considering multiple viewpoints.

> Force yourself to consider opposing arguments, especially if they challenge your best-loved ideas.
> CHARLIE MUNGER

Ways of concluding

Your conclusion is where you get to wrap things up and to leave your audience thinking about what you've said. Here are some ways of doing that:

- By reiterating your main point
- By issuing a call to action
- By saying why your point matters
- By inviting response

Chapters 8 and 24 provide more tips on writing memorable CONCLUDING sentences.

Come up with a title

Titles are important. On the one hand, they need to tell readers what your piece is about and give some sense of what you're going to say about it. At the same time, you'll want to come up with a title that will get your readers' attention and make them want to read on. Whatever your purpose, you should always think about your rhetorical situation when deciding on a title, to be sure it will appeal to your AUDIENCE and reflect your STANCE.

Some titles simply indicate the topic:

- "When Doctors Make Mistakes"
- "The Sanctuary of School"
- "My Life as an Undocumented Immigrant"
- "Stop Coddling the Super-Rich"
- "Listening to Taylor Swift in Prison"

Other titles are more provocative, saying something surprising or asking a startling question. Such titles often reflect a strong point of view—and make readers want to read on (or not):

- "Well-Behaved Women Seldom Make History"
- "Have Smartphones Destroyed a Generation?"
- "What My Bike Has Taught Me about White Privilege"
- "Is Google Making Us Stupid?"
- "How to Tame a Wild Tongue"

Some TITLES include a subtitle, usually to explain the title or indicate the author's stance:

- "*Hispanic, Latino, Latinx*: One Word Can't Define Us All"
- "Minority Student Clubs: Segregation or Integration?"
- "Extra Lives: Why Video Games Matter"
- "Utopian Dream: A New Farm Bill"
- "Goldenrod and Asters: My Life with Plants"

Get response and revise

One good thing about writing, according to author Robert Cormier, is that "you don't have to get it right the first time, unlike, say, a brain surgeon. You can always do it better." That's for sure! And a good first step to doing it "better" is to get a little help from your friends. Once you have a draft, you'll want to get feedback from some readers. The following questions can help you or others read a draft with a critical eye and think about how it might be revised:

- How does the OPENING get your AUDIENCE's attention? Does it make clear why your topic matters?

- Is your point stated explicitly in a THESIS—and if not, should it be?

- Have you provided sufficient REASONS and EVIDENCE to support your thesis? If not, do you need to find more evidence? Or do you need to QUALIFY your thesis to make it one you can support?

- Have you noted any COUNTERARGUMENTS or views other than your own—and represented them accurately and respectfully? What other positions should you consider?

- Have you cited any sources? If so, have you clearly distinguished what they say from what you say—and provided DOCUMENTATION? Are any QUOTATIONS introduced with a SIGNAL PHRASE?

- Is the text organized in a way that's easy to follow? Have you provided TRANSITIONS to help readers follow what you've written? Are there headings to help readers see the main parts—and if not, should you add some?

- Does the text include any VISUALS? Is there any data that would be easier to understand if you presented it in a pie chart or bar graph—or illustrated it with a photo?

- How does the text CONCLUDE? What does it leave readers thinking? How else might you conclude?

- Does your title announce the topic and give some idea of what you have to say about it—and will it get your audience's attention? If not, might it help to add a subtitle?

If it's permitted, you might ask AI to respond to your draft. You'll want to give it some guidance about what to look for and to be sure it's aware of your genre, audience, purpose, and anything your assignment requires. You might try uploading the above guidelines for getting response to tell AI what to look for.

I try to leave out
the parts that
people skip.
ELMORE
LEONARD

Once you've gotten feedback and read over your draft yourself, put it aside for a day or two if you can. The above questions will have identified plenty of specific things to consider as you revise, but be sure to keep your RHETORICAL SITUATION firmly in mind as you work, especially your AUDIENCE and PURPOSE.

You want to make your text as readable as possible, and to be sure that everything in the draft contributes to your point and will help you achieve your purpose. Take seriously any advice you've gotten from other readers, but don't feel that you have to do everything they suggest. You're the author!

Edit!

Cheryl Strayed may be the author of a best-selling book called *Wild*, but it seems that she's rather cautious when it comes to her writing, saying that she writes to find out what she has to say—and that she edits "to figure out how to say it right." Good advice! So once you've written and revised what you want to say, you need to fine-tune your text to be sure that it says precisely what you want it to say, and that your readers will be able to follow and understand what you say. There's no single recipe for doing that, but here are some tips that can help guide you.

Editing paragraphs

- Check each paragraph to be sure it contributes to your point in some way.

- Try to focus each paragraph on one point—and to include a TOPIC SENTENCE that tells readers what it will focus on.

- Make sure that each paragraph is developed in enough detail.

- If any paragraphs are especially long, check to see if they might be split into two paragraphs—or if there's any excessive detail you can edit out.

- Pay special attention to your OPENING paragraph (will it grab your audience's attention?) and CONCLUDING paragraph (will it solidify your message?).

Editing sentences

- Be sure that your sentences *are* sentences, starting with a capital letter and ending with a period, question mark, or exclamation point; and including a subject and VERB.

- Check for sentences beginning with *it is* or *there is*. These can be good ways of emphasizing or introducing an idea, but often they simply add unnecessary words. Why say "It is essential that we speak up" rather than "We need to speak up"?

- Check for any unnecessary words—words like *very* or *really*.

- Count up the words in each sentence. If too many are pretty much the same length, see if you can combine some sentences, add details, or vary the sentence structure in some other way.

- Pay attention to the way your sentences open. If sentence after sentence begins with a subject, try varying them by adding PREPOSITIONAL PHRASES or TRANSITIONS.

Chapter 25 offers advice for writing good sentences.

Editing words

- DEFINE any terms that your readers may not understand.

- Think about what TONE is most appropriate for your audience and purpose—serious? playful? casual? academic?— and be sure that the words you use reflect that tone.

- Check to be sure that your language is respectful. Especially when you're writing about a controversial topic or discussing positions you disagree with, use words that demonstrate RESPECT—and not disrespect. Civility matters!

Words matter,
tone matters,
civility matters.
JEN PSAKI

- Use gender pronouns according to the way people want to be called: *he/him/his, she/her/hers, they/them/their,* or some other pronouns (*ze* or *hir,* for example). If you're writing in generalities, or about someone whose pronouns are unknown, use SINGULAR *THEY* (as in "Nobody would admit they were wrong.").

Give some thought to design

You're almost there: you've written out a draft, gotten response, and edited your text. It says what you want it to say. So now you need to think about what you want it to look like, and whether there are any design elements that will help your readers follow what you say. As usual, you'll need to think hard about what will work best for your AUDIENCE, PURPOSE, and the rest of your RHETORICAL SITUATION.

- Choose FONTS that suit your purpose and reflect the TONE you want to convey. And think about whether there are any words you want to emphasize with *italics* or **boldface**.

- Think about whether you should add headings to help readers see (or scan) your main points.

- Is there any text that would be easier to understand if it were set off in a list?

- If you're presenting numerical data, would it be easier to see in a pie chart or bar graph?

- If you haven't included any VISUALS, might you add images, charts, or other graphics that would help to illustrate a point?

- Be sure to provide CAPTIONS for any images, charts, or graphs and to refer to them in the text so that readers know how they relate to your point.

Chapter 27 gives advice on designing what you write.

Don't forget to proofread

Read over your text slowly, start to finish. If at all possible, print it out; mistakes can be hard to spot on a computer screen. Then read it aloud bit by bit.

- Read each sentence to be sure it begins with a capital letter and ends with a period, question mark, or exclamation point.
- If you've included headings, be sure they're all in the same font and with the same amount of space above and below.
- If you've included any VISUALS, be sure they are all referred to in the text.
- Check for PARALLELISM to be sure that all headings or all elements in a series or list have the same structure: all NOUNS, all GERUNDS, all PREPOSITIONAL PHRASES, all commands, and so on.
- Check your spelling. Use a spellchecker, but be aware that it won't catch wrong words that are spelled correctly. For example: if you write *principle* when it should be *principal*, a spellchecker would not likely catch the mistake.
- If your text is in MLA, APA, or another style, make sure that your title, margins, spacing, page numbers, and documentation follow the requirements of that style.

Take time to reflect on your own writing process

Once you've finished writing something, it's a good idea to take stock of what you've written—and of your writing process. Here are some questions that can help you get started:

- What did you do well?
- If you could do one more draft, what would you change?
- What did you find challenging? easy? satisfying? fun?
- What response did you get from others, and how did it help?

- Did you do any research for this project? If so, how did it contribute to what you wrote? Did it change your mind in any way about your topic?

- If you cited other sources, how many different perspectives did you include? Did you incorporate positions that differ from your own, and how fairly did you represent those views?

- If you used AI, what kind of help did it provide, and how helpful did it prove to be? In what ways might you use it again, and is there any way you would not use it again?

- How did your audience affect what you wrote?

- What is your favorite sentence or passage, and why?

- What was your purpose for writing, and how well do you think you achieved that purpose?

Finally, think about what you've learned about yourself as a writer. What do you want to work on?

> I think I did pretty well, considering I started out with nothing but a bunch of blank paper.
> STEVE MARTIN

REFLECT! "Forget a room of one's own—write in the kitchen, lock yourself up in the bathroom. Write on the bus or the welfare line, on the job or during meals." Cultural critic **Gloria Anzaldúa** wrote these words in 1981, long before cell phones allowed us to write pretty much anywhere. Picture her on a bus, pad of paper in one hand and a pen in the other, *writing*. Where do you do most of your writing—on a bus or train? in an armchair? at breakfast? And how do you do it—on a laptop? a mobile phone? a pad of paper? Think about your circumstances today: where you write and how that allows you to do your best writing.

9 Arguing

Fight for the things that you care about.
But do it in a way that will lead others to join you.

—RUTH BADER GINSBURG

Come now, let us reason together.

—ISAIAH 1:18

College athletes should be paid. Climate change is a reality, and one cause is the burning of fossil fuels. Corporate tax cuts enable companies to pay their workers more. These are all arguments, not facts. They make claims that are debatable and with which we may agree or disagree—so anyone making such claims needs to support them with good reasons and evidence. Think for a moment about some of the claims that surround us, coming from social media, podcasts, newspapers, even song lyrics and movies (think "We Are the Champions" or *Barbie*). So we're surrounded by argument—what we read and see, what we hear, what we talk about, and especially

125

what we write. We need to look and listen with an open mind but a critical eye, to present our own arguments carefully, and to respond to those of others respectfully. This chapter provides a roadmap for reading, writing, and thinking about the arguments you'll encounter in college, at work, and everywhere in between.

A GUIDE TO DEVELOPING AN ARGUMENT

You'll often be assigned to write an essay that argues a position of some kind—to stake a CLAIM that you then support with REASONS and EVIDENCE. Here now is some advice that will make you aware of the various choices you'll have and that will help you make good choices. It's designed to be used *as you write*. Keep it close at hand!

Identify a topic that matters

If you get to choose your topic, choose one that matters to you and will matter to others. But even if you're assigned to write about a specific topic, try to come up with some aspect that interests you— or that will be of interest to others.

Think about your rhetorical situation

Once you have a topic, give some thought to who your audience is, what you hope to accomplish, and the rest of your rhetorical situation.

Purpose. What do you hope to accomplish by writing about this issue? What do you hope to learn? What do you want to persuade your audience to think or do? How can you best achieve these purposes?

Audience. Whom do you want to reach? What do they know about your topic, and what if any background information will you need to provide? Are they likely to think your argument matters, or will you have to convince them? How sympathetic are they likely to be to your argument? What kinds of evidence will they find persuasive? What values do they hold, and how are they different from yours?

Stance. How do you want to come across as an author—as curious? well-informed? sympathetic?—and how can you establish your credibility to write on this topic? Why do you care about the topic? Do you have any preconceived ideas about it? Where did these ideas come from? How else might you think about it?

Context. What's motivating you to write about this issue? What is being said about it: what are the various perspectives? If you're writing in response to an assignment, what's your time frame and are there any requirements you need to keep in mind?

Language. What kind(s) of language will best suit your genre and purpose? If you're writing for an academic assignment, does it have any language requirements? If not, do you think it should be formal or informal—and are there specific languages or dialects that will help you connect with your audience? Standardized English might (or might not!) be expected in an essay for a composition class, but if you're giving a speech hoping to be elected president of the Spanish club, you might want to include some Spanish in your talk—or to speak entirely in Spanish.

Medium and design. How will your argument be delivered—in print? online? as a speech? How does the medium affect the way it will be designed and the kinds of evidence you can provide—can you include images? audio? links to other sources?

Be sure the topic is arguable—and one you can approach with an open mind

Begin by making sure that the topic is arguable—not an easily verified fact or a mere opinion, but a subject about which there are a number of different perspectives. Think about whether it's worth discussing: Is it a topic that matters, and one that others (including your audience) will care about? Be sure the topic is manageable, given the time and resources you have. Finally, ask yourself whether it's a topic you can investigate with an open mind. If that's not the case, find another topic.

Let's assume you're intrigued by a topic you've read about in your campus newspaper: whether NCAA athletes should be paid. A quick search reveals a wide range of viewpoints on this topic, suggesting that it is timely and not a matter of simple facts or mere opinions. So this topic appears to be arguable; so far, so good. The sources you've identified in your quick search suggest that it's also manageable, that you'll be able to find informative arguments on all sides of the issue that will be readily available to you online or through your library. Finally, since you have no preconceived idea about whether or not athletes should be paid, you believe you can approach the topic with a fair and open mind.

In an interview about how he came to write his 2016 book *Indentured: The Rebellion against the College Sports Cartel*, Joe Nocera reflects on how he first became interested in the topic of pay for athletes in 2011, when he wrote an article in the *New York Times Magazine* arguing that college athletes should be paid:

> I got interested in this subject around rights, much more than the issue of pay. I did write the first story with an idea of how to pay the players, but it was more of a thought exercise. And I did it five years ago, when I was just starting to get into this, and before the widespread criticism of the NCAA really gained steam. So, I hadn't really thought much about it. And in the course of doing that story . . . I began to realize how pervasively the life of an athlete is controlled.
>
> —JOE NOCERA, "Let's Start Paying College Athletes"

Note that Nocera started with a question for which he had no answers, and one he hadn't "thought much about." So he began with a topic that intrigued him rather than one he had already made up his mind about. And the research he then did led him to understand how many perspectives there are on the topic and how many lives are affected by it.

College athletes are still not paid, but they're now allowed to earn money from endorsements. Here's Caitlin Clark on a Hy-Vee cereal box—and the proceeds all go to a foundation whose mission is to "uplift and improve the lives of youth through education, nutrition, and sport," three things she believes have been foundational to her success.

Research your topic with an open mind

Start by thinking about what you already know about the topic—and what you don't know. What questions do you have? What do you think about the topic, and why? Finally, think again about whether you can explore this topic with an open mind.

Do some research. If you're exploring a current topic, you'll likely find a lot of sources online; but if you're studying a topic from the past, you'll probably find many of the sources you'll need in the library. And for some topics you may need to conduct interviews, observations, or other field research. Whatever research you do, keep in mind that your goal is to learn about the topic, not simply to find evidence to support ideas you already have.

Identify the various positions on the topic. You'll want to learn about all the PERSPECTIVES you can find. Especially if you have an idea of your own position on the topic, keep an open mind. What are some of the issues that are being discussed, and what are the various positions on those issues? What are others saying, and why?

Formulate an explicit position, and state it as a working thesis

When you feel you understand the topic well and have enough information to work with, you'll need to formulate a position that you'll be able to support. And once you can articulate your position, write it out in an explicit THESIS, one that clearly identifies your topic and makes a claim that will get your audience's attention. For example:

> Artificial intelligence will be the death of humans as we know them.
>
> Professional athletes today are shuffled around like pawns.

Be careful, however, not to overstate your thesis: you may need to QUALIFY it using words like *sometimes*, *might*, or *in some cases*, which will limit your position to one that you'll be able to support. For example:

> Artificial intelligence *may well be* the death of humans as we know them.
>
> Today, professional athletes are *too often* shuffled around like pawns.

See pp. 114–15 for more detail on coming up with a thesis. Such qualifying words and phrases show that you are arguing seriously and cautiously, rather than making absolute claims that you may not be able to substantiate. So be sure to ask yourself whether your thesis needs to be qualified—and if so, in what ways. And keep in mind that at this point in the process, this is a *working thesis*; it may change as you continue to work on your draft. Here's how one author team stakes out their position on whether higher education is for everyone:

Study after study reminds us that higher education is one of the best investments we can make. We all know that, on average, college graduates make significantly more money over their lifetimes than those with only a high school education. What gets less attention is the fact that not all college degrees are equal. There is enormous variation in the so-called return on education depending on factors such as institution attended, field of study, whether or not a student graduates, and post-graduation occupation. While the average return on obtaining a college degree is clearly positive . . . it is not universally so. For certain schools, majors, occupations, and individuals, college may not be a smart investment.

—STEPHANIE OWEN and ISABEL SAWHILL,
"Should Everyone Go to College?"

Their position is clear: higher education is not always a good investment. Notice, however, how careful they are to qualify their argument, noting that while college graduates earn more "on average," it is "not universally so," and that in certain cases college "may not be a smart investment." By saying that higher education *may* not be a good investment, the authors have limited their position to one they will be able to support.

Present your position as a response to what others say

Whatever your topic, you will rarely if ever be the first one to say something about it. What you say will be part of a larger conversation, one that began before you got there. It's a good idea, therefore, to start your essay by noting something else that has been said about the issue and then presenting your position as a response. Framing your ideas in this way is a means of engaging with the ideas of others, of weaving their ideas in with yours, and of entering that conversation.

In the following example from an op-ed column in the *New York Times* arguing that community colleges need more support, the president of LaGuardia Community College opens by noting

The entrance to LaGuardia Community College. New York.

something that many of those who read the *Times* probably assume about American college students: that they divide their time between "classes, parties and extracurricular activities":

> You might think the typical college student lives in a state of bliss, spending each day moving among classes, parties and extracurricular activities. But the reality is that an increasingly small population of undergraduates enjoys that kind of life.
>
> Of the country's nearly 18 million undergraduates, more than 40 percent go to community college, and of those, only 62 percent can afford to go to college full-time. By contrast, a mere 0.4 percent of students in the United States attend one of the Ivies.
>
> The typical student is not the one burnishing a fancy résumé with numerous unpaid internships. It's just the opposite: Over half of all undergraduates live at home to make their degrees more affordable, and a shocking 40 percent of students work at least 30 hours a week. About 25 percent work full-time and go to school full-time.
>
> —GAIL O. MELLOW, "The Biggest Misconception about Today's College Students"

Mellow responds to what readers "might think" by questioning that assumption, noting that very few students live "that kind of life"—and that more than 40 percent attend a community college and work at least thirty hours a week. She then points out that public funding for community colleges is "significantly less than for four-year colleges"—and states her position clearly and explicitly:

> Community colleges need increased funding, and students need access to more flexible federal and state financial aid, enhanced paid internships and college work-study programs. . . . It's time to put public and private money where more and more students are educated, and remove the real, but surmountable, obstacles that stand between them and a degree.

Whenever you argue a position, you're responding to something someone else said or did that has motivated you to speak up. Especially in academic writing, you're expected to do more than just assert your own position; you need to let your readers know what larger conversation you're responding to.

Come up with support for your position

With so much misinformation flying around today, it's more important than ever for the arguments you make to be backed up by solid support. Even in everyday arguments—say over a claim that Impossible Burgers are tastier than the real thing—you'd better be prepared to prove that the new meatless wonders are really, really good—or face skeptics who will say, simply, "Says who?" or "Can you prove it?" Answering such questions persuasively is the key to supporting your claim. The ancient Greek philosopher Aristotle long ago wrote that we should use "all the available means" we can to persuade an audience, and suggested three in particular: providing good reasons and evidence, demonstrating credibility, and appealing to emotion.

You're entitled to your own opinions but not your own facts.
DANIEL PATRICK MOYNIHAN

Provide good reasons and evidence

Whatever your thesis, it needs to be backed up by REASONS that explain *why* you take that position. One way to think about that is to write out your thesis and then answer the question *why*? For example:

> Artificial intelligence may well be the death of humans as we know them. *Why?* Because robots will be able to do what humans do now—and more.

> Too often today, professional athletes are shuffled around like pawns. *Why?* Because most contracts give more rights to teams and owners than to players.

You likely have other reasons as well, ASSUMPTIONS that explain why your reasons justify the claim. In this argument about artificial intelligence, the assumption is that nothing can replace humans, and in the one about professional athletes, that constantly shuffling around players is detrimental to both the players and the game.

If you can't come up with good reasons for taking a position, you may need to revise your thesis, or find another topic. But once you have a list of reasons, think about which ones best suit your PURPOSE, and which ones your AUDIENCE is likely to accept.

See pp. 61–65 for examples and advice on using each of these kinds of evidence.

Then you need to provide EVIDENCE to support those reasons. While there are many kinds of evidence you can use to good advantage, some of the most common ones used in academic contexts are facts and statistics, expert testimony, surveys, observations, interviews, experiments, and personal experience—as well as charts and other visuals.

Keep in mind that what counts as evidence varies from discipline to discipline. Facts and statistics may be required in some disciplines but not in others. Data from observations and interviews is expected in an ethnographic report for a *sociology* class, whereas textual evidence is expected in much writing about *literature*. Results from experiments are required in some *science* writing. Personal experience may count as evidence in *education* courses, but not in *engineering*. Just about everyone values expert testimony.

See how June Jordan, professor of English and African American Studies, uses *facts and statistics* to build support for a claim.

> What we casually call "English" less and less defers to England and its "gentlemen." "English" is no longer a specific matter of geography or an element of class privilege; more than thirty-three countries use this tool as a means of "intranational communication." Countries as disparate as Zimbabwe and Malaysia, or Israel and Uganda, use it as their non-native currency of convenience. Obviously, this tool, this "English," cannot function inside thirty-three discrete societies on the basis of rules and values absolutely determined somewhere else, in a thirty-fourth other country, for example.
>
> In addition to that staggering congeries of non-native users of English, there are five countries, or 333,746,000 people, for whom this thing called "English" serves as a native tongue. Approximately 10 percent of these native speakers of "English" are Afro-American citizens of the U.S.A. I cite these numbers and varieties of human beings dependent on "English" in order, quickly, to suggest how strange and how tenuous is any concept of "Standard English."
>
> —JUNE JORDAN, "Nobody Mean More to Me Than You and the Future Life of Willie Jordan"

Jordan builds up to her claim with facts and statistics about English. That it's spoken by non-native speakers in more than thirty-three countries, countries "as disparate as Zimbabwe and Malaysia, Israel and Uganda." And in five more countries, by 333,746,00 native speakers. Obviously, she says, the "English" spoken by all these people in all these places is not going to adhere to rules formulated "somewhere else."

And then she tells us her point: to suggest that the idea that millions of people spread across so many "disparate" countries would speak one "Standard English" is, at best, "strange" and "tenuous."

You can also find evidence to support an argument by using some familiar rhetorical strategies: analyzing CAUSES AND EFFECTS, CLASSIFYING, COMPARING AND CONTRASTING, DEFINING, DESCRIBING,

See pp. 51–58 for examples and advice on using each of these strategies.

providing **EXAMPLES**, and **NARRATING**. These are strategies that you probably use all the time, and they come in handy for both developing and supporting an argument.

Consider how environmentalist Benji Backer uses three of these common strategies to support his argument that we need a number of different solutions and perspectives to deal with "complicated environmental problems."

> Threats to the environment are real—we are facing a dramatic increase in global carbon emissions, our air quality impacted by wildfires is making the West less hospitable, and droughts are causing immense water scarcity concerns. As we've seen these and many other issues come to fruition over the past few decades, we've learned a lot about the causes. One of the elephants in the room is the reality that carbon production has contributed in a negative way to a few of our globe's severe environmental concerns.
>
> But instead of vilifying vulnerable communities that had no idea that their production of affordable, abundant energy would be contributing to environmental problems, we should be utilizing their talents, background and brainpower to come up with next-generation solutions. After all, to solve complicated environmental problems, we need a diverse set of solutions and knowledgeable voices.
>
> —BENJI BACKER, "The Conservative Case for Environmentalism"

Notice how he starts with three *examples* of threats to the environment (carbon emissions, wildfires, droughts) and then goes on to acknowledge two *causes* (the drought causes water scarcity, carbon production contributes to "severe environmental concerns"). Last, he offers a *contrast*, arguing that instead of vilifying those who produce coal we should use their talents and "brainpower" to find solutions. In sum, these rhetorical strategies provide powerful evidence for Backer's argument that we face "real" threats to the environment and need "diverse" and "knowledgeable" voices to come up with solutions.

Images can also be a powerful way to support an argument. Think about how advertisements use images to get our attention and to argue that we should buy this kind of laptop or that kind of

shampoo. Consider this National Park Service poster, which makes an argument about wildlife safety, specifically about what we should and should not do around animals—and "good luck" if we do the wrong thing.

Demonstrate your credibility

You need to establish your own AUTHORITY as a writer: to show that you know what you're talking about by citing trustworthy sources, and to demonstrate that you're fair by representing other positions evenhandedly and accurately. Be careful, though, not to overdo it, and to demonstrate respect as well as credibility. You don't want to come across as boastful. You might want to acknowledge those you've learned from, noting that you're building on their work.

When Jaron Lanier, often said to be the "father of virtual reality," decided that social media—for which he'd been an advocate—had become a monster we now can't control, he wrote a book called *Ten Arguments for Deleting Your Social Media Account RIGHT NOW.*

Anticipating criticism of his position, Lanier acknowledged and addressed that criticism in the opening chapter:

> Plenty of critics like me have been warning that bad stuff was happening for a while now. . . . For years, I had to endure quite painful criticism from friends in Silicon Valley because I was perceived as a traitor for criticizing what we were doing. Lately I have the opposite problem. I argue that Silicon Valley people are for the most part decent, and I ask that we not be villainized; I take a lot of fresh heat for that. Whether I've been too hard or too soft on my community is hard to know.
>
> The more important question now is whether anyone's criticism will matter. It's undeniably out in the open that a bad technology is doing us harm, but will we—will you, meaning *you*—be able to resist and help steer the world to a better place?
>
> —JARON LANIER, *Ten Arguments for Deleting Your Social Media*

In this passage, Lanier comes across as straightforward and honest: he's telling it like it is, even if he gets criticized for doing so. But then he takes an unexpected turn: rather than condemning "Silicon Valley," he argues that most people working there are in fact decent (and he includes himself in this "we") but then points to an even larger issue: Is it possible that by now, no one will be able to make "bad stuff" stop happening? Lanier suggests that such a goal can only be achieved if everyone who uses social media takes action, and he closes by addressing us directly—as *you*.

Readers will know Lanier's credentials: they are detailed on the inside cover of the book. This passage increases his credibility by including himself in the group he's criticizing and by accepting responsibility, suggesting that we can trust him to be giving us his most thoughtful and best advice.

Establish a responsible stance and a trustworthy tone

In a time of arguments based on fake news, misleading headlines, and downright lies, it's more important than ever that you aim for honesty and truth, take full responsibility for what you say, and establish a reasonable, trustworthy tone. After all, your audience must trust that you know what you're talking about and believe that you have their best interests at heart if they're to listen carefully to what you say, much less accept what you want them to think or do.

See how Kamala Harris establishes a trustworthy TONE in a speech at Howard University, a school that she herself attended:

> I've had the honor of speaking at many commencements. But this one is particularly special for me. Because decades ago, I sat just where you sit now, feeling the embrace of my Howard family.
>
> Our Howard family.
>
> And a family, at its best, shares common values and aspirations. . . . A family looks for ways to support and inspire one another. . . .
>
> You are . . . part of a legacy that has now endured and thrived for 150 years.
>
> Endured when the doors of higher education were closed to Black students. Endured when segregation and discrimination were the law of the land.
>
> But over the last 150 years, Howard has endured and thrived. Generations of students have been nurtured and challenged here—and provided with the tools and confidence to soar.
>
> —KAMALA HARRIS, Howard University commencement address

It's not hard for Harris to win her audience's trust, having graduated from Howard University herself. But she makes the most of it, noting that she's "had the honor" of speaking at many commencements, but that "this one is particularly special." In fact, she still recalls "feeling the embrace" of "Our Howard family." A family shares common values and aspirations, and her words suggest that she and her audience have much in common beyond having attended the same school. And when she tells them they have "the tools and confidence to soar," she speaks from personal experience: she's been where they are now and assures them that they have what it takes "to soar." Her words demonstrate that she knows what she's talking about—and both understands and cares about the members of her audience.

There are other ways to establish trustworthiness and credibility, of course. Harris could have, for example, cited statistics about how many generations of successful graduates Howard has sent forth to uphold its values. Or she could have drawn on testimony from other scholars who can also speak to Howard's ability to help students "soar." But in this instance, she draws on her own authority—as a highly successful former prosecutor, attorney general of California, and senator (she was not yet vice president)—and her own experience to build a sense of trust with her audience.

REFLECT! Find a speech on *YouTube* given by someone who interests you, perhaps an author or a candidate for office, and listen for how that speaker establishes credibility. What does the speaker do (or fail to do) to come across as trustworthy (or not)?

Appeal to your audience's emotions and values

Good reasons and evidence provide powerful support for an argument, but sometimes it helps to appeal to an audience's emotions, moving hearts as well as minds. Emotional appeals can stir strong feelings and evoke values that members of your audience can be expected to hold. Images are especially effective at evoking emotions. Consider the photograph on the next page of someone asking for money at a Christmas market in Germany. Our eyes are drawn first to the sign with its stark but simple message: *Ich habe hunger* (I'm hungry). And then we see the person's outstretched hand, asking for help and showing us quite literally that they need a

helping hand. It's an image that appeals to our emotions and to our values, that no one should go hungry.

Be careful when you make an emotional appeal that it suits your argument and purpose, and think about what you want your audience to think or do in response. Also, take care not to overdo it, pulling at their heartstrings so hard that your audience feels manipulated. Remember that if used inappropriately, emotional appeals may turn your audience off!

Consider other perspectives respectfully, and look for common ground

No matter what your position, others may have different views or even offer COUNTERARGUMENTS. You need to acknowledge views other than your own accurately and respectfully and to answer any objections—whether to explain why you disagree, concede that they have a point, or some of each. Doing so shows that you've done your homework and are aware of what else has been said, enhancing your authority to write on the topic and demonstrating to your readers that you're a writer they can trust. And including views that are contrary to your own shows you to be confident enough of your own views to acknowledge other perspectives that are also worth considering.

Acknowledging the views of others is also a way of establishing **COMMON GROUND** with those who hold positions different from yours. Showing that you're trying to understand where they're coming from will also increase the likelihood that they'll take seriously what you say, and finding some point of agreement will always increase the likelihood that your own argument will be heard.

> Successful arguments include a healthy consideration for other views.
> JOHN DUFFY

Sometimes building common ground is a matter of choosing the right words. Calling someone who doubts the existence of climate change a "climate denier," for example, is likely to end the conversation. Better instead to say they're skeptical of all the claims about climate change—and to avoid any labels.

See how journalist Clive Thompson considers other points of view and builds common ground in arguing that technology is making our minds and our lives better:

> Some people panic that our brains are being deformed on a physiological level by today's technology: spend too much time flipping between windows and skimming text instead of reading a book, or interrupting your conversations to read text messages, and pretty soon you won't be able to concentrate on anything—and if you can't concentrate on it, you can't understand it either. In his book *The Shallows*, Nicholas Carr eloquently raised this alarm, arguing that the quality of our thought, as a species, rose in tandem with the ascendance of slow-moving, linear print and began declining with the arrival of the zingy, flighty Internet. "I'm not thinking the way I used to think," he worried.
>
> I'm certain that many of these fears are warranted. . . . Today's multitasking tools really do make it harder than before to stay focused. . . . One of the great challenges of today's digital thinking tools is knowing when *not* to use them, when to rely on the powers of older and slower technologies, like paper and books.
>
> —CLIVE THOMPSON, *Smarter Than You Think: How Technology Is Changing Our Minds for the Better*

The title of Thompson's book lets readers know that he is an advocate for new technologies: they are "changing our minds for the better." Yet he takes time to seek out those like Nicholas Carr who disagree with him, considering his opinion and quoting him, letting Carr speak for himself—a sign of respect. Thompson goes on to build common ground with those readers by acknowledging Carr's position as worthy of respect. He even heeds Carr's warning to some degree, noting that it's important to know when and when *not* to use digital tools.

Invite response

Whatever your topic, you are not likely to be the first one to write about it. If in writing about an issue you're joining a larger conversation, then you should invite your readers to do the same—to respond to what you say and add their voices to that conversation. One way to do this is to conclude by calling on readers to do something specific, as civil rights activist Michelle Alexander does in the introduction to her book *The New Jim Crow*:

> A new social consensus must be forged about race and the role of race in defining the basic structure of our society, if we hope ever to abolish the New Jim Crow. This new consensus must begin with dialogue, a conversation that fosters a critical consciousness, a key prerequisite to effective social action. My writing is an attempt to ensure that the conversation does not end with nervous laughter.
>
> —MICHELLE ALEXANDER, *The New Jim Crow: Mass Incarceration in the Age of Colorblindness*

Here Alexander calls on readers to act, to join a conversation that she hopes her book will begin, one that she says is "prerequisite to effective social action."

See on the next page how she concludes an op-ed on the same topic published in the *New York Times*. Like many newspapers, the *Times* explicitly invites readers to respond by sending in letters to the editor or posting comments online, and Alexander concludes by naming specific goals and how they should be met—and then challenging her readers to respond to a direct question.

> If our goal is *not* a better system of mass criminalization, but instead the creation of safe, caring, thriving communities, then we ought to be heavily investing in quality schools, job creation, drug treatment and mental health care in the least advantaged communities rather than pouring billions into their high-tech management and control. Fifty years ago, the Rev. Dr. Martin Luther King Jr. warned that "when machines and computers, profit motives and property rights are considered more important than people, the giant triplets of racism, extreme materialism and militarism are incapable of being conquered." We failed to heed his warning back then. Will we make a different choice today?

In this conclusion, Alexander calls directly on readers to reject mass criminalization and instead to invest in education, job creation, and health care as the best way to create "safe communities." To underscore this position, she notes that citizens failed to act when Martin Luther King Jr. urged them to take action against the "giant triplets" that have led to mass criminalization, closing with a potent rhetorical question she very much hopes will be answered by a resounding "yes."

Ways of organizing an argument

While there are various ways of organizing anything you write, here is one way you might go about organizing an argument.

Introduce your topic in a way that will get your AUDIENCE interested. You might start with some background information and then ask a provocative question that your essay aims to answer, as Gabriela Moro does in her essay on page 147 on "Minority Student Clubs: Segregation or Integration?" You could also start by quoting or summarizing what others have said about the topic and then responding with what you say. Or sometimes you might open by simply stating your thesis.

Provide good reasons and evidence to support your claim. If you're following TOULMIN style, you may want to state any ASSUMPTIONS that explain your reasoning.

Acknowledge any counterarguments or other perspectives accurately and fairly, and respond to what they say. Try to find COMMON GROUND with positions that are different from yours.

Look for places throughout where you can demonstrate your credibility (perhaps by citing trustworthy sources and multiple perspectives), and ***appeal to your audience's emotions*** (some of your evidence might do that).

Conclude in a way that leaves your audience thinking about what you've said—reiterating your main points, explaining the implications of your argument, or saying why it matters. Sometimes you might want to conclude with a call for action, as Moro does in calling for further research to determine ways of promoting "meaningful diverse interactions among the student body."

Read your draft with a critical eye, get response—and revise

Now's the time to read over what you've written to see that you've made your position clear, supported it with good reasons and evidence, and considered carefully what others have said—and then to ask a classmate to read it over as well. The following questions can help you or someone else to read over a draft that takes a position:

- Have you DESCRIBED the issue clearly and in a fair-minded way?

- Have you stated your POSITION explicitly and as a response to what others have said about the topic? Is there a THESIS— and if not, is one needed?

- What good REASONS have you given for your position, and what EVIDENCE have you provided as support? Is your evidence factually accurate? How likely is it that your AUDIENCE will find it persuasive?

- What's your STANCE? Is it trustworthy and appropriate to your audience and purpose?

- What background information have you provided? What more might your readers need?

- How reliable are any sources you've cited? What kinds of sources are they—scholarly? popular? Who published or sponsored them? What's their purpose—to inform? sell? persuade? entertain? What can you learn about them? Do other sources say the same thing?

- What COUNTERARGUMENTS and other perspectives have you considered, and have you described them fairly and accurately? How have you addressed what they say?

- How will your OPENING make your audience want to read on? How else might you begin?

- Is it clear why the issue matters? Why do you care, and who else should care?

- Does the CONCLUSION make clear what you want readers to think or do? Have you invited them to respond?

- Is your argument easy to follow? If not, would it help to add TRANSITIONS or headings?

- Consider your title. Does it tell readers what the topic is, and will it make them want to read on? Think about whether there's a better title.

Now take a deep breath—and REVISE! If you've analyzed your draft and gotten advice from others, you've got a plan. You know what you need or want to do. But remember: you're writing an ARGUMENT, which needs to take a clear POSITION supported by REASONS and EVIDENCE—and to acknowledge other positions as well. Here's what *you* think and why!

REFLECT! Examine something that you've written—an essay, an email, a presentation, whatever. Have you made clear that what you wrote about mattered to you, and should matter to others? If not, how would you now revise what you wrote to make that explicit?

A STUDENT ARGUMENT

GABRIELA MORO

Minority Student Clubs: Segregation or Integration?

Gabriela Moro wrote this essay in her first-year composition class at the University of Notre Dame. It was later published in Fresh Writing, *an online archive of exemplary first-year writing by students at Notre Dame. Moro graduated in 2018 with a major in neuroscience and behavior and is pursuing a career in medicine.*

Minority representation on US college campuses has increased significantly in recent years, and many schools have made it a priority to increase diversity on their campuses in order to prepare students for a culturally diverse US democratic society (Hurtado and Ruiz 3–4). To complement this increase, many schools have implemented minority student clubs to provide safe and comfortable environments where minority students can thrive academically and socially with peers from similar backgrounds. However, do these minority groups amplify students' tendency to interact only with those who are similar to themselves? Put another way, do these groups inhibit students from engaging in diverse relationships?

Many view such programs to be positive and integral to minority students' college experience; some, however, feel that these clubs are not productive for promoting cross-cultural interaction. While minority clubs have proven to be beneficial to minority students in some cases, particularly on campuses that are not very diverse, my research suggests that colleges would enrich the educational experience for all students by introducing multicultural clubs as well.

To frame my discussion, I will use an article from *College Student Journal* that distinguishes between two types of students: one who believes minority clubs are essential for helping minority students stay connected with their cultures, and another who believes these clubs isolate minorities and work against diverse interaction

Provides background information and introduces topic.

Poses questions that guided her research.

Summarizes what others say.

States claim as a response to what's been said.

among students. To pursue the question of whether or not such groups segregate minorities from the rest of the student body and even discourage cultural awareness, I will use perspectives from minority students to show that these programs are especially helpful for first-year students. I will also use other student testimonials to show that when taken too far, minority groups can lead to self-segregation and defy what most universities claim to be their diversity goals. Findings from research will contribute to a better understanding of the role minority clubs play on college campuses and offer a complete answer to my question about the importance of minority programs.

Discusses opposing views.

Before I go further, I would like to differentiate among three kinds of diversity that Patricia Gurin and colleagues identify in their article "Diversity and Higher Education: Theory and Impact on Educational Outcomes." The first type is *structural diversity*, "the numerical representation of diverse [racial and ethnic] groups." The existence of structural diversity alone does not ensure that students will develop valuable intergroup relationships. *Classroom diversity*, the second type, involves gaining "content knowledge" or a better understanding about diverse peers and their backgrounds by doing so in the classroom. The third type of diversity, *informal interactional diversity*, refers to "both the frequency and the quality of intergroup interaction as keys to meaningful diversity experiences during college." Students often encounter this kind of diversity in social settings outside the classroom (Gurin et al. 332–33). Informal interactional diversity is the focus of my research, since it is the concept that leads colleges to establish social events and organizations that allow all students to experience and appreciate the variety of cultures present in a student body.

Defines key term, "diversity."

In a study published in *College Student Journal*, three administrators at Pennsylvania State University explore how biracial students interact with others on a college campus. The authors conclude that views of minority clubs and related programs, which the authors call race-oriented student services, tend to fall into two groups: "Although some argue that these race-oriented student services are divisive and damage white-minority relations, others support these services as providing a safe place and meeting the needs of minority students to develop a sense of racial pride, community and importance" (Ingram et al. 298). I will start by examining the point of view of those who associate minority clubs with positive outcomes.

A study by Samuel Museus in the *Journal of College Student Development* finds that minority student programs help students to stay connected with their culture in college and help ease first-year minority students' transition into the college environment. The study also shows that ethnic student organizations help students adjust and find their place at universities that have a predominantly white student body (584). Museus concludes that universities should stress the importance of racial and ethnic groups and develop more opportunities for minority students to make connections with them. This way, students can find support from their minority peers as they work together to face academic and social challenges. Museus's findings suggest that minority student groups are essential for allowing these to preserve and foster connections to their own cultures.

In another study, Wendell Hall and colleagues evaluate how minority and non-minority students differ in their inclinations to take part in diversity activities and to communicate with racially and ethnically diverse peers at a predominantly white university. These scholars conclude that "engagement [with diverse peers] is learned" (434). Students who engaged with diverse students before going to college were more likely to interact with diverse peers by the end of their sophomore year. Minority students were more predisposed than their white peers to interact with diverse peers during their freshman year (435). These findings indicate that minority student clubs can be helpful for first-year minority students who have not previously engaged with other minority students, especially if the university has a predominantly white student body.

Cites evidence from published studies.

Cites evidence showing benefits of minority clubs.

Cites further evidence of positive effects.

Professors and scholars are not the only ones who strongly support minority clubs. For example, three students at Harvard College—Andrea Delgado, Denzel (no last name given), and Kimi Fafowora—give their perspective on student life and multicultural identity on campus to incoming students via *YouTube*. The students explain how minority programs on campus have helped them adjust to a new college environment as first-year students. As Delgado puts it:

Quotes student testimony on the benefits of such clubs.

> I thought [cultural clubs were] something I maybe didn't need, but come November, I missed speaking Spanish and I missed having tacos, and other things like that. That's the reason why I started attending meetings more regularly. Latinas Unidas has been a great intersection of my cultural background and my political views. ("Student Voices")

The experiences these minority students shared support the scholarly evidence that minority clubs help incoming students transition into a new and often intimidating environment.

While the benefits of these clubs are quite evident, several problems can also arise from them. The most widely recognized is self-segregation. Self-segregating tendencies are not exclusive to minority students: college students in general tend to self-segregate as they enter an unfamiliar environment. As a study by Nathan Martin and colleagues finds, "Today, the student bodies of our leading colleges and universities are more diverse than ever. However, college students are increasingly self-segregating by race or ethnicity" (720). Several studies as well as interviews with students suggest that minority clubs exacerbate students' inclination to self-segregate. And as students become comfortable with their minority peers, they may no longer desire or feel the need to branch out of their comfort zone.

Considers problems with minority clubs.

In another study, Julie Park, a professor at the University of Maryland, examines the relationship between participation in college student organizations and the development of interracial friendships. Park suggests, "if students spend the majority of time in such groups [Greek, ethnic, and religious student organizations], participation may affect student involvement in the broader diversity of the institution" (642). In other words, if minority students form all of their social and academic ties within their minority group, the desired cultural exchange among the student body could suffer.

Cites research pointing out problems with many clubs.

So what can be done? In the Penn State study mentioned earlier, in which data were collected by an online survey, participants were asked to respond to an open-ended question about what they think universities should do to create a more inviting environment for biracial students (Ingram et al. 303). On one hand, multiple students responded with opinions opposing the formation of both biracial and multiracial clubs: "I feel instead of having biracial and multiracial clubs the colleges should have diversity clubs and just allow everyone to get together. All these 'separate' categorizing of clubs, isn't that just separation of groups?" "Having a ton of clubs that are for specific races is counter-productive. It creates segregation and lack of communication across cultures" (304–05).

Considers views opposing biracial and multiracial clubs.

On the other hand, students offered suggestions for the formation of multicultural activities: "Encourage more racial integration to show students races aren't so different from each other and to lessen stereotypes" (305). "Hold cultural events that allow students of different races to express/share their heritage" (306). Patreese Ingram and colleagues conclude that while biracial and multiracial student organizations are helpful in establishing an inviting college environment for minority students,

Cites student testimony in support of multicultural activities.

> creating a truly inclusive environment . . . requires additional efforts: these include multicultural awareness training for faculty, staff, and students, and incorporation of multicultural issues into the curriculum. In addition to the creation of biracial/multiracial clubs and organizations, the students in this study want to increase awareness of the mixed heritage population among others on college campuses. (308)

Quotes research on the need for an inclusive environment.

The two very different opinions reported in this study point to the challenges minority student programs can create, but also suggest ways to resolve these challenges. Now that evidence from both research studies and student perspectives confirms that these clubs, while beneficial to minority students' experiences, can inhibit cultural immersion, I will continue with my original argument that the entire student body would benefit if campuses also implemented multicultural advocacy clubs, rather than just selective minority clubs. Gurin and colleagues, the researchers who identify the three types of diversity in higher education, contend that even with the presence of diverse racial and ethnic groups and regular communication among students formally and informally, a greater push from educators is needed:

Sums up evidence on both sides of the issue. Reiterates claim.

> In order to foster citizenship for a diverse democracy, educators must intentionally structure opportunities for students to leave the comfort of their homogenous peer group and build relationships across racially/ethnically diverse student communities on campus. (363)

This suggestion implies that participation from students and faculty is needed to foster cultural immersion in higher education.

Another way to improve cross-cultural exchange is by developing a diverse curriculum. An article on multiculturalism in higher education by Alma Clayton-Pedersen and Caryn McTighe Musil in the *Encyclopedia of Education* reviews the ways in which universities have incorporated diversity studies into their core curriculum over the last several decades. The authors report that the numbers of courses that seek to prepare students for a democratic society rich in diversity have increased (1711, 1714). However, they recommend that institutions need to take a more holistic approach to their academic curricula in order to pursue higher education programs that prepare students to face "complex and demanding questions" and to "use their new knowledge and civic, intercultural capacities to address real-world problems" (1714). My research suggests that a more holistic approach to the importance of diversity studies in the college curriculum, as well as multicultural advocacy clubs, are necessary in order to prepare *all* students, not just minority students, for the diverse world and society ahead of them.

Thus, even though minority student clubs can lead to self-segregation among students and result in less cross-cultural interaction, their benefits to minority students suggest that a balance needs to be found between providing support for minorities and avoiding segregation of these groups from the rest of the student body. Besides sponsoring minority student programs, colleges and universities can implement multicultural events and activities for all students to participate in, especially during the freshman year. An initiative like this would enhance the diverse interactions that occur on campuses, promote cultural immersion, and garner support for minority student clubs.

Beyond the reach of this evaluation, further research should be conducted, specifically on the types of cultural events that are most effective in promoting cultural awareness and meaningful diverse interactions among the student body. By examining different multicultural organizations from both public and private institutions, and comparing student experiences and participation in those programs, researchers can suggest an ideal multicultural program to provide an optimal student experience.

Concludes by calling for response in the form of further research.

Works Cited

Clayton-Pedersen, Alma R., and Caryn McTighe Musil. "Multiculturalism in Higher Education." *Encyclopedia of Education*, edited by James W. Guthrie, 2nd ed., vol. 5, Macmillan, 2002, pp. 1709–16.

Gurin, Patricia, et al. "Diversity and Higher Education: Theory and Impact on Educational Outcomes." *Harvard Educational Review*, vol. 72, no. 3, 2002, pp. 330–63. *ResearchGate*, https://doi.org/10.17763/haer.72.3.01151786u134n051.

Hall, Wendell, et al. "A Tale of Two Groups: Differences between Minority Students and Non-Minority Students in Their Predispositions to and Engagement with Diverse Peers at a Predominantly White Institution." *Research in Higher Education*, vol. 52, no. 4, 2011, pp. 420–39. *Academic Search Premier*, https://doi.org/10.1007/s11162-010-9201-4.

Hurtado, Sylvia, and Adriana Ruiz. "The Climate for Underrepresented Groups and Diversity on Campus." *Higher Education Research Institute*, 2012, heri.ucla.edu/briefs/urmbrief.php.

Ingram, Patreese, et al. "How Do Biracial Students Interact with Others on the College Campus?" *College Student Journal*, vol. 48, no. 2, 2014, pp. 297–311.

Martin, Nathan D., et al. "Interracial Friendships across the College Years: Evidence from a Longitudinal Case Study." *Journal of College Student Development*, vol. 55, no. 7, 2014, pp. 720–25. *Academic Search Premier*, https://doi.org/10.1353/csd.2014.0075.

Museus, Samuel D. "The Role of Ethnic Student Organizations in Fostering African American and Asian American Students' Cultural Adjustment and Membership at Predominantly White Institutions." *Journal of College Student Development*, vol. 49, no. 6, 2008, pp. 568–86. *Project MUSE*, https://doi.org/10.1353/csd.0.0039.

Park, Julie J. "Clubs and the Campus Racial Climate: Student Organizations and Interracial Friendship in College." *Journal of College Student Development*, vol. 55, no. 7, 2014, pp. 641–60. *Academic Search Premier*, https://doi.org/10.1353/csd.2014.0076.

"Student Voices: Multicultural Perspectives." *YouTube*, uploaded by Harvard College Admissions and Financial Aid, 7 Aug. 2014, www.youtube.com/watch?v=djIWQgDx-Jc.

Thinking about the Text

1. What do you take away as the main CLAIM of Gabriela Moro's argument?

2. How well do you think she supports this claim? Show examples from the text that you find most persuasive.

3. How does Moro take COUNTERARGUMENTS into consideration? Do you think she deals fairly and evenhandedly with all sides? Cite examples from her text.

4. What does Moro do to convince you that she is CREDIBLE and trustworthy? What more might she have done?

5. Moro obviously cares deeply about this topic. Think of a topic that is equally important to you, and write a paragraph or two introducing the topic and summarizing an ARGUMENT you'd most like to make about it.

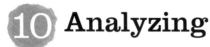 Analyzing

I'm a huge fan of teaching you to think,
analyze, and communicate, then sending you out
into the world to cause trouble.

—HILARY MASON

Wise policymakers analyze issues carefully
and look at facts and probabilities
instead of just hoping for the best.

—LAURA INGRAHAM

W hy have you lost five pounds in the last month? What has made *Abbott Elementary* so popular? Which candidate should you vote for? Answering such questions calls for analysis, for examining something in detail in order to understand it in some way. In analyzing why you've lost weight, you might begin by detailing your eating patterns: At what time of the day do you eat? How often do you eat? What prompts you to eat—or what keeps you from eating? What foods do you favor, and which ones do you avoid? Has your caloric intake gone down, and why? As you gather data on what and when you eat, and on your reasons for eating as you do, you are generating evidence you can use to begin finding answers to your original question.

Thinking about the popularity of *Abbott Elementary* will probably lead you to examine the features that have made the show so popular: especially the characters, teachers who are just trying to take care of their students in spite of many obstacles; the dialogue, which is both authentic and genuinely funny; the storyline, which argues for the importance of public schools; and the setting itself.

And in order to decide which candidate to vote for, you'll need to consider *all* the candidates, their policies, the issues you care about, and so on. Whatever your subject, conducting a detailed analysis—looking at "facts and probabilities" rather than "hoping for the best," in Laura Ingraham's words—will help you answer questions and understand your topic better as a result.

Every field uses analysis. *Engineers* carry out detailed analyses to understand whether a bridge can be built in a specific location. *Scientists* use quantitative data to analyze causes and effects. *Social scientists* use qualitative analysis to help them understand human behavior. *Literature students* analyze poetry in order to understand how various aspects of a poem or novel lead us to understand it in a certain way. This chapter provides guidelines for doing a rhetorical analysis, focusing on texts of various kinds and the strategies an author or artist uses to communicate a message to an audience.

REFLECT! Think of an issue that's being discussed and debated now—on campus, in a local community, in the world. What are people saying? What do the various sides think, and why? What kinds of analysis are they doing or citing as support for what they think?

A GUIDE TO ANALYZING A TEXT

A speech, a novel, an ad, a painting, a music album, a contract: all are *texts* of one kind or another. You might be assigned to analyze one of them; or you may have other reasons to conduct an analysis: for a job, to make financial or political decisions, to better understand yourself or the world around you. Here's some advice that will help you analyze texts of various kinds. As you'll see, it's designed to be used *as you write.* Keep it close at hand!

Identify a text you want to understand

Whether you're assigned to analyze a specific text or get to choose one yourself, you'll do your best work if the topic or text is of interest to you. But all analysis is driven by a question of some kind, something you're curious about, so a good way to begin is by looking for a question that you really want to know the answer to: What was the best Super Bowl ad this year? What makes K-pop so popular? Why do so many people say that *Moby-Dick* is the greatest American novel? These questions all call for analysis, for looking closely at these texts to tease out answers.

Joanna Robinson, Dave Gonzales, and Gavin Edwards, all longtime observers of the Marvel Cinematic Universe, set out to answer a puzzling question: "How did Marvel conquer the world?" To answer this question, the trio analyzed historical and financial data as well as over 100 original interviews with producers, stars, directors, writers, and the head of studio Kevin Feige. The result: a book-length study, *The Reign of Marvel Studios,* arguing that the studio's new take on the "old Hollywood system" was at the heart of their success:

> It signed up actors for long-term contracts, cultivated trusted staff writers, and brought on a small army of visual artists who sometimes determined the look of a movie before a director was even hired. The result was a string of hits without parallel in the annals of moviemaking.
>
> —JOANNA ROBINSON, DAVE GONZALES, and GAVIN EDWARDS,
> *The Reign of Marvel Studios*

As these authors show just how these steps led to unparalleled and ongoing success, they also tell a compelling series of stories, full of

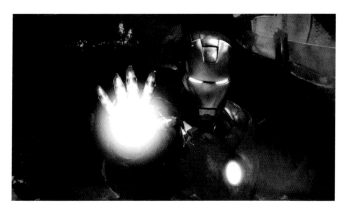

From *Iron Man 2*, Iron Man fires up his repulsor glove to blast War Machine. 2010.

insider insights and scenes that surprised even those who thought they knew everything there was to know about Marvel. That's what deep research and careful analysis can provide!

Think about your rhetorical situation

Once you have chosen a text to analyze, take time to consider your rhetorical situation.

Purpose. What do you want to happen as a result of your analysis—a more thorough understanding of a complex text? a certain interpretation of a poem? a decision about a proposal? How can you best accomplish your goals?

Audience. Who will be reading your analysis, and what do you know about them—their age, gender, cultural background? What are they likely to know about the text you're analyzing, and what background information will you need to provide? Can you assume they'll be interested in your subject? If not, how can you frame your analysis in a way that they will relate to? If you're analyzing the official statements your college has made on freedom of speech for an essay in your composition class, for instance, you might analyze any ETHICAL APPEALS they make and look for evidence they provide to support them. If instead you were writing on X, you might simply link to one of the college's statements along with a question asking what it ignores or leaves out.

Stance. How do you want to come across to your readers—as well informed? objective? enthusiastic? Whatever it is, how can your writing reflect your stance? And how are you approaching the text you're analyzing—as a student? a serious reader? a critic? something else?

Context. What else has been said about the subject of your analysis? What are the various perspectives? You'll need to provide some of that larger context in your analysis. And what's *your* context—if you're writing in response to an assignment, what's your time frame, and are there any requirements that you need to keep in mind?

Language. Think about the tone you want to establish: serious? authoritative? something else? Consider too whether you will need to use any foreign or technical terms and if so, whether you'll need to define them for your readers.

Media and design. Think about how you will deliver your analysis. Will it be a print text? a digital text? an oral presentation? Your medium will affect the way it is designed: for an oral presentation, you might use slides; for a print text, headings would probably be useful to help readers follow the major points of your analysis.

Be sure it's a text you can manage— and approach with an open mind

Think carefully about how much time you have to complete your analysis before you decide definitively on a text. A student in a course on the history of the Bible who was interested in the Book of Judges proposed doing an analysis of that book. This student quickly realized, however, that such a task was far from manageable given the due date, and so he chose to analyze one story in that book that he had always been curious about, the Samson and

Delilah story. Consider as well what resources you may need to carry out your analysis, and whether you have access to them. The student analyzing the Samson and Delilah story had access to several different translations as well as to a bibliography provided by the instructor that included other scholarly analyses of this story. Finally, think about how open-minded you are about the subject of your analysis. The purpose of an analysis is to gain some kind of insight about the subject, not to confirm something you already believe about it.

Think about what you want to know about the text

You may need little but the text itself to conduct a rhetorical analysis, especially in cases where the text is assigned in class. Sometimes, however, you will need to do some research to find out more about the topic. Wesley Cohen grew up in a household that would never have subscribed to *Cosmopolitan*, a magazine she therefore assumed was all fluff and no substance—the kind of thing you'd pick up while waiting for a dental appointment. But once she got to college and was free to read anything, including *Cosmo*, she was surprised to see that it now includes articles about some very serious issues, such as domestic violence, equal pay, right alongside horoscopes and fashion advice. So for an assignment to write a feature in a journalism class, she decided to look at what was happening "over at *Cosmo*." Noting that "It's rare to find a magazine that covers domestic violence and celebrity fashion on equal footing," she set out to analyze the changes that have taken place there in recent years.

If you want to read about what's happening at *Cosmo*, see Wesley Cohen's essay on p. 175.

You might not always begin with an explicit question as Cohen did, but your analysis will always be prompted by a question of some kind, by something that you're curious about.

Conduct a preliminary rhetorical analysis

A rhetorical analysis looks closely at a text (whether it is verbal, visual, or uses some other medium) in order to see what it says and how it does so. When you analyze a text, you examine each of its parts systematically to show how it engages the attention of readers and leads them to understand the text in a certain way.

If you take any humanities courses, you'll surely be asked to analyze various kinds of texts. Imagine, for example, how you might go about analyzing the following short but powerful poem:

> A word is dead
> When it is said,
> Some say.
> I say it just
> Begins to live
> That day.
>
> —EMILY DICKINSON

In analyzing this poem, you might begin by summing up the meaning as you see it and then showing how each line builds to that meaning. You'd consider why Dickinson breaks lines where she does, how rhyme and repetition contribute to the meaning, and what the contrast between living words and dead words suggests about spoken words.

Now imagine how you might do a rhetorical analysis of an article about Beyoncé by Michael Eric Dyson. The title immediately catches your attention: "Beyoncé. Amen." Why Amen? Then you read the opening sentence, which makes a startling claim:

> Beyoncé is not only the world's greatest entertainer, a feminist and a principled advocate of Black culture, but also something of a religious prophet.
>
> —MICHAEL ERIC DYSON, "Beyoncé. Amen."

Beyoncé a religious prophet? There's a claim that calls for analysis! You might first follow all the other religious allusions in the article and think about how they help support Dyson's claims that Bey is a "religious prophet" and her stadium a "sanctuary." You could also note that he quotes Beyoncé speaking about her goals for providing spiritual nourishment. You'd likely note that he builds his own credibility by referring to his personal experience as a preacher and his love for the Black church—as well as acknowledging that the church sometimes fails to live up to its own ideals.

This kind of rhetorical analysis is a good way to understand what the article says, and how well this author supports his claim that Beyoncé is "something of a religious prophet." It will be up to you to decide if you're convinced—and if not, why not.

You might also be assigned to analyze a visual text. One assignment I've often given to my first-year students asks them to analyze the campus map. Ours is a huge university, and they need to learn their way around campus. Analyzing the map gets them thinking about what's where and why. Why are certain buildings in one place rather than another? What is at the center of campus and what is on the periphery? What are the largest buildings? the smallest? Does one area of the map seem dominant? If so, what does that area represent—science and technology? the humanities? the administration? sports arenas? Analyzing the map reveals a lot!

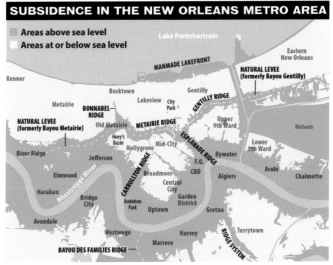

A map of New Orleans showing areas above sea level and those at or below sea level.

Suppose you are working on a presentation for an environmental engineering course on what the city of New Orleans should consider doing to prepare for any future hurricanes. You might include a slide of a map in your presentation showing which areas of the city lie at or below sea level, as part of your analysis of the potential problems, along with specific suggestions for what needs to be done now to ensure the safety of those who live in those low-lying neighborhoods.

Whether the text you're analyzing is written or visual, you'll need to examine it carefully to see how it supports what it says. Asking the following questions will help you to do so systematically.

Analyzing a written text

- What is your overall impression of the text, and what specific elements lead you to that impression?
- What CLAIM is the text making, and how do you know?
- What REASONS and EVIDENCE does the writer provide to support the claim? How convincing do you find them?
- What has motivated the writer to take on this topic? What's the larger conversation this text is responding to?
- How has the writer acknowledged and responded to COUNTERARGUMENTS—other points of view on the subject? Are they presented fairly and honestly?
- Does the writer use any EMOTIONAL APPEALS?
- How does the writer establish AUTHORITY and CREDIBILITY to address this topic?

Analyzing a visual text

- What does your eye go to first, and why has the designer chosen to draw your eye to that spot?
- What seems most important or interesting?
- Who do you think the visual aims to reach—who is its AUDIENCE—and how do you know?

- What is its PURPOSE? How well does it achieve its goal?
- Even if there are no words, what does the visual *say*? What is its ARGUMENT, and how do you know? Is the argument implicit or explicit?
- If there are words, how do they help get the message across? What's the font, and how does it affect the TONE?

What does your preliminary analysis show?

By the time you've completed a preliminary analysis, you should be immersed in your subject, so it's time to step back and look not at the trees but at the forest: What does your analysis reveal about the text? What most interests you about what you've discovered, and why does it seem important? Begin by making notes answering these questions and looking for patterns that may emerge.

In studying the notes she had taken on our campus map, for example, one of my students found that the very center of the campus houses the administrative offices but that two very large areas, the medical complex and the sports complex, take up the biggest part of campus. She found that the engineering and science area is next both in the space it occupies and in its prominence on the map, and that student dorms are on the outer periphery of the campus. These findings got her wondering if it had always been this way, so she went to the library and found the original campus map, showing classroom buildings in the center and only one small office devoted to administration. The library was the largest and most prominent building on campus. As she continued to think about the data she'd gathered, she thought hard about what her analysis revealed about the university and its values. How do these values play out in terms of campus layout and building design? Do changes in the development of the campus suggest a shift in what the university values?

Come up with a working thesis

Once you've analyzed your subject, you need to determine what your analysis shows. What have you learned about the subject, and what can you now say about it? Try writing that out as a working

See pp. 114–15 for more on coming up with a working thesis.

thesis, saying what you've analyzed and what you can now claim about it. Here's what my student wrote: "Our campus map is a work in progress, constantly changing in ways that reflect shifting priorities and financial realities."

Remember that you may need to qualify your thesis

On reflection, my student worried that she was overstating her case, saying that shifting priorities are always linked to financial realities. Such overstatements can hurt a writer's credibility and make an analysis less persuasive, or perhaps even cause people not to take it seriously. Be careful to QUALIFY if need be. Here's how my student did that: "Our campus map is a work in progress, constantly changing in ways that reflect shifting priorities that are often linked to financial realities."

Develop support for your analysis

Every textual analysis depends on support. There are three questions you can ask to begin gathering support: What evidence will support your analysis? How can you establish credibility? Will the text make any emotional appeals?

What evidence supports the analysis?

Any analysis of a text needs to examine its use of facts and other evidence. In her 2018 book, *Dopesick: Dealers, Doctors, and the Drug Company That Addicted America*, Beth Macy analyzes the factors that led up to the current opioid epidemic in the United States. Macy, an award-winning journalist, has the credentials to make her account trustworthy and credible; and her interviews with addicted people and those who love them provide very strong emotional appeals. But she also relies on facts and other evidence drawn from research.

Consider how she uses facts presented in two research studies. The first, by researchers at Princeton, supports Macy's finding that opioid addiction has now reached a crisis point: this study found that US mortality rates "had quietly risen a half-percentage point annually between 1999 and 2013 while midlife mortality continued to fall in other affluent countries." She then turns to results of a poll conducted by the Kaiser Family Foundation showing that today "56 percent of Americans now know someone who abused, was addicted to, or died from an overdose of opioids." Indeed, Macy's book-length analysis piles up facts and statistics that make her conclusions inescapable: America is "dopesick."

In addition to facts and statistics, Macy draws on the expert testimony of doctors and medical researchers, who support her analysis of the complicit role the medical community unwittingly played in exacerbating the opioid epidemic. And she provides one major example—Purdue Pharma, which introduced OxyContin after it gained FDA approval in 1995 and advertised it as completely safe: "If you take the medicine like it is prescribed, the risk of addiction is one half of one percent." Many people using OxyContin, however, ignored the "if." Within two months of its release, Macy shows, the drug was "on the streets" in large amounts. This extended example supports Macy's analysis and the argument she is making about the opioid crisis.

The kinds of evidence that you provide as support for an analysis will depend on your topic, but could include ANALOGIES, ANECDOTES, COMPARISONS, EXAMPLES, FACTS, QUOTATIONS, DEFINITIONS, statistics, personal experience, and so on.

How can you establish credibility?

We tend to believe people who seem credible, trustworthy, and honest, and establishing such credentials has never been more important than it is today. When you are writing an analysis, then, you need to come across as believable and to demonstrate that you're someone whose work can be trusted.

In an analysis of Juneteenth, celebrating the announcement, on June 19, 1865, in Galveston, Texas, that "all slaves are free," Clint Smith traces the effects of that proclamation on the Black citizens of Galveston and Texas today. Smith argues that "it is not enough to study history" or "to celebrate singular moments of our past" without understanding their effects "on the world around us today." In this essay, Smith establishes credibility not just by talking the talk of Juneteenth but by walking the walk—reporting from Galveston, on the spot where history was made, joining the crowd, and "soaking in the words" their ancestors heard in 1865. Standing on that very same spot, he says, he "felt the history pulse through my body." Then he continues his pursuit of understanding how that day's announcement reverberates down through the decades by going to visit Emancipation Park, which marks both the celebration of "our greatest emancipation" and a "wake-up call" for how much remains to be done to establish true freedom for all. As he walks the park, Smith stops to talk with residents and to listen to their stories, to see the current "racial chasm" in Texas through their eyes.

The rhetorical choices Smith makes—to speak in the first person, to attend the celebration in person, to explore Galveston himself, and to listen to its Black citizens—all build his credibility and the trustworthiness of his analysis.

Analyzing whether or not you can trust an author or speaker will lead you to carefully consider the words they use to see what kind of TONE they establish (careful and cautious? angry and belligerent? evenhanded?). Likewise, in analyzing a visual text, the use of fonts and colors and even layout might give you a sense of whether it's taking its subject seriously or not.

Should your analysis make any emotional appeals?

Any rhetorical analysis should carefully consider whether the text appeals to its audience's emotions, and if so, to what effect. Appeals to emotions are often misused: think of ads that suggest that buying a certain skin care product will make us as gorgeous as the model using it, for example. But EMOTIONAL APPEALS can also tug at our heartstrings in positive ways, persuading us to appoint a designated driver when we've been drinking, for instance, or to contribute to the life-saving work of Doctors without Borders.

Congresswomen in white at the 2019 State of the Union address.

See how Vanessa Friedman, a fashion critic at the *New York Times*, appealed to readers' emotions in her analysis of the role that clothing played at President Trump's 2019 State of the Union address:

> When the television cameras came up on the buzzing House chamber as Congress awaited President Trump's entrance, the most striking sight was not the grandeur of the room (though it is pretty grand) or the nerves and excitement of the special guests, but rather the unmistakable block of Congresswomen practically aglow in white on the Democratic side of the aisle.

—VANESSA FRIEDMAN, "A Sea of White, Lit by History"

A photo underscores Friedman's point: no one, she said, could "miss the message in what they wore: one of gender equality and pride, the long arc of history and the fight for women's rights, commitment to an agenda and, in the background, joy." The photo captures that moment of joy and appeals to readers to share in that joy and the message it delivers.

When you are analyzing any text, look carefully for emotional appeals, and think about how the author uses them. Are they used to create empathy? to arouse outrage? to change minds? to help establish the author's credibility? Or are they used negatively, to call out or humiliate someone, or to stoke divisiveness or even hatred? Perhaps they're simply indicating why readers should care about the topic. In each case, think about how any emotional appeal supports or relates to the argument the text is making, and whether it does so fairly.

Consider the larger context— and perspectives other than your own

If you're analyzing a text or topic that you think matters, chances are that you won't be the first one to do so. That means you should try to look *beyond* your own reaction and consider other perspectives. Being open to the ideas of others will help you produce a stronger analysis and will underscore your credibility as someone who's open to what others think and doesn't rush to judgment.

In an analysis of American exceptionalism, Jake Sullivan, a senior fellow at the Carnegie Endowment for International Peace, sums up the perspectives of others before offering his own conclusion:

> Some argue that the United States is fractured beyond repair— ... that you can no longer make arguments to the American people based on higher purpose—they are too angry or too cynical.
>
> I see it another way.... Let's not forget that, throughout American history, the path forward has been determined not in times of disruption but in their aftermath.... As for the American people, I believe that they would welcome a renewed form of exceptionalism that addresses their concerns, speaks to their aspirations, and restores confidence that their country can be a force for good in the world.... American exceptionalism is not a description of reality but the expression of an ambition. It is about striving, and falling short, and improving. This is the essence of a patriotism that every American can embrace.
>
> —JAKE SULLIVAN, "Yes, America Can Still Lead the World"

Thus does Sullivan's lengthy analysis of anger lead him to move beyond those who think we cannot recover from the current divisiveness, arguing that his analysis shows that Americans are very likely to keep working toward the goal of improving, always improving.

Invite response

Whatever the topic of your analysis, if you're writing about something that you find important, chances are that others will find it important as well. And if as we've said writing is a way of joining a larger conversation, it is also a way of starting one. So one way of concluding an analysis is to invite your readers to respond to what you say. See how Erin Hawley does this in a post to *The Geeky Gimp*, her blog about disability in comics, games, and TV shows. Here's how she opens a post about writing while disabled:

> "Are people telling me this thing I wrote is good because it's actually good, or are they praising it because they have such low expectations of me?" . . . [As] a disabled writer, I question other people's reactions to my work.
>
> —ERIN HAWLEY, "Writing While Disabled: The Damage of Ableism"

And here's how Hawley concludes her post:

> I am curious if other disabled writers experience similar thoughts, or have any tips on how to keep writing while disabled. Please let me know in the comments!

In this conclusion, she asks readers directly to respond to some questions she has. You can benefit by doing the same, and inviting response to what you write.

Read Erin Hawley's full post and find a link to her blog at letstalklibrary.com.

Ways of organizing an analysis

While there's no one way to organize an analysis, here's one way you might go about it.

Introduce your analysis in a way that will get your audience's attention and have some sense of what your analysis is about. Think hard about the opening sentence, which needs to draw them in. See, for example, how Wesley Cohen starts her analysis of *Cosmopolitan* on page 175 by saying, "Open up the March 2016 issue of *Cosmopolitan Magazine*, and you'll find tips for flirting with a guy at work."

And here's how Gloria Anzaldúa opens a famous essay about language: with a dentist telling her that "We're going to have to control your tongue." These are sentences that grab readers' attention, and make them interested to read on.

Then you'll want to say what you'll be analyzing and what's prompted you to look into this subject. Sometimes you'll need to provide contextual information for your readers, perhaps by first summarizing what others have said, and then responding with what you say. You may want to state an explicit THESIS in your introduction, saying what you claim as a result of your analysis—or you may want to save that until later in your essay.

Provide evidence that supports your analysis. If you're writing about a text, written or visual, much of your evidence will come from the text itself. But you may also present evidence from other sources. The kinds of evidence you show will depend on the subject of your analysis. Cohen includes examples from *Cosmo*, quotations from its editors and others, as well as anecdotes from her own experience.

Acknowledge perspectives other than your own. Be sure to include viewpoints other than your own, and to present them fairly. Even if you're analyzing something no one else has written about, acknowledge other possible perspectives.

Demonstrate your credibility by maintaining a fair and evenhanded TONE and by citing sources showing that you have done your homework and know what you are talking about!

Conclude by summing up what your analysis reveals, what you want your audience to understand about your topic, and why it matters—to you, and hopefully to them. Cohen concludes her analysis of *Cosmopolitan* on a personal note: "I want to read about face gloss and I want to know about domestic terrorism. . . . As a woman, and as a person, I should not have to choose just one story." And here's a more straightforward conclusion, of a data analysis on why so many action heroes are named Jack, James, or John: "These characters have been overcoming seemingly insurmountable odds for more than half a century, and I for one will not be betting against them." Just as you want your introduction to grab readers' attention, your conclusion can leave them with something to think about.

Want to read about why so many action heroes are named Jack, James, or John? Go to letstalklibrary.com.

Read your draft with a critical eye, get response—and revise

Now's the time to read over what you've written to make sure that the question that has driven your analysis is absolutely clear and that you've provided sufficient evidence to support the conclusion you come to in your analysis. Then you'll want to ask others to read over your draft. Here are some questions that can help you or others read and respond to the draft.

- How will your OPENING grab readers' attention? If you aim to reach a specific AUDIENCE, will your opening make them want to read on? How else might you begin?

- Have you DESCRIBED or SUMMARIZED the text in enough detail for readers to follow your analysis? Is there more background information you need to add?

- Have you made clear what your analysis revealed about the text—and have you stated it explicitly in a THESIS? If not, should you do so?

- What EVIDENCE supports your analysis? Is there any other evidence that could add to the strength of your analysis?

- Have you made any EMOTIONAL APPEALS—and if so, how do they support your analysis?

- How have you established your CREDIBILITY to write on this subject?

- Have you addressed PERSPECTIVES other than your own— and if not, should you do so? Have you considered such perspectives fairly? If you've cited any sources, have you DOCUMENTED them fully?

- How effective is your CONCLUSION? What does it leave your audience thinking? How else could you conclude?
- Consider your title. Does it make clear what your analysis is about, and will it engage readers' interest? How might you make the title more engaging?

Now's the time to REVISE! If you've analyzed your analysis (!) and gotten advice from others, you've got a plan. You know what you want to do. But remember what you *need* to do: to explain what your ANALYSIS shows and provide EVIDENCE that supports your conclusions. And as always, keep in mind your AUDIENCE and the rest of your RHETORICAL SITUATION.

REFLECT! Set your analysis aside for a few days. Then come back to it with fresh eyes and read it again. What do you find most effective about your analysis? What is your favorite sentence or passage, and why? What spots might call for further revision, and why? How well do you think you conveyed your point(s) to your audience? Write a paragraph or two in which you sum up what you've learned—both about the text you've analyzed, and about the process of analysis itself.

A STUDENT ANALYSIS

WESLEY COHEN

What's Happening over at *Cosmo*?

Wesley Cohen wrote this essay for a journalism class at the University of California at Davis. It was later published in Prized Writing, *an annual book of exemplary writing from across the disciplines done by students at Davis. The version included here has been revised to include MLA documentation, something that was not required in her journalism class.*

Open up *Cosmopolitan Magazine*'s March 2016 issue and you'll find tips for flirting with a guy at work ("Text him a funny follow-up!") and a fashion-infused profile of actress-slash-beauty mogul Jessica Alba (titled "Billion Dollar Babe").

The title and opening sentences capture readers' interest.

Between these pieces is an eight-page feature on the intersection of gun rights and domestic violence in America. The article includes an eye-catching graphic of a chocolate gun in a candy box surrounded by brightly striped truffles, and a handy flowchart for talking with a new romantic partner about gun ownership. There are also stark warnings and statistics.

Summarizes the contrast that she'll explore in her analysis.

According to the piece's author, Liz Welch, "8,700 women were shot to death by their partners between 2000 and 2013" (162) and women are 200 percent more likely to be killed when a physically abusive relationship involves a gun. The article frames gun control as a women's issue, chronicling the stories of several young women who were murdered by abusive partners or ex-partners (Welch).

It's rare to find a magazine that covers domestic violence and celebrity fashion on equal footing—and this wide editorial scope is largely the work of the former editor-in-chief Joanna Coles. *Cosmo*'s shift toward more diverse content goes against decades of editorial tradition in a brand famous for its focus on sex, celebrities, and fashion—and its racy covers, as figure 1 shows.

First claim.

Provides background information.

Cosmo started life in 1886 as a women's magazine that published Willa Cather, Upton Sinclair, and Kurt Vonnegut. Chief editor Helen Gurley Brown was brought on in the 1960s in response to weak sales, and she recreated the magazine as a sex-centered, single woman's guidebook to the fab life.

Brown pledged to keep *Cosmo* "frisky and fresh" over her three-decade reign. She acknowledged in her November 1995 letter from the editor that women may be interested in subjects other than "sexual pleasure, passion, friendship, love, achievement," but told readers that "we let the newspapers, TV shows, and newsmagazines deal with them" (30). But Joanna Coles eschewed this either-or approach to writing for women, telling NPR's Rachel Martin, "I have no problem understanding that women are interested in mascara and the Middle East" (*Morning Edition*). (Indeed, figure 2 shows Coles speaking at a *Cosmo* event that was sponsored by Maybelline, a company known for its mascara.)

Fig. 1. 2006 cover names Beyoncé
the "Fun, Fearless Female of the Year."
www.getty.com

Fig. 2. Editor-in-chief Joanna Coles speaking at a *Cosmopolitan* event in 2015 that was sponsored by Maybelline. www.getty.com

Since 2014, *Cosmo* has endorsed political candidates based on whether they support equal pay, birth control access, and reproductive rights. Coles doesn't see a conflict in presenting pro-choice political endorsements alongside stiletto recommendations: "I feel that these are about lifestyle issues for women. The biggest single decision which will impact your life is when you have a child. I want women to have control over that" (qtd. in Gold).

Provides examples to support the claim that Cosmo tackles serious issues.

Coles's *Cosmo* is all about diversifying what counts as "women's interest." A new header, Cosmopolitan.com, next to "LOVE," "CELEBS," and "BEAUTY," reads—in appropriate millennial format— "#COSMOVOTES." Under this tab, readers can find *Cosmo*'s political endorsements, updates on polls and primaries, and opinion pieces on candidates and issues. It makes no secret of *Cosmo*'s political leanings.

In her same 1995 letter from the editor, Brown laid out her reasoning for leaving hard-hitting subjects out of *Cosmo*'s pages, writing, "We're not big on scaring you" (30). But Jill Filipovic's November 2015 piece about anti-abortion violence seems pretty scary to me.

Filipovic, a UN Foundation Fellow and award-winning contributor to *The Guardian*, *The New York Times*, *Al Jazeera America*, and *Time* magazine, is no lightweight. But in the margin by Filipovic's byline, there's a picture of Mary-Kate and Ashley Olsen as toddlers above a link offering to show me "A Photo from Every Year of Their Lives."

This new *Cosmo* balances pithy quizzes about Hannah Montana and critiques of the hyper-sexual portrayals of African American women in film and TV. How does one women's magazine make it all work?

Poses a question that will guide the analysis.

First of all, *Cosmo*'s new direction rejects the idea of women's-interest journalism as a niche market. On CNN's *Reliable Sources*, Joanna Coles pushed back against host Brian Stelter's suggestion that working with women's magazines to reach voters—instead of reaching out directly through social media or relying on hard news reporting—was a way that political candidates use "alternative media."

"Well, I don't think of women's magazines with 53 million readers as being 'alternative media,'" said Coles, nearly breaking into a laugh. "I think it might be as big, if not bigger, than the footprint of *Reliable Sources*, Brian" (Coles, *Reliable Sources*).

Coles noted instead that she believes her "very large" readership has been underserved by mainstream media. It's hard to argue with her. While men's-interest magazines like *Esquire* publish hard-hitting cultural essays alongside fiction by the likes of George Saunders and Stephen King, the news that *Cosmo* had won a National Magazine Award in 2014 for an extensive piece on contraception was met with astonishment. Coles seems to carry her sense of humor in her purse, however. About a story titled "It's Time to Start Taking *Cosmopolitan* Seriously," she tweeted "Start?????" (*Twitter*).

A different *Reliable Sources* interview featured host Brian Stelter asking two uncomfortable-looking female journalists "Are women's magazines serious?" Roberta Meyers, editor-in-chief at

Elle, was set up against *Rolling Stone* writer Janet Reitman, who worried aloud that female writers who focus on women's-interest writing often never "break out" of women-only journalism. Meyers noted that she started out at *Rolling Stone* before taking the lead at *Elle* and pointed out that many of her writers are also published in *The New Yorker, New York Magazine*, and *Rolling Stone*. Reitman responded by saying that she appreciates and reads women's magazines herself, but reiterated her earlier concern about the "ghettoizing" of female-interest journalists. This time, Reitman said, eyes focused and concerned, that many women journalists "just literally cannot, somehow, make it to write for larger men's magazines or general-interest magazines" (Meyers and Reitman).

Introduces another perspective: Can women's magazines be serious?

It seems that this, in Reitman's mind, is the ladder that female journalists must climb: women's magazines, men's magazines, then general-interest magazines. Or perhaps: women's magazines/general-interest magazines. Because in many ways, male interests are considered general interest.

While writing about romance or fashion puts a journalist into the "ghetto" of trivial feminine pursuits, typically masculine interests are widely considered respectable reading material. As Joanna Coles noted in her NPR interview, "Men are allowed to talk about sports relentlessly, and yet we still take them seriously. I don't understand why women can't talk about fashion, or sex, or love, or wanting more money and not be taken as seriously as men" (*Morning Edition*).

In her *Reliable Sources* appearance, *Elle*'s Roberta Meyers looked fabulous: her blow-out great, her makeup subtle and professional, her poise unshakeable. But she looked worn down, too. She spoke of a perceived gap between her readers and the rest of the world, "the idea that there's a divide between people who care about fashion and only fashion," and everybody else. She then went on to say "I find it sad . . . that we're still talking about women as a whole separate kind of people, you know?" (Meyers and Reitman). Meyers spoke brightly of her love for her readers, but to Reitman and Stelter, choosing to write for *Elle* instead of *Rolling Stone* is apparently a real comedown.

It's hard to find an article discussing *Cosmo*'s long history without reading contemptuous descriptions of its past content. As *Jezebel*'s managing editor Kate Dries said, *Cosmo*'s new focus on career advancement and female empowerment has been a "slow climb out of lipstick-and-lasagna land" ("The New *Cosmopolitan*").

Cosmo was forbidden to my sisters and me when we were growing up. My parents didn't want us encountering this male-centric view of sexuality or developing such a shallow image of female beauty. They even tried to ban Barbie from the premises before she snuck in inside wrapped birthday presents and well-meant hand-me-downs. I don't blame them.

Cosmo still passes down narrow ideas of what a woman is and does and wants. Women of color, transgender women, and queer women are not addressed as *Cosmo*'s central audience, and the women who star on its covers month to month are overwhelmingly thin and pale and provocatively dressed. My parents didn't want to limit the type of woman I could be while I was still a girl.

So instead I learned how to be like a boy. I learned how to play hockey and laughed at the sorts of girls who wanted to be princesses. I learned not to cry when I got hurt, and I learned to love reading about boys, or girls who pretended to be boys, in *Eragon* and *To Kill a Mockingbird* and *The Woman Who Rides Like a Man*. And in many ways this was an honest expression of who I was and who I wanted to be.

But perhaps these behaviors also came from an understanding that it was possible—easy, even—to be too feminine. That uber-femininity could be shallow, or stupid, or mean. That it could be dangerous.

Now I am learning to look hard at the books that I read and the movies that I watch and the people that I admire. I am learning not to dismiss femininity for its own sake, but this is hard when feminine books and speech patterns and movies are constantly

Acknowledges Cosmo's earlier reputation.

Cites her own experience to support the claim that Cosmo once presented shallow views.

Explores the view that Cosmo presents a narrow view of women.

Makes an emotional appeal.

dismissed by the cultural outlets I admire. The shock with which media outlets have responded to Joanna Coles's work at *Cosmo* is yet another example of this dismissal. But still I have learned to love Taylor Swift and horoscopes and eyeshadow, as well as weight lifting and science fiction and neuroscience, Walt Whitman and Suzanne Collins. And *Cosmo* has helped.

Cites personal experience to establish her credibility to write on this topic.

I am not saying that *Cosmo* is above critique. It continues to sideline the experiences of women who do not fit its target audience. It builds prehistoric concepts of femininity into its columns, and tells women implicitly or explicitly to trim down, dress up, and make themselves beautiful. Its advertisements and photosets build a fantasy of femininity in which woman is pale and thin and glossy. This does real damage.

But *Cosmo* is not beneath contempt. When we close the door to *Cosmo* for its perceived frivolity or irrelevance, we close the door to women's voices, their interests and concerns and desires. By assuming that women's journalism cannot be real journalism, Brian Stelter and others declare that women cannot know what journalism looks like, that we don't even know which stories are important and which are stupid. That we earn the right to tell our own stories only by making them unfeminine.

Why her analysis matters.

That femininity cannot be universal.

But femininity is universal. It always has been.

And universal experiences are feminine. As long as men are taught, like I was, that femininity is saccharine and silly and toxic, they are also taught to hate a part of themselves.

Reiterates claim that Cosmo can be both progressive and not progressive.

Nobody wins this fight.

Making room for femininity in feminism means recognizing that outlets like *Cosmo* can be progressive as well as problematic.

I want the right to criticize *Cosmo* when it writes harshly about female celebrities' bodies and the right to relish its fashion slideshows. I want to read about face gloss and I want to know about domestic terrorism. I want the right to be unfeminine without recourse, and the right to delight in my femininity. As a woman, and as a person, I should not have to choose just one story.

Do I contradict myself?
Well then I contradict myself,
(I am large, I contain multitudes.)

Works Cited

Brown, Helen Gurley. "Step into My Parlor." *Cosmopolitan*, Nov. 1995, pp. 28, 30.

Coles, Joanna. Interview with Brian Stelter. *Reliable Sources*, CNN, 7 June 2015. Transcript.

———. Interview with Rachel Martin. *Morning Edition*, NPR, 14 Oct. 2014. Transcript.

———. "Start?????" @JillFilipovic: Time to take @Cosmopolitan seriously." *Twitter*, 2 May 2014, twitter.com/joannacoles/status/462312728812863488.

Dries, Kate. "The New *Cosmopolitan* & the Slow Climb Out of Lipstick-and-Lasagna Land." *Jezebel*, 9 Dec. 2014, jezebel.com/the-new-cosmopolitan-the-slow-clim-out-of-lipstick-a-1666538526.

Gold, Hadas. "The New *Cosmo*: Love, Sex, Politics?" *Politico*, 9 Apr. 2014, www.politico.com/story/2014/09/the-new-cosmo-love-sex-politics-110586.

Meyers, Roberta, and Janet Reitman. Interview with Brian Stelter. *Reliable Sources*, CNN, 30 June 2013. Transcript.

Welch, Liz. "Love and Guns." *Cosmopolitan*, Mar. 2016, pp. 158–66.

Thinking about the Text

1. Wesley Cohen has a lot to say about *Cosmopolitan*, but what is her primary CLAIM about what's "happening over at *Cosmo*"?

2. How well do you think she supports that claim? Point out examples of the EVIDENCE she provides that you find most persuasive, and explain why you find them so persuasive.

3. Cohen includes a lot of personal information; how do you think it contributes to her analysis?

4. You might say that this essay analyzes more than one text—that which is found on the pages of *Cosmopolitan* and that which has been said (and written) about it. How effectively does Cohen weave it all together?

5. Go to cosmopolitan.com and see for yourself "what's happening" over there now. Find some EXAMPLES that support—or contradict—what Cohen concludes about *Cosmo*, and draft an email to her about what you find.

11 Summarizing & Responding

Effective academic writing resides
not just in stating our own ideas but in
listening to others, summarizing their views,
and responding with our own ideas in kind.

—GERALD GRAFF AND CATHY BIRKENSTEIN

Your linguistics instructor assigns you to read Gloria Anzaldúa's "How to Tame a Wild Tongue." Your job: to summarize this text and write an essay responding to it. In your environmental science class, the instructor asks students to read the Environmental Justice for All Act of 2021–22 and then to summarize its major goals, followed by a response that suggests ways the act could be strengthened or criticized. And in your first-year writing class, it's presentation week! You're assigned to listen to a presentation given by two classmates and then to respond. The assignment specifies that you start by briefly summarizing what they say before responding with what you want to say.

Instructors who give these assignments know that one way to fully understand a text and remember what it says is to summarize it in our own words—and then to talk back to it, engaging with what it says and offering ideas of our own in response. That's why it's often said that such assignments are "where writing meets reading." And these moves—read-understand-respond—are fundamental to much of the work you do in college, and wherever you engage with the ideas and words of others.

A GUIDE TO SUMMARIZING AND RESPONDING

Summarizing and responding to a text is a common college assignment, a way of demonstrating that you've engaged with the text, that you understand what it says, and that you have something to say as a result. Following is some good advice on how to write effective summaries and responses, so listen up: these tips will help you!

Read the text you'll be responding to

Begin by reading the text straight through in order to get the big picture—the most important point the text is making.

Then reread, underlining or jotting down the major CLAIMS and ideas and the main EVIDENCE supporting those ideas. If there's an explicit THESIS, put it in brackets. And put quotation marks around any words or phrases that are written so well that you think you may want to QUOTE them.

Whatever the text says, read it with an open mind. Especially if you disagree with what it says, think about where the author is coming from and why they think differently than you do. And while you're at it, think about why *you* think the way you do. Most important, be sure that you understand exactly what the author is saying so that you'll be able to present it from their perspective rather than yours.

Write out a few sentences in your own words stating the text's main points. It can be rough, but just imagine you're telling a friend about what you've just read; the idea is to give the gist of what the author has said.

Think about your rhetorical situation

Once you've carefully read the text you'll be summarizing and responding to, stop and think about who your audience is and the rest of your rhetorical situation.

Purpose. If you've been assigned to write a summary/response essay, one purpose will likely be to demonstrate that you understand what the text says. But responding also gives you the opportunity to engage with what it says, and to add your own thoughts to the conversation. What do you think about what the text says, and what would you like to say back to the author?

Audience. This is a common college assignment, so your audience will likely include your instructor. But other students may read what you write; if so, how will that affect what you write and how you write it?

Genre. There are various ways you might respond. If you respond to what the text says, you'll be writing an argument. If you respond to the way it's written, that will call for ANALYSIS. Or maybe the text just gets you thinking, in which case you might write a REFLECTION.

Stance. What is your attitude about the text? Are you a critic? a fan? something else? Think about how it will affect your response.

Context. What are the requirements of your assignment—length, due date, and so on? And what's the larger context surrounding the text you'll be writing about? Are you permitted to use AI?

Language. Think about the REGISTER of language that would be most appropriate. If you're speaking on a serious topic for a class presentation, you may want to use formal language, but if you're writing about the latest Adam Sandler movie for your college newspaper, you'll likely choose informal language. If you're writing about a topic that includes technical language for readers who are not familiar with the topic, you will likely need to define some terms. The same goes for texts that use foreign words. In short, the language you use depends on your audience, purpose, and topic.

Media and design. If you get to choose, is there a medium that will work especially well for your subject? If you're writing about a film, for instance, doing so online would enable you to include audio or video clips. Whatever the medium, will your essay need headings, images, or any other design elements?

Summarize accurately, fairly, and concisely

Reread the text slowly, making a list of the main ideas. Then go back and check to see that you've noted all the ideas that matter, ones that you'll need to account for in your summary.

Write out a sentence stating the text's main message. You could then start your summary with this sentence, and it will function as a kind of THESIS sentence.

Focus on the main ideas, leaving out unnecessary details. Keep in mind that you just need to give readers enough information so that they'll understand what you're responding to. And be sure that you capture the main ideas accurately and fairly.

Use your own words, but leave out your own opinions. This should be a SUMMARY of what the text says, not of what you think about it. (You can get to that when you *respond* to what it says!) Use neutral, nonjudgmental language—say "the author's point," for example, rather than "the author's questionable point." Once you've drafted your summary, go back to the text to make sure that you haven't inadvertently copied any of the original wording or sentence structures.

If you QUOTE *any words or phrases*, be sure to enclose them in quotation marks and introduce them with a SIGNAL PHRASE to clearly distinguish what the author says from what you say. And while you could use neutral words ("the author says," "according to the author"), it's better to use words that reflect the author's STANCE. Here, for example, is how you might quote a line from Joy Harjo's blog:

> As former Poet Laureate Joy Harjo argues in a blog post about music, "The saxophone is so human. Its tendency is to be rowdy, edgy, talk too loud, bump into people."

But quote sparingly, and only when you need to use the author's exact wording for accuracy, or because the wording is so memorable that you want to call special attention to it. For example, here's a sentence you might well want to quote if you were summarizing Sojourner Truth's "Ain't I a Woman?": "Nobody ever helps me into carriages, or over mud-puddles, or gives me any best place!" This sentence is so powerful and clear in its message that it's hard to imagine how you could summarize it, so this is definitely one to quote.

If you're permitted to use AI, it can help provide a recap of complex texts, but remember that it makes mistakes and might even leave out crucial details. You'll need to check everything it says for accuracy—and to be sure that the words and structures of your summary are yours and not AI's.

See Ch. 30 for tips on using AI carefully and ethically.

Name the author and title of the text you're summarizing, usually in the first paragraph. If you're summarizing a lengthy work, you'll need to provide IN-TEXT DOCUMENTATION giving the pages you've summarized. And if you've consulted additional sources, you'll need to DOCUMENT them in a list of works cited or references.

A model summary. See how Taylor Jordan, a student at North Carolina A&T, sums up an op-ed about college admissions. You can read the op-ed on page 196.

> In a *New York Times* opinion piece, "I Learned in College That Admission Has Always Been for Sale," Rainesford Stauffer argues that college bribery schemes, a huge test prep industry, and big-time donors strip opportunities from those students who actually work hard on

their own. She begins with a personal narrative about a friend who had a "personalized standardized test tutor" while applying for college—and recalls her shock at realizing that some of her other friends even had professional editors and college admission coaches. She notes that the current college admissions scandal with celebrities engaging in bribery and other illegal acts is only one example of what some rich people do to help their children get into college—and that it's "no more abhorrent than what happens every day." Still, she acknowledges her own privileges as a white student with parents who went to college and says that what really makes her mad is thinking about those who have fewer privileges than she does.

Stauffer seems most angry about the fact that there's a huge industry of tutors and essay writers and college admission coaches for those who can afford them—and that it's all perfectly legal. Citing the work of a Harvard education professor, she points out that it's a system that results in "working class and poor students, black, Latino, Native American and first generation students [being] underrepresented on most campuses." To sum up, Stauffer's central argument is with the unfairness of the college admission system, and the signal it sends to students that their hard work counts for less than their parents' money.

—TAYLOR JORDAN, North Carolina A&T State University

Note that this summary begins by naming the author of the text being summarized and summing up the author's main ideas. Subsequent sentences in the first paragraph point to the author's use of her own experience and provide additional details to back up the main ideas. Jordan includes brief quotations directly from the article, enclosed in quotation marks and integrated smoothly into her own sentences. Note also that she is careful to leave her own opinions out of the summary, which focuses solely on the article she is summarizing, and that she is careful to qualify statements ("Stauffer *seems* most angry") rather than putting words in the author's mouth. Finally, note that Jordan quotes a memorable sentence from one of the article's sources, which sums up the author's central argument.

REFLECT! Choose a text that you really like—a film, an episode in a TV series, a comic book, a favorite podcast or book, whatever. Then summarize what you've chosen so that someone who isn't familiar with it will get a good sense of what it's about. Ask a classmate for their response: How well did you capture the essence of the text you summarized? Then, if your instructor allows the use of AI, ask a chatbot to summarize the same text, and compare it with yours. Does it focus on the same main ideas? include the same detail? Which summary seems more accurate? Which summary do you prefer, and why? How might you revise your summary as a result?

Develop your response

Responding to something you've read (or heard or seen) gives you the opportunity to speak up—to ask questions, point out details you think were overlooked, analyze the way the text was written, agree, disagree. There's more than one way of responding to a text, but often you'll be assigned to respond in one of three ways:

- to respond to *what* the text says
- to respond to *how* the text is written
- to respond to the way the text affects *you*

If you're responding to what the text says

In this case you'll likely be making an **ARGUMENT**. You could agree or disagree with the author's ideas, or both; whatever you do, you should do so explicitly. In general, it's a good idea to provide a **THESIS** sentence that makes your overall response to the text clear. And then you need to give reasons and evidence to support what *you* say: facts, examples, textual evidence, data the author overlooked, and so on. Even if you agree with what the author says, you need to do more than just restate views you share. Perhaps you could

See pp. 51–58 and 61–65 for examples and advice on using various kinds of evidence.

point out evidence the author didn't mention, some personal experience that's pertinent to the conversation, or counterarguments that need to be mentioned. Here are some questions that will help you think about what a text says:

- What's the CLAIM?
- What good REASONS and EVIDENCE support that claim? Remember that evidence can include VISUALS as well as words.
- Does the text include any COUNTERARGUMENTS or other PERSPECTIVES? If not, are there some that should be acknowledged?
- What's *your* response? Do you agree, disagree, or both agree and disagree with the author's conclusions? Why?

If you're responding to the way the text is written

Here you'll be writing a RHETORICAL ANALYSIS. You could analyze the text's use of language, its sentence patterns, the way it's organized, or other elements of its style, and how these things affect the way you understand or respond to the author's message. In any case, you'll need to support your analysis with examples from the text. Here are some questions that will help you think about the way a text is written:

- How would you describe the author's STYLE—humorous? serious? conversational? passionate? logical? something else?
- What words, sentence structures, layout, or images help to establish this style? How do they affect the way you respond? You'll need to show EXAMPLES in the text that help create this style.
- Does the author use any METAPHORS, ANALOGIES, repetition, or other figures of speech—and how do they help get the point across?
- How does the way the text is written contribute to the effectiveness of its message?

If you're writing about your personal response

This kind of response gives you the opportunity to REFLECT on how the text affected you personally. You could go in many directions. What did the text make you think about—and are you still thinking about it? Did the author make you think the subject matters or make you care about it? As with any kind of writing, you'll need to give reasons and evidence to help your audience understand your reactions, and care about what you say. Here are some questions that may help you reflect on your own reaction to a text:

- What was your first reaction to this text?
- Did anything in the text surprise you? make you laugh? annoy you? mystify you? Show some EXAMPLES!
- Did it make you think or change your thinking about something? If so, in what way?
- Do you now want to learn more about the topic? If so, what would you like to find out?
- What would you say about this text if you were telling a friend about it? What REASONS would you give to explain your reaction?

No matter which of these three approaches you take, responding to what the text says, how it says, or how it affects you, you will want to think hard about how best to begin, how to support what you say, and how to conclude your response.

Ways of organizing a summary/response essay

There's no one way to organize a summary and response essay, but here's one common way.

Begin your essay in a way that gets readers' interest

If you're responding to a text about an unusual issue, you might want to begin with a question, a quotation, or a dramatic statement about that subject. If you're responding to what a text says, you might begin with a sentence that first **SUMMARIZES** what the text says before responding with what you think. If you're analyzing the way a text is written, you could start by **QUOTING** a line that exemplifies what you'll be writing about. Or perhaps you're responding to a text that touches on something you yourself have experienced; in that case, you might begin with a personal **ANECDOTE** that shows how you are connected to the topic in question. No matter how you begin, be sure to name the author and the title of the text you're responding to somewhere—ideally, in the first paragraph.

For more on ways of beginning, see p. 116.

Conclude in a way that leaves readers thinking

Here's your chance to leave your audience thinking about the implications of what you've said. If you're responding to the text's argument, you could **REITERATE** your main point; if you're analyzing the way the text was written, you might remind readers about how the writer's **STYLE** affects the message; if your response is a personal one, you might note some insight you got from reading the text.

Sometimes you might conclude by **QUOTING** something memorable from the text that your essay is all about. One student who summarized an interview with rapper Nipsey Hussle and responded to what he said about luck and hard work concluded by quoting a famous line from that interview: "Luck is just bein' prepared at all times, so when the door opens you're ready."

For more on ways of concluding, see p. 117.

Regardless of how you conclude, you might also invite your audience to respond. Keep the conversation going!

Come up with a title

If you've written an argument, your title should indicate the topic; if you've written an analysis, your title should indicate something about what you analyzed; if you've written a reflection, the title should indicate what the text has led you to think.

For more on coming up with a title, see pp. 117–18.

Read your draft with a critical eye, get response—and revise

Now's the time to read over what you've written to see that you've summarized the text accurately, fairly, and concisely, and responded cogently and persuasively.

- Does your title make clear what the essay is about? Can you think of a better title?

- How will the OPENING make readers want to read on? Does it mention the author and title of the text you're responding to? If not, are they mentioned elsewhere?

- Is the summary written in your own words? Check to be sure. Have you SUMMARIZED the text in a fair-minded way, and without indicating your own opinion, before going on to give your response?

- Have you provided enough detail so that readers will understand what you're responding to? Is all the detail you've included actually necessary?

- If you've quoted anything, is the wording so memorable or important that it needs to be QUOTED? Is it enclosed in quotation marks?

- If you've quoted a full statement, is it introduced with a SIGNAL PHRASE—and does the verb suit the quotation? If you've used *said*, is there a more interesting or accurate verb you might use instead—*claimed*? *pointed out*? *declared*?

- Is the point of your response clear? Have you stated it in a THESIS sentence? If not, should you do so?

- What EVIDENCE have you provided to support your response—facts? examples from the text? personal experience? counterarguments or viewpoints the author didn't mention?

- Have you included any VISUALS? If not, is there anything that could be presented in a photo, a chart, or a graph?

- Have you provided **DOCUMENTATION** for any additional text you've summarized or quoted?

- How does the essay **CONCLUDE**? This is your chance to help readers engage with the ideas *you* think are worth thinking about.

Now **REVISE**! If you've analyzed your draft and gotten advice from others, you've got a plan: you know what you need to do. But remember that you're writing a **SUMMARY/RESPONSE** essay, which means summing up a text succinctly and fairly and then responding in some way. Here's what *you* think about the text—and why!

AN OP-ED, AND A RESPONSE

This chapter concludes with an essay written by Julia Latrice Johnson, a student at North Carolina A&T State University. Following the guidelines in this chapter, she responded to a *New York Times* op-ed about the college admissions scandal of 2019, in which dozens of wealthy parents, celebrities, and coaches were involved in a nationwide fraud and bribery scheme that resulted in some students getting into the colleges of their dreams because of their parents' checkbooks rather than their own work or talent. As you might expect, response to this scandal was swift, especially among college students. First comes the *Times* piece, and then comes the summary/response essay.

RAINESFORD STAUFFER

I Learned in College That Admission Has Always Been for Sale

Rainesford Stauffer is a writer whose work has been published in the New York Times, *the* Atlantic, GQ, *and* Teen Vogue. *She is the author of* An Ordinary Age, *a book about the challenges of young adulthood in the United States. The piece here was first published in the* Times *in 2019.*

Shortly after my freshman year of college, when I was debating whether to transfer to another college or drop out and venture into the work force sans degree, I met with an older friend who had attended an Ivy League-adjacent school. I wanted her advice on whether to apply to her alma mater.

I'd love it there, she assured me, with one caveat: You have to be really smart, she said. It became evident that her "smart" and my "smart" were different things. She casually rattled off hours she'd logged with a personalized standardized test tutor, paid to boost her score. Her parents opted not to pay an editor to work with her on her application essay, but plenty of her classmates' families had.

I suddenly felt as though I'd failed a test I didn't know I was taking. I was even more gobsmacked when I realized how common her experience was. Asking around, I learned that a subset of my peers had been carefully groomed with tools I hadn't even known existed. I came to realize that my "A" in Literature from my freshman year and a job between classes and on weekends were not going to compete with pedigrees buffed to application perfection thanks to highly compensated college admissions coaches.

I did end up transferring, not to my friend's school but to The New School, where I finished my degree remotely while working full time, and I graduated in January 2017. Now I talk to young people, including my own sister, who agonize over the fact that no matter how hard they study, they will never compete with students who have test and application boosts. Even so, I know I've enjoyed benefits that many other students haven't because I'm white and have parents who are college graduates. I'm more angry on behalf of those with fewer resources than me who have to compete with those gaming the system.

So when news broke that celebrities, top university coaches and other ultrarich individuals were accused by the Justice Department of engaging in college admissions bribery, my initial thought was that this latest round of revelations is no more abhorrent than what happens every day.

It's obviously a scandal when rich people are accused of breaking the law to get their kids into top schools. But the bigger outrage should be that a legal version of purchasing an advantage happens every college application season and that there's an entire industry supporting it.

Anyone can see the kinds of things outlined in the indictment—bribes paid by wealthy parents in exchange for their children's admission to top universities, and accompanying schemes to secure athletics scholarships for teens who didn't even play high school sports—are unacceptable. But what about the standardized test prep industry, worth around $840 million, which involves parents forking over up to $200 an hour for Ivy League tutors tasked with increasing their children's scores. That doesn't include application essay writers, who coach students on what to write about, edit their writing and, in some cases, write for them. It doesn't include college coaching firms, which charge up to $40,000 to strategize an applicant's entire process.

Donations made to schools by the parents of legacy students can essentially buy acceptance letters. Meanwhile, there are some students who don't have a parent to skim their essay for typos or can't afford to pay to enroll in a prep course or to repeatedly take a standardized test until their score rises.

Natasha Warikoo, a professor at Harvard Graduate School of Education and the author of *The Diversity Bargain*, says while there's no debate that the actions the people involved in this week's admissions scandal are accused of are reprehensible, there's actually very little agreement among Americans or admissions officers about what is and isn't O.K. in terms of application assistance.

"A fair system to me would produce an outcome in which people who are selected are representative of 18-year-olds overall in the United States," Ms. Warikoo said, noting that while wealthy students are overrepresented, working class and poor students, black, Latino, Native American and first generation students are underrepresented on most campuses. "We don't have consensus in the United States about what is a fair system of selection."

"If you had to design a system that would give rich, white kids the best odds of getting into prestigious colleges and universities, look no further than the current system," said Nikhil Goyal, author of *Schools on Trial* and a doctoral candidate at the University of Cambridge. His research has found that universities ending legacy admissions and making standardized tests optional "would boost class and racial diversity and signal to youth that their worth is less defined by test scores and more by their creativity and passions." It's no coincidence that one of these can be bought: the test scores. Creativity and passion cannot.

Perhaps it wouldn't sting so much if we scrapped the college rankings, or if we didn't bill college as the foremost experience for young people, one that sets the tone for their entire lives.

This newest admissions scandal is infuriating, but the ongoing, perfectly legal one that lets wealthy families pay for the things that lead to greater chances of admission hurts even more. It sends a message to any student who can't take advantage of the current system that no matter how hard he or she has worked, it will always be possible for someone else to buy a better life.

A STUDENT SUMMARY/RESPONSE ESSAY

JULIA LATRICE JOHNSON
Can Money Buy Almost Anything?

Julia Latrice Johnson was a student at North Carolina A&T State University when she wrote this essay. She earned a master's degree in English and African American literature from there in 2019 and is now a content reviewer and proofreader at Binary Fountain/Press Ganey, an online platform that provides data analytics based on patients' feedback to healthcare organizations.

What do you do when you desire to further your education, but your writing sucks? You know that there are better writers out there because they all have received acceptance letters from colleges where personal statements are a requirement. But how would you feel if you knew that those writers had professional tutors and editors to fix and maybe even write their work? This was the frustration described by Rainesford Stauffer in her *New York Times* op-ed, "I Learned in College That Admission Has Always Been for Sale."

Stauffer speaks distinctively about privilege—her own privilege in being white and having parents who graduated from college, and the privilege of others who have monetary advantages that essentially "buy acceptance letters." Paid tutors and admission essay editors can help "buy" college admission. Rich parents who bribe admission officers can "buy" college admission. Rich parents who donate large sums of money can "buy" college admission.

Stauffer makes it her business to talk to students who cannot "buy" admission and "who agonize over the fact that no matter how hard they study, they will never compete with students who have test and application boosts." Those boosts include essay editing, test tutoring, and admission coaching, advantages paid for by parents with money. All are common practices, and perfectly legal.

Title and opening sentence pose provocative questions that get readers' attention.

Names author and title in the first paragraph.

Summarizes major ideas in the op-ed.

Quotes a memorable statement to underscore the unfairness Stauffer is concerned with.

Lori Loughlin departing from federal court, April 2019.

Bribery, however, is not legal—but still practiced. Stauffer describes "rich people . . . breaking the law to get their kids into top schools" as an unacceptable scandal that sparked outrage. But even worse, she says, are the legal ways of buying advantages: the tutors and editors and coaches and large donations. What most enrages Stauffer is that it's an unfair system, one that privileges wealthy students but that works against "working class and poor students, black, Latino, Native American, and first generation students."

Leaving her own opinion out, focuses on what motivated Stauffer to write her op-ed.

Reading Stauffer's article made me think of Lori Loughlin, Aunt Becky from *Full House*, one of the actresses currently involved in the admissions scandal. She and her husband have been accused of paying over a half million dollars to secure their daughters' admission to the University of Southern California (USC). Perhaps in response, Dr. Dre, rapper, producer, and another celebrity parent, took to *Instagram* to congratulate his daughter on her acceptance to college while also making note of the recent college scandal: "My daughter got accepted into USC all on her own. No jail time!!!" (qtd. in Amiri).

Opens her response by giving her own first reaction to the op-ed.

And yet . . . while he may not have bribed the admissions team, his daughter still had advantages other students did not thanks to her father's $70 million donations to USC. The only difference between Lori Loughlin and Dr. Dre is that he wrote his check as a donation and she wrote hers to an organization that paid USC to admit her daughter. *Both famous parents exhibit privilege that screams for attention and response.*

Stauffer's article also puts into perspective a part of college that not many people can bring themselves to discuss. There are advantages that certain individuals have. I did not have such advantages. I did not have access to paid tutors or essay editors. I had to study and write on my own and pray that my parents were not too tired after long days at work to help me edit my essays. And I have had to focus in on what I can do myself rather than thinking about the unfair advantages others have. Despite not having any particular advantages, much less donating a million dollars, I was still able to gain admission to Coastal Carolina University and even to pursue a second degree at North Carolina A&T State University.

Offers her own experience as an example of what privilege do to get into college.

Dr. Dre and his daughter.

Michelle Obama speaking at North Carolina A&T State University.

Considers the op-ed in broader context, noting how others may respond to it.

This article will probably get multiple responses, depending on the readers. One response, similar to Stauffer's and my own, will most likely be shared widely among the many students who do not have access to the advantages wealthy people have, but are still working as hard as they can to get to where they hope to be. Another response may possibly come from students who are okay with the scholastic advantages they have because of their parents' money. And there will probably be a lot of privileged students who see nothing wrong with their parents using their money as a means of admission, but who still choose to work hard and go the extra mile to not have mommy or daddy's money follow them throughout life.

Introduces major claim and supports it with evidence from the op-ed.

In any case, it is not the fault of students, whether they have certain advantages or not. It's the system that is unfair in granting opportunities to some students just because their parents can "buy" them. Stauffer is right to be angry on behalf of those with fewer resources than she has "who have to compete with those gaming the system."

Reflects on what the op-ed has helped her realize about her own experience.

The system is unfair. Knowing that I may be refused admission in favor of those with rich parents or those who have essentially had the work done for them might discourage me from even applying to certain schools. Realizing that my hard work and that of my parents can be overshadowed by other people's money is disheartening, and yet it also leads me to constantly persevere in my studies.

What resonated with me the most in Stauffer's article comes at the very end when she says that the way college admission works now "sends a message to any student who can't take advantage of the current system that no matter how hard he or she has worked, it will always be possible for someone else to buy a better life." Any students who pride themselves on grasping and mastering any concept, including the college admission process, have reason to resent those who have been fortunate enough to have college and other such things gifted to them. Speaking for myself, however, knowing that anything I achieve is the result of my own hard work is highly rewarding, and that is one of the most important lessons that I learned from reading Rainesford Stauffer's op-ed.

Concludes by articulating the lesson she learned from reading this op-ed.

Works Cited

Amiri, Farnoush. "Dr. Dre Deletes Post about Daughter's Acceptance to USC after $70M Donation Resurfaces." *NBC News*, 25 Mar. 2019, www.nbcnews.com/2019 /3/25/.../dr-dre-deletes-post-about-daughter-s-acceptance -usc-after-n986906.

Stauffer, Rainesford. "I Learned in College That Admission Has Always Been for Sale." *The New York Times*, 13 Mar. 2019, www.nytimes.com/2019/03/13/opinion/college-admission -scandal-celebrities.html.

Thinking about the Text

1. What is the main ARGUMENT that Julia Johnson is making in response to Rainesford Stauffer's op-ed?

2. How does Johnson support her argument: What EVIDENCE does she provide? How does she use her own experience to support her argument?

3. What do you think makes Johnson's OPENING especially effective (or not)?

4. What do the three VISUALS add to the effectiveness of her response?

5. Write a letter responding to Johnson in which you share your own thoughts or experiences about the college admissions process.

REFLECT! Think about the experiences **Rainesford Stauffer** and **Julia Johnson** had with college admissions. How do your own experiences compare with theirs? What do you think about Stauffer's claim that college is always "for sale"?

Synthesizing & Reporting

The capacity to synthesize becomes ever more crucial
as information continues to mount at dizzying rates.

—HOWARD GARDNER

Effective reports present information
that readers can and will trust to be accurate.

—KEITH WALTERS

W hat's it take to be a good reporter? Surely near the top of the list is curiosity, the desire to discover something important and to share that something with others. Some reports have galvanized the entire country, as was the case with Rachel Carson's report on the dangers of pesticides in 1962. In the 1940s and '50s, the Kinsey Reports on human sexual behavior led to changes in the way people think about sex. And in 2024, a report on the impact of generative AI on health care, found evidence of several substantial risks, including the danger of inaccurate recommendations and the "deskilling" of health-care workers, findings that led to changes in medical policy.

So good, solid reports can play a crucial role in making important things happen. But good, solid reports don't spring up magically. Instead, they are the result of careful, thorough research and the mental work of synthesizing, bringing together bits and pieces from numerous sources that provide an overview of your topic or even lead to new insights. You do this kind of thinking all the time: when you're trying to decide which section of a course to take, you might read up on the various teachers on *Rate My Professors*, ask classmates about them, and then decide based on your synthesis of all that information.

Synthesizing sources involves combining the words of others to provide new insights. EOGHAN RYAN

Much of the writing you do in college will call for this kind of thinking, which begins with careful research, moves through a synthesis of the sources and ideas that research turns up, and concludes with some kind of report. Whether for an informational speech in *public speaking*, an ethnographic report in *sociology*, or a research report in *history*, you will need to put your synthesizing skills to work. In many ways, then, Reports R Us, providing much of the information that we rely on to understand topics that matter to us and to make sense of the world.

A GUIDE TO RESEARCHING, SYNTHESIZING, AND DEVELOPING A REPORT

Whatever kind of report you're writing, you'll need to think carefully about the different perspectives others have taken on the topic, as well as about who will be reading the report, what they know about the topic, and what information you'll need to provide. And since reports are expected to provide factual information, you'll need to do some research—and to demonstrate that the information you report is accurate and trustworthy. Here now is a guide to the process of researching a topic, synthesizing the many sources and ideas you'll find, and then writing a report. It's designed to be used *as you write*, so keep it close at hand.

Choose a topic that interests you

Sometimes you may be assigned a specific topic. If so, find an angle that interests you—and one that you think will interest your audience. Say you're assigned to write a report for an economics class on supply and demand in a particular industry. Choose an industry you want to know more about—skin care, craft beer, whatever. On other occasions, you may be able to choose a topic. If so, spend some time BRAINSTORMING about topics or issues that interest you, that you feel you can research with an open mind, and that you want to spend some time learning about. Here's a chance to do so!

Think about your rhetorical situation

Once you have a topic, spend some time thinking about the audience for the report, what you hope the report will accomplish, and the rest of your rhetorical situation.

Purpose. What do you want to accomplish with this report—provide information? inspire your audience to take some kind of action? What can you do in your report to achieve this purpose?

Audience. Who will be reading your report? Stakeholders of some kind? Your superiors in an organization? Fellow students? Think about what your target audience already knows about the topic and what background information you may need to provide. Will they be interested in the topic—or will you have to get them interested?

Stance. How do you want to be perceived as the author—as an authority on the topic? an interested and knowledgeable observer? How can you establish that stance—and how will you establish your credibility to report on this topic?

Context. What have others said about the topic, and do you need to take their perspectives into account in your report? How will your report contribute to the larger conversation about the topic? How much time do you have to complete the report, and what kind of research will you need to do? Reports are often written by a team. Will you be collaborating with other writers? Are there any other requirements you need to keep in mind?

Language. The language you use will depend on your audience. Is there a kind of language they are likely expecting, or that will appeal to them? If you're presenting an important report to a group at work, you'll likely want to use fairly formal language, whereas a report that will be read by classmates might be more conversational. It also depends on your purpose: What kind of language will be most effective for what you're trying to accomplish?

Medium and design. How will your report be delivered—in print? as an oral report? online? How does the medium affect the way you'll design the report? If it will include information that's best presented in a graph or charts, will that affect the medium you use?

Research your topic and decide on a focus

The heart of most reports is the information they provide, so a big part of your job as a report writer will be to gather as much relevant data as possible. Whatever your topic, your report will only be as strong as the information it provides. Begin with any information you already have about the topic, and make notes about what more you need to find out. What questions do you have? What will your readers want to know or need to be told?

Do some research

You might start with REFERENCE WORKS that give an overview of the topic. If you're reporting on a current issue, you'll likely find a lot of sources online; *Wikipedia* can be a good place to start, for it often includes links to other sources. If you're permitted to use AI, it can suggest and provide links to some sources to start with. You'll also find help in this book—check out Chapter 16: Starting with Questions, Finding Sources.

What are the various perspectives on your topic?

What are others saying about it? Reporting calls on you to maintain an evenhanded, objective STANCE, but others are sure to have various viewpoints on the topic, and you need to be aware of them.

Focus on an angle that interests you

Once you have a general understanding of your topic, think about what aspect you want to focus on. Here's where you need to narrow the scope of what you research, and to consider the constraints of your assignment. Which sources provide the most relevant and helpful information on your topic? How much can you cover in your report, given the time you have to complete it? And think about your audience and how much the angle you are choosing will interest and matter to them. Most of all, though, think about what interests *you*!

Synthesize the information and ideas you find

Now comes some fun: use your mental muscles to synthesize what your sources say. Identify the various ideas and perspectives they present, and think about their similarities and differences. What can your synthesis add to your understanding of the topic? There's no one way to synthesize a bunch of different facts and ideas and examples and whatever else your research turns up, but here's how the author who also writes as Lemony Snicket describes how he does it:

> Here is what I do: Little bits from all over the place, mostly literature—scurry into my mind and I scurry after them. They are not original ideas—not because they are not original, although of course they aren't; it's because they're not ideas. Not yet. In the beginning they are just *things*. . . . As I survey those scraps in my mind, . . . I try to get them in some kind of order. I put them together, so they stop dashing around and start clinging to something.
>
> —DANIEL HANDLER, *And Then? And Then? What Else?*

Whether or not you find yourself scurrying around after ideas, you'll probably find yourself working with bits and pieces of information, a process that can lead to a broad understanding of your topic—and might lead you to new ideas about that topic. Here are some tips that will help you get started.

Identify patterns and themes

Once you have chosen sources you expect to use in writing your report and have read them carefully to be sure you understand what they say, skim through them again, this time looking for patterns and themes:

- *Reread each source with an open mind.* Don't think about whether you agree or disagree with what they say. Take notes, summarizing what each source says, looking for patterns in what they address and say.

- *Are there any ideas, issues, or controversies* that are addressed in more than one source? Facts? Statistics? Anecdotes?

- *Note any people or sources* that are mentioned in more than one source. If there are, think about whether you should check them out as well.

- *Then identify significant differences:* points on which some sources disagree, take different STANCES, or cite different kinds of EVIDENCE.

This kind of synthesizing will give you a deeper understanding of your topic, and may well get you thinking about it in a new way. You might find that two or three of your sources generally agree about one point but disagree about another point, or that there's a new angle that you now need to investigate. In any case, the process will surely give you a lot to think about, and will help you decide what you want to focus on.

For more on synthesizing, see Ch. 19.

Moving from what your sources say to what *you* want to say

While learning about what many others have written about the topic and synthesizing the ideas in a number of different sources will help you see the big picture of your topic, it might also get you thinking about the topic in new ways. This in turn will affect what you then will write about it. Remember, though, that you shouldn't just report what others have said; your report needs to be about what *you* say. So you'll want to be careful to weave ideas from your sources in with your own.

See on p. 350 how one writer weaves ideas from multiple sources into his article on the effects of "Other People's Vacations."

Here are some questions that can help you move from what your sources say to what you say:

- Have your sources turned out to support your initial ideas about the topic? Or are you now starting to question some of your ideas?

- If they've changed your mind in some way, do you now need to do further research?

- If your sources reflect a number of different PERSPECTIVES, do you agree with some sources and disagree with others?

- What new ideas or insights has your research led you to?

- What information do you find most interesting about your topic? Does it suggest an angle to focus on in your report?

Based on your understanding of your sources and your own thinking, what is most significant about your topic? How can your report make the topic compelling to your audience and get them interested in reading what you write?

Formulate a working thesis

Say what you plan to report about the topic. For example, if you're reporting on food insecurity on campus, your working thesis might start out broadly, with something like this:

> Hunger is a big problem in the United States today.

Then think about whether you need to QUALIFY that statement—to make it one that you'll be able to support, and that will interest your audience. Here's one way to qualify the statement that hunger is a big problem in the US today:

> Hunger is a growing problem on our campus today.

If you're reporting on a controversial topic, your research may lead you to develop an opinion about the issue. But remember that your goal is to present information on the topic, not to tell readers what you think about it.

See how a report written for the general public summing up the findings of an annual survey presents its facts and data. The survey measured who people in 2019 trusted the most. Read on: you may be surprised by what it found.

> Employers are now the most trusted institution, according to the 2019 Edelman Trust Barometer, with 75% of respondents saying they trust "my employer"—25 points more than business in general, 40 points more than government, 20 points more than a peer or expert and 10 points above traditional media.
>
> Of the 33,000 people surveyed in 27 countries for the 19th annual Trust Barometer, more than three quarters (76%) say they want CEOs to take the lead on change instead of waiting for government. And 73% believe a company can take actions that both increase profits and improve economic and social conditions in the community where it operates.
>
> A similarly high number of employees expect their employer to actively join them in advocating for social issues (67%), and 71% expect that their work will shape the future of society in a meaningful way.
>
> Stephen Kehoe, Edelman's global chair of reputation, told the Holmes Report: "Overall, people are pessimistic about the future, and they are also concerned about fake news, and don't trust the media and government, so 58% say they are looking to their

employer as being a trustworthy source of information about headline issues where there is not consensus in society, such as gun control, #MeToo, or immigration."

—MAJA PAWINSKA SIMS, *The Holmes Report*

Note how much data the reporter packs into this passage: we know that these findings are based on a survey of 33,000 people, for instance, from 27 countries. Note too the use of statistics to support the findings: 76 percent of those 33,000 people reported that they wanted CEOs "to take the lead on change," rather than "waiting for government." Finally, see how this reporter uses quotations to support the findings she reports, quoting the "chair of reputation" of the firm that conducted the original research. As readers, we know this is information we can trust.

Tailor your report to a target audience

Some reports are written for very specific audiences: a company's annual report to stockholders, for example, will address a group of people who have a stake in the company's performance, attempting to provide a clear and positive overview of the firm's accomplishments in the preceding year. A report to members of a synagogue on how their funds have been used to reduce poverty in a partner community will present data documenting the use of funds and may include photos showing the effect that the funds had on those in need. Whatever your audience, you'll want to think hard about what they already know about your topic and what information they'll be looking for.

The annual report for Girls Who Code, a national non-profit working "to close the gender gap in technology," addresses two audiences: contributors to the organization, and those people who might contribute in the future. See how the author of the report, the founder and CEO of the organization, speaks directly to these two audiences in a letter on the following page.

When I started Girls Who Code, I never imagined that we would grow to become a movement reaching almost 90,000 girls of all backgrounds in all 50 states. And now, just six years into our work, we've reached a tipping point. We are on track to achieve gender parity in computer science by 2027. And we know why: because our work is as much about quantity as it is about quality. We scale our programs to reach more girls in more places, and to give them the chance to forge lifelong bonds so they may persist in computer science.

It's incredible. But for us, parity is really just the beginning. We've reached a moment unmatched in our history, a moment as full of anger and anguish as it is promise and potential. Women and girls across the country are coming together to correct centuries-long power imbalances across lines of gender, race, sexuality, and more.

Girls Who Code is proud to be a part of this movement, and even prouder because our girls—girls of all races and ethnicities and abilities and zip codes—are leading it. They are solving problems in their communities . . . and defining the future of our world.

We're thrilled to be giving them the tools they need to get there.

I hope you'll join us and make sure every girl has the chance to change her world—our world—for the better. Thank you for your support.

—RESHMA SAUJANI, Annual Report of Girls Who Code

Girl coders.

GIRLS WHO CODE, 2017–2018

- 📍 SIPs
- ● 1–10
- ● 11–50
- ● 51–100
- ● 101–150
- ● >150

In her report, Saujani engages supporters and potential donors by summarizing the remarkable strides the group has made in its six years of operation—now working with "girls of all races and ethnicities and abilities and zip codes"! And she includes a map showing that the organization (as of 2018) has programs in all 50 states. Note too that girls don't just get coding skills: they get coding skills that can help them "change our world." Finally, Saujani concludes her report with a thank-you, another way of acknowledging and encouraging donors.

Demonstrate your credibility, and that of the information you're reporting

In an age of misinformation and even outright lies, it's more important than ever to demonstrate that you are knowledgeable, trustworthy, and fair—and that the information in your report can be trusted as well. You can build credibility by demonstrating that you've read up on the topic, by citing reliable sources, and by documenting your sources. And you can demonstrate fairness by being evenhanded in the information you present—by citing sources that reflect various perspectives.

In an essay reporting on food production, Sam Forman compares two kinds of farms in Iowa—large industrial farms and small family-owned farms. As a student at Grinnell, a college in Iowa, he had some firsthand knowledge of both kinds of farms, but see how he presents information in ways that make readers feel we can trust both him and what he reports:

Proponents of large-scale agriculture argue that it is cheaper and more efficient to produce food following an industrial model. Judging by price tags, they may be right. Often vegetables at a farmer's market fetch a higher price than those in the supermarket do. But the supermarket is not the only place we pay for industrially produced goods.

Iowa State professor Mark Honeyman pointed out to me, citing work by J. E. Ikerd, a professor of agricultural economics at the University of Missouri, that many of the costs of mass-produced agriculture are hidden. For instance, we all pay taxes to the government, which in turn spends billions of tax dollars a year subsidizing the industrial food system. Between 2003 and 2005 the government spent an average of $11.5 billion per year on crop subsidies, 47 percent of which went to the top 5 percent of beneficiaries ("Crop Subsidy"). This means we are subsidizing a lot, and mostly the biggest agri-businesses.

Most family farmers receive no government subsidies. So when I told Barney Bahrenfuse and Suzanne Costello, who run B & B Farms in Grinnell, that I repeatedly heard from people involved in large-scale agriculture that family farming is nice but ultimately not very profitable if even viable at all, Costello was quick to respond: "You take away the industrial farms' government subsidies—they don't work. We don't take any government subsidies, so who's viable?"

In fact, the CEO of Fremont Farms, which holds about 9 million hens, pointed out to me that they receive no government subsidies, which I verified online; according to the Environmental Working Group's website, which gets its statistics from the US Department of Agriculture, except for a paltry $5,361 in corn subsidies between 1999 and 2000, Fremont Farms has gotten no subsidies at all. No direct subsidies, that is. It is important to remember, however, that their operation is indirectly subsidized by the artificially low price of corn in their chickens' feed.

—SAM FORMAN, "The Future of Food Production"

Note that Forman interviewed and quotes an Iowa State professor, the owners of a small family farm, and the CEO of a large industrial farm—and that he even did the work of verifying what one of them told him. He also cites (and documents) data from a policy analysis database. He's clearly done his homework—and synthesizes what he learned from a number of different sources! See also how carefully he qualifies his information, noting that those who say food produced by large-scale farms is less expensive than food sold at farmer's markets "may be right" and that family farmers for the most part receive no subsidies. And while he quotes one family farmer who says that industrial farms wouldn't work without government subsidies, he also notes that the CEO of a large-scale poultry farm said they get no government subsidies. Forman may well have his own opinions, but he's careful here to report only what he has learned about his topic, leaving readers free to reach their own conclusions.

It's important to note that reports are supposed to be objective, "just the facts." But while you should strive to be as objective as possible, most of the people you cite will have a particular point of view. And even as it's important to keep objectivity as a goal, it's also worth noting that reports are rarely if ever completely neutral: think of a fact-filled infographic reporting on the quality of local water sources, which will probably lead readers to favor one viewpoint more than others. Remember, however, that readers will expect you to provide some kind of information, not to tell them what you think about it—or what they should think. Remember too that bringing in more than one viewpoint or perspective can help you aim for fairness and objectivity.

REFLECT! Reread the excerpt from **Sam Forman**'s report on food production. How would you describe Forman's TONE? What words in his text help you decide what his tone is? And how would you describe his STANCE toward the topic: can you spot any places where he is less than objective—and if so, does that affect how you respond to the report? Write a paragraph reflecting on the challenges of maintaining objectivity when you have your own opinions about a topic you're reporting on.

Establish a confident stance and an engaging tone

One of your tasks as a writer reporting information is to engage your readers, to make them interested in reading about your topic. In an era when we're all constantly bombarded with information, getting readers' attention is more important than ever. And then to keep their attention, you'll need to demonstrate confidence, to show that you know what you're talking about.

Jean Twenge sure got readers' attention in 2017, when she wrote an article for the *Atlantic* on the question, "Have Smartphones Destroyed a Generation?" That's a title that grabs attention, and the article that follows includes some startling facts:

The arrival of the smartphone has radically changed every aspect of teenagers' lives, from the nature of their social interactions to their mental health. These changes have affected young people in every corner of the nation and in every type of household. The trends appear among teens poor and rich; of every ethnic background; in cities, suburbs, and small towns. Where there are cell towers, there are teens living their lives on their smartphone. . . .

You might expect that teens spend so much time [on their phones] because it makes them happy, but most data suggest that it does not. The Monitoring the Future survey, funded by the National

Institute on Drug Abuse and designed to be nationally representative, has asked 12th-graders more than 1,000 questions every year since 1975 and queried eighth- and tenth-graders since 1991. The survey asks teens how happy they are and also how much of their leisure time they spend on various activities, including nonscreen activities such as in-person social interaction and exercise, and, in recent years, screen activities such as using social media, texting, and browsing the web. The results could not be clearer: Teens who spend more time than average on screen activities are more likely to be unhappy, and those who spend more time than average on nonscreen activities are more likely to be happy.

There's not a single exception. All screen activities are linked to less happiness, and all nonscreen activities are linked to more happiness. Eighth-graders who spend 10 or more hours a week on social media are 56 percent more likely to say they're unhappy than those who devote less time to social media. Admittedly, 10 hours a week is a lot. But those who spend six to nine hours a week on social media are still 47 percent more likely to say they are unhappy than those who use social media even less. The opposite is true of in-person interactions. Those who spend an above-average amount of time with their friends in person are 20 percent less likely to say they're unhappy than those who hang out for a below-average amount of time.

—JEAN TWENGE, "Have Smartphones Destroyed a Generation?"

Twenge is clear, straightforward, and unequivocal, and she provides data to support the connection between time spent on phones and general unhappiness and stress. She tells it like it is, with confidence: "The results," she says, "could not be clearer: Teens who spend more time than average on screen activities are more likely to be unhappy." Her tone throughout is serious but not alarmist: she reports information her readers need to know, and she comes across as a confident, steady, reliable reporter who provides some very interesting and thought-provoking information.

Without data, you're just another person with an opinion. W. E. DEMING

Ways of organizing a report

The way you organize and design a report depends on the information you're presenting and the medium you'll use. Some topics call for COMPARISONS or DESCRIPTIONS, while others may call for you to cite expert testimony or present many EXAMPLES, and still others may lead you to present numerical data in a bar graph. So it's not possible to specify one generic way to organize all reports. Regardless, you'll want to organize your report in a way that your audiences can easily follow, whether it's using headings to guide readers from topic to topic, presenting some information in a list to make it easier to follow, and so on.

Consider the findings from a 2018 General Social Survey on the attitudes of pet owners, focusing on attitudes and feelings of four kinds of people: those with pet dogs, those with pet cats, those with both dogs and cats, and those with no pets at all. How did the groups compare, in terms of happiness? And the winner was . . . people with pet dogs reported being the happiest! In fact, people with dogs were twice as happy as cat owners, while those who had both cats and dogs fell somewhere in the middle. (Here's a surprise: people with no pets at all were almost as happy as those with dogs. Go figure!)

This summary presents the findings in words, but the same findings would perhaps be easier to see if they were presented visually, as the graph below shows. Which one do you find easier to understand?

DOGS OR CATS?
Which Ones Make Us Happier?

Dogs only	😺😺😺😺😺😺😺😺😺😺😺😺😺😺😺😺😺😺 36%
Cats only	🐱🐱🐱🐱🐱🐱🐱🐱🐱 18%
Dogs and cats	😺🐱😺🐱😺🐱😺🐱😺🐱😺🐱 28%
No pets at all	⊘⊘⊘⊘⊘⊘⊘⊘⊘⊘⊘⊘⊘⊘⊘⊘ 32%

Source: General Social Survey, 2018.

Or let's say you're writing a report comparing the two teams in the NBA finals that are most favored to win the championship. You could organize your report in two sections, one on Team A and the other on Team B, and examine each team's star players, post-season statistics, and other factors that point toward winning or losing. Or you might choose to organize the report around key statistics—rebounds per game, number of turnovers, and so on—and then compare Team A and Team B in each category. Either method of organization should yield a clear and reader-friendly result.

Finally, when it comes to organizing a report that you're assigned to do for a class, make sure to find out if there are any requirements for how to organize your work. Some fields in the sciences and social sciences require an organization known as IMRAD for the headings it includes: introduction, methods, results, and discussion. Engineering instructors may require you to include a title page and organize your report around methods, results, discussion, conclusions, and references. Other disciplines may require different organizations.

Consider whether to include any visuals

Many reports include information that is best presented as visual text. The annual report for Girls Who Code, for example, includes a map to show all the states where that organization has chapters. And the *Atlantic* article on smartphones includes a number of graphs showing ways that smartphones have affected teenagers' behavior. The one here draws attention to how much less they've been hanging out with friends since the iPhone was released.

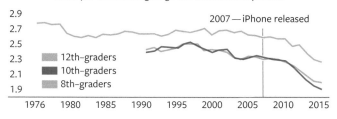

Not Hanging Out with Friends
Times per week teenagers go out without their parents

Read your draft with a critical eye, get response—and revise

Once you have a draft, it's time to read over what you've written to be sure that your report will engage readers and tell them what you want them to know about your topic. If at all possible, get feedback from a classmate or friend. The following questions can help you or others read a report with a critical eye.

- Does the TITLE make clear what the report is about—and will it engage readers' interest? What other title might you use?

- How well does the report address your intended AUDIENCE? Will they see why the topic matters?

- Have you indicated in a THESIS what the report is about and said anything about how it is organized?

- How have you established your CREDIBILITY? How many PERSPECTIVES does your report represent?

- How have you demonstrated that the information in your report is accurate and trustworthy? Have you FACT-CHECKED to be sure?

- Have you incorporated any facts, statistics, examples, or other material from your research—and if so, have you acknowledged the sources where you found these both in your text and in a list of WORKS CITED or REFERENCES?

- How would you characterize your report's TONE? Does it reflect your STANCE and the way you want to come across to your readers? If you have an opinion about your topic, have you kept it out of the report?

- Is the organization clear and appropriate to the topic? Have you included headings and TRANSITIONS to help readers follow the report easily?

- Have you included any VISUALS or presented any text graphically? If not, is there any information that would be easier to understand in a chart or table or list?

- How does the report CONCLUDE? What do you want to leave readers thinking, and does the conclusion do that? How else might your report conclude?

And now it's time to REVISE. If you've analyzed your draft and gotten advice from others, you've got a plan. You know what you *want* to do—but think about what you need to do. Remember that you're writing a REPORT, and that means providing factual information—"just the facts," some would say—but that however you present these facts—with EXAMPLES, DEFINITIONS, COMPARISONS, ANALOGIES, and so on—they need to support what you say about the topic. You're also writing to a particular AUDIENCE about something that you think matters, so now's your chance to make them care as well.

REFLECT! Choose a topic you are very interested in, and then browse the web to find someone who is reporting on that topic. Read the report carefully, and reflect on how effective the reporting is: How trustworthy is the information it provides? How objective is it? How credible is the author? How well does the report engage you and make you want to read on (or not)? If you could revise the report or give advice to the writer, what would you do or say?

A STUDENT REPORT

STEPHANIE POMALES

For Better or Worse: *Spotify* and the Music Industry

Stephanie Pomales wrote this essay for an introduction to computers class when she was a student at the University of Califoria at Davis, and it was a winner of the school's annual Prized Writing competition. She majored in communication studies at Davis and is now an Internal Communications Associate at Meta. Her essay is documented using APA style.

Opens with questions that engage her audience of college students.

When you want music, where do you turn? Are you a purist who demands vinyl? Or do you go online to *Pandora*? *YouTube*? *Apple Music*? *Tidal Music*? *Spotify*? If so, you are one of millions upon millions of people who access music digitally. But how much do you really know about the digital streaming services you are using? If streaming is the way most of us now listen to music, what issues does this shift raise for artists and the music industry? This report sets out to explore that question.

Announces the purpose of her report.

Establishes a conversational tone.

Let's consider *Spotify*, the most popular streaming music service in the United States today. Founded in 2008 by Swedish entrepreneur Daniel Elk, *Spotify* was first made available here in 2011. Since then, *Spotify* has created a new way for people to consume music and has had a huge impact on the music industry's business model. With over 40 million paying subscribers, *Spotify* currently ranks number one as the most popular music service in the world, with more users than *Apple Music*, *Tidal*, or *Pandora*.

Provides background information.

However, with popularity has come a critical backlash. The company, and its CEO, have been on defense ever since *Spotify* was first introduced into the US music marketplace, facing public opposition from recording artists, labels, and music industry executives. Piracy concerns, a decline in physical record sales, and *Spotify*'s pay-per-stream model have been major points of discord between the music industry and streaming companies. Most everyone in the industry acknowledges that streaming services are not going away, but many are still concerned about the ethics of streaming and whether musicians, especially independent artists, are being treated fairly. Despite these criticisms, streaming services are likely here to stay—at least until a new technology that is better, faster, or cheaper comes onto the marketplace.

States thesis.

In fact, *Spotify* was once a new technology, one that was invented to be "better" than existing technology. You might say it all started with *Napster*, a peer-to-peer service that let people share and receive music files online or through email. It made music available for free, and thus was hugely popular. Its site was shut down after intense legal battles with copyright holders, but Napster had already changed the face of the music industry (Swanson, 2013). Apple's *iTunes*, *Rhapsody*, and *Pandora* all came shortly thereafter, each helping to further the digital music sphere into a more legitimate way of listening to music online (Marshall, 2015). And then, in 2008, along came *Spotify*.

Provides a short narrative about the history of streaming.

Spotify is an "on demand" streaming service that operates on two plans. The first level, *Spotify Free* ("freemium"), lets users listen to music for free but with advertisements and with limited options. For example, they can listen to music only on shuffle mode and cannot access the higher quality sound that comes with a paid subscription. They also cannot listen to songs on demand and are limited to a certain number of skips in shuffle mode. For $9.99 per month ($4.99 for students), users can upgrade to the second tier, *Spotify Premium*, which gives them consistent, high quality, on-demand music. The music is considered "on demand" because users can listen to specific music that they choose instead of having music chosen for them by a computer-generated formula. *Spotify* licenses access to millions of songs by making deals with labels and independent artists for a certain percentage of its profits, money that comes from advertisements in the *Spotify Free* tier or from subscription fees in *Spotify Premium*. These funds go into a pool that is distributed based on how often songs are played and other

Describes the services Spotify provides.

popularity factors; "think of it like having your paycheck fluctuate based not only on your own performance, but on the performance of everyone else in your industry as well" (Luckerson, 2019). According to an article in *Quartz*, song rightsholders make anywhere from $.006 to $.0084 cents per play, and these earnings can be divided up between the label, the producers, and the artists (Livni, 2018).

Streaming services are currently locked in a heated debate with music industry professionals over whether or not the pay-per-stream model is adversely affecting the industry and the artists. As the top streaming service in the world, *Spotify* takes up much of the spotlight, especially after Taylor Swift pulled all her music from *Spotify* in 2014. Swift added her albums back in 2017, but her absence on the site for many years raised serious questions about the ethics of *Spotify*'s free model. Many artists and music industry professionals believe that the backlash is warranted, while others argue that *Spotify* provides a legal alternative to pirating that justifies its existence (Swanson, 2013).

Provides statistics.

Introduces alternative views of streaming services.

Taylor Swift raised red flags about *Spotify* when she removed her albums from *Spotify* in 2014.

Spotify started with good intentions: to combat the music piracy that *Napster* had unleashed, as people began to see peer-to-peer sharing as a way of owning free music. Daniel Elk, *Spotify*'s founder, believed that streaming services could simply monetize already existing consumer behavior, and that it would be a legitimate alternative to the global issue of pirating.

In spite of the criticism, *Spotify* has lived up to much of its early promise. Streaming services are in fact saving music sales, which have been declining in recent years in part because of struggles with piracy (Shaw, 2016). Even Carl Sherman, the president of the Recording Industry Association of America, has spoken out on the subject. In a recent blog article reporting on the music industry midway through 2016, Sherman admitted that much of the growth in the music industry in recent years has been brought about by music subscription services (Sherman, 2016), saying that 2016 was the first time that music professionals had seen consistent sales since 1999, when record sales reached their peak (Singleton & Popper, 2016). Sherman even acknowledged that streaming had contributed a lot to these record-high sales numbers, noting that it "accounted for almost half of all recorded music revenue in the first half of 2016" (Sherman, 2016). Since *Spotify* is the streaming service with the most subscribers, and the main contributor to the industry's increased sales, its impact on the music marketplace is considerable. Approximately $1 billion was spent on streaming services in the first half of 2016, with more people than ever opting for paid subscription plans. Music spending in total for the same year, including record sales and online sales, was more than $3.4 billion according to industry statistics (Shaw, 2016). The three major record labels—Universal Music Group, Sony Music Entertainment, and Warner Music Group—have all seen improved sales, largely due to the popularity of streaming services in the United States (Shaw, 2016).

Provides evidence of Spotify's positive effects.

Many still believe, however, that *Spotify* is not doing enough to help musicians earn a living wage, especially in the case of indepen-

Spotify's billboards celebrate its listeners and inspire others to join the fun.

dent artists. Many common arguments state that music buying is decreasing. During the heydays of CDs and records, buying music was a more public, even social, experience. Now that big box stores are reducing their CD sections and there are fewer music stores around, music buying takes place mostly online and in the privacy of one's home. While it's easy to assume that fewer people are willing to pay for music, data shows that people who pay for streaming services will spend more over time than those who bought physical CDs in the 1990s (Shaw, 2016). A typical CD buyer in 1990 spent $50 per year on music, while a *Spotify* subscription could cost as much as $120 per year (Singleton & Popper, 2016). With 25% of all *Spotify* "freemium" users converting to paid subscriptions (Singleton & Popper, 2016), more people than ever before are paying for their music.

Many of *Spotify*'s defenders believe that critics are simply looking at streaming services in the wrong way, saying that streaming services and store-bought albums are different things. Streaming,

Provides evidence of Spotify's negative effects.

Notes counterarguments to Spotify's critics.

they say, needs to be taken seriously as a new technology that cannot be compared to previous technologies. Vinyl, cassettes, and CDs each had a moment in which they were the most in-demand technology, and streaming is now having its moment. This suggests that a major change is overdue concerning how people view the streaming model. When radio DJs play a song, they are sending music over airwaves to hundreds or even thousands of people at the same time. On the other hand, streaming occurs on a one-to-one basis with individual people accessing a song they want to hear whenever they want to hear it. This explains why the payment per stream is so low, and why *Spotify* simply can't be compared with *AirPlay*.

Compares streaming with earlier technologies.

Spotify's Daniel Elk has a response to all the criticism that his company has faced. Most industry professionals see music sales on a per-unit basis, he says, like buying an individual song on an online music store. Elk suggests that the music industry needs to move away from a unit-based business model and to a streaming model. People do not buy music from streaming services—instead, they pay for access to music for a designated period. Over an extended period, the small payments for music access will result in more money for both artists and industry professionals (Marshall, 2015).

But *Spotify*'s biggest problem is not the complaints of artists or industry bigwigs. Indeed, it is piracy, in the form of illegal music downloading. The switch to streaming has many researchers trying to determine whether it has resulted in more or less music piracy. After all, one of the main reasons Elk started *Spotify* was to make streaming a viable alternative to piracy in the digital age. If piracy has decreased, then one could say that streaming services have fulfilled a valuable goal for the music industry; if piracy has risen, it may be that streaming services are adding to digital piracy.

Introduces the music industry's main problem: piracy.

The Federation of the Phonographic Industry estimates that 20 million Americans are pirating on a regular basis (Carman, 2016), and it seems that the "exclusives" that some streaming companies offer may be partly responsible. When popular music is available only on specific streaming services, users are less able to get all their music on one service, resulting in widespread pirating of that music (Singleton & Popper, 2016). For example, when Kanye West's *Life of Pablo* album was available only on *Tidal*, it is estimated that 500,000 people illegally downloaded the album from various file-sharing websites (Carman, 2016). Each of the illegal downloads resulted in loss of income for the artist, the streaming services, and the industry professionals behind the production and creation of the album. Although exclusive content may help to bring more business to a specific streaming service, ultimately, they may be doing more harm than good to the industry and to *Spotify*'s efforts to eradicate pirating.

Provides evidence of the damage done by piracy.

Academic research offers conflicting viewpoints about music streaming services and their influence on pirating. In their paper "Streaming Reaches Flood Stage: Does *Spotify* Stimulate or Depress Music Sales?" Aguiar and Waldfogel (2015) conclude that Spotify has been revenue-neutral for the music industry, stating that "losses from displaced sales are roughly outweighed by the gains in streaming revenue" (p. 1). Their research also shows that *Spotify* has helped to decrease the amount of music piracy in the United States and across the globe, but does not do much to raise the net profit of the music industry (Aguiar & Waldfogel, 2015). Borja and Dieringer (2016), however, conclude that streaming services like *Spotify* increase instances of pirating by 11%, with more streaming directly correlated with higher rates of music pirating. This might have to do with the fact that most people "do not view streaming as a low-price substitute for pirating," as many complain that streaming services are still too expensive (Borja & Dieringer, 2016, p. 91). In fact, Borja and Dieringer found that the two most predictive factors for pirating were peer pressure and a high tendency toward risk taking. College students seem to be the population most inclined to this behavior, as students have little income and many expenses.

Cites research about Spotify's effects on piracy.

Citing scholarly research helps build the author's credibility: she's done her homework!

With higher levels of risk taking, students are more likely to pirate from illegal file-sharing websites because they have less money to buy music and are more susceptible to the considerations of others.

While peer pressure surely plays a significant role in piracy behavior, internet users may have more complex reasons behind why they resort to pirating even when low-cost alternatives like streaming are available. In 2016, Russ Crupnick, a writer for <u>MusicWatch. com</u>, conducted a survey with 1,000 respondents between the ages of 13 and 50 and found that the reasons for music pirating are varied between different age categories. Some people surveyed simply stated that they want to own the music, rather than only have access to it for a brief period, while others only pirate music if they do not like the track enough to purchase it on a digital music site (Crupnick, 2016). Many of the respondents stated that they wanted to have "on demand" music on their smartphones, a feature that *Spotify Free* does not offer. Somewhat surprisingly, many of the people surveyed who pirated music claimed that they spend a fair amount of money buying music from legal sources; in fact, the amount they spend on legal music is only slightly less than the amount spent by average, non-pirating music buyers (Crupnick, 2016).

Considers other perspectives on piracy.

Although criticism of streaming continues and research gives conflicting information concerning piracy, streaming services have made their mark on the music industry. Those using these sites, including both premium and "freemium" subscribers, have grown accustomed to accessing large quantities of music for free, or for incredibly cheap prices. Music labels must adjust to these changes and work accordingly with streaming services in order to stay relevant into the 21st century, especially given the potential for streaming services to independently contract with musicians in the near future. The more subscribers join, the more money artists will see in their pockets and the less irritated music executives will be with *Spotify*'s cut of the profits. This not only applies to big name artists receiving millions of streams, but indie artists as well. Longer

Sums up the findings of her research.

free trials, special discounts, and family memberships are all ways that streaming services can get more paid subscribers. Any money that goes to the music industry is still better than having musicians' work be pirated. Marketing toward older generations on the benefits of streaming services may also prove to be useful in increasing the number of paid subscription members. With *Spotify* holding a high conversion rate of users from free to paid plans, it is likely that streaming services will become more normalized in music history and will begin to secure a stronger reputation in the eyes of industry professionals.

States the conclusion supported by research.

If you're someone who gets your music via *Spotify*, *Pandora*, or another streaming service, do you subscribe or take the free-mium options? Or do you find a way to download what you want for free? What do you think you *should* do, and why? As subscribers, or potential subscribers, these are all issues that you should consider when you stream your next song. As this report has demonstrated, these are decisions we all need to think about.

Challenges readers to think about where they get music; invites response.

References

Aguiar, L., & Waldfogel, J. (2015). *Streaming reaches flood stage: Does* Spotify *stimulate or depress music sales?* (NBER Working Paper No. 21653). The National Bureau of Economic Research. http://doi.org/df3d

Borja, K., & Dieringer, S. (2016). Streaming or stealing? The complementary features between music streaming and music piracy. *Journal of Retailing and Consumer Services, 32,* 86–95. http://doi.org/gc8qv8

Carman, A. (2016, April 10). *How music streaming service exclusives make pirating tempting again*. The Verge. http://www.theverge.com/2016/4/10/11394272/music-streaming-service-piracy-spotify-tlop-tidal

Crupnick, R. (2016, February 22). *Bad company, you can't deny*. MusicWatch. http://www.musicwatchinc.com/blog/bad-company-you-cant-deny/

Livni, E. (2018, December 25). *Mariah Carey's record-breaking day shows how little musicians make from* Spotify. Quartz. https://qz.com/1507361/mariah-careys-record-breaking-day-shows-how-little-musicians-make-from-spotify/

Luckerson, V. (2019, January 16). *Is Spotify's model wiping out music's middle class?* The Ringer. https://www.theringer.com/tech/2019/1/16/18184314/spotify-music-streaming-service-royalty-payout-model

Marshall, L. (2015). "Let's keep music special. F—*Spotify*": On-demand streaming and the controversy over artist royalties. *Creative Industries Journal, 8*(2), 177–189. http://doi.org/gc3chw

Shaw, L. (2016, September 19). *The music industry is finally making money on streaming.* Bloomberg. https://www.bloomberg.com/news/articles/2016-09-20/spotify-apple-drive-u-s-music-industry-s-8-first-half-growth

Sherman, C. (2016, September 20). *The modern music business midway through 2016.* Medium. https://medium.com/@RIAA/the-modern-music-business-midway-through-2016-f74e22ecff42#.geo4odf4s

Singleton, M., & Popper, B. (2016, September 20). *The music industry is on the rebound thanks to paid streaming.* The Verge. http://theverge.com/2016/9/20/12986980/music-industry-apple-spotify-paid-streaming

Swanson, K. (2013). A case study on *Spotify*: Exploring perceptions of the music streaming service. *MEIEA Journal, 13*(1), 207–230. http://doi.org/gfvxmh

Thinking about the Text

1. Stephanie Pomales has obviously done a lot of research on *Spotify* and other streaming services. What is her major CLAIM and where is it stated?

2. What examples, facts, and reasons does she offer to support the major claim? How well do you think she supports that claim? What EVIDENCE do you find most informative and persuasive—and what leads you to that conclusion?

3. How does Pomales deal with COUNTERARGUMENTS and alternative viewpoints? Do you think she does so fairly?

4. Make a rough outline of this report. What does it reveal about how she has organized all her information? How effective is that organization? How else could it be organized?

5. Pomales concludes her report by asking readers how they get music—by subscribing to a streaming service, using a free streaming service, or downloading what they want for free—and then asking what they think they should do, and why. Write a paragraph or two describing how *you* get music, and REFLECTING on what you now think you should do—and why.

13 Narrating

What unites people? Armies? Gold? Flags? Nah. *Stories*.
There's nothing more powerful than a good story.
Nothing can stop it. No enemy can defeat it.

—TYRION LANNISTER

Why would telling a story be "more powerful" than everything else in the world? Is it because millions of people have watched *Game of Thrones*? Or read about the adventures of Odysseus, or Harry Potter? It's much more than that. Storytelling is a universal genre: "the one true democracy we have," says novelist Colum McCann. "It goes across borders, boundaries, genders, wealth, race—everyone has a story to tell." A good story can even change minds. These are all reasons that stories mean so much to our lives and to the work we do as readers, writers, and speakers.

If you're a *biology* major, you'll learn a lot through stories about how major discoveries were made, from Watson and Crick's quest to solve the structure of DNA to the epic journeys that led Charles Darwin and Alfred Wallace to their theory of evolution. If you're a *business* major, you're likely to work with case studies, narratives about situations that real companies faced in which you might be assigned to be the CEO (the protagonist) and have to figure out how to deal with the situation. And if you are a fan of Shakira, you've likely watched or listen to *Las Mujeres Ya No Lloran*, an album filled to the brim with vivid stories about her personal struggles and why "women no longer cry."

So narratives are all around us, not just in literature and on TV. It's no surprise then that they will play a role in your composition class. You might open an argument with a personal narrative that makes a point about your topic—and perhaps return to that story in your conclusion. Or you might compose a narrative as a way to make a point. And you may be assigned to write a literacy narrative about how you learned to read or write or do something else. This chapter aims to guide you in creating a narrative of your own.

Shakira sings "Puntería." Times Square, New York, 2024.

A GUIDE TO DEVELOPING A NARRATIVE

Put most simply, a narrative tells about something that's happened in order to make a point of some kind. A personal narrative focuses on something that happened to the person writing it. That's you, and here are some steps to get you started.

Identify an event that matters

The first step is to come up with an event that matters—to you, and hopefully to others as well. Think about what happened, and why. When and where did it happen? Who was involved, and what roles did they play? Why does it matter to you, and why have you chosen to write about it? How can you write about it in a way that will interest others—especially if it's something they wouldn't ordinarily read about?

If you're assigned to write a LITERACY NARRATIVE, you'll focus on how you learned to do something—read, write, knit, play the guitar, whatever. Just be sure it's something you care about. Start by thinking about what you learned, and who else was involved. Was it easy? challenging? fun? something else? Why has it mattered enough to write about it?

When Melissa Hicks was assigned to write a personal narrative for her writing class at Lane Community College, in Oregon, she found herself thinking over and over about making butter on her family's farm as a young girl and her fondness for butter now as an adult. Writing about those experiences prompted her to think about why they've been so important to her:

> In my house we have butter and margarine. The butter is for cooking. The margarine is for macaroni and cheese. I swear that it's the butter that makes everything taste so good. My favorite foods that remind me of my mother and my own childhood. In the grocery store aisle, I stand under the harsh white lights of the dairy case, margarine in one hand and butter in the other.... I weigh them in my mind, thinking of the high cost of butter. No matter how long I

stand and weigh, I always put the butter in my cart. I remember the times when I was a girl—the taste of sweet, fresh butter melting on my tongue. I remember the work it took, and I know the price is more than fair.

—MELISSA HICKS, "The High Price of Butter"

The story Hicks goes on to tell moves back and forth between her present grown-up self and her past childhood. She meditates on the honest, hard work on the farm where she took care of the cow and made butter, and reflects on how those experiences shaped the values that she still holds today.

And here's Savion Glover, now a famous tap dancer, telling the story about how learning to play the drums at a young age got him started "making too much noise":

I started playing drums in Suzuki class when I was three or four. I'd go in there and start banging on some drum or on the piano or the xylophone, and they eventually moved me up a level into the regular drum class, I think because I was just making too much noise. I just couldn't stop banging around. Meanwhile at home I used to play everything, just everything, my mother tells me. I do remember putting

A close-up of Savion Glover, making music and noise with his feet.

on shows for her. She would come home from work, and I'd have the knives and forks out from the drawers and the pots and the pans set up like drums. I figured out you could get different tones out of the big pots and the little pots and the teakettle and the colander.

—SAVION GLOVER, *My Life in Tap*

Note that Glover's narrative implicitly tells readers that this sequence of events matters a great deal to him: it captures his commitment to and near obsession with making music (and noise!) since he was a toddler, using red highlighting to underscore that he "**just couldn't stop banging around.**" Creating sound and performing for his mother seem like the most important things in his life! This paragraph draws readers in and invites us to find out what happens next.

Think about your rhetorical situation

When you've decided on the event your narrative will focus on and considered the point you want the narrative to lead up to, it's time to consider your rhetorical situation.

Purpose. Think again about why you want to tell this story. Will telling it help you understand yourself and what has happened to you in your life in new ways? Will it help you connect with a particular audience? Or maybe your narrative is meant to entertain—to get your audience laughing along with you. Whatever your purpose, keep it in mind from start to finish.

Audience. Who will read your story? Why would it interest them— or how can you get them interested? What do you want them to take away from it? What do you know about them, and how much background will you need to provide? What do you know about their age, gender, cultural heritage, basic values and beliefs, and so on? How might such factors influence the way you tell your story—and how you present yourself?

Stance. What stance will you take? How do you want to come across—as knowledgeable? thoughtful? funny? something else?

Whatever stance you adopt, think about how the words you choose and the way you put them together will help establish that stance.

Context. What else has been said about your topic? Does your narrative relate to any larger social or political or economic issues (or educational ones, if you're writing a literacy narrative), and if so, what will your audience need to know about that context? Finally, think about your own context—the requirements of an assignment, the time you have to complete your narrative, and so on.

Language. What languages or dialects might you use? If you include dialogue, for example, you'll want to let people speak in whatever languages or dialects they use. See how Rachel Kondo uses Hawaiian Creole in her story "Girl of Few Seasons," when a father gives some advice to his son who's about to leave for Vietnam: "'Some kine advice. I know. Soljah to soljah. But only get one ting fo say . . . Duh ting you gotta do,' said Daddy, 'is . . . no die.'" Just imagine how the narrative would be different if Kondo had paraphrased what he said into standardized English.

Media and design. How will your narrative be delivered—in print? online? as an oral presentation? How does your medium affect the way your narrative is designed and the kinds of examples you can provide? Can you include visuals—photos and captions? video? audio? Would headings help readers follow the story? Your decisions about media and design should aim to help your audience follow your story and understand the major points you want to make with that story.

Try to recall details that will make your story come alive

Start by writing down everything you can remember about the event that's at the heart of your narrative—just start writing and keep going until you run out of memories and words. *What* happened? *When* and *where* did it take place? *Who* was there? What were they wearing, what did they say or do? Can you recall any specific sounds, smells, colors, or tastes? What vivid or quirky details can you add that will help bring your story to life so that others can experience it along with you? Can you add some dialogue—conversations or even just words that will let your audience listen in on what was happening? *Why* does this story matter?

See how Lynda Barry incorporates visual details and dialogue in her narrative essay recalling how important good teachers have been to her success as a cartoonist, author, and now a teacher herself. Here she is at age seven, sneaking out of home and in a panic about "needing to get to school":

I was 7 years old the first time I snuck out of the house in the dark. . . . It was quiet outside. Stars were still out. Nothing moved and no one was in the street. It was as if someone had turned the sound off on the world.

I walked the alley, breaking thin ice over the puddles with my shoes. I didn't know why I was walking to school in the dark. . . . All I knew was a feeling of panic, like the panic that strikes kids when they realize they are lost.

That feeling eased the moment I turned the corner and saw the dark outline of my school at the top of the hill. My school was made up of about 15 nondescript portable classrooms set down on a fenced concrete lot in a rundown Seattle neighborhood, but it had the most beautiful view of the Cascade Mountains. You could see them from . . . the windows of my classroom—Room 2. . . .

"Hey there, young lady. Did you forget to go home last night?" It was Mr. Gunderson, our janitor, whom we all loved. He was nice and he was funny and he was old with white hair, thick glasses and an unbelievable number of keys. I could hear them jingling as he walked across the playfield. I felt incredibly happy to see him.

And I saw my teacher, Mrs. Claire LeSane, walking toward us in a red coat and calling my name in a very happy and surprised way, and suddenly my throat got tight and my eyes stung and I ran toward her crying. . . .

It's only thinking about it now, 28 years later, that I realize I was crying from relief. I was with my teacher, and in a while I was going

to sit at my desk, with my crayons and pencils and books and class-mates all around me, and for the next six hours I was going to enjoy a thoroughly secure, warm and stable world....

Mrs. LeSane asked me what was wrong and when I said "Noth-ing," she seemingly left it at that. But she asked me if I would carry her purse for her, an honor above all honors, and she asked if I wanted to come into Room 2 early and paint.

—LYNDA BARRY, "The Sanctuary of School"

Barry is a master cartoonist and storyteller, and this passage is full of colorful, quirky details. We wonder, along with her, why she is going to school in the dark, but that thought is swept aside as she turns a corner and sees her school—her "sanctuary," even though the school is just a bunch of "nondescript portable classrooms." Then she sees the janitor, with his "unbelievable number of keys" jingling a greeting—and then her teacher, Mrs. LeSane. Note the colorful images (red coat, thin ice over puddles) and how Barry's dialogue helps make the passage more vivid and immediate, and thus carries readers along. Finally, notice how Barry's cartoon image helps tell the story: she's literally cradling her school, her sanctuary, in her arms—and with a smile on her face—as she declares, "I'm home."

Ways of telling a story

At this point, you should think about creating a scratch **OUTLINE** or **STORYBOARD** for your narrative. You might think of the narrative as a big arc, with a dramatic event or something else at the beginning that will get your audience's attention and then lead to the details—the what, who, where, when, how, and why of your story—and eventually to some kind of conclusion. Then plot points along this arc where you'll bring in particular information.

See Ch. 24 on ways of getting and keeping attention.

Begin in a way that will grab your audience's attention and hold it. Melissa Hicks starts with a single sentence: "In my house we have butter and margarine." It's a surprisingly simple statement, and one that gets our attention and keeps us reading.

Decide on a point of view. If you're writing about something that happened to you, your narrative should be written in first-person singular (*I, me*), as Lynda Barry does, on page 241. If, however, the narrative is about someone else, you'll probably want to use the third person (*he, she, they*). You might also consider organizing your narrative around changes in point of view, moving the story along through the eyes of different people.

Think about the details that will bring your story to life. What happened? When and where? Who was there? See how Lynda Barry tells us all that: how she was "walking to school in the dark," and saw her teacher and "ran toward her crying." And note the DESCRIPTIVE detail: the janitor's "unbelievable number of keys . . . jingling as he walked across the playfield," the teacher's "red coat," the "honor above all honors" of being asked to carry the teacher's purse. These are the kinds of concrete detail that bring a narrative to life, and make it one that readers will remember.

Think about how you'll move the story along. Most narratives are written in CHRONOLOGICAL ORDER, and in past tense, starting at the beginning and continuing straight through to the end. See how Melissa Hicks tells her story:

> For my fourteenth birthday I got a cow. I did not ask for a cow. I had very clearly asked for a horse. While every girl-child wants a horse, I felt that I had earned mine. I had worked at a farm down the road for the last two summers. I rode my bike to the stables. I would shovel the manure, feed the horses, ride for hours, and then pedal home exhausted. I knew how to take care of a horse. The life my family had worked and sweated for, clearing our little spot in the Maine woods, was . . . well suited to horse-raising. . . . The fact was, I didn't know beans about cows.

If you want readers to experience the narrative as very immediate, you might use the present tense. Here's Hicks later in the narrative, making butter:

> As my arms tire, I alter the motion. Instead of shaking the jar up and down, I go side to side. My youngest sister . . . asks for the jar. My mother, setting the milk back in the fridge, tells her to wait her turn.
>
> —MELISSA HICKS, "The High Price of Butter"

The present tense takes readers right into the scene: we are there with her as she does the hard work of making butter.

Conclude in a way that will leave your readers thinking. There are many good ways of concluding an essay, but in the case of a narrative, one especially good way is by saying why the story matters. Remember that a narrative essay needs to make a point, not simply tell a story. So your conclusion is when you can leave your readers thinking about that point. Read on now about various ways that three authors go about telling readers why their story matters—and why their readers should care.

See Ch. 24 on other ways of concluding.

Indicate why the story matters

Readers expect more from a personal narrative than just a good story. We want to know why the subject of the narrative matters to the author—and why those of us reading it should care. You can't assume that readers will know why your story matters, so you need to make that clear. There's no simple formula for how to do that, other than to say what *not* to do: don't simply *say* why it matters. Let's see how some of the authors in this chapter show us why their story matters.

In her essay about how school was a "sanctuary" for her, Lynda Barry writes about more than just herself, noting that while we know that "a good education system saves lives," we are still told that "cutting the budget for public schools is necessary, that poor salaries for teachers are all we can manage." She wants to change our minds about that. Here's how she concludes her essay:

> The best arguments in the world won't change a person's mind. The only thing that can do that is a good story.
> RICHARD POWERS, *The Overstory*

> Mrs. LeSane asked us to please stand, face the flag, place our right hands over our hearts and say the Pledge of Allegiance. Children across the country do it faithfully. I wonder now when the country will face its children and say a pledge right back.
>
> —LYNDA BARRY, "The Sanctuary of School"

And here's how Melissa Hicks shows us why her essay is about more than just the price of butter:

> To me the cost of butter is more than a price tag. The cost of butter reminds me of my childhood, and how my family struggled to be pioneers in the twentieth century. The cost of butter reminds me of the value of hard work, and how that brought my family together. . . . Yet the cost of butter is more than a symbol of hard work and quality. The fact that I buy it is an affirmation of my own choices in life. Because of my childhood, I know the cost in sweat of butter. As an adult, I choose to pay that price in cash.
>
> —MELISSA HICKS, "The High Price of Butter"

Finally, here's high school teacher Brent Peters, near the end of a book about a food literacy program he and colleagues developed, reflecting on the larger meaning of their work:

> Working in the garden, I know I am just a steward. In that space, students have found passions, developed a love for learning, grieved while hugging chickens, shared meals, learned how to use tools, discovered what it means to build, cut themselves and bled, been trusted with dangerous things, laughed with one another, and seen the progress of their work, whether it grew green out of the ground, came together with screws, became palatable with fire, or returned to the earth through decay. I am there to keep those sacred things safe and to tell the stories that make them sacred. Each time we go there now, students know the garden is a special place. One can't help but recognize the passion, thought, and time that has made it a landscape of expressed learning and compassion.
>
> —JOSEPH FRANZEN and BRENT PETERS, *Say Yes to Pears*

In all three of these examples, the writers show just why their story matters, why it's important to them and should be to us as well.

Read your draft with a critical eye, get response—and revise

Once you have a draft, ask others to read it over and talk with you about it. Ask them to be frank: What did they get out of your story? Was anything confusing? What did they like best? Did they find it engaging? easy to follow? Try to get response from people who represent your intended audience—and some who might not: Now's the time to hear as many diverse perspectives as possible. Now's the time to do so!

Eventually, of course, you need to be your own best critic. After all, you know what you were aiming for. So get out your magnifying glass, and take a very close look at what you've produced.

- How will the OPENING capture the audience's attention and make them want to read on? How else could the narrative begin?

- How well has the scene for the story been DESCRIBED? Is it clear when and where the story takes place?

- If there are shifts in time in your story, are they signaled by the use of different verb tenses?

- Will readers be able to follow the narrative easily? Are there TRANSITIONS from one part of the story to the next? If not, should there be?

- What vivid details help the story come alive?

- Does the narrative include dialogue or direct quotation? If not, should you add some?

- Are there any VISUALS? If so, what do they contribute to the narrative? If not, would adding some help carry the story along?

- How would you describe the TONE, and what words, visuals, or other elements help establish that tone? Will the AUDIENCE you want to reach find this tone engaging?

- Is the point or significance of the story clear? What makes it clear? Have you stated it explicitly—and if not, should you do so?

- How does the narrative CONCLUDE? What does it leave readers thinking? How else might it end?

- Try to come up with a TITLE that will readers' attention, and make them want to read what you've written.

Now's the time to REVISE. If you've analyzed your draft and gotten advice from others, you've got a plan. You know what you need to do, and what you *want* to do. So now's your chance! But remember that you're writing a NARRATIVE: you're telling a story. And you're telling it to an AUDIENCE, and they will want to know *why* you're telling this story. Be sure to tell them why the story matters to you—and why it might matter to them.

REFLECT! "Tell me a fact and I'll learn. Tell me the truth and I'll believe. But tell me a story and it will live in my heart forever." This **Native American proverb** sets a high standard for the stories we tell. Think of a story that has stayed with you for a long time. What made it so memorable: the subject? the way the story was told? the message? Then write a paragraph or so about what makes a narrative live on "forever."

A STUDENT NARRATIVE

YAZMIN CARBAJAL
Living the Narrative My Abuelita Wrote

Yazmin Carbajal is a student at Sonoma State University, California, where she is studying business marketing and Spanish. She met Andrea Lunsford in a writing workshop at her high school and wrote this narrative specifically for Let's Talk.

Who would you say has influenced your life in a permanent way or perhaps even created a narrative that your family has lived out or lived up to? In my case, the answers to these questions go back a long way. Ever since I can remember, my parents—especially my dad—have encouraged me and my siblings to get a college education. My dad's immigration status prevented him from pursuing some employment opportunities, but even so, he has always told me that it is possible to dream big and achieve my goals by working hard. But where did his values and beliefs come from? They are all part of the story that my abuelita—my grandma—told my dad and then me, and that I hope to tell the next few generations.

The title gets our attention—how is the writer living the narrative?—and the first sentence asks a question that draws us in.

I currently attend Sonoma State University, studying business marketing and Spanish, with a plan to graduate in 2026. As a first-generation student, I have faced and continue to face many obstacles, and I constantly have to battle the feeling that I don't belong. There are moments when I think I'm the only one who finds my accounting class material unclear or confusing, but then I remember that my dad and grandma always told me that I would never learn to conquer obstacles without a little uncertainty or hardship. When they came to an unknown country in the hope of a better life, they had to not only conquer their fears but also overcome a language barrier, and they had to find a way to live in a country where they were often faced with ridicule.

Provides background information to help readers follow the story.

Points out one reason the narrative is so important.

One-word sentence ("Right!") helps establish a friendly tone.

Flashback to her grandmother's youth provides poignant details that explain her character. Notice the shift to past tense.

I want to lead by example, just like my grandmother did, since I have siblings who look up to me in the same way that her siblings looked up to her. So when it came time to think about college, and how to ease the financial strain on my family, I thought, "What would Grandma do?" Right! I made a list of all the scholarships I qualified for during my final year of high school and started applying for them, hoping they would help me reach my goal. For me and my siblings, getting an education means everything, since my grandparents and parents never had the opportunity to do so. You might wonder why I've been so determined to pursue a college degree, but the reason is pretty simple: it's because of my grandmother's unwavering desire to provide a better life for us. Without her, our lives here in the United States would not have existed.

But I'm getting ahead of myself, so let's back up and meet my grandma, Juana Ramirez, who was born in San Pedro Cahro, Mexico. As a girl, my grandmother worked to provide for her siblings and her parents by taking on small jobs and even cooking for other families just to get the leftover food. Taking on grown-up responsibilities made her want to write a new story for herself and her family: she didn't want them to struggle the way she had to. In fact, she intended to support them! She had a dream, and her mind was made up. She was determined to rewrite the family's future by finding a way to move to the United States with my dad and all my uncles. My grandpa Antonio was already in California a couple months out of the year, taking on odd jobs and working in the fields to provide for his family. But before Grandpa had even thought about bringing my dad and all five of his brothers to California, Grandma had already made up her mind: our family would join him there. And so they did.

In February of 1994, with that dream still strong in her heart, my grandma and her family set out for the United States, making the long voyage by bus from San Pedro Cahro to Guadalajara, where they took a flight to Tijuana. Once they landed in Tijuana, they were greeted by my grandma's brother Esteban, who then drove her and my uncles to Madera, California. A couple days later, one of my grandma's sisters, Laura, drove them north to the small town of Gualala, California, where they settled in, the brothers sharing a single room and taking turns sleeping on the floor in a tiny two-bedroom apartment. Through some pretty rough times—when they had to deal with poor wages, and a major language barrier—my grandma never gave up. She was creating the new life she had always dreamed of.

My grandma always had a plan. When Esteban picked up the family in Tijuana—my grandma along with my dad, and my uncles Antonio, Jorge, Javier, Gustavo, and Oscar, he laughed and asked, "What are you going to do with all these kids?" My grandma just smiled back and said, "You'll see what I'll do with my basket of eggs!" That was Grandma's way of telling him that she had a plan, a story all worked out for our family. It was a narrative she had been creating from the moment she decided to be everything our family needed, both physically and financially. She steeled herself to be encouraging, to instill in us her work ethic, and to push us to dream big—writing the story of how we were going to fulfill her goals and create dreams of our own.

Dialogue helps bring the story to life, as does the metaphor of the basket of eggs.

But she didn't stop there. Although the family had no experience whatsoever with restaurants, my grandmother decided they should start one, urging my uncles to take a risk and start a restaurant of their own—and some years later, she encouraged my uncles to buy property; instead of renting, they would be owners. On her Mexican food nights, the restaurant would be bursting with people waiting to try her food—enchiladas, albondigas, posole, carne en chile—and wanting to come back for more. Her cooking became a way to connect with the community and bring together our family and so many other families. For many years now, my family has owned and operated a popular restaurant in our community, where locals and visitors alike come to socialize and where they can count on getting a friendly greeting—and some very good food.

The food names remind readers that the family's Mexican culture is alive and well!

Juana Ramirez, 1972 (left); high school graduation (right): "Thanks to my family for your support, love, and sacrifice. This is for you."

As I look back, I know that we would not have made the choices or the decisions we did if it weren't for Grandma's unwavering support and fierce perseverance. She made sure to instill tenacity in us and to challenge us to add our dreams to hers. That's one big reason that when I graduated from high school, with my own dreams of higher education about to come true, my grandma's photo was with me on my graduation cap. And it's the reason she will continue to guide me as I complete college and launch my own career.

My abuelita wrote our family story and gave us the inspiration and strength to dream big and without fear. *Todos nuestros logros son para ella*: All of our achievements for her.

Conclusion reiterates her point and echoes her title. Use of 2 languages echoes the focus on 2 countries and 2 cultures.

Thinking about the Text

1. Yazmin Carbajal draws on personal experience to support her CLAIM that her pursuit of education and a better life for her family is a reflection of her grandmother's persistence and determination. Do you see any places in her narrative where she could have reached beyond her own experience to bring in information from other sources? If so, what kind of information would that be, and do you think it would strengthen her essay, or might it distract from the focus of the narrative? Explain your reasoning.

2. Identify the EMOTIONAL APPEALS Carbajal uses in this narrative. Which ones do you find most effective, and why?

3. Carbajal chooses not to organize her essay CHRONOLOGICALLY, but rather moves back and forth in time. Re-read the essay paying attention to those time changes: What effect do they have on your reading of the essay? Do they make it more engaging? easier (or harder) to follow? How else could she have organized her narrative?

4. Carbajal's essay includes two direct quotations, her uncle's question and her grandma's response. Why do you think she chose to use direct quotations in that particular passage? Do you see other places in the narrative where direct quotations might have been effective?

5. The pursuit of higher education as one way to lead to a better life is the driving force in Yazmin Carbajal's narrative, one she says she inherited from her grandmother. Think about one or more guiding forces in your life. Who or what has helped to shape the story of your life? Then write a brief NARRATIVE that introduces and explains what is driving the story of your life.

14 Reviewing

Reviewing makes of reading a participation sport,
not a spectator sport.

—PATRICIA HAMPL

We are inundated with reviews, every day, everywhere, in print, audio, and digital. Think *TikTok*, where influencers review products 24/7. Or think of the reviews of movies, TV shows, books, music, restaurants, and countless products we encounter on a daily basis. You may well have done some reviewing yourself, perhaps on *Reddit* or *Amazon*. If not, read on.

Imagine having the power to guide someone toward a favorite new book, a totally binge-worthy TV series, or a great new Thai restaurant—with just your written words. That's the kind of power you can have when you write a review. Say you want to convince a friend to check out *Bluey*, the cartoon about a family of dogs in Australia. "Really?" says your friend. "Yes, really," you reply, and go on to explain that it's about a puppy named Bluey and her sister Bingo and their parents Bandit and Chilli—and that it's the most hilarious, clever, and comforting cartoon you've ever seen. Ryan Gosling loves it! So does your dog!

Whether or not you convince your friend, what you've done is to provide a brief review of the show: describing it (a cartoon about a family of dogs), giving some reasons to support your claim that it's a must-see series (it's hilarious, clever, and comforting; famous people love it, and so do dogs), and implying that your friend will love it too. You could go on to produce a more formal written review, setting out additional reasons for the show's success, giving examples that support those reasons, and concluding with an invitation to check it out.

In fact, you may find yourself writing reviews in your classes, from a review of a lecture you are assigned to attend for a *history* course to a review of several experimental studies for *biology*. And in many courses, you may be assigned to write a LITERATURE REVIEW of important research done on a particular subject. In each case, you'll need to describe what you are reviewing, set forth the criteria you

Bluey's sister chases Bandit.

used to assess it, provide examples and good reasons to support your review, and explain why it matters. This chapter aims to get you thinking about the opportunities you will have as a reviewer, and to serve as a handy and helpful guide as you do so.

A GUIDE TO DEVELOPING A REVIEW

For any review you are writing, in any medium and in any genre, you will need to think about the audience you want to reach and what background information you should provide to help them understand your review. You'll also need to think carefully about the CRITERIA you'll use to evaluate whatever you're reviewing, and the EVIDENCE you'll need to provide to support your review.

Choose a subject that intrigues you

Sometimes, the subject of a review will be assigned by your instructor. If so, look for some aspect of the subject that grabs your attention or for an angle that matters to you. Say you are assigned to write a restaurant review: you can make it fit your interests by thinking about what kind of cuisine you would most like to try out for the review—the supposedly best burger joint in town? a favorite food truck? a new vegan restaurant? The more you feel connected to the topic, the more you'll engage with what you write. If you're free to choose the subject of your review, think about what you would most like to learn about: kinds of bikes that would be most useful for getting around a sprawling campus? a new book that everyone seems to be reading? an indie film that's attracted widespread praise, and criticism? In any case, spend some time choosing a subject that you'll want to spend time thinking about.

Think about your rhetorical situation

Once you've settled on a specific subject for your review, it's time to think about the audience you want to reach and the other elements of your rhetorical situation.

Purpose. What purpose will your review serve? Will you be review-ing something in order to decide whether to recommend it (or not)? Or are you simply aiming to evaluate it, decide whether it's good, interesting, trustworthy, or something else? What do you want your audience to do in response to your review: Buy a product and help spread the word about it? Attend an event? Form an opinion, or change their mind about the subject? Maybe just have a good laugh? What can you do to make sure you achieve your purpose?

Audience. Who will read (or watch, or listen to) your review, and what do you know about them? What are they likely to know or think about the subject of your review, and what information about it will you need to provide? What values do they hold and what kinds of appeals are they most likely to respond to? What criteria of evaluation will they most likely look favorably on—or disregard? Do you think they will be interested in your subject? If not, how can you get them interested?

Stance. How do you want to come across to your audience—as knowledgeable about the subject? intrigued by the subject and wanting to explore it? a consumer who wants to share information? an advocate for an important issue? How will you go about estab-lishing this stance?

Context. What have others said about your subject? What are the varying perspectives on it? And what about the context you are writing in: When is your review due? How much and what kind of research may you need to do? Who can you consult for advice?

Language. As with most kinds of writing, the language you use will depend on what best suits your purpose and audience. Think about what expectations or needs your audience may have with regard to language. Sometimes the subject of your review will lead you to use certain languages or dialects—using some Spanish in a review of a new taqueria, for example.

See Ch. 26 for guidance on thinking about your use of language and dialects.

Medium and design. How will you distribute your review—in print? online? as an oral presentation? And how do your media affect the way you design your text? What design decisions do you need to make about layout, use of color and images, charts or graphs, video or audio clips, possibly even animation? What will each add to the overall effectiveness of your review?

Explore your subject

The more you know about the subject of your review, the more likely you will be able to evaluate it thoughtfully and make recommendations to your readers about it.

Look closely at your subject

If you're reviewing a film, watch it; if you're reviewing a gadget, use it; if you're reviewing a story, read it. Jot down notes about what you already know about what you are reviewing and what you find most impressive or memorable about it, including any quotations you may want to use. Then make a list of questions you have about it. Most of all, look closely, more than one time, at whatever you are reviewing: re-read, re-observe, re-examine it from various angles, making sure you know it well.

Do some research

In most cases, the subject of your review will be your primary source, but you should also find out what others have said about it. You may also need to learn more about the topic in order to write about it yourself. If you are reviewing a film, for instance, you might need to learn more about the director, or where the film was shot, or how the special effects were conceived and executed.

Consider multiple perspectives

Try to find out what many others have had to say about your subject. For a film review, you can search for reviews from a range of sources, from quick takes noted on *Rotten Tomatoes* to full-length reviews in newspapers or magazines. If you find contradictory or controversial views, all the better. Think about what they say, and about how they affect what you then will say.

Provide relevant background information

You'll need to provide enough information about the subject of your review so that your audience can understand and follow the review. What's "enough" will depend on your rhetorical situation. If readers are likely to be familiar with what you are reviewing, you may need just a sentence or two; if not, you'll need to tell them enough about the film or music or book or whatever so they can follow what you say about it.

Sometimes you'll want to include an image, or a link to audio or video clips. In an article about why *Gilmore Girls* is still so popular almost twenty years after it first aired, journalist Saul Austerlitz briefly summarizes what the show is about for readers who include both those who've been watching it for years and those who were not even born when that show first aired:

> [*Gilmore Girls* tells] the story of a bookish teenage girl whose best friend is her 30-something mother. The backdrop is an idyllic Connecticut town full of oddballs and eccentrics, and the tone is a blend of character-driven comedy and drama, all set to a screwball pace.

Lorelai Gilmore (front row, in the red sweater) next to her daughter Rory and the rest of their family and friends in *Gilmore Girls*.

And he provides some detail to give a sense of what makes the Gilmore girls "eccentric," detail that will help those who haven't seen the show follow his review:

> Popular culture was the lifeblood of the series. . . . A single episode might reference Nikolai Gogol, *The Brady Bunch*, the punk band Agnostic Front, the Velvet Underground, *Fiddler on the Roof*, David Hockney, and the Franco-Prussian War.
>
> —SAUL AUSTERLITZ, "Why *Gilmore Girls* Endures"

Establish criteria for evaluating your subject

Reviews need to be based on clear criteria, standards you can use to evaluate your subject. Sometimes the criteria will be obvious: if you are evaluating a film, such criteria might include the quality of the directing, the acting, the cinematography, any special effects, and so on. But in some cases, your criteria will be shaped by your audience or purpose. If you were writing a review of *Barbie* for a sociology class, you'd more likely focus on what it says about gender, class, consumerism, and so forth. As you work to develop the criteria for your review, you might want to check out other reviews of the same subject to see what criteria they use. One other approach is to sum up your initial evaluation of your subject in a few words and then to list the reasons you have for that evaluation; those reasons can very likely be stated as criteria.

Take a look at a recent review of some headphones published in *The Verge*, which states the criteria near the beginning of the review:

> No matter how you're using them, the criteria for picking the best noise-canceling headphones haven't changed.
>
> | | |
> |---|---|
> | Comfort | Battery life |
> | Noise cancellation | Multipoint pairing |
> | Sound quality | Bonus features |
>
> The "best" headphones for you will differ based on which of those factors you prioritize and care about most, but our overall pick for

the best noise-canceling headphones remains Sony's WH-1000XM5. They offer a combination of sound quality, comfort, and great noise cancellation that's hard to beat.

—*The Verge*

Notice that while this review provides clear criteria, it also tells readers that they will be the final deciders: the particular criteria that are most important to them should be the ones that govern their decision to buy, or not buy.

Or consider part of a review of Beyoncé's 2023 *Renaissance* tour. Writing in *Esquire,* Bria McNeal calls this tour Beyoncé's "greatest achievement," noting several criteria for that claim, including that "it's an athletic feat, a work of art, and even a pseudo-communion." On that last point, McNeal describes the atmosphere of the concert as being communal, almost like a family reunion:

The whole thing exudes rich aunt energy. Pure fun. No rules. And the atmosphere? Well, it's like a reunion. After all, the last time the Beyhive convened was during 2016's Formation Tour.

Three fans arrive early for Beyoncé's Renaissance concert. Landover, Maryland. 2023.

You know that moment at a family party, when you see someone you don't recognize, but feel an intrinsic connection to? That's what attending *Renaissance* is like. Everyone is a stranger, yet also a cousin. I suppose that makes Beyoncé our matriarch. Just ask the troves of fans yelling "Mother!" during her set.

—BRIA McNEAL, "Beyoncé's Renaissance Tour
Is Her Greatest Achievement"

Elsewhere in the review, McNeal offers support for two other criteria, demonstrating Beyoncé's athleticism and artfulness. These attributes, along with the strong sense of community, help us understand why McNeal concludes that this concert tour is the singer's "greatest achievement." You may agree with McNeal's assessment, or maybe you do not; but Beyoncé has additional tours in her projected trilogy, so you may even have the opportunity to reconsider what you think, and perhaps to write your own review.

Read Bria McNeal's review at letstalklibrary.com.

Decide what your review will claim about your subject

The criteria you've established will help you decide what you think about your subject and figure out what you want to claim about it. Your claim may be primarily evaluative: the best film that you've seen all year—or the worst, or good in some ways and not so good in others. Or your review may focus on something *about* your subject—for example, on why an old TV show is once again popular, twenty years after it last aired; or how a new device improves on other similar devices. Whatever your focus, now's the time to start thinking about how you'll be able to support what you claim. It's one thing to say to a friend that "*Poor Things* is the worst film I've seen in a long time" and another to write a review of the film that goes on to offer support for what you say. Once you've got an idea about your claim and how you'll support it, try writing it out as a preliminary THESIS statement.

Here's a claim that critic Mike Scott made about the film *Killers of the Flower Moon*:

> Armed with a strong vision, a great ensemble cast and a compelling story, 81-year-old Martin Scorsese does in his *Flower Moon* what he can be counted on to always do: deliver one of the most well-told stories of the year.
>
> —MIKE SCOTT, *The Times-Picayune*

Note that this claim contains the three specific criteria Scott used to come to his judgment: "a strong vision, a great ensemble cast, and a compelling story."

Think about whether you need to qualify your claim

Few if any subjects are all good or all bad, so you will want to think carefully about qualifying what you claim. *Poor Things* might have a few good qualities going for it after all—for example: Emma Stone's Oscar-winning performance, the costumes and sets, the dance scene with Stone and Mark Ruffalo! So you might qualify what your claim to say "In spite of some plot inconsistencies and a lot of gratuitous sex, *Poor Things* is worth seeing for the costumes and sets, Emma Stone's Oscar-winning performance, and especially the dazzling dance scene with Stone and Mark Ruffalo."

Watch Emma Stone and Mark Ruffalo dance at letstalklibrary.com!

Consider perspectives other than yours

As you develop the overall claim you want to make, remember to consider alternative points of view. Others may have quite different views on your subject, so you need to think about them, decide which ones you should acknowledge in your review, and how you want to respond to them. Here's a question that film analyst David Chen asks in his review of *Flower Moon*:

> So *Killers of the Flower Moon* is an incredible movie about awful white people doing terrible things. . . . But to what end?
>
> —DAVID CHEN, *decodingeverything.com*

Read David Chen's review at letstalklibrary.com.

From *Killers of the Flower Moon*, Mollie Kyle (played by Lily Gladstone) sits with her sisters.

To answer that question, he takes into consideration the views of Osage language consultant Christopher Côté, whose reaction to that film went viral:

> As an Osage, I really wanted this to be from the perspective of Mollie and what her family experienced, but I think it would take an Osage to do that. Martin Scorsese, not being Osage, I think he did a great job representing our people, but this history is being told from the perspective of [a white man] Ernest Burkhart.
>
> —CHRISTOPHER CÔTÉ

These comments, and those of several other indigenous reviewers, lead Chen to agree that

> *Killers* is ultimately a movie from a white perspective, centering the feelings of white people who are involved in committing atrocities against people of color.
>
> —DAVID CHEN

Chen takes these comments to heart in his review, fully acknowledging them. Yet he concludes the review by saying that in spite of very clear "qualms" about the movie, his ultimate judgment is that Scorsese is "one of the greatest filmmakers . . . still making work as vibrant as ever at the age of 80."

Provide good reasons and evidence to support your claim

Developing strong criteria for evaluation and crafting a clear claim to anchor your review are crucial steps. But any claim will only be persuasive if you support it with good reasons and verifiable evidence. Here is broadcast journalist Anderson Cooper making a claim about the graphic memoir by Canadian artist and cartoonist Maurice Vellekoop that tells the story of growing up gay in Toronto:

> *I'm So Glad We Had This Time Together* is that rarest of things: a book about coming out to a loving yet conservative family that is as heartrending to read as it is to look at. It's an incredibly moving, funny, and ultimately triumphant account (spoiler alert!) of what can only be described as a magical fairy tale (pun totally intended).
>
> —ANDERSON COOPER

This recommendation appears on the *Amazon* page advertising the memoir—the kind of brief recommendation you will see on the back covers of many books. Were Cooper to go on to write a complete review of Vellekoop's memoir, he would need to provide evidence to support the reasons he gives for recommending the memoir: that it is "moving" and "funny" and "triumphant." In this case, such evidence could come, first of all, from the memoir itself, but also from what critics have had to say about the book, from readers' comments about it, or from Anderson's own personal experience.

See pp. 51–58 and 61–65 for examples and advice on using various kinds of evidence.

Now take a look at how cartoonist Irene Velentzas opens her review of another graphic memoir, *Family Style: Memories of an American from Vietnam,* by Thien Pham:

> What forces bind us together? Are they biological, cultural, shared experiences? Are they forces tangible or intangible? Good or ill? These are the questions at the heart of Thien Pham's *Family Style*, a poignant and disarmingly humorous graphic memoir about Pham's formative refugee experience. According to the UN Refugee Agency (UNHCR), during 2022, 108.4 million people were "forcibly displaced" around the globe due to "persecution,

conflict, violence, [or] human rights violations," 35.3 million of which were refugees. A whopping 43.3 million of these displaced persons were children, a number that's doubled in the past decade alone per UNICEF; this is equivalent to about 13% of the population of the United States. In 2022, the US resettled about 25,500 refugees through its Refugee Admissions Program, a rate dramatically lower than its 125,000-spot maximum. It's difficult to care about one statistic among many, but *Family Style* takes what might have otherwise remained a faceless number and turns it back a living breathing human being. Cleverly disguised as a food memoir, the book tells a compelling story about the structures—both large and small—that hold society together, and how they can collectively nourish or malnourish us.

—IRENE VELENTZAS

Velentzas begins with several questions, which she says are "at the heart" of *Family Style*, a book she claims takes a "poignant" and "disarmingly humorous" look at refugee experience. She then introduces statistical evidence from several sources that underscores the enormous problems faced by refugees, asking readers to consider the dire seriousness of Pham's subject and supports the major claim of her review, that the book "tells a compelling story about the structures—both large and small—that hold society together."

Further along in the review, Velentzas focuses on a small but powerful "structure" that nourishes young Thien: a magnet. Hoping to win this treasure in a game of "throwing slippers" that children play in the refugee camp, he instead wins a friend, who later gives him the magnet:

Young Thien, with his magnet.

When his family also arrives in the US, as he struggles to find the words to connect to his new world, *magnet* becomes one of the first English words Thien learns—a word he shares with his mother. Pham's repeated image of Thien sticking a steel washer to the magnet elegantly echoes the image of his mother holding onto him.

In this passage, Velentzas offers evidence from the memoir itself to back up her claim, noting that interweaving the small detail of the magnet through the story adds to the poignancy she mentioned earlier and helps build connections that "hold society together."

Consider the ethical aspects of your review

Words have consequences. And the words of reviewers can have more consequences than most. That's why it is so important that you really know what you are talking about, and that the information you share is accurate and fair-minded. Reviewers wield considerable power! Tom Shales, a TV analyst for the *Washington Post* for decades, once said that reviews could make or break a series. As a colleague noted after Shales's death, he "struck terror in the greedy hearts of TV executives while delighting countless dazzled readers."

Terrorizing greedy executives is one thing, but hurting the feelings of students in a high school musical or of a classmate whose essay you're reviewing is another matter altogether. As a reviewer, you will have power, and you need to use it responsibly—to keep in mind the feelings of whoever created or contributed to whatever you're reviewing. That's not to say you should offer only praise, but that you need to think about how your words will affect others.

Jesse Green, chief theater critic for the *New York Times*, may well have had the feelings of those he was writing about in mind when he reviewed the musical *How to Dance in Ohio*. Here's how he opened his review:

> It would have been enough of a first for a Broadway musical to tell a respectful or even vaguely authentic story about autistic people. . . . So it is a welcome change that the seven autistic characters in *How to Dance in Ohio* are presented, without condescension, as young adults a lot like most others, albeit with unusual gifts and challenges. That they are also played by autistic performers makes the feel-good show, which opened on Sunday at the Belasco Theater, more than a first: It's a milestone.

> —JESSE GREEN, "In *How to Dance in Ohio*, Making Autism Sing"

The opening scene in *How to Dance in Ohio*. New York. 2023.

Green goes on to praise the actors and the music, but he also has criticisms to offer, saying that the show is "very conventional, sometimes dispiritingly so" and that its focus on "cheerful persuasion" comes at the expense of the "depth and complexity" it could have aimed for. Still, Green's tone is respectful and evenhanded, even in his most critical comments.

How to Dance in Ohio got plenty of kudos for casting actors who were themselves autistic from people who wrote reviews of their own or responded to those written by others. But it also elicited some potent criticism. Here is one person, responding on *Reddit*, who has ethical questions about the production:

> My only problem is, neither of the two writers for the musical is autistic. In my opinion, writing a story about what it's like being autistic and not actually having gone through the daily experience seems fundamentally wrong, even if there was a ton of research and consulting done on their end.

Others disagreed:

> I'm autistic, and I think that it's okay for neurotypical writers to write autistic characters if they put in the research. The fact that there are

> so many autistic people on the creative team, including consultants, is a good sign. I don't like the idea of limiting the kinds of stories we can tell just because we haven't lived particular experiences.

There are no clear-cut right or wrong answers to questions like the ones raised here: the issue for you as a reviewer is to anticipate such questions and think hard about how your words will affect others. And remember that when you are peer-reviewing something written by one of your classmates, you want to be honest in your assessment but to keep in mind that you're addressing a real live person who has feelings.

Ethical issues abound on *TikTok*. Just take a look at all those influencers shouting out for your attention about things they are essentially reviewing. Sometimes they will have done careful research, considered ethical implications, and worked hard to produce a video review that is fun, well informed, and based on solid evidence. But not always. They may be writing about something they're being paid to review and may or may not know (or care) much about the products they are reviewing.

You may have occasion to post some *TikTok* video reviews yourself, and if so, you'll need to think about your ethical responsibilities: to your audience, those who will view your video, to those who created what you are reviewing. And to yourself: What does your review say about you, your values, and your credibility?

REFLECT! How much of what you watch on *TikTok* is a review of one kind or another? Are there influencers that you follow? Take some time to track and take notes on what and who you are watching: What attracts you to these posts or videos? What holds your attention, and why? How much do you trust the people who made the videos, and why or why not? Do any of the video reviews raise ethical questions for you, and if so, how do such questions affect your overall response to what they say?

Ways of organizing a review

You've got a claim and lots of good reasons and evidence to support it: a big stack of notes. Now what? You've wished for a fairy godmother to wave a wand and organize the review for you. Apparently she's taken the day off—you're on your own! But we can help. We looked at dozens of student reviews of Beyoncé's and Taylor Swift's albums and concerts and noticed two ways they were often organized.

Some students open with a personal anecdote about how they first heard an album or attended a concert, showing how they were personally connected to the artist and her music, which then led up to their claim and the criteria for their evaluation. Then they organized the rest of the review systematically, song by song, evaluating each one to showing how it supported their claim. To conclude, many of these students returned to the personal note they began with, reflecting on the concert or music or looking forward to what the artist might do next.

Other students started right off with a claim, often stated as a thesis, and then organized the rest of the review around the criteria for their evaluation, using features of particular songs to illustrate and support each of the criteria. These writers then tended to conclude by pulling together all the evidence to reiterate their claim.

Of the many reviews we read, well over half included images, most often of Swift or Beyoncé in costume but others of the sets or special effects. Photos can act like exclamation points in a review, riveting the attention of readers and providing visual support for the claim. If you use visuals in your review, remember to caption each one and to introduce it in the text of your review to let readers know how it supports the points you are making.

Read your draft with a critical eye, get response—and revise

Once we're finished with a draft, we're tempted to congratulate ourselves and go out for ice cream. But not so fast. While it's good to let a draft sit for a little while so that you can clear your head and come back to it with fresh eyes, getting response to what you've written is one key to success. You may be in a peer group in your class, and if so they can give you helpful feedback. Your instructor may also give you some pointers on how to revise the draft. In addition, why not ask a couple of friends you trust to be honest and helpful to read and respond to what you have written. Seeing your draft through other people's eyes will help you read and revise. Here are some questions that can help you or someone else look at your draft with a critical eye:

- How does your OPENING grab and hold your audience's attention? Does it let them know what the review is about—and why it matters? What other openings might you consider?

- Is your CLAIM stated explicitly, as a thesis? If not, why not—and should it be?

- What do you do to establish your CREDIBILITY, to let the audience know you can be trusted to give an accurate and fair review?

- Have you provided background information SUMMARIZING or DESCRIBING the subject of your review well enough for your audience to understand it and follow your reasoning?

- What CRITERIA have you established for your review, and have you stated them explicitly in your draft? Have you forgotten any important criteria?

- What REASONS and EVIDENCE have you provided to support your claim? Can you provide anything more?

- Have you considered any COUNTERARGUMENTS or perspectives in addition to your own? If so, how have you responded to them?

- How would you describe your STANCE and TONE? What words and phrases signal the stance and tone?

- How is your draft organized? Do you state your criteria one by one along with the pertinent reasons and evidence? Or do you focus mostly on your reasons and evidence? Which would be better for your subject and audience?

- What kind of **LANGUAGE** have you used? Is there reason to use any languages other than English? Any dialects that would speak to your audience? And how would you describe your style overall—formal? informal? friendly? what else?

- Have you included any photos or other images, and if not, should you? How do (or would) they support your argument?

- Are there any ethical issues with the subject of this review, and have you been fair to all concerned?

- How does your review **CONCLUDE**? What do you leave your readers thinking about? How else might it conclude?

REFLECT! How much of what you watch on *TikTok* is a review of one kind or another? Are there influencers that you follow? Take some time to track and take notes on what and who you are watching: What attracts you to these posts or videos? What holds your attention, and why? How much do you trust the people who made the videos, and why or why not? Do any of the video reviews raise ethical questions for you, and if so, how do such questions affect your overall response to what they say?

A STUDENT REVIEW

AUDREY ASHDOWN

There's a New Girl in Town—and She's Still Here!

Audrey Ashdown was a sophomore at Appalachian State University in North Carolina when she wrote this review specifically for this book. A psychology major and a member of the a cappella group Treble Attraction, she plans to pursue a graduate degree in psychology in order to help children and adolescents struggling with OCD.

> "It's a weird life but it's where I'm at right now."
> —Nick Miller, in *New Girl*

New Girl, a Fox sitcom that aired from 2011 to 2018, was a big hit, gathering a robust fanbase, racking up eleven Emmys, and getting accolades for what a *New York Times* critic calls its comedic consistency (Lyons). But then it ended—or did it? Today, seven years after the series closed up shop, it's arguably more popular than ever, with 155,000 subreddit followers, ten of whom are online as I write this. I myself have watched the streaming show numerous times—and that's coming from someone who barely has the attention span to watch a show once, let alone over and over again. So I set out to examine why *New Girl* has attracted such an enthusiastic and loyal audience.

    I didn't watch *New Girl* when the show was actually airing, discovering it only after its final season had ended. But soon enough, I was hooked. Getting to know the *"new girl"* Jess (Zooey Deschanel) as she moves in with three single guys—classic underachiever Nick (Jake Johnson), obsessive wannabe cool guy Schmidt (Max Greenfield), and lovable goofball Winston (Lamorne Morris)—soon had me feeling like one of the family. Even though all the characters, including Jess's best friend Cece (Hannah Simone) and part-time roommate Coach (Damon Wayans Jr.), use flip phones and watch DVDs, I can relate to the challenges they face and the joys they share without getting caught up in the disconnect between the time the show was set and the time when I am watching.

Taking a tip from the opening to this chapter, the author includes an intriguing epigraph.

Cites statistics supporting her major claim.

Notes the question that inspired her research and her purpose—to answer this question.

Reveals her stance on this topic: she's a fan.

Introduces first reason (and criterion) for the show's ongoing popularity.

This brings me to my first reason for *New Girl*'s ongoing popularity: it can be enjoyed by people of all generations. The show is defined not by the time in which it is set but rather by its themes of friendship, "found family," and coming of age, all of which are timeless aspects of the human experience. At the beginning of the first season, the characters are all in their early thirties, but even as a fourteen-year-old, I still saw myself in them. As I've gotten older, I've come to appreciate the show even more as I'm now learning how to be an adult alongside some of my favorite characters. Recently, I even showed a compilation of *New Girl*'s funniest scenes to my great-aunt, who laughed with me despite our sixty-five-year age gap.

Clearly, *New Girl* is beloved by a broad audience, in large part due to the universal themes that resonate throughout the main characters' wild adventures. Thanks to the outstanding writing of Elizabeth Meriwether and the improvisational chops of the six main actors, every episode puts the characters in ridiculous (and hilarious) situations. Taken at surface level, the happenings of each episode might seem like a clever script written merely to get a laugh. But look deeper, and the plot of just about every episode relates to a bigger, heartwarming theme or a growth opportunity for the characters.

From the left: Winston, Schmidt, Cece, Jess, and Nick in *New Girl*.

Take, for example, "Background Check," episode 6 of season 4, which is arguably one of the funniest and most chaotic *New Girl* episodes. When Winston, who is in training at the police academy, informs everyone in the loft that an officer is coming over to do his background check, Jess confesses to the others that she has a bag of meth in her closet. In their scramble to figure out how to get rid of it, Jess throws the bag, which explodes all over the apartment minutes before the officer comes in. Jess then stuffs some of the drugs into her bra; Cece flushes the rest of them in the toilet and floods the bathroom; Nick confesses his most embarrassing moments to the officer in an attempt to distract her; and Coach, hoping to convince the officer that Winston contributes positively to the community, finds a random man to pretend to be Winston's teenage brother from the Boys & Girls Club. When Winston finds out what's going on, Jess says that she didn't tell him about the meth because she never imagined him making it this far in his police training. Just as Winston is about to take the fall for Jess, she tells the officer that Winston wasn't involved at all and apologizes to Winston for not believing in him. Only then does the officer inform everyone that the white crystals Jess had in her closet were aquarium rocks, not meth. Despite the doubts of Winston's friends about his abilities, the officer tells them that Winston not only passed his background check, but is one of the academy's most promising cadets and will make "one hell of a cop." The happy ending is capped by Jess's sincere apology to Winston, which not only strengthens their friendship but also helps her grow as a person. As wildly hilarious as this episode is, it also reminds audiences about the importance of believing in our friends, who just might end up surprising us. Full of random bits of slapstick and purely comedic scenes, at its core this episode offers touching moments and lessons about friendship.

Another relatable aspect of *New Girl* is its unique and lovable characters, each of whose silly quirks are on constant display. Winston, for example, is surprisingly good at playing the handbells, while Nick never washes his towel, claiming "the towel washes me."

Summarizes episode, supporting the claim that growth of character is a universal theme.

Another good reason the show remains popular: the characters are lovable.

The characters all have well-established personalities from the start of the show, and throughout the seasons we are constantly learning funny little bits of lore from their lives.

But that isn't to say that the characters are all perfect—along with their lovable quirks come their flaws, which the show doesn't shy away from exploring. Each character has their own individual challenges, which often get in the way of their love lives, friendships, and careers. While the situations these flaws get them into are often comical, they all present learning opportunities for the characters (whether they are heeded in the moment or not).

What I appreciate most about the show is how I get to see the characters I love and identify with grow each season, making mistakes and getting back up again. Schmidt, for example, starts out as a shallow, sex-crazed "douchebag" (who has to put money in a jar every time he says something inappropriate), but by the end of the show he has grown into a loving husband and caring father. Granted, it takes him countless bad decisions to end up there (like when he dates two women simultaneously because he doesn't have the strength of character to choose), but he gradually begins to accept accountability for the hurt he has caused others and lets his scumbag façade fall away. It is so easy to get attached to and root for these characters, making it all the more satisfying when they help each other become better people.

Even after taking all of these "deeper" themes and aspects of the show into consideration, I still come back to my favorite thing about *New Girl*: it is comforting and rewatchable. There's something reassuring about finding a show that I (and lots of others) can enjoy whether I'm watching intently or just listening while doing laundry or making notes for one of my classes. Hearing the familiar jokes and dialogue almost makes me feel like I'm part of the family, hanging out in loft 4D with my thirty-year-old BFFs. I often come back to *New Girl* when I'm a little sad or need a pick-me-up because it is one of the few pieces of media that never fails to make me laugh—no matter how many times I've seen it.

Offers further examples of character growth and development.

Names a final reason: the show is comforting.

Colloquial language ("hanging out," "BFFs") establishes a friendly, conversational tone.

As much as I enjoy and admire *New Girl*, however, I recognize that, like all television shows, it is open to criticism. One common complaint is the show's use of racism and microaggressions as part of its humor. One *Reddit* thread has heavily debated this point, and in my opinion one of the best responses comes from a user who points out that when "any clunky racial comments are made, it's always to showcase the ineptitude of the speaker" (U/spooky_upstairs). Many of these questionable jokes come from Schmidt, who always ends up shooting himself in the foot and looking stupid. I find myself agreeing with this *Reddit* user that these comments are a way to satirize or make fun of those who make racist jokes rather than a way to endorse the stereotypes behind the jokes. Additionally, three of the six lead characters—Winston, Cece, and Coach—are people of color, and they are well-developed, multifaceted characters with their own interests and subplots that are vital to the show's storyline and success. Compared to many popular American sitcoms of its time, *New Girl* is actually pretty diverse, and not just in a performative way.

So while I recognize criticisms of *New Girl* and find many of them thoughtful, in the end, I remain a fan. In a time full of anxiety and uncertainty, I think it's increasingly important to have media that just makes people feel good. Take it from Nick: it's a weird life, and we need uncomplicated, joyful TV now more than ever.

Takes alternate perspectives into account.

Responds to criticisms of the show.

Conclusion says why the show is more than just popular today: it's important!

Works Cited

"Background Check." *New Girl*, created by Elizabeth Meriwether, season 4, episode 6, 20th Century Fox TV, 4 Nov. 2014.

Lyons, Margaret. "*New Girl* Returns, Up to Its Old Tricks." *The New York Times*, 9 Apr. 2018, www.nytimes.com/2018/04/09/arts/television/new-girl-zooey-deschanel.html.

U/spooky_upstairs. Comment on "*New Girl*'s Racist Undertones." *Reddit*, 2023, www.reddit.com/r/NewGirl/comments/18aazoc/new_girls_racist_undertones.

Thinking about the Text

1. Audrey Ashdown's review provides an answer to the question that got her interested in this topic: What keeps enthusiastic audiences coming back to *New Girl*, seven years after the series ended? While she offers good REASONS as an answer, she does not state them in an explicit THESIS. Working with one or two classmates, come up with an explicit thesis for Ashdown's review, one that encompasses all of the reasons she offers.

2. Ashdown cites some of her own personal experience to support the claims she makes about the show's success. She also cites statistics from *Reddit*. What if she had cited more outside sources, perhaps quoting from other reviews? How would that have affected her argument? Would it be more or less persuasive, and why?

3. How does Ashdown address COUNTERARGUMENTS or other points of view on *New Girl*? Can you think of other counter-arguments she might have considered? How does she respond to the counterargument that she does cite? Do you agree with her assessment of the counterargument she discusses, and if so, why?

4. If you've never before watched *New Girl*, has this review made you want to start watching it? If not, why not?

5. Whether or not you yourself have watched any episodes of *New Girl*, make time to watch a couple of episodes, maybe including one of the ones Ashdown mentions, and then write a brief response to her, explaining which of her claims you agree or disagree with, and why.

15 Writing in Multiple Modes

This is a time for exploration, for experimentation:
when we can create and risk, write graffiti
on the walls and color outside the lines. . . .

—ADAM BANKS

Check out an article or blog post on the web and you will probably find links to videos, databases, and other sources. Go to a sales presentation and you will no doubt encounter a speaker using slides and maybe audio or video clips—or even an old-fashioned print handout. Attend a poster session on campus and you'll see student presenters offering infographics that they introduce and then answer questions about. Read a film review online and you'll probably be able to click on a link to watch a trailer. Even a traditional essay assignment may call on you to use photos or drawings and to provide other information visually in pie charts or graphs. That's writing in multiple modes.

In many ways, writing in multiple modes is nothing new: just google "illustrated manuscripts and maps," for example, and you'll find pages with decorative initials and miniature drawings written over a thousand years ago.

Today writers can produce texts that combine words, images, colors, sounds, and even videos, and that can be delivered through print, spoken, and digital media. This chapter will help you take advantage of the opportunities offered by writing in multiple modes—so get ready to deliver your messages as you've never delivered them before!

Consider the modes you could use

Rhetorician Cynthia Selfe identifies five modes that writers and speakers can use to convey our messages:

> *Linguistic*—words, titles, headings, captions, ALT TEXT
> *Visual*—photos, drawings, charts, graphs, colors, fonts
> *Audio*—speech, spoken dialogue, sounds, music, tone of voice
> *Gestural*—facial expressions, body language
> *Spatial*—how text and visuals are arranged on page or screen

Your media will dictate which modes you will be able to use—you can't include audio in a print text, right?—but your AUDIENCE and PURPOSE will often determine which modes you will want to use.

Take a look at the following passage from an article about Olympic gymnast Simone Biles that depends entirely on words.

> On Sunday, during the all-around, Simone Biles, her hair trailing behind her like an exclamation point, became the first woman to perform a triple-double—two flips and three twists—in competition during a floor routine. Only a few men can do it, and the way Biles does it is better than the way most of them do. The triple-double is so difficult that U.S.A. Gymnastics has argued that a new tier needs to be added to the code of points, gymnastics' rule book, to account for it.
>
> —LOUISA THOMAS, "The Unlimited Greatness of Simone Biles"

Simone Biles
warms up, 2019.

Now let's see how this passage might be brought more fully to life with additional modes. You could use the *visual* mode, for example, by including an image like the one here. As for the *audio* mode, how about an audio clip of her talking about doing a triple-double—or the roar of the crowd as she sticks the landing? And just imagine the ways you could show the *gestural* mode: with a link to a video of her doing a triple-double, showing her facial expressions as she flips and twists—or as she breaks into a big smile as she lands. Finally comes the *spatial* mode. You could start with the words and then add an image or a video to illustrate what you say. Or you could do the reverse: start with an image showing her doing a triple-double, and then describe with words what she did, and what an astounding accomplishment it was.

REFLECT! Select something you've written that uses words only, and think about how you could use additional modes to illustrate or elaborate on what you wrote. Try doing it! And then write a paragraph comparing the two versions. Which one do you prefer, and why?

A GUIDE TO WRITING IN MULTIPLE MODES

Students tell me that they love doing multimodal projects. They say they're a lot of work, but a whole lot of fun too. This guide aims to help you do that work—and to have some fun along the way!

Identify a topic

You may be assigned a topic, but if you get to choose, start by making a list of questions that really intrigue you, questions you genuinely want to answer. Chances are one of these questions will lead you to an important topic, one that you care about and that will bring out the best in you as a thinker. Lauren Rose Reyes was assigned to develop a research-based argument on a subject related to public health. Reyes had been thinking for some time about her beloved grandmother's formative encounter with US medical services, so she decided to take this opportunity to investigate further.

She learned that her Mexican Indigenous grandmother, pregnant with Lauren's mother, was almost pushed into signing papers that would have led to a tubal ligation, a procedure she would never have wanted or agreed to and did not at all fit into her cultural value system. This fact of family history led Reyes to compare traditional US health care practices with Indigenous ones and to develop an argument for finding ways to bring the two systems in contact with one another.

She decided that this topic, which was potentially very important, was worth investigating. But her assignment was to write using multiple modes, and so she then needed to consider what modes (and what media) she would work with. After talking with her instructor and assessing the resources available, Reyes decided to prepare an oral presentation supported by print or digital materials. Her multimodal project was on its way!

Think about your rhetorical situation

Multimodal writing calls for the same close attention to rhetorical principles that all writing and speaking does. Whatever your topic, you need to think carefully about your purpose, audience, stance, context, language, and genre—in addition to modes and media.

Purpose. What are your goals for this project? To fulfill an assignment? To raise awareness about a problem? To convince others to support a cause? To provide information? Ask yourself what you want to happen as a result of your project; what actions do you want to see taken, or what ideas do you hope to convey? What modes and media will be most useful for achieving your goals?

Audience. Whom do you want to reach? What are they likely to know about your topic, and what background information will you need to provide? Will they be interested in your topic—and if not, are there certain modes that will get them interested—photos (visual mode)? music (audio mode)? a provocative title (linguistic mode)? If you want to reach students on your campus, then you might choose an online campus bulletin board or *Facebook* group. If your audience is limited to people you know, you may be able to make some assumptions about what they're likely to respond to—but most projects you put online may well be seen by people you don't know, so you can't make any such assumptions. Finally, consider how you can make your project accessible to those who have limited vision or hearing. Do you need to provide ALT TEXT?

Stance. What's your attitude toward your topic, and how do you want to present yourself to your audience—as a well-informed observer? a stern critic? a puzzled inquirer trying to figure something out? Then consider how you will reflect that stance: For an oral presentation, what facial expressions and gestures will convey your stance? What will you wear? For written projects, think about what fonts and tone will help establish your stance.

Genre. The kind of text you're writing may affect the modes you can or should use. If you're ANALYZING a scientific text or REPORTING information, you may have reason to present data visually, in graphs or pie charts. If you're writing a NARRATIVE, you may want to add photos or include some dialogue in audio. If you're making an ARGUMENT in a print essay, you might want to choose a font and write in a manner that reflects the seriousness of your subject.

Context. When is the project due, and can you manage to complete the project you have in mind in the time available? What resources will you need to complete the project? What modes would you like to use? If you plan to give an oral presentation, make sure to check out the space and equipment that will be there and find out what you will need to bring (a laptop and a particular dongle, an easel to display photographs, and so on).

Language. You might think first of what REGISTER will be most effective for your project. Should it be fairly academic and formal? Informal, avoiding jargon and using everyday, accessible language? Then think about whether you will use English or whether you will write or speak, at least partially, in another language, along with your reason for doing so. In the same way, consider what dialect(s) of English you think will be most effective in reaching your audience and addressing your subject.

Medium and design. How will your project be delivered—in print? online? as a speech? or through some combination of media? How does the medium affect the way it will be designed and the modes you can or cannot use? Will you be able to include images? audio? video? links to other sources?

Choose a primary medium of delivery

Most multimodal projects have at their core one medium of delivery—oral, print, or digital. Class presentations, for example, are primarily oral, though the spoken words can be enhanced by print text (handouts) or digital ones (audio or video clips; *Power-Point* slides). An informative REPORT, on the other hand, might be primarily a print text, though one augmented with images, charts, graphs, or other visual material. A BLOG will always be delivered digitally, though it can include links to both oral and print texts.

"Moby Dick? Let's see ... Would you like the DVD, the podcast or the interpretive dance?"

CartoonStock.com

Spend some time, then, thinking about how best to deliver your message to your particular audience.

Explore your topic, do some research

Whether your primary medium is print, oral, or digital, you'll need to immerse yourself in your topic, exploring it in various ways and likely doing some research. Your goal is to examine the topic from multiple PERSPECTIVES, not only to understand the topic but to be aware of the conversation surrounding it, of who's talking about it and what they're saying. Here too you can use various modes to explore the topic. You might start by FREEWRITING about it or even try drawing a picture of it. If your topic is a current issue, there may be a podcast about it. And there could also be some people on campus with expertise in the topic who you could interview.

For more detail on exploring a topic, see pp. 112–13.

Come up with a working thesis

Once you have some idea about what you want to say about your topic, take some time to craft a working thesis, a clear statement identifying the topic and the claim you will make about it. Keep in

See pp. 114–15
for detail on
coming up with
a thesis.
mind that this **THESIS** may well change (and get better and more precise!) as you continue to work.

Lauren Reyes began by wondering about her grandmother's experience of the extreme mismatch between her Indigenous values regarding health care and those of the US medical establishment. As she began researching this topic, she found more and more evidence that revealed large disparities in health care between Native and other communities in general and in maternal and infant health care in particular:

> Native Americans are 4.5 times more likely to die from pregnancy- or childbirth-related causes than white mothers are.

As Reyes dug deeper, she found additional research supporting the existence of these disparities, but she also found research to suggest that they could be addressed by bringing in traditional Indigenous maternity and birthing practices to work with typical current US medical practices. Here's the working thesis she started off with:

> To address the extreme disparities Native mothers experience in maternal health, I recommend integrating traditional Indigenous birthing practices with Western medicine.

Whatever media you're using, you need to make your major point very clear. Don't make your audience search for it! In a spoken presentation, you'll want to state your thesis clearly up front, near the beginning of your talk. You may want to put it on a slide so that your audience will both hear it and see it. You have more options in a print text: you may state your claim in your introduction, or you may have reason to withhold it until further into your text.

Ways of providing evidence

See Ch. 4 for tips
on providing
evidence.
As with any text, a multimodal one will be only as good as the information you put in it. But a multimodal text gives you many ways to

present that information. You can present data in a paragraph—or on a line graph. You can describe something with words, or with an image—or even a video. If you want to compare two or more things, you can sometimes do so with words alone, but especially if you're comparing several things, you can also make the comparison easy to see and understand with a bar graph or pie chart. And think of all you can link to in a digital text.

Lauren Reyes presented the evidence for her written essay about Native American maternal health in paragraph form. But then in her spoken presentation (and the video, which was then posted online), she highlighted key questions and points on slides that often included images, making it easy for her audience to follow her thoughts. The slide below presents a graph that shows, at a glance, the huge disparity between the rate of maternal mortality in the United States and that in thirteen other countries:

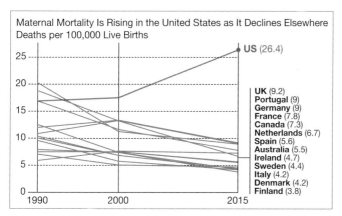

Source: Global, regional, and national levels of maternal mortality, 1990–2015: a systematic analysis for the Global Burden of Disease Study, 2015.

Ways of organizing a multimodal project

Multimodal projects include a number of different elements, which must be carefully organized. In fact, you may well be organizing throughout the process of developing a multimodal project. You might start with a stack of sticky notes, jotting down major points, evidence, images, video and audio clips on each note, which you can then organize and arrange as they'll be used. Some students like to use 3 × 5 cards, each card with a main point or idea, and then tape them together in a chain to spread out on the floor. Going from top to bottom, one card at a time, lets this student see all the points and whether they follow logically from one to another or need to be rearranged, revised, and so on. Lauren Reyes used the traditional Native American medicine wheel in her presentation to organize and provide an overview of points she was going to make.

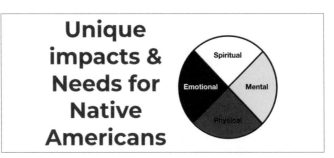

For a video essay, you might start out with a **STORYBOARD**, sketching out the parts of your project so that you can see how they fit together logically and systematically. For an audio essay, you'd likely develop a script that accounts for both words and other sounds. For print texts, you might use a good old **OUTLINE**, using major points as heads and supporting points as subheads.

How to begin?

Whether your text is delivered in a print document, a speech, or online, it has to begin somewhere. Whatever the medium, you might begin with a provocative question or quotation, or by sum-marizing what's been said about your topic and then responding with what you think—these are all strategies that work in any medium. But when you're writing with multiple modes, you have some additional options. In a presentation, for example, you could not only begin by asking a question—you could have the question on a slide, in large type, for your audience to see.

Ways of beginning are covered on p. 116.

Now imagine you're writing a digital narrative about a frisky lit-tle dog. You could start by saying, "Once upon a time, I had a frisky little dog. His name was Gus." You might insert a photo of him right there—or even better, a video of him chasing a ball. And if your text lets readers decide where to begin, you'll want to have a menu with a button that says "Introduction." These are just some ideas; the point is that multiple modalities present a number of ways to get an audience's attention.

How to conclude?

Whatever your medium, you can conclude by summing up your argument, explaining what you hope your audience will take from what you've written or said, or calling for some kind of action. You can also invite response. If you're giving an oral presentation, you'll probably follow that by saying thank you and then asking if there are any questions. If you're writing on the web, you can add your email address or social media handle and invite readers to respond. You can even invite response in a print document by telling readers how to reach you through text or email: you've had your say, so let readers know that you'd like to know what they think and would welcome their response.

Ways of ending are covered on p. 117.

Don't forget transitions

While you may understand precisely how the parts of something you write fit together, you need to make certain that those reading and especially those listening will be able to follow what you say. This means providing explicit transitions from point to point, and explicit references in your text to any images, audio or video clips,

See p. 497 for a list of common transitions. and other elements. Transitions like *first*, *then*, *also*, and *for example* smooth the way for your audience to follow your argument and move from point to point.

To provide a transition from one paragraph to another, you can also write a sentence that links the two. For example, here is a transition sentence from Lauren Reyes's essay:

> In general, maternal health outcomes throughout the United States are disgraceful in comparison with peer countries.

This transition sentence refers back to what has just been discussed (maternal health outcomes in the United States) and then forecasts what is coming up next (those outcomes in peer countries).

For multimodal projects, transitions need to be even more explicit: you can't just insert an audio clip into a digital report, for example, and assume that your audience will know why the audio clip is there and what it contributes to the overall point you're making. Just as you would use a signal phrase to introduce a quotation in a print essay ("they declared," "the author responded"), you need to introduce images, audio or video clips, or other such elements explicitly ("Figure 1 shows," "as you'll hear in the following audio clip"). You also need to explain explicitly what they add to your overall point ("this graph demonstrates my point that," "as you can see in this brief video").

The best way to be sure that your organization works, that all the parts fit together smoothly and your transitions are explicit enough, is to try it out on a friend or classmate, asking them if they can follow what you say. And ask them directly if there's any place where they got confused, needed a clearer transition, or had any other difficulties.

Document sources

As with any academic assignment, you should document any sources you refer to or cite. For projects that are delivered in print, this means including a list of works cited (MLA) or references

(APA). And for digital projects, you can simply link to any sources you've used that are accessible online, enabling readers who want to check them out to do so. For presentations, oral or digital, this usually means including a slide at the end that lists all sources; you might also distribute this list in print, as a handout.

REFLECT! "This is a time for exploration, for experimentation: when we can create and risk, write graffiti on the walls and color outside the lines. . . . we must expand our notion of academic discourse." That's the challenge that **Adam Banks** issued to an audience of college writing teachers, and that opens this chapter. How would you answer his challenge? Find a piece of academic writing you have done, and then imagine how you could rewrite it using multiple modes. Describe that revised piece in a brief paragraph, and explain what you especially like about it.

A MULTIMODAL PROJECT IN THREE MEDIA

LAUREN ROSE REYES

Where Have Our Mothers Gone?
Remedying Native American Maternal Health Disparities with Traditional Birthing Practices

Lauren Rose Reyes, who is studying human biology at Stanford, is of Mexicana, Diné (Navajo), and Mescalero Apache descent. She created this multimodal project for her second-year rhetoric and writing class. Her assignment began with a research-based argument, delivered as a print *document. She then developed an* oral presentation *with* PowerPoint *slides on the same topic. Finally, her presentation was videotaped and posted to the web as a* digital *text. Here is her written essay—and as you'll see, it's been annotated to suggest ways it could use multiple modes and media.*

Print

Rosa, a Mexican and Indigenous woman, was in labor at a hospital in Los Angeles. This was supposed to be a time of great support and compassion as she brought new life into the world, but that was far from what she received. Instead, the medical staff asked how many kids she already had and pushed her to sign medical forms written in English that she could not read. Little did she know at the time that they were trying to get her to sign a consent form for tubal ligation! If she had signed those papers, I would not be here. Rosa was my grandmother, and her fighting spirit (and luck) allowed for three more generations of strong Mexican and Native women to be born and live on. Others were not as lucky. The forced sterilizations of many Mexican-American women in Los Angeles during the early 1970s were an atrocious act of eugenics (Manian).

In fact, Western medicine has in numerous ways consistently failed these women and their families. As a result, disparities in maternal and infant health care between Native and white communities are still all too common today. To remedy this situation, traditional Indigenous birthing practices should be integrated with Western medical practices to fulfill the needs of both expectant mothers and their babies.

The Disparity: Native American Maternal Health Outcomes

In general, maternal health outcomes throughout the United States are disgraceful in comparison with peer countries. The United States has a maternal mortality rate of 26.4 deaths per 100,000 live births in comparison to 3.8 to 9.2 deaths among peer countries (Kassebaum et al., 1784–86). These dismal health outcomes in the United States are particularly prevalent among marginalized communities, namely among people of color and those from rural communities. While some researchers are studying the existence and impacts of such outcomes on various racial communities, they seldom include Native Americans.

Some of the statistical information here and elsewhere in the essay might be easier to comprehend in a chart or graph (visual mode).

Native American women are especially underrepresented in such research. Their exclusion is often justified by the belief that since the Native population is so small comparatively, it is not statistically significant. This omission, however, creates a large gap in knowledge about the severity of the maternal health disparities Native women face.

The limited information we do have on Native American women's health outcomes is bleak. We know, for example, that Native women are 4.5 times more likely to die from pregnancy and childbirth-related causes than white mothers (Dominguez et al.). But why? Such outcomes may be the result of limited access to hospitals. About one in five Native American women in rural areas live at least thirty miles away from a hospital with obstetrics, which is exceedingly alarming considering they are the most susceptible to maternal morbidity and mortality (Truschel and Novoa). It may be because the clinics and hospitals they go to do not provide maternal care. Many Native Americans go to Indian Health Service (IHS) hospitals and clinics, run by the Bureau of Indian Affairs. The mission of the IHS is to provide quality health care to Native Americans in federally recognized tribes, but their services are severely under-funded. Mary Smith, a former principal deputy director of the IHS, writes that in order to provide the same level of care that federal prisoners receive, funding would need to double, and it would need to be even more than doubled to reach the same coverage that Medicaid provides. It is unfortunately unsurprising that maternal health-care services are rarely available at IHS clinics. Even with designated clinics for Native Americans, albeit with limited services, around 75% of Natives go to white health-care centers for giving birth. And finally, the fact that only 0.4% of U.S. physicians are Native American may help explain why Native mothers experience neglect and racial discrimination in the delivery room (Hassanein).

Looking at the Missing and Murdered Indigenous Women (MMIW) crisis in conjunction with these health disparities reveals a connection between the crisis and the current health outcomes for pregnant Native women. Native Americans are 2.5 times more likely to experience violent crimes and two times more likely to experience rape or sexual assault when compared to all other ethnicities (Addington). Native women are ten times more likely to be murdered than all other races or ethnicities combined (Bartley and Pueblo). In addition, homicide during or shortly after pregnancy is the leading cause of maternal mortality in the United States, a fact that disproportionally affects Native women, who are more likely to be the victims of homicide than others (Wallace et al.). Finally, setting maternal health disparities in the context of the MMIW crisis provides a fuller picture of the suffering that Native mothers face not only in health-care systems but also as a result of other discriminatory behavior and outright crimes.

What Was and Is: Traditional Indigenous Wellness Practices and the Impact of Colonialism

Traditional religious and healing ceremonies were banned from our communities in 1883, and anyone who continued these practices was put in prison (Price). This prohibition continued until 1978, when the American Indian Religious Freedom Act allowed Native Americans once again to practice these ceremonies (United States, Congress). Yet even then, Natives still received inferior medical care. This limited access to adequate care, the banning of traditional wellness practices, and the ongoing colonialist subjugation of Native Americans have severely harmed the health of our communities.

Before colonialism stripped Indigenous communities of traditional wellness practices, they used a holistic form of community-based care. While specific practices vary across communities, they all share some common values, the first of which is holistic practices aimed at mental, emotional, and spiritual wellness (*Legal Status*). As Diné (Navajo) midwife Nicolle Gonzales explains, traditional wellness does not mean just going to a doctor or a clinic. It is a lifestyle and a relationship between patient and provider. As she further elaborates, "You don't just wake up one day and [decide] to have a traditional ceremonial birth." Instead, according to Patrisia Gonzales, you research traditional practices and then work to build a relationship with a midwife and others in the community, who collectively care for expectant mothers (65). Across the Southwest, tribes use various birthing practices, from religious ceremonies to herbal and natural medicines. Within Diné traditions, for example, the Blessingway ceremony—a re-enactment of the creation involving songs, chants, and stories—provides the mother with spiritual strength and welcomes the new baby into the world. As the baby is being born, the medicine man chants:

> The Early Dawn found a baby
> To the East, he found a baby;
> When he had found the baby
> He spoke to the baby;
> The baby heard him.
> When he spoke to the baby
> The baby was eager to be born.
> The baby has a happy voice;
> He is an Everlasting and Peaceful baby.

Setting this quotation off in a distinctive font or in a box would call special attention to it (visual, spatial modes).

Adding a link to a medicine man chanting this ceremonial verse would help bring it to life (audio mode).

These comforting words welcome the baby to the world in a loving, positive way. R. Cruz Begay describes the Blessingway ceremony as

> bring[ing] the pregnant woman and her family into a symbolic identification with their ancestors; to the traditional Holy People and to the universal forces of life. This means that in giving birth to a new person, she is spiritually joined to both the past and the future! Through the words and chants of the Singer, she is made to feel these spiritual connections and to feel good and holy as a result. (249)

This ceremony brings peace and spiritual strength to the mothers who are welcomed in this way.

A Solution: Combining Indigenous Wellness Practices and Western Medicine

Integrating traditional Indigenous birthing practices such as the Blessingway with Western medical practices has the potential to mitigate maternal health disparities among Native women. Instead of a cold room with unfamiliar people and medicinal odors, Native women can be surrounded by community members and the comforting scent of sage smudge while preparing to have a ceremonial birthing experience. The World Health Organization advocates such integration, noting the efficacy of traditional healing practices and calling for increased access to this type of care (*Legal Status*). Reclaiming traditional healing and cultural practices can begin to undo the traumatic effects of colonialism on Native women. And thanks to Diné midwife Nicolle Gonzales, the non-profit Changing Woman Initiative (CWI) is one organization that aims to improve maternal health outcomes in the Native American community by revising traditional wellness practices and upholding the matriarchal values of many Southwestern tribes. Currently, CWI is providing education about traditional Indigenous midwifery, home-birth services, and easy access to women's health clinics.

Adding a link to the CWI website or including a screen shot of the site would lead readers to more information (digital media, visual mode).

In an interview, Nicolle Gonzales acknowledges the challenges that come with creating integrated birthing practices:

One is some people are not aware of what their traditional birthing practices are. Two, a lot of Tribes are in the Southwest, but if you live in an urban area, . . . you see people from all over, so you can't integrate just one traditional birthing practice. You kinda have to honor all of them, and every community has different teachings.

In other words, the needs of Indigenous women are multiple and varied, due to colonial trauma, differing health-care systems, and the loss of traditional lands, practices, and identity. In addition, many Native women come to the CWI clinic with pre-existing health issues; over 50% of them need the kind of medical support that hospitals can provide. In short, widespread health disparities among Native communities continue to create obstacles to traditional birthing practices (United States, Department). As Gonzales points out, "We get some very sick women who get sick during their pregnancy who need to go to the hospital."

Despite such serious challenges, Gonzales notes that she has seen miracles and the healing of trauma within traditional sacred spaces, and she continues to envision a world in which Indigenous women can experience a traditional birth if that's what they desire. If traditional models of care can be used in hospitals, ceremonies like Blessingway may not be conducted in a traditional Diné Hogan—but that's a sacrifice that may be necessary in order to develop an integrated model. Evaluating how best to balance traditional practices within Western hospitals calls for keeping elders and knowledge keepers at the forefront of the integration of our traditions into clinical practice.

Conclusion

Integrating traditional birthing practices into health care for Native women can serve as a conduit for cultural healing from historical and current traumas, but still there is a serious need for systemic change in the health care that serves Native people. Researching and identifying the public health disparities among Native communities, and specifically among Native women, is essential to bring healing to Native American mothers and reduce the maternal mortality rate. Birth is sacred, and it is how we as Indigenous people ensure that our medicines, ceremonies, and traditions carry on. If we revitalize birth, then we can help ensure that new generations of healthy Native children can enter this world as a miracle against the colonialism that tried—but failed—to eradicate us, and grow up to thrive.

Works Cited

Addington, Charles. "MMIW Crisis: Reviewing the Trump Administration's Approach to the Missing and Murdered Indigenous Women (MMIW) Crisis." U.S. Dept. of Justice, 11 Sept. 2019, www.doi.gov/ocl/mmiw-crisis.

Bartley, Felicia, and Isleta Pueblo. "Murdered & Missing Indigenous Women." *Native Womens Wilderness,* www .nativewomenswilderness.org/mmiw/. Accessed 6 Oct. 2023.

Begay, R. Cruz. *Navajo Childbirth.* 1985. U of California, PhD dissertation.

Dominguez, Adrian, et al. *Community Health Profile.* Urban Indian Health Institute, Oct. 2016, www/uihi.org/wp-content/uploads /2017/08/UIHI_CHP_2016_Electronic_2017082 5.pdf.

Gonzales, Nicolle. Interview with the author. 17 Feb. 2023.

Gonzales, Patrisia. *Red Medicine: Traditional Indigenous Rites of Birthing and Healing.* U of Arizona P, 2015.

Hassanein, Nada. "Pregnant but Unequal: Native Americans Given Promise of Health Care. For Rural Moms, It's an Empty One." *USA Today,* Aug. 2022, www.usatoday.com/in-depth /news/health/2022/08/11/rural-native-americans-suffer-lack -maternal-health-care-access/10084897002/.

Kassebaum, Nicholas J., et al. "Global, Regional, and National Levels of Maternal Mortality, 1990–2015: A Systematic Analysis for the Global Burden of Disease Study 2015." *The Lancet,* vol. 388, no. 10053, 8 Oct. 2016, pp. 1784–93, https//doi.org/10.1016/S0140-6736(16)31470-2.

Legal Status of Traditional Medicine and Complementary/
Alternative Medicine: A Worldwide Review. World Health
Organization, 2001, apps.who.int/iris/handle/10665/42452.

Manian, Maya. *The Story of* Madrigal v. Quilligan: *Coerced*
Sterilization of Mexican-American Women. 2018. U of San
Francisco School of Law, Research Paper No. 2018-04. *SSRN,*
papers.ssrn.com/so13/papers.cfm?abstract_id=3134892#.

Price, Hiram. *Rules Governing the Court of Indian Offenses.* U.S.
Dept. of the Interior, 30 Mar. 1883. *UND Scholarly Commons,*
commons.und.edu/indigenous-gov-docs/131.

Smith, Mary. "Native Americans: A Crisis in Health Equity."
Human Rights Magazine, vol. 43, no. 3, 1 Aug. 2018, www
.americanbar.org/groups/crsj/publications/human_rights
_magazine_home.

Truschel, Lucy, and Cristina Novoa. "American Indian and
Alaska Native Maternal and Infant Mortality: Challenges
and Opportunities." *Cap20,* 9 Jul. 2018, www.american
-indian-alaska-native-maternal-infant-mortality-challenges
-opportunities/.

United States, Congress. Public Law 95-341. *United States Statutes*
at Large, vol. 92, 1978, pp. 469–70. *U.S. Government Printing*
Office, www.govinfo.gov/content/pkg/STATUTE-92/pdf
/STATUTE-92-Pg469.pdf.

United States, Department of Health and Human Services, Centers
for Disease Control and Prevention. "Chronic Diseases."
Tribal Health, 3 Mar. 2023. *Internet Archive,* web.archive
.org/web/20240226125731/https://www.cdc.gov/tribal/data
-resources/information/chronic-diseases.html.

Wallace, Maeve, et al. "Homicide During Pregnancy and the
Postpartum Period in the United States, 2018–2019."
Obstetrics and Gynecology, vol. 138, no. 5, 2021, pp. 762–69,
https://doi.org/10.1097/AOG.0000000000004567.

Oral

The essay Lauren Reyes wrote was in a way only the beginning. From there she continued her research and then developed and gave an oral presentation. Now let's look at the way she OPENS her presentation—and then compare it with how she begins her essay.

Yá'át'ééh shik'éí dóó shidine'é. Shí éí Lauren yinishyé. Naashgalí dine'é nishłį Naakaii dine'é báshíshchíín.

Hello and Hola. My name is Lauren and I am Diné, Mescalero Apache, and Mexican. To start off, I'd like to tell you a story about a Mexican Indigenous woman named Rosa and her experience giving birth in a Western hospital in Los Angeles. While Rosa was expecting a smooth birthing, that's not what she received. She was bombarded with questions. And the medical professionals kept pushing her to sign a form that she couldn't read because it was written in English and she spoke Spanish! It was only later that she learned that if she had signed this form, she would have been unknowingly sterilized. If Rosa had not been so lucky, I would not be here today. Because Rosa was my grandmother.

Reyes opens her spoken presentation by addressing class members and her instructor in the Diné (Navajo) language. Note, too, that she chooses not to translate this passage. Next she greets her audience in both English and Spanish, before introducing herself with her first name only, appropriate choices for the rhetorical situation of a classroom presentation. Finally, she names her own ethnicities, providing background information for what is to come. Only then does she begin to tell the story of her grandmother, using a narrative to introduce her argument. Throughout the presentation, she uses everyday language, with short sentences to break up longer ones, and ends her introduction with a sentence fragment for special emphasis. These are all rhetorical strategies that help keep her in-class audience engaged and with her.

To engage a more distant audience, her written text opens with a dramatic scene: a woman giving birth in a hospital. Using longer and more complex sentences, Reyes provides details and facts intended to get readers' attention, and then reveals that the woman in the hospital was her own grandmother, which leads into a claim about an "atrocious act of eugenics" that sets the scene for her argument to come.

Turn to p. 292 to see how Reyes begins her essay.

Now let's look at how she **CONCLUDES** her presentation:

Moving forward, there needs to be more research on the disparity and its connection to the Missing and Murdered Indigenous Women Crisis. We also need to uplift Native medicine and Native medicinal practitioners and understand that the solution is both policy- and health care–based—and that we can both bring these traditional practices into clinical settings and also create specific birthing centers that have these practices at the forefront. Overall, addressing this issue will lead to less violence against Native mothers and more healthy Native moms and babies.

Thank you, Gracias, and Ahéhee!

Reyes concludes her spoken presentation by touching on the three major parts of her argument, her words backed by a slide that names the three parts. This simple slide, which she used early on to give an overview of the structure of her presentation, returns here as a shorthand way to remind her audience of the ground she has covered. Accompanying her last sentence are images that illustrate the contrast she is invoking between violence against Native women and healthy, happy Native mothers and babies. In Reyes's spoken presentation, the slides expertly echo the substance of her words, embodying them and making them easy for her audience to understand and to remember.

And she concludes her written essay by reiterating her thesis, calling for the integration of traditional Native birthing practices with Western medicine. Her final sentences reaffirm the sacred nature of birth in Native cultures and stress the endurance of

Native people who will continue to defy colonialist attempts to "eradicate" them. Revitalizing birthing practices, she concludes, is a good way to begin this hard work. Written in formal academic English, the conclusion provides an accurate summation of her argument.

Digital

You can see the video of Lauren Reyes's presentation on letstalk library.com. As you'll see, she uses all five modalities: linguistic (her words), audio (her voice), gestural (her movements and facial expressions), visual (her slides), and spatial (her position in the room, the elements on her slides). Pay attention in particular to how she uses the visual mode—her slides—to help her audience follow her presentation and to put special emphasis on some things she says.

Outline

The Disparity   What Was   A Solution
                 & Is

Thank you!
(English)

¡Gracias!
(Español)

Ahéhee'
(Díné Bizaad)

Thinking about the Text

1. Lauren Reyes began this project by drafting a print argument. What is her CLAIM? Take a look at the facts and studies she mentions in the introduction to her essay: How well do you think they support the claim she makes as her thesis?

2. Compare the OPENING of her oral presentation with the opening of her print essay. Her research question is the same in each: "Where have all the mothers gone?" But note the differences in the two versions: What do you see as the strengths of each? Which one do you find to be more memorable, and why?

3. Reyes uses the Native American medicine wheel to organize her presentation and to help her audience follow what she says. Why might she have made this rhetorical choice, and how effective do you think it was in helping to get her points across?

4. How is the CONCLUSION of her oral presentation organized, and what transitions does she use to link one point to the next in her final paragraph? What do you find most memorable about the conclusion, and why?

5. Look at an essay you have written with an eye for how you would adapt it to be an oral presentation. How would you change the introduction you wrote for readers in order to get the attention of a live audience?

PART FOUR

RESEARCH

FIND OUT

Starting with Questions, Finding Sources

Research is formalized curiosity.
It's poking and prying with a purpose.

—ZORA NEALE HURSTON

The important thing is not to stop questioning.
Curiosity has its own reason for existence.

—ALBERT EINSTEIN

You, it turns out, are a born questioner. In fact, research shows that humans differ from non-human primates in just this way: we ask questions! In addition, humans have evolved to spend lots of time, brain space, and brain power articulating questions—and then searching for and creating knowledge that will help provide answers. And we do so not just because of everyday needs like food and shelter but also because, well, because *it's just what we do*. This chapter recognizes the questioner and researcher in all of us and provides guidance as you engage in these distinctly human activities.

Being curious and asking questions are at the very heart of the "poking and prying with a purpose" that Zora Neale Hurston associates with research. So doing research calls on you to immerse yourself in new ideas and topics you want to know more about, searching out what other people have said about them, and considering a wide range of perspectives—including those that differ from any ideas about the topic you already have.

Tracking down answers to important questions (another way of saying "research") is crucial to getting and creating knowledge. While most of us grew up accepting ideas handed down to us by others, at some point we begin to question some of those ideas, to want to understand and evaluate them on our own rather than accepting them as "just the way it is." We start to think about and search for answers to questions that excite or puzzle or even frighten us. In short, we become researchers.

In fact, you are probably already a pretty experienced researcher. The reading you do and the questions you ask before buying a new smartphone; the time you spend exploring your college's website to decide what courses to take; the hours and hours you spend looking for early recordings by BTS, Taylor Swift, Metro Boomin, or someone else. All research. During your college years, you will have the opportunity to do research in many courses and on many topics. Take advantage of these opportunities to put your curiosity and imagination to work, to discover things you couldn't have imagined before now, and to add to your own knowledge. This chapter will help get you started on any research you set out to do.

> No one person is the authority on anything.
> CLEO KEAHNA

STARTING WITH QUESTIONS
Choose a topic that matters to you

Sometimes a topic chooses you, one you're so fascinated by that you've been thinking about it for a long time. If so, chances are good that this is a topic you should take time to explore. Other times, you may be assigned a topic to research—particularly in a class you're

Never stop being a kid. This will guarantee that the world—even the universe itself—becomes and remains your playground of curiosity.

NEIL DeGRASSE TYSON

taking or a job you hold. But even when topics are assigned, they are often broad enough to let you focus on one aspect that seems most important to you or that really piques your curiosity. Still other times, the choice of topic may be left open to you as long as it somehow relates to the course content. In each of these cases, you need to zero in on an aspect of the topic so that its importance is absolutely clear and that it in some way matters to you.

In one first-year seminar on environmental science, students were assigned to write a research-based essay on some aspect of sustainability. In response, one student who lived in a dorm chose to pursue a question that had been bothering him: How many plastic straws and bottles and aluminum cans were fellow students tossing into the trash rather than recycling? So he decided to do a little field research, counting the number of straws, bottles, and cans he found in the trash cans on three floors of his dorm. The number was even higher than he had imagined; and when he thought about how many more floors there were in this one dorm, he was even more alarmed. The question he had started with led him to this basic research of his own, which he then followed up with research using online databases and

How NOT to do research!

"I'm sorry, sir, but this survey does not allow for that opinion."

other sources in order to find out what others have reported about the growing amount of recyclable material that ends up in landfills and dumps and even in the ocean. This student was certain he had identified an important topic, one that mattered and that was worth researching and writing about.

Think about your rhetorical situation

Once you've identified a topic to research, take time to think carefully about your purpose, audience, and the rest of your rhetorical situation. Jotting down some notes on the following elements of the rhetorical situation will come in handy when you begin shaping your topic into a RESEARCH QUESTION and eventually a THESIS.

Purpose. Why have you chosen this topic, and what do you hope to accomplish in researching and writing about it? What do you want to happen as a result of your work?

Audience. Who will read what you write, and what are they likely to know about your topic? What background information will you need to provide? What kinds of EVIDENCE or sources will they find most persuasive?

Stance. What do you know about the topic, and what do you think and believe about it? How would you describe your attitude on the topic—neutral? curious? passionate? something else? How do you want to come across to your audience, and how can you establish your credibility to write on this topic? Your TONE (serious? humorous? conversational?) will be important for establishing this stance.

Context. Who is doing research on the topic, and how could their work inform what you write? Identifying this part of your rhetorical situation brings you into a conversation that's already taking place about your topic and that will be very important to you as you begin your own research. And what about your assignment: When is it due? Are there any requirements about the length of what you write and the kinds of sources you should consult?

Genre. Have you been assigned to write in a particular genre—an ARGUMENT? a REPORT? an ANALYSIS? a MULTIMODAL presentation of some kind? If not, what genre best suits your topic and purpose?

Language. What kind of language will be most effective for your purpose and genre—formal? businesslike? conversational? something else? Should you use more than one language or dialect—and if so, why?

Media and design. Are you required to use a certain medium? If not, which mediacy will best suit your topic and purpose and help you reach your audience? Will you need to include photos or other images? graphs or charts? Will you need headings? Does your assignment have any format requirements?

Even if you can't answer all these questions right now, they'll get you thinking about your topic. And do take notes: it's amazing what good ideas may pop into your head as you think systematically about your rhetorical situation.

Do some research to get an overview of your topic

At this point, you might use ChatGPT SEARCH to get a sense of who has written about your topic. *Wikipedia* can also be a particularly good place to start, a site where you'll likely encounter various perspectives on your topic, find links to sources you may want to consult, and read about any controversies.

See Ch. 30 for advice about using AI carefully and ethically.
Check to see if you're permitted to use generative AI in your class—and if so, you might ask *ChatGPT* or another chatbot about who has written on your topic and what's been said about it. Keep in mind, however, that you'll need to check any information AI gives you for accuracy.

For now, you should cast a wide net for good ideas, dipping into a few sources to see what they have to say about your topic. Make some notes about what sources you might use.

Focus your topic

Once you've gathered some basic information and have some sense of the larger conversation surrounding your topic, think about whether you need to narrow the topic to make it more manageable. One good way to begin is to jot down what you now know about the topic. Then highlight the points that are most interesting to you: the more the topic matters to you, the better your research and writing about it will be.

Suppose you've been following some online threads about the dangers of social media, discussions that have generated a lot of agreement, as well as some pushback. This topic gets you thinking about the pros and cons of social media, so you decide to pursue it, beginning with a broader topic: "effects of social media." But you quickly realize that you can't possibly cover such a huge topic, so you begin to narrow what you try to cover. Because you're especially interested in what effects social media might be having on you and your college work, how about "cognitive effects of social media on college work"? Still pretty unmanageable. So you focus in a little more closely: "negative cognitive effects of social media use on college students in the United States." This is still a big topic, but it is now narrow enough that you can at least begin to gather information in a somewhat focused way.

Come up with a research question

Once you have a manageable topic, you can turn it into a question that will guide your research as you look for compelling ways to answer it. Your question should be clear and succinct, and not one that can be answered with a simple "yes" or "no." "Does social media affect the cognitive abilities of college students?" Well, yes it does or no it doesn't, and you're left with a one-word response that won't help you at all to engage the large body of work that exists on the negative effects of social media.

Here are two ways that the topic on the negative effects of social media can be recast as a research question:

What are the negative cognitive effects of social media use on college students in the United States?

How does the use of social media negatively affect the cognitive abilities of college students in the United States?

These are questions that can guide you as you begin to research this topic. They are also questions worth investigating, because the answers will be very important not only to you but to others as well. As you begin your research to answer your research question, remember to do so with an open mind, ready to consider sources that present many different perspectives. You don't want to choose only sources that you agree with: take a look at what researchers and scholars with many varying, even conflicting opinions have to say.

Plot out a working thesis

Once you have a research question, the next step is to come up with a working thesis that can help guide your research. Keep in mind that you'll keep asking your question, and you may well modify the thesis as you continue the research, but your working thesis will function as a **HYPOTHESIS**, your best guess at this point about what you will claim in writing about your topic.

See pp. 114–15 for more on drafting a thesis.

As someone investigating the negative effects of social media on college students, you might begin with a working thesis like this:

> College students in the United States seem to be negatively affected by the use of social media, and excessive use has been shown to lead to troubling cognitive results.

This thesis will almost surely change as you dig into research on the topic: Will your research turn up credible evidence to support the statement that college students are "negatively affected" by social media use? If so, are the most troublesome effects cognitive ones? What is the correlation between the increasing use of social media and various behaviors among college students? These are questions that careful and systematic research will answer and that may then lead you to further revise your thesis statement.

REFLECT! Take some time to jot down some of the things you worry about, or things you wish you knew more about. **BRAINSTORM** about these things for ten or so minutes, until you've identified a few ideas. Which ones are most important to you, and which ones might have the greatest impact on others? Choose one, and write a paragraph introducing this topic to a friend and explaining why you want to carry out research on it.

FINDING SOURCES

Elizabeth Winkler began musing about all the strong, resourceful, and memorable women in Shakespeare's plays back in 2018, when she was following the #MeToo movement. As she attended and reread these plays, she kept finding more and more instances of remarkable women characters, so much so that she decided to research the controversy over who actually wrote "Shakespeare's" plays. So she immersed herself in the arguments various scholars had put forward in favor of possible authors—an all-male cast including Francis Bacon, Christopher Marlowe, and Edward de Vere—and then turned again to the plays themselves. And they led her to ask a most provocative question: What if Shakespeare was a woman? From there, she was off on the research adventure of a lifetime.

Winkler's experience shows how research often works: you start out with a focus on a topic, even with a preliminary thesis, but a simple turn of the kaleidoscope can reveal an entirely new way of looking at the topic. And that new way of looking can then lead you to consider sources that might not have seemed relevant before.

Was "Shakespeare" a woman?

In this case, Winkler's question led her to turn to primary sources—Shakespeare's own plays—with a new eye, which in turn led her to discover things in the plays that the "real" Shakespeare would have been hard-pressed to know, but that *would* have been known by a particular woman poet living at the same time: Amelia Bassano. From there, Winkler set off to hunt for everything she could find out about Bassano. And she found a lot—enough to support her claim that "Shakespeare" may well have been a woman.

In doing her research, Winkler used time-tested methods: careful, critical reading both of the plays, and of secondary sources on the question of authorship. She also did some field research, interviewing one of the scholars who's theorized that Bassano was the actual author. But in addition, she relied on her own imagination and intuition. Most important of all, she kept her mind wide open to new possibilities, and looked for sources from a very wide range of viewpoints.

Like Winkler, you may draw on both primary and secondary materials when you conduct research—and may even gather information from field research.

What kinds of sources do you need?

Deciding on the sources that will be most helpful is a challenge today, when there are so many to choose from, from books and articles and databases to video and audio files of all kinds—all readily available through your school library. So it's wise to spend some time thinking about the kinds of sources your topic calls for. Like Winkler's, your topic might call for consulting primary sources and historical documents. But contemporary topics require a different approach. If your topic is, say, about the environment, you probably need current sources from scientific and environmental journals, perhaps along with interviews of people strongly affected by environmental change. You might also want to schedule an interview with an environmental studies professor. Whatever your topic, look for sources that represent different perspectives on it, including ones that challenge your own thinking on the topic. Remember that research is about INQUIRY: to learn about the topic, not simply to find support for what you already think about it.

Primary and secondary sources

Primary sources are original works, like Shakespeare's plays. They are firsthand accounts, diaries, historical documents, personal narratives, and materials generated from FIELD RESEARCH like interviews or surveys. *Secondary sources,* in contrast, REPORT on or ANALYZE primary sources—and provide secondhand knowledge. So *Beloved* is a primary source, while a critic's analysis of that novel is a secondary source.

Sometimes your purpose determines whether a source is primary or secondary. Suppose you are writing an essay on Kendrick Lamar, who won the 2023 Grammy for best rap album of the year. That album is your primary source, while a critic who has written a review of Lamar's album is a secondary source. But suppose you decide to write an essay on that particular critic's work: then the review of Lamar's album would be a primary source for your research.

Scholarly and popular sources

Scholarly sources are those written by experts for an academic audience. Whether they're journal articles, books, conference papers, or some other publication, they've usually been peer-reviewed by experts and include full documentation of their sources. *Popular sources*, in contrast, are written for a general audience; while they can be authoritative and cite scholarly research, they haven't been as fully vetted as academic sources, nor do they usually include documentation.

In the field of psychology, the journal *Psychology of Consciousness: Theory, Research, and Practice* is a scholarly source, while *Psychology Today* is a popular source. Even though both kinds of sources can provide excellent information, you'll want to be sure that the sources you use are appropriate to your PURPOSE and AUDIENCE. If you're writing about tax policy for a business class, the *Wall Street Journal* might be a useful source, but its movie reviews would not usually be appropriate sources in a film analysis for a class on the history of film.

See examples from popular and scholarly sources on pp. 316–17.

SCHOLARLY SOURCE

Published in an academic journal.

Contents lists available at ScienceDirect

Marine Policy

journal homepage: www.elsevier.com/locate/marpol

Human footprint in the abyss: 30 year records of deep-sea plastic debris

Multiple authors who are academics.

Sanae Chiba[a,b,*], Hideaki Saito[c], Ruth Fletcher[b], Takayuki Yogi[d], Makino Kayo[d], Shin Miyagi[d], Moritaka Ogido[d], Katsunori Fujikura[e]

[a] Japan Agency for Marine-Earth Science and Technology (JAMSTEC), 3173-25 Showamachi, Kanazawaku, Yokohama 2360001, Japan
[b] UN Environment World Conservation Monitoring Centre, 219 Huntingdon Road, Cambridge CB3 0DL, UK
[c] Global Oceanographic Data Center (GODAC), Japan Agency for Marine-Earth Science and Technology (JAMSTEC), 224-3 Toyohara, Nago 9052172, Japan
[d] Marine Works Japan, Ltd., 224-3 Aza-Toyohara, Nago 9052172, Japan
[e] Department of Marine Biodiversity Research, Japan Agency for Marine-Earth Science and Technology (JAMSTEC), 2-15 Natsushimacho, Yokosuka 2370061, Japan

ARTICLE INFO

Keywords:
Deep-sea debris
Marine litter, plastic pollution
Single-use plastic
Database
North Pacific

ABSTRACT

Includes an abstract.

This study reports plastic debris pollution in the deep-sea based on the information from a recently developed database. The Global Oceanographic Data Center (GODAC) of the Japan Agency for Marine-Earth Science and Technology (JAMSTEC) launched the Deep-sea Debris Database for public use in March 2017. The database archives photographs and videos of debris that have been collected since 1983 by deep-sea submersibles and remotely operated vehicles. From the 5010 dives in the database, 3425 man-made debris items were counted. More than 33% of the debris was macro-plastic, of which 89% was single-use products, and these ratios increased to 52% and 92%, respectively, in areas deeper than 6000 m. The deepest record was a plastic bag at 10898 m in the Mariana Trench. Deep-sea organisms were observed in the 17% of plastic debris images, which include entanglement of plastic bags on chemosynthetic cold seep communities. Quantitative density analysis for the subset data in the western North Pacific showed plastic density ranging from 17 to 335 items km^{-2} at depths of 1092–5977 m. The data show that, in addition to resource exploitation and industrial development, the influence of land-based human activities has reached the deepest parts of the ocean in areas more than 1000 km from the mainland. Establishment of international frameworks on monitoring of deep-sea plastic pollution as an Essential Ocean Variable and a data sharing protocol are the keys to delivering scientific outcomes that are useful for the effective management of plastic pollution and the conservation of deep-sea ecosystems.

Table 1
Summary of the total and plastic debris occurrences during deep-sea surveys by remotely operated vehicles and submersibles of the Japan Agency for Marine-Earth Science and Technology (JAMSTEC) in the six oceanic regions for 1982–2015. The information is based on the Deep-sea Debris Database of Global Oceanographic Data Center (GODAC) of JAMSTEC (updated on July 3rd, 2017) (http://www.godac.jamstec.go.jp/dsdebris/e/). Single use plastics are plastic bags, bottles and packages.

Describes research methods, includes numerical data.

Oceanic Region	Year of observation	Geographical range (Latitude - Longitude)	Dive depth range (m)	Debris depth range (m)	Max. depth (m) of plastics	Total dive number	Total debris number	Plastic debris number	% Single use plastic
Western North Pacific	1982–2015	1°15' - 45°34'N 122°42' - 163°15'E	100- 10,899	100-10898	10,898	4552	3370	1108	89
Eastern North Pacific	1998–2002	17°12' - 24°24'N 154°14' - 159°13'W	1714–5569	3879–4684	4684	85	8	2	100
South Pacific	1990–2013	3°10' - 34°53'S 149°52'E - 112°12'29'W	499–6498	1846–4460	1986	168	12	1	100
North Atlantic	1994–2013	14°44' - 36°14'N 33°54' - 81°48'W	2265–6024	2300 – 4935	-	68	17	0	N.A.
South Atlantic	2013	20°38' - 31°06'S 34°03' - 41°39'W	921–4219	2493–2721	-	16	5	0	N.A.
Indian Ocean	1998–2013	4°02'N - 32°57'S 57°04' - 105°53'E	1276–5290	1923–3264	2573	121	13	4	100
Total						5010	3425	1115	89

Cites academic research with consistent documentation style.

at maximum, and on surveys conducted in areas relatively close to the coast. There are only a few cases of long-term observation records on deep-sea plastic pollution [18,25,26] and of surveys conducted in areas more than 1000 km off the coast of the mainland [13,19,27]. Information on deep-sea debris in the western North Pacific Ocean is also very limited [15,28]. Because high concentrations of plastic debris were

2. Material and methods

2.1. Data

The data used in this study were from the Deep-sea Debris Database updated on July 3rd, 2017 (http://www.godac.jamstec.go.jp/dsdebris/e/). The debris data were obtained by visually analysing video footage

from various aspects. The Deep Ocean Observing Strategy (DOOS) (http://www.deepoceanobserving.org) is being developed under the auspices of the Global Ocean Observation System (GOOS), with the aim of promoting and integrating physical, biogeochemical, and biological observation in the deep sea (> 2000 m) of the global ocean. In accordance with the guideline of the Framework for Ocean Observation [52], agreed upon by the global ocean science community at the OceanObs'09 meeting in 2009, DOOS is preparing to identify Essential Ocean Variables (EOVs) to measure deep-sea environments globally (http://www.goosocean.org/index.php?option = com_content&view = article&id = 14&Itemid = 114). The density or occurrence of plastic is one of the possible deep-sea EOVs. It is particularly recommended to

Includes complete reference list.

References

[1] UNEP, GRID-Arendal, Marine Litter Vital Graphics, United Nations Enviroment Programme and GRID-Arendal., Nairobi and Arendal, 2016.
[2] United Nations, The Sustainable Development Goals Report. doi:http://dx.doi.org/dx.doi.org/10.18356/3405d09f-en, 2017.
[3] M. Bergmann, M.B. Tekman, L. Gutow, Marine litter: sea change for plastic pollution, Nature 544 (2017), http://dx.doi.org/10.1038/544297a (297–297).
[4] F. Galgani, G. Hanke, T. Maes, Global Distribution, Composition and Abundance of Marine Litter, Springer International Publishing, 2015, pp. 29–56, http://dx.doi.org/10.1007/978-3-319-16510-3.2 (in: Mar. Anthropog. Litter).
[5] LITTERBASE, Online Portal for Marine Litter. (www.litterbase.org).
[6] D.K.A. Barnes, F. Galgani, R.C. Thompson, M. Barlaz, Accumul. Fragm. Plast. Debris Glob. Environ. 364 (2009) 1985–1998, http://dx.doi.org/10.1098/rstb.2008.0205.

POPULAR SOURCE

Published in a general-interest periodical.

Author is a journalist.

Catchy, provocative title and photo.

Every year, an estimated <u>eight million metric tons</u> of land-based plastic enters the world's oceans. But when marine researchers have measured how much of this plastic is floating on the water's surface, swirling in offshore gyres—most notably, the so-called Great Pacific Garbage Patch, between Hawaii and California—they have only found quantities on the order of hundreds of thousands of tons, or roughly *one per cent* of all the plastic that has ever gone into the ocean. Part of the explanation for this is that all plastic eventually breaks down into microplastic, and, although this takes some polymers decades, others break down almost immediately, or enter the ocean as microplastic already (like the synthetic fibres that pill off your fleece jacket or yoga pants in the washing machine). Scientists have recently found tiny pieces of plastic falling with the rain in the high mountains, including France's <u>Pyrenees</u> and <u>the Colorado Rockies</u>. British <u>researchers</u> collected amphipods (shrimplike crustaceans) from six of the world's deepest ocean trenches and found that eighty per cent of them had microplastic in their digestive tracts. These kinds of plastic fibres and fragments are smaller than poppy seeds and "the perfect size to enter the bottom of the food web," as Jennifer Brandon, an oceanographer at the Scripps Institution of Oceanography, told me. "They have been shown to be eaten by mussels, by coral, by sea cucumbers, by barnacles, by lots of filter-feeding plankton."

Academic experts and studies cited but not documented.

How to determine if a source is scholarly or popular

- *What's the title?* Scholarly titles sound academic and often include subtitles. Popular titles are more likely to be catchy, sometimes provocative.

- *What are the author's credentials?* Scholarly sources are written by academics or researchers. Some academic authors also write books or articles for a general audience. These would be considered popular rather than scholarly.

- *Who's the publisher or sponsor?* Look for academic presses or organizations.

- *Does it include* DOCUMENTATION? Scholarly sources cite research and document their sources, both in in-text documentation within the text and on a list of works cited or references.

- *If it's online, what's the URL?* Colleges and universities use *.edu.*

- *Does it look scholarly?* Academic sources tend to have a one-color, conservative design and often include tables and charts. Popular texts are more likely to have a colorful design and to include photos and other illustrations.

- *Are there ads?* Popular sources often include many ads; scholarly ones have few if any ads.

All that said, keep a very sharp eye out for sources that claim to be credible scholarly sources, and look scholarly. Because they may not be! In this age of FAKE NEWS, we now have to worry about fake scholarly sources as well, especially those that pop up in a *Google* search. Such sites are written and designed to sound and look scholarly. Check to see who's sponsoring the site: Is it an academic institution or an advocacy group? And check out *Snopes* or another fact-checking site to see what they say about it. And finally, remember that scholars and other experts are not the only people with valuable knowledge that can be useful to your research: roommates and friends and family may also offer relevant expertise!

See Ch. 17 for advice on how to determine whether unfamiliar sources should be trusted.

Finding sources on the internet

Many of us turn to the internet whenever we need to find some kind of information. A click of a few keys and whammo—a long list of sources!

Search engines. Many of us begin research by using search engines like *Bing* or *Google*. These are all powerful tools for research, but they can quickly become overwhelming. Typing in "plastic in oceans" on *Google*, for example, recently yielded over 300 million possible sources—in less than a second. Still, using a search engine as a starting point can give you an overview of what's out there— and help you discover photographs, videos, blogs, maps, and other materials related to your topic.

Google is not a synonym for research.
DAN BROWN

But the results you get from any search engine are affected by algorithms designed to give you what they think you want—which is not going to help you find the multiple perspectives on your topic that you need. Be especially careful about clicking on the first items that appear: many of them are "sponsored" sources, which means someone has paid to have them come up at the top of a search. These results may not even be related to the topic you're searching for—as happened to a friend whose *Google* search for the Cluny Museum brought up twenty offers for private tours of Paris before the museum's own site came up. In short, the "good stuff" may appear farther down in the list.

And get to know *Google Scholar*, a search engine that will direct you to scholarly literature across an array of disciplines: journal articles, books, technical reports, court opinions, and more. (What you won't find here: news and magazine articles, book reviews, or editorials.) Many of the sources available on *Google Scholar* aren't available for free, but you can access them if your college library subscribes to the databases that contain them—and most likely it does.

Running searches on the web. Whatever search engine you use or whatever you're searching for, choosing KEYWORDS will be a key to focusing your search to get the sources you need. Say you're interested in race car driving. Searching for those three words yields an unmanageable number of results, so you try "race car drivers." Still too much. Further thinking leads you to wonder about the gender of drivers—and more specifically, about women NASCAR drivers. So you narrow your search and type in "women NASCAR drivers." There are various ways of focusing what a search engine looks for, but here are a few that work with many engines:

- Use *quotation marks* to search for an exact phrase ("women NASCAR drivers"). If you enter those same words without quotation marks, you'll get sources with all three words but not only in that order.

- Use *and* to retrieve texts using all of the words ("women and NASCAR and drivers").

- Use *or* to retrieve texts using any of the words ("women or NASCAR or drivers").

Wikipedia is a free online encyclopedia that can give you a sense of what is being written and debated about your topic. But because virtually anyone can edit what's on *Wikipedia*, its information is always changing—which means it's a source you usually won't want to cite. Still, most of its entries include links and bibliographies that will lead you to other sources, so it can be a good starting point for researching a topic.

Government sites. Are you looking for information about Ameri-Corps? the Census Bureau? the Justice Department? the Library of Congress? the National Archives? the Supreme Court? Go to *USA .gov*, where you can access sites for these and many other government agencies and departments.

News sites. Many newspapers and magazines offer free access to at least some of their online content. And your college library might well subscribe to some of those that don't; if so, you'll be able to access them through the library's portal. In addition, some newspapers allow you to search their archives, so you can look for articles relevant to your topic that have been published in the past.

And now there are various news aggregators, websites, and apps such as *Flipboard, Feedly, SmartNews, Pocket, News360,* and *Google News* that collect news content from multiple sources—in some cases, thousands! Some include links to the original articles and many of them provide personalized news based on your interests.

Social media sites such as *Instagram, TikTok,* and *Facebook,* as well as blogs and podcasts, can be useful sources—or not. I follow the work of cognitive psychologist Steven Pinker on *X,* for example, as a way of keeping up to date on the work in this field, and I also follow linguist Dennis Baron's deeply researched and informative blog, *The Web of Language.* In these cases, I know some of the writers and their expertise and can generally trust what they say to be credible sources of information. I'm much less likely to use information provided by sources whose reputation I don't know. As we all know, there's a lot of misinformation being retweeted and reposted on social media every minute of every day. So if you cannot trust or verify information you find on *X,* it's wise to pass it by, and not to cite it in anything you write.

Image, video, and audio banks. Free images, audio, and even films are available in a number of sources on the web. For photos, check out *StockSnap.io, Unsplash, Reshot,* or *Shutterstock.* For videos, consult *Pexels* and *Storyblocks.* And for audio files, check out *AudioJungle, Audioblocks,* and *Freesound.* Remember, though, that while some of these sources are free of charge, you still need to acknowledge and DOCUMENT any that you use in your own writing.

REFLECT! Together with a partner, do a search for the same term using the same search engine—but each on your own computer. Compare what the two searches turn up. Most likely they will be different. Why? Spend some time BRAINSTORMING about this, and how it might affect the way you think about search results.

Finding sources using AI

If you're permitted to use AI, *ChatGPT* and other such bots can help you find sources. As this book goes to press, chatbots that have the capability to search the web (such as *ChatGPT4* or *Copilot*) can provide up-to-date sources. Free versions (such as *ChatGPT3.5*) can refer us to general or historical sources, ones that existed before their "knowledge cutoff" date (September 2021, for 3.5). In May of 2024, I posted this prompt in *ChatGPT3.5*.

You

Can you help me find sources on the topic of negative cognitive effects of social media on college students in the US today?

ChatGPT3.5

Certainly! While I can't provide real-time or the most up-to-date sources, I can guide you on where to find information on the negative cognitive effects of social media on college students. Here are some suggestions:

1. **Academic Journals:** Use academic databases like *PubMed, JSTOR,* or *PsycINFO* to search for peer-reviewed articles. Keywords could include "social media," "college students," and "cognitive effects."

2. ***Google Scholar*:** Conduct a search on *Google Scholar* for recent articles and research papers related to the negative cognitive effects of social media on college students.

3. **Research Institutions:** Check the websites of research institutions such as Pew Research Center, RAND Corporation, or other organizations that focus on social behavior and technology impact.

4. **News Outlets:** Look for articles from reputable news outlets that cover recent studies or findings on the topic. Some examples could be the *New York Times, The Atlantic,* or *Wired*.

5. **Books:** Explore books written by experts in the field of psychology, sociology, or technology. They may provide in-depth analyses on the impact of social media on cognitive function.

6. **Government Reports:** Check reports from government agencies or departments that focus on education or health. These reports may contain relevant statistics and findings.

7. **Conference Proceedings:** Look for conference proceedings from academic conferences focused on psychology, sociology, or communication. They often contain the latest research findings.

8. **Social Science Databases:** Use social science databases like *Social Science Research Network* (*SSRN*) to find working papers and preprints on the topic.

Remember to critically evaluate the sources you find and check for the credibility of the authors and the publication. Additionally, consider the date of publication to ensure you are accessing the most recent information.

ChatGPT can make mistakes. Check important info.

This is sound advice: in this case, *ChatGPT3.5* did not make up information or sources (which it sometimes does) but offered examples of reputable databases and websites we might consult, and even suggested some keywords to use. Notice, however, that it includes a note cautioning us that "ChatGPT can make mistakes" and to "check important info." So while this free version of *ChatGPT* could not help identify specific sources on the topic, it did offer good general advice on where to go to find such sources.

Here is what the subscription-based *GPT4* offered in response to the same question:

ChatGPT4

From a quick search using *Bing*, here's what I discovered.
Research indicates that excessive social media use can negatively affect college students by decreasing their interpersonal competencies in initiating offline relationships, leading to unfinished daily tasks, and impacting their mental health. It can also reduce cognitive reappraisal ability and increase emotional suppression, which adversely affects emotion regulation. Furthermore, there's evidence that social media use can influence students' academic performance, health, overall well-being, and university practices. For instance, it presents a constant temptation that detracts from academic tasks, suggesting

324 RESEARCH | Find Out

a need for academic environments to promote positive social media usage strategically.

You

Can you provide the sources for that information?

ChatGPT4

The information comes from a study detailed on ResearchGate, discussing the impacts of social media use among college students. This research highlights the negative cognitive effects related to social media usage, including decreased interpersonal competencies, unfinished tasks, and impacts on mental health, academic performance, and overall well-being. For comprehensive details, please refer to the source directly: "Impact of Social Media Use In College Students" on ResearchGate.

Note that *ChatGPT4* first provided what looked like a summary of research based on a "quick search" that linked to dozens of sources on the web. But it took a further prompt to determine that the information was indeed a summary—and that the summary was actually based on only one source, which we would then have to look up to check for accuracy. And further prompts would be needed to get at additional sources on the subject, or sources that take different perspectives on the question.

The bottom line for now seems to be that chatbots can indeed be helpful in turning up potentially useful sources, but that you will almost certainly have to write several prompts to get the information you need, and even then you will need to check the sources the bot identifies to make sure they are credible and accurate—and real. In short, you will have a lot of work to do.

Using your college's library

Learn how to use your school's library—the physical library on campus and the library's website that gives access to all that's in the library. Take a tour, or try to meet with a reference librarian, and come prepared with questions: Where can you find encyclopedias, almanacs, and other general reference works? What special collections (of art, film, music, audio, and video) does the library have? How can you access library resources online? And once you've settled on a topic, see if there's a librarian who specializes in the field that you're researching.

The library catalog. The books, the encyclopedias, the films, the audios, and more: they're all accounted for in the library catalog, with information about where they're located. At most colleges, the catalog is digital; you can search by author, title, subject, and keyword. Do an *author search* if you want to find out everything in the library written by that author. Do a *title search* if you know the complete title of what you're looking for. If you don't know a specific author or title, you can do a *subject* or *keyword search* that will give an overview of all the materials in the library related to that topic.

Your library probably uses the Library of Congress Subject Headings (LCSH), so you may need to experiment for a while to make sure you're using a word that LCSH also uses. For example, if you enter "American Civil War" as a subject heading, you might get a notice telling you that this is not a LCSH subject heading— but that "United States History Civil War" is. Then you'll be on the right track to do a successful subject search.

Databases. These are large digital collections of journal, magazine, and newspaper articles and other sources. Although many are only available by subscription, they are likely available through your college library.

General databases that cover a wide range of fields and include both scholarly and popular sources can be a good place to start:

- ***Academic Search Complete*** offers access to thousands of journals and magazines, including many that are open access.

- **JSTOR** provides access to millions of academic journals, books, and primary sources in seventy-five disciplines.
- **Lexis/Nexis Academic** offers documents from business, government, legal, and news sources.
- **ProQuest Central** provides access to thousands of its "most used" academic journals, newspapers, magazines, dissertations, and more. Look here for the *New York Times*, the *Wall Street Journal*, *The Economist*, and more.

Subject-specific databases come in handy once you have a research question. If, for example, you are researching the effect of changing rules in pro basketball, check with a reference librarian to recommend specific sports-related databases. Here are several subject-specific databases that are often very useful:

- **AGRIS** is a public domain database for accessing millions of resources in agricultural science and technology.
- **ERIC** gives access to journals, conference papers, and other publications related to education.
- **IEEE Xplore** provides access to publications in computer science, electrical engineering, and related fields.
- **MLA International Bibliography** indexes scholarly articles and books in the fields of literature, language, linguistics, rhetoric, and folklore.
- **PsychINFO** provides abstracts of peer-reviewed articles in psychology and the behavioral sciences.

Conducting field research

You can learn a lot at the library and on the web, but some topics might lead you to do your own firsthand research: to interview someone with expertise in your topic, to conduct a survey to gather information, or to observe people in a particular place or situation. Field research involving people as subjects can bring up ethical issues. Academic and other institutions have Institutional Review Boards

(IRBs) to help deal with these issues before research is begun. When planning a field study, talk to your instructor to determine whether you need to consult with your college's IRB to make sure that your study will not be harmful to any of its participants.

Interviews

You can sometimes get information by interviewing someone with expertise or experience in the area you're researching. Say you're looking into the incidence of pandemics in this century. You might interview a microbiology professor on your campus to help launch your search. Here are some tips for conducting a successful interview:

- *Request and schedule the interview* well in advance, either by email or with a telephone call. Be sure to explain your PURPOSE and ask how much time the person would be willing to grant you for the interview.

- *Prepare a list of questions* in advance. You might begin with some questions about the person's work. But then move to open-ended questions that will elicit full answers. Avoid questions that can be answered with a simple "yes" or "no" ("Do you follow the Spurs?") or that prompt certain answers ("Don't you agree that student athletes should be paid?").

- *Take notes* or ask permission to record the interview—or do both. If you are recording, be sure to test all equipment in advance!

- *Write down the person's full name* and title along with the date, time, and place.

- *Say thank you*, both at the end of the interview and later in a written note or email.

Conversations

While interviews are often formal and structured, you may find that more informal, unstructured conversations can sometimes be

The best primary sources are often sitting right next to us.
CLINT SMITH

useful for gathering information. It's worth following the practice of many Indigenous researchers, who stress respectful, engaged silence and listening as a way of coming to understand and appreciate the information that someone is sharing with you. Here are some tips for having such conversations:

- *Try to meet in a comfortable setting* where you can do something together—knit, cook, garden, and so on.
- *Ask permission* to record or take notes.
- *Share some of your own experience* with the topic.
- *Respect the other person's silence*, and be patient waiting for response.
- *Listen carefully* and intently, letting the person know that you're paying close attention. Do not interrupt.
- *If you do ask questions*, do so only for clarification.
- *Express gratitude* for the time spent together.

Observations

You can observe a lot by watching.
YOGI BERRA

Some research questions will lead you to do firsthand observation. Say you're researching how the arrangement of desks in a classroom affects participation. You might observe several classrooms—one with desks in rows, another where they're in a circle, and a third where they're in small clusters. This kind of observing calls for intense and purposeful attention, looking to catch every detail you can and recording the data accurately. Here are some tips to help you do so:

- *Think about your* PURPOSE. What do you want to find out? And how will you use what you learn?
- *Plan ahead*. What will you observe, and when? What materials will you need—a notebook? a camera? If you will be recording information on your phone, what video or

audio apps do you need? Do you need to ask permission in advance to observe, and to take photos or videos?

- *Take notes*. DESCRIBE the place, who's there, what they're doing. Don't start analyzing what you see; just record what you observe. Be sure to note the date, time, and place.

- *After the observation*, take time to jot down any additional details as well as your thoughts about what you saw, along with any questions you may have.

- *Review your notes* and any recorded material carefully, noting any recurring patterns. What have you learned? Did anything surprise you? How can you use the findings when you write up your research?

Surveys

Sometimes your research will require you to get information from a large number of people. Suppose you want to get student response to the latest hike in tuition fees. The best way to do that is with a questionnaire. Here are some tips for planning a survey and creating a questionnaire:

- *Think about your* PURPOSE. What are you trying to learn, and how will you use the results?

- *Decide who to contact*, and how. Will you email them a questionnaire? use *Survey Monkey*? conduct the survey on the phone?

- *Write out your questions*. It's best not to ask too many questions. Multiple-choice questions are easy to answer and then tabulate, but you may also need to ask some open-ended questions to get the information you're seeking.

- *Begin by saying thanks* for taking the time to respond to your questions, and be sure to explain what you're trying to learn. End by again saying thank you and saying when the survey is due.

- ANALYZE *the responses*, looking for patterns and what they reveal about your topic. Think about how you can use the information in reporting on your research.

REFLECT! What have you learned about your topic so far? At this point in the process, which sources seem the most promising, and why? Are you finding enough sources to answer your research question? If not, might you need to revise your question? Have you looked at your topic from a number of different perspectives? If so, have they got you thinking? If not, get to work!

Evaluating Sources, Checking Facts

You may have read that I went to MIT. In 1982 I filled out a *Who's Who* survey with joking responses, and they never bothered to check the facts.

—CHEVY CHASE

Those of us who got our first personal computers way back in the 1980s heard a lot about *GIGO*: "garbage in, garbage out," shorthand for saying if the data you put into a computer is faulty, the outcome will be equally faulty. That phrase is still in use, and its warning is as timely as ever in an even broader context: especially in an age of AI, if the authors and sources you rely on in your writing are "garbage" (or hallucinations?)—well, then, your writing is in danger of being garbage too. And today, when distinguishing fact from fiction, truth from lies, the real from the "deep fake," is more and more difficult, writers need all the help we can get in making sure that the information we find in sources is honest and trustworthy, and that any source we cite in our own work is too.

Florida governor Ron DeSantis should have checked his sources before he quoted Winston Churchill in a speech that ended his campaign for the Republican presidential nomination in January 2024. The sentence DeSantis quoted—"Success is not final, failure is not fatal: it is the courage to continue that counts"—was one that Churchill never spoke or wrote. According to the International Churchill Society, no one knows quite how the quotation came to be associated with Churchill, but the director of Hillsdale College's Churchill Project notes that the ease of quoting and misquoting on the internet has made Churchill, known for his wit and wisdom, "the king of fake quotes." So no matter where you find a quotation that seems perfect, especially from the internet or AI, remember to make sure it is worded accurately—and *not* a fake!

As you begin your search for useful and credible sources, remember that *all* sources have a point of view and so will inevitably reflect at least some of the assumptions and preferences of those who create them. Even the most careful authors can never be all-seeing and all-knowing: while they can aim to present information accurately and fairly, they can't possibly see the topic from every perspective. Pure objectivity is just not possible. But we must still try hard to be as accurate and truthful as possible. It's up to you then to carefully assess all the sources you consult to determine whether you can trust and believe what they say. This chapter will help you make sure the sources you rely on are worthy of your attention—and your trust.

IS THE SOURCE USEFUL?

Once you find sources that seem promising, you need to decide whether they're likely to be useful: how they'll serve your purpose, whether your audience will find them persuasive, and so on. Here are some questions to ask of sources you're considering.

How useful is the source for your research? Check out any table of contents, abstracts, or introduction to get a sense of what the source covers. Then think about what it might contribute to your research. Does it include a bibliography that would lead you to other sources on the topic? Does it include CITATIONS or links that will lead you to other sources?

What is the source's major CLAIM—and does it make sense to you? If you find it hard to believe, see if you can find any other sources that make similar claims. If the claim does seem reasonable, what kinds of EVIDENCE does it provide as support?

What's the genre? Is it REPORTING information or ARGUING a certain position? Chances are you'll need both kinds of sources; but if a source is advocating a particular POINT OF VIEW, you'll want to find sources that provide other PERSPECTIVES as well.

When was the source published or last updated? Keep in mind that more recent does not necessarily mean more useful; the kinds of sources you need will depend on your topic. If you're writing about free speech on campus, you'll likely need to find recent sources with up-to-date information—but you might also want to see what the US Constitution has to say about freedom of speech.

Who are the authors, and what are their qualifications for writing on the topic? Are they affiliated with a particular organization that might affect their viewpoint or goals? If the source doesn't include any information about the author, do a web search to see what you can learn.

Who's the publisher or sponsor? If it's a university press, scholarly journal, or government organization, you can assume that the information has been peer-reviewed; if it's a mainstream news publisher, it's likely been fact-checked. If it's an online source, the URL will help you determine what kind of organization is sponsoring the site: *.org* is used by non-profits, *.gov* by government agencies,

.edu by colleges and universities, *.us* by US government offices, and *.com* by commercial enterprises. No matter who the publisher or sponsor is, do they have a point of view or an agenda you should be aware of?

How might you use this source in your own writing—for background information? as support for your claims? as a counterargument or an example of another perspective?

IS THE SOURCE RELIABLE?

Writers today need to make sure that any sources we use are trustworthy. But that's easier said than done, now that anyone with a computer can post whatever they think—and want others to think. And when entire websites and news organizations present information deliberately slanted to favor one side and denigrate another, sorting through what's accurate and what's not is often a tough call.

Just take a look at the left-leaning *Media Matters for America* and the right-leaning *Accuracy in Media* and you'll find them "reporting" the same information, but often spinning it in radically different ways. That's one reason you need to check out who sponsors such sites and do enough research on them to determine whether they have any biases you need to be aware of. This section provides strategies for checking facts and determining whether—or not—a source should be trusted.

Checking facts

Trust, but verify.
RONALD REAGAN

Ukrainian president Volodymyr Zelenskyy was once seen belly dancing in a skin-tight gold costume. Steph Curry parted ways with Nike because they wouldn't let him write Bible verses on his shoes. Californians are no longer allowed to take a shower, do laundry, and flush the toilet on the same day. These are all stories that were once reported as facts—and were then researched and disputed by various fact-checking organizations.

If you're working with academic sources, you may not encounter too many claims as outlandish as these. But then again, you just might. And given all the misinformation, deliberately misleading news reports, and outright lies that exist these days, you'll want to check the facts if you have any doubts. Thank goodness, there are now a number of sites dedicated to fact-checking. *Snopes*, *Fact Check.org*, and *PolitiFact.com* are three sites dedicated to investigating what's a fact, and what's not—all nonpartisan, meaning they lean neither left nor right.

Snopes

Checking everything from facts to news stories to images, *Snopes* is an internet source for determining "what is true and what is nonsense." It also accepts submissions if you find something you want fact-checked.

 FACTCHECK.ORG

A non-profit site run by the Annenberg Public Policy Center at the University of Pennsylvania, *FactCheck.org* monitors the factual accuracy of what is said by major US political players in ads, debates, speeches, interviews, news releases, and other statements.

PolitiFact.com
Sorting out the truth in politics

PolitiFact.com, a fact-checking website run by the Pointer Institute for Media Studies, includes a "Truth-O-Meter" that rates claims as true, mostly true, half true, mostly false, or false. In spite of its name, this site covers more than just politics. (In fact, it's where we found the story about Steph Curry's shoes!)

Sites like these can go a long way toward helping you choose sources that are credible, and toward being confident that any sources you cite, and thus pass on to others, are trustworthy and accurate.

REFLECT! Choose a website that you've identified as potentially useful for a topic you're researching or are interested in learning about. Using one of the fact-checking sites listed above, decide whether the information on the site is trustworthy. Write a brief paragraph summing up how reliable the site seems.

Reading laterally

Researchers at Stanford asked a number of students, historians, and professional fact-checkers to study various websites to determine which ones were credible and trustworthy. What they discovered was alarming: the historians and the students were largely unable to determine which sites were credible. The professional fact-checkers, on the other hand, identified the credible sites every time. Their secret? They would quickly look over the site, but then they would open a number of additional tabs and search to see what others had to say about the site. As the authors of the study say:

> Historians and students often fell victim to easily manipulated features of websites, such as official-looking logos and domain names. They read vertically, staying within a website to evaluate its reliability. In contrast, fact checkers read laterally, leaving a site after a quick scan and opening up new browser tabs in order to judge the credibility of the original site. Compared to the other groups, fact checkers arrived at more warranted conclusions in a fraction of the time.
>
> —SAM WINEBURG and SARAH McGREW

In short, the students and historians read *vertically*, focusing on the site they were checking—its author, its sponsor, its links, its claims—whereas the professional fact-checkers read *laterally*, leaving the site to find out what other sources had to say. Specifically, they tried to verify *if* anyone else was saying what the source they were checking said; and they also tried to find out *what* if anything other sources had to say *about* the site or its author.

And that's what you should do. When you're researching something online and find a website you know nothing about, take a tip from the pros: open several tabs in the same browser at the top of your screen to search for information about the site or the text.

- ***Enter the title of the site,*** and add keywords like "sponsor" or "funding" to find out if the site has a particular agenda.
- ***If you're investigating a specific article,*** enter its title to see if it's discussed on other sites, and if so, what they're saying.
- ***Enter the name of the author*** to see what you can find out about their expertise and STANCE on the topic.
- ***Enter any claims that seem questionable.*** See if any other sources make similar claims. And pay special attention if a claim pops up on *Snopes* or another fact-checking site.

By studying a number of other sites on the same topic, you'll find information that you wouldn't likely spot by simply studying the site itself—and you'll find it more quickly to boot.

REFLECT! Look again at the website you evaluated on page 336. This time look beyond the source, opening several browser tabs to see what other sites claim about the same topic. Does reading laterally turn up any new information about the source's reliability?

Triangulating

Experienced researchers know to raise a caution flag when they find information in a source that can't be verified by other sources. That's a pretty good sign that the source may not be trustworthy. To avoid falling victim to such sources (especially those that have been identified by AI, which sometimes makes up sources that don't even exist), it's always wise to "triangulate" sources—that is, to check at least three other credible, verifiable sources that are reporting the same information. If it is accurate, you should find a number of other sources reporting on it.

Likewise, if you can find only one or two pieces of evidence to back up a claim that you yourself want to make, you'd better re-evaluate your claim: you may be on shaky ground.

But triangulation is about more than validating the accuracy of a source or its claims. In addition, it will take you deeper into the topic you're exploring, leading to a richer understanding of it and helping you see the topic from several different perspectives. Finally, triangulation is one more way to uncover and counter biases, including your own.

Reading with a critical eye

Once you've determined that a source seems reliable, read it very carefully for what you can learn about your topic and how it might inform what you yourself write.

- What's the CLAIM? Is it clearly stated? Does it support your own thinking about your topic? Or does it provide a different perspective, one that might get you thinking differently?

- What REASONS and EVIDENCE support that claim: Facts? Expert testimony? Data? Personal experience? Analogies? Look here for reasons and evidence that you might use in your own argument.

- Does the source acknowledge and respond to any COUNTERARGUMENTS or other PERSPECTIVES? If it cites other sources, does it provide DOCUMENTATION? Should you check out any of these other sources?

- What's motivating the author? If there's no author, who's the sponsor, and what's their interest in the issue? What are their PURPOSES for sponsoring the site, and are they clearly stated?

- Are you convinced that the argument is one to take seriously? Is this a source you'd want to CITE?
- How would it contribute to your own argument?

Finding the good stuff

You've checked facts, triangulated, read carefully and laterally. You're pretty sure the information you've found is reliable. But is it good? Take it from Howard Rheingold: the good stuff is there—we just have to know how to find it. Here are some things he says that we should look for:

> The good stuff is out there if you know how to find and verify it.
>
> HOWARD RHEINGOLD

- *The authors are identified.* It's even better if they provide a way to respond or contact them. If they're academics, check *Google Scholar* to see if their work has been cited by other scholars.
- *The site is .edu, .gov, or .org* and the author or site is affiliated with a college or university, government agency, or some other trustworthy institution.
- *The source cites or links to other sources* as support for any claims.

These are all signs of information you can trust. But don't forget about your own good common sense: if a source sounds outlandish or ridiculous or too good to be true, it very well may be. Just remember that in this age of misinformation, you probably need to confirm even your own good judgment!

Checking your own firsthand research

You also need to take a good look at any FIELD RESEARCH you yourself have done. If your research has led you to conduct experiments, interviews, observations, or surveys, then you need to do some double-checking of that work, assessing it with a critical eye. Begin by checking to be sure you've provided necessary details—exactly when and where the research took place, the instruments you used (such as questionnaires or questions for interviews), and how you went about analyzing the results. Make sure that you have also clarified your own part in the research and taken into account how your own beliefs or assumptions might have unconsciously influenced the findings. Double-check the data you gathered to make sure your calculations are accurate and the conclusions you draw are fully supported by the data. Finally, if you have quoted the words of any participants, check to see that these are absolutely accurate.

REFLECT! Choose two websites on a topic you're exploring or want to explore. Then use the various methods provided in this chapter—fact-checking, lateral reading, and triangulating—to assess the reliability of each site. Which method works best, and why? Finally, write a paragraph describing the steps you took to assess the sites and what you learned by doing so.

Building an Annotated Bibliography

An annotated bibliography can be a researcher's best friend—and a shortcut to identifying great sources.

—SHIRLEY BRICE HEATH

A s a researcher, you may have several reasons for compiling an annotated bibliography. Building one can help you narrow and focus your topic, or help move you toward a thesis or major claim. Or it can help you decide which sources will be the most useful for your project, or compare several sources on the same topic, or reveal varying perspectives on a topic. Annotating a source will surely help you read it carefully and critically and thus understand it more fully. And the more sources you annotate, the more you will be able to understand the larger conversation surrounding your topic, the range of

341

perspectives on it, and the way the sources relate to your own research. Finally, compiling an annotated bibliography will help separate the sources you have found into those that are credible, timely, and useful, and those that are not. In one of my classes, students decided they would "annotate" some sources and "detonate" others they found to be less useful, or misinformed, or even fake!

In any case, an annotated bibliography demonstrates that you've done your homework, that you are familiar with what others have had to say about your topic, and that the sources you've identified are trustworthy and credible. Unlike the student in the cartoon on this page, you will not be relying on "anonymous" sources!

There are two ways to annotate a bibliography: by describing sources and by evaluating them. *Descriptive annotations* primarily summarize the contents of a source and explain how you expect it to contribute to your research. *Evaluative annotations* do that as well, but they also explain what you see as a source's strengths and weaknesses. This chapter provides guidelines and examples for doing each one.

"I would have done a bibliography, but my sources
prefer to remain anonymous."

A GUIDE TO ANNOTATING A BIBLIOGRAPHY

Annotations vary in length, usually between 150 and 300 words in one or two paragraphs: you're trying to capture the essence of the source as succinctly as possible. You will be expected to DESCRIBE each source and explain what it will contribute to your research—and you may be assigned to EVALUATE sources as well.

Begin with complete documentation for the source, following the style assigned by your instructor or used in your field—MLA, APA, or some other style. This information will help you or your readers locate the source easily, and it can also be cut and pasted into your list of WORKS CITED, REFERENCES, or other bibliography.

Identify any authors, along with their credentials. If they have a particular STANCE, note that as well.

Briefly SUMMARIZE ***or*** DESCRIBE the source's main points and any details that are relevant to your research, making sure to do so accurately and fairly. Note how the source contributes to your research and informs your thinking on the topic, and how you expect to use it in what you write.

If you're writing an evaluative bibliography, consider things that matter to your project: How AUTHORITATIVE is the source? Does it consider multiple views, or a certain view you need to learn about? Does it include a bibliography or CITE sources you didn't already know about? Be sure to note both its strengths and weaknesses.

Alphabetize entries in your bibliography by the lead author's last name; if there is no author, use the first word of the title (excluding *a*, *an*, or *the*).

Present all the annotations in a bibliography consistently: if one is written in complete sentences, they should all be.

If you're following MLA or APA style, see the formats they each require on pages 344 and 345.

TWO KINDS OF ANNOTATIONS

Olivia Steely is a student at the University of Missouri, St. Louis, where she is majoring in English with a minor in Spanish. The following examples are from an annotated bibliography she compiled while researching the empathetic rhetoric of Dorothy Roudebush, an educator and activist for women's rights. The first is a descriptive entry she wrote for her class, and the second is an evaluative one she wrote for this book.

A descriptive annotation*

Leake, Eric. "Writing Pedagogies of Empathy: As Rhetoric
 and Disposition." *Composition Forum*, vol. 34, Jan. 2016,
 compositionforum.com/issue/34/empathy.php.

> This article by a rhetoric professor at Texas State
> University answers the calls for teaching empathy
> and discusses ways that it can be taught in writing
> classes. Leake discusses two theories of empathy
> and how they can be taught—as rhetoric, and as a
> disposition. Rhetorical empathy, he says, focuses
> on the "enticements" and "limitations" of
> empathy as a means of persuasion, while
> dispositional empathy teaches "habits of mind"
> aimed at helping students better understand and
> engage with others. Leake also reviews multiple
> definitions of empathy and perspectives on it,
> which provides much more context and adds to
> my own understanding of what empathy can and
> cannot do.

*The annotated bibliography on this page follows **MLA** style.

An evaluative annotation*

Leake, E. (2016). Writing pedagogies of empathy: As rhetoric and
disposition. *Composition forum, 34*. https://compositionforum.
com/issue/34/empathy.php
This article by a professor of rhetoric addresses the calls for
teaching empathy and discusses ways that it can be taught in
writing classes. Leake discusses two theories of empathy and
how they can be taught—as rhetoric, and as a disposition.
Rhetorical empathy, he says, focuses on what he calls the
"enticements" and "limitations" of empathy as a means of
persuasion, whereas dispositional empathy teaches "habits of
mind" aimed at helping students better understand and engage
with others. Even though the many detailed suggestions he
offers for incorporating empathy in a writing class do not
pertain to my project, the multiple perspectives and definitions
he provides will broaden both my understanding of empathy
and the way I think about it. In addition, he's made me aware
of what Carl Rogers, Krista Ratcliffe, John Duffy, and other
scholars have said about empathy; I plan to pursue their work
as well.

*The annotated bibliography on this page follows **APA** style.

REFLECT! See if you can find an annotated bibliography on a topic
you're researching. If you do, does it include any sources you haven't
found yourself? And if it's an evaluative one, is it helpful to you, and in
what ways? If you cannot find an annotated bibliography on your topic,
search on the web for annotated bibliographies about empathy. Take a
look at one, and see how it compares with the examples in this chapter.

Synthesizing Ideas

Should a college education be free? That's your research question. You get started, and your research turns up many different answers: Yes, college should be a universal right, just like K–12. And a free college education is offered in Finland, Germany, Sweden, and a number of other countries. College needs to be affordable, but not free. Making college free would be a "needless windfall" for affluent students; financial aid should be given only to students who really need it. College would never actually be free; the cost would be borne by taxpayers.

These are answers that reflect many different positions and present various kinds of evidence and data, giving you a lot to think about. As a researcher, you'll need to *synthesize* what your sources say, looking for connections, patterns, ideas, examples, controversies, and more—all things that will help you figure out what you think about your topic and then to support what you say about it. This chapter will help you think about the ideas you find in your sources and then weave some of them in with your own.

Identifying patterns and themes

As a researcher, you will often contend with ideas and information from varying points of view, and need to think about how they connect to one another (or not) and how they inform, support, or challenge what *you* want to say. That means reading carefully and purposefully, and *with a critical eye but an open mind*. It also means taking notes as you read, noting any similarities or differences, recurring patterns, ideas, citations, or other things.

When you work with sources in this way, you're synthesizing. Think of synthesizing as a way of putting your sources in conversation with one another and letting them talk back and forth as a way of helping you understand your topic more fully. Here are some questions to help you synthesize information:

- *What do your sources have in common—***how do they agree?** Are there any recurring facts or examples? ideas? issues or controversies? Is there any data that's cited in more than one source?

- *Are there any disagreements among your sources?* Do they take different POSITIONS? Use different methods? Serve different audiences or purposes? Present different kinds of EVIDENCE? Rely on different sources?

- *Do any of your sources cite or refer to one another?* Do they respond to one another in any way, and if so, are they critical of each other? complimentary? a little of each? Does any source build on the research cited in another?

- ***Are there any links*** found in more than one of your sources?

- ***Are there any sources cited that you haven't seen***—and that you should check out?

- ***How would you characterize the conversation among your sources?*** Does it seem cooperative? antagonistic? guarded? Does the nature of the conversation affect how you feel about using any of these sources?

- ***Have you encountered any surprising ideas or*** EVIDENCE—things that you now need to investigate?

- ***What*** GENRES ***are your sources?*** Magazine articles? Newspaper op-eds? Scholarly arguments? Blog posts? Books? Speeches? If they're all from the same one or two genres, consider checking out other genres as well.

Moving from what your sources say to what you say

The work you do identifying common patterns, themes, and differences among your sources is the first step in synthesizing the information you've found. You may note, for example, that almost all your sources call for one particular solution to a problem—or that each source identifies a different solution to that problem. Synthesizing this information, you could say that there is general agreement (or very little agreement) on how to solve the problem. And of course you'll likely have sources that present sharply different positions. Making sense of it all is a challenge, but it will make you aware of

The mind's synthesizing powers at work!

what many others have said about your topic—and get you thinking more about your own position.

In short, the work of synthesizing multiple ideas and perspectives will help you think about (or rethink) your own POSITION. Now is the time to go back to your working THESIS: In light of all you've learned from your sources, do you need to revise it—to focus on one aspect of the topic, or to QUALIFY it in some way? Here are some questions that can help you think about how your sources have affected your thinking about your topic:

- How exactly do your sources relate to your topic or THESIS? What does each source contribute to the points you are making about the topic?
- Are there any ideas or positions in your sources that you want to respond to?
- Do any sources present data or examples that you want to cite or challenge?
- Have your sources changed your views or made them more nuanced—and if so, how?
- Have any sources brought up questions you hadn't considered and now want to explore?

If so, yay! Good solid research is supposed to open our minds to new possibilities and lead us to see things more clearly and comprehensively. Such insights can even lead you to see your topic in a new light and to have new ideas about what you want to say about it.

If, as Zora Neale Hurston says, research is "poking and prying with a purpose," such poking and prying will inevitably lead to new discoveries, new ideas, and new understandings. Most important, synthesizing your sources systematically will help you to discover and clarify your own ideas and to come up with your own conclusions—and then to make your own contribution to the conversation.

REFLECT! If you are permitted to use *ChatGPT* or another AI tool, ask it to synthesize several sources for you—*after* you have already gotten a good start on synthesizing them yourself. Then compare your synthesis with the one produced by AI, carefully noting similarities, differences, and discrepancies. What about the AI-generated synthesis strikes you as most helpful? What if anything seems off the mark or inappropriate in some way? What does the comparison teach you about how you could make your own synthesis more effective?

Writing that synthesizes information

You will see signs of synthesis at work in much of what you read. Here, for example, is the opening of an article that synthesizes information drawn from multiple sources on the effects that vacations can have on the health of those who take them:

> Beyond souvenirs and suntans, the best reason to take a break may be your own health. For the Helsinki Businessman Study, a 40-year-old cardiovascular-health study... researchers treated men at risk of heart disease. From 1974 to 2004, those men who took at least three weeks of vacation were 37 percent less likely to die than those who took fewer weeks off (Strandberg et al.).
>
> Even if we don't view time off as a matter of life and death, people who take more of their allotted vacation time tend to find their work more meaningful (West et al.). Vacation can yield other benefits, too. People who took all or most of their paid vacation time to travel were more likely than others to report a recent raise or bonus (U.S. Travel Association).
>
> —BEN HEALY, "Hell Is Other People's Vacations"

So far, so good. But Healy goes on to synthesize information from other sources that share another common theme—concern for how vacation travel is affecting our planet:

Tourism's carbon footprint grew four times as much as expected from 2009 to 2013, and accounted for 8 percent of all greenhouse-gas emissions in that period (Lenzen). What's more, the travel industry is expected to consume 92 percent more water in 2050 than it did in 2010, and 189 percent more land. In other news, people are less likely to recycle while on vacation (Oliver).

The patterns and themes Healy synthesizes into these paragraphs lead him to draw an ironic conclusion of his own:

So for your own health and sanity, book that vacation. But for everyone else's, please travel as sustainably as you can, and take it easy with *Instagram*.

And notice that he includes IN-TEXT DOCUMENTATION for the sources he cites. You need to do that as well.

Here's one more example. Researcher Peggy Orenstein spent two years talking to more than 100 young men between the ages of 16 and 21 about what they think it means to be a man and about how they view masculinity. In the following paragraph, she synthesizes information drawn from these interviews and from a recent survey.

[W]hen asked to describe the attributes of "the ideal guy," these boys appeared to be harking back to 1955. Dominance. Aggression. Rugged good looks (with an emphasis on height). Sexual prowess. Stoicism. Athleticism. Wealth (at least some day). It's not that these qualities, properly channeled, are bad. But while a 2018 national survey of more than 1,000 10- to 19-year-olds conducted by the polling firm PerryUndem found that young women believe there were many ways to be a girl . . . young men described just one narrow route to successful masculinity. One-third said they felt compelled to suppress their feelings, to "suck it up" or "be a man" when they were sad or scared, and more than 40 percent said that when they were angry, society expected them to be combative.

—PEGGY ORENSTEIN, "The Miseducation of the American Boy"

See Ch. 12 on researching and synthesizing ideas for a report.

What Orenstein has done is to study the responses of these 100 young men, looking for patterns and themes and trends—and then reporting the results of that synthesis, in this case the characteristics these young men claim make up "the ideal man." Note that she does not cite the interview sources because they are her own research. In addition, she does not cite the source of the 2018 national survey because she is publishing this article in a magazine (*The Atlantic*) that doesn't include formal documentation. In the writing you do in your academic classes, you would cite both of these sources—your own research as well as the national survey.

REFLECT! Why not take a cue from **Peggy Orenstein**'s question ("What do you think are the attributes of the 'ideal guy'?") to make up a question of your own: "What are the attributes of the ideal roommate?" "ideal partner?" "ideal pet?" Then interview five people who are themselves roommates, partners, or pet owners. With their permission, record their responses and then look for patterns, similarities, differences, and so on—and synthesize your findings into one brief paragraph.

Quoting, Paraphrasing, Summarizing

To quote? to paraphrase? or to summarize?
That is the question.

—CAROLE CLARK PAPPER

ood researchers are part detective, part adventurer, and part explorer. Their sources provide clues and point to new leads; they identify new directions that delve deeper and deeper into knowledge about the topic of research. But researchers are also part orchestra conductor, gathering sources, bringing them together to make beautiful music—not in a symphony but in a compelling, eye-opening research project.

As the conductor, you are in charge of your project—the one who discovers a new way of looking at your topic, the one who decides what conclusions can be drawn from the evidence you consider, who moves from a challenging research question to a thorough exploration of the question and its implications, and eventually to staking your claim, developing a thesis and supporting it. And just as an orchestra's conductor decides when to cue the string section or turn to a flute soloist, so you decide when to bring in your sources for greatest effect.

The sources you bring in act like supporting players or voices, highlighting the points you are making but without overpowering your own voice. You can bring these supporting voices in with a quotation (the precise words of a source, enclosed in quotation marks), a paraphrase (ideas in a passage from a source, in your own words), or a summary (a brief statement of a source's major points).

A way to establish your authority

Bringing the ideas and voices of others into your writing shows that you understand the context surrounding your topic, that you know what others have said about it and the varying perspectives they bring. In other words, it helps build your credibility and trustworthiness to write on the topic: you know what you're talking about and are now a part of the conversation. And finally, judicious quoting, paraphrasing, and summarizing allow you to be the conductor, to direct the action in your research essay to the desired end.

Deciding whether to quote, paraphrase, or summarize

While there are no strict rules for choosing whether to quote, paraphrase, or summarize, here are some tips that can help you decide.

Quote

- If an idea is so important and powerfully stated that rewording it might weaken or distort it
- When it's a passage you intend to analyze
- To call attention to the author's expertise in order to help establish your own credibility

- To make sure you are presenting a source fairly and accurately, especially if it's one you do not agree with

Paraphrase

- When the precise words aren't important, but there's a point or some details you want to include
- If the original wording will be hard for your audience to understand

Summarize

- A lengthy passage when the point is important but the details are not

QUOTING

Quoting someone's exact words helps ensure that you're representing their ideas accurately. By quoting sources directly, you show that you're being careful and respectful, letting those you quote speak for themselves rather than interpreting what they say. Be sure to use the exact words of your source, and to enclose them in quotation marks. And make sure to frame the quotation by introducing it and then explaining how it relates to your point.

Enclose short quotations in quotation marks within your text. If you're following MLA style, short quotations should be no longer than four typed lines. If you're following APA style, short means no more than forty words. The following example is in MLA style.

> In their introduction to *Identity and Story: Creating Self in Narrative,* Dan McAdams, Ruthellen Josselson, and Amia Lieblitch offer an instructive perspective for using narrative to support progress and change. Stating "We are all storytellers, and we are the stories we tell" (3), they suggest that the stories we tell (and that are told about us) become the stories of who we are.
>
> —JACQUELINE JONES ROYSTER, *Making the World a Better Place*

And here's an example in APA style:

> In the Afterword to his 2002 book *Next: The Future Just Happened*, Lewis (2002) said that he "began writing this book after the Internet had become a commercial joke." In raising his voice in opposition to that view, Lewis felt he was being "ridiculously brave," though in retrospect neither he nor those whose views he was challenging seem to have gotten the Internet's significance right (p. 237). Today, two decades after his book came out, theorists and pundits are still trying to determine that significance.

***Set off long quotations as* BLOCK QUOTATIONS.** Block quotations are not enclosed in quotation marks, but instead, the whole block is indented five spaces (or one-half inch). What counts as a long quotation varies: it's more than four lines for MLA or forty words for APA. Here is Professor Jabari Mahiri using a block quotation (APA style) in a study of the language used by high school coaches:

> As one technique for focusing on players' accomplishments and improvements, coaches gave extended turns of praise both to the team as a whole and to individual players, as when Coach LeRoy Crowe pulled a player to the side after a game to say:
>
> > You played a good game out there my man. You know that? People weren't recognizing what you were doing, but the coaches saw what you were doing. You were playin' that point guard position. You were looking down low. You hit Kendall with a nice pass down there. You remember that pass he scooped up? You weren't hitting your free throws. But, I mean, we recognized that you stayed under control. (p. 34)
>
> —JABARI MAHIRI, *Shooting for Excellence: African American and Youth Culture in New Century Schools*

In this passage, Mahiri uses a long quotation to let the coach speak for himself, providing an example of the kind of coach-player interaction Mahiri is studying. Note too that when setting a block quotation the parenthetical documentation comes after the quotation's final punctuation.

Quoting poetry

You can quote up to three lines of poetry in your text, enclosed within quotation marks. Separate the lines with slashes, leaving one space on either side of the slash.

> Appointed in 2019, Joy Harjo was the first Native American Poet Laureate of the United States. In "Remember," a poem about what is most important to remember in life, she encourages readers to "Remember you are all people and all people are you. / Remember you are this universe and this universe is you" (lines 9–10). Here Harjo suggests that our memories should encode our common humanity.

If you're quoting four or more lines of poetry, set them off in a BLOCK QUOTATION, indented five spaces from the left margin. Set the lines as they appear in the original poem, with the same line breaks and indentations as the original poem.

> Alas, rhetoric can be used for harmful purposes: to humiliate and confuse, to distort and mislead. In W. B. Yeats's haunting words, written amidst the horrors of the great war in 1919:
>
> > Things fall apart; the centre cannot hold;
> > Mere anarchy is loosed upon the world,
> > The blood-dimmed tide is loosed, and everywhere
> > The ceremony of innocence is drowned;
> > The best lack all conviction, while the worst
> > Are full of passionate intensity. (lines 3–8)
>
> Today it may well seem that the worst among us are the ones whose "passionate intensity" is being heard. But giving in to that vision would mean giving up on rhetoric as ethical communication. And that we cannot do.

Changing a quotation to fit into your text

Put ELLIPSES in places where you omit words from a quotation because they're unnecessary for your point. Use three dots with a space before each one and after the last dot. If, however, you omit an entire sentence or more, add a period before the ellipses.

> In 1879, the Scottish philosopher Alexander Bain wrote one of the few nineteenth-century grammars to approve of singular *they* . . . declaring, "When both genders are implied, it is allowable to use the plural. . . . Grammarians frequently call this construction an error, not reflecting that it is equally an error to apply *his* to feminine subjects. The best writers furnish examples of the use of the plural as a mode of getting out of the difficulty."
>
> —DENNIS BARON, *What's Your Pronoun?*

Put brackets around any words that you insert in a quotation to make it fit grammatically into your text, or that you add to clarify something that might otherwise be unclear.

> In 1885, the linguist Fred Newton Scott observed that pretty much everyone used the singular *they*, both people who care about good grammar, and those who don't, noting, "The word *they* is being used as a [common gender] pronoun every day by millions of persons who are not particular about their language, and every other day by several thousands who are particular" (qtd. in Baron 167).

Punctuating quotations

When a quotation is followed by other punctuation, that punctuation goes inside the final quotation mark in some cases and outside in others. Following are some guidelines on where it goes:

Commas and periods go *inside* the closing quotation mark, even if they are not part of the original quotation.

> "Rap is definitely poetry," Latto tells me. "We just do it to a beat."
>
> —ADAM BRADLEY, "Dismantling the Barriers between Rap and Poetry"

When there's in-text documentation, however, the documentation goes after the closing quotation mark, and the end punctuation that's part of your sentence goes after the parentheses.

> Nothing in my education had provided me with strategies for resisting certain versions of whiteness that may privilege me but oppress others. I state this lack and unearned privilege . . . simply because I want to make them visible. For "only by visualizing this privilege and incorporating it into discourse can people of good faith combat discrimination" in ways that prevent their doing "more harm than good" (Wildman and Davis 660, 661).
>
> —KRISTA RATCLIFFE, *Rhetorical Listening: Identification, Gender, Whiteness*

Exclamation points and question marks go *inside* the closing quotation mark if they are part of the quoted text. But they go *outside* the closing quotation mark if they are a part of the sentence you're writing, not a part of the quotation.

> Noting that most people are more likely to cheat on their taxes if they believe others are not paying a fair share of what they earn, Rene Chun asks "So why are Americans still paying?" One answer—that taxpayers now have to list a Social Security number for every dependent—has meant that "the number of dependents nationwide shrank by millions." It's worth noting, however, that "some of the disappeared had names like Fluffy"!

Colons and semicolons always go *outside* the closing quotation marks.

> "Despite deep IRS budget cuts," Rene Chun says, "most Americans still pay their income taxes every year"; indeed, he goes on to say that "most of us feel *obliged* to pay."

> Way back in 1789, Benjamin Franklin declared that "Nothing is certain except death and taxes": How right he was!

With parenthetical documentation

See p. 418 (MLA) and p. 460 (APA) on punctuating parenthetical documentation with long quotations. If you provide parenthetical DOCUMENTATION for a quotation, it goes after the closing quotation mark, and put the end punctuation that's part of your sentence after the parentheses.

> The restaurant became the place where Rosie studied human behavior, puzzling over the problems of her regular customers and refining her ability to deal with people in a difficult world. She took pride in "being among the public," she'd say. "There isn't a day that goes by in the restaurant that you don't learn something" (451).
>
> —MIKE ROSE, "Blue-Collar Brilliance"

Notice that this example follows MLA style; if it followed APA style, the parenthetical documentation would say (p. 451).

Explaining how a quotation relates to your point

When you insert a quotation into a text you're writing, you need to explain what it means and how it relates to what you are saying. If you were writing an essay about how race affects college admissions, for instance, here's something you might quote, and how you'd explain it.

> Educators are now beginning to understand the degree to which schools often operate on the basis of contradictory principles. Professor Carmen Kynard has pointed out that American colleges and universities have often practiced exclusionary policies while claiming to do the opposite, a move Kynard's grandmother referred to as "runnin with the rabbits but huntin with the dogs" (19). Such contradictions, in other words, are anything but accidental.

Imagine that this paragraph ended by quoting Carmen Kynard's grandmother: Would you be able to understand what she said—and what it has to do with college admissions? Maybe you would, or maybe not. The point is that you'll usually need to explain a quotation and to tell readers explicitly how it relates to what *you* are saying.

PARAPHRASING

When you paraphrase, you restate information from a source in your own words and your own sentence structures. Paraphrase when there are ideas you want to convey but the original wording is not important. Be careful not to use the same words or structures, which could be seen as plagiarism. At the same time, make sure that you represent the original text accurately.

A good paraphrase demonstrates that you have read the source carefully—and that you understand what it means! And even though you're using your own words, be sure to acknowledge where the ideas came from by naming the author and including parenthetical documentation.

Here's a paragraph from an article in *The Atlantic*, followed on the next page by two possible paraphrases:

> For 23 years starting in 1885, Belgium's King Leopold II was the "proprietor," as he called himself, of the misnamed Congo Free State, the territory that today is the Democratic Republic of Congo. Exasperated by the declining power of European monarchs, Leopold wanted a place where he could reign supreme, unencumbered by voters or a parliament, and in the Congo he got it. He made a fortune from his privately owned colony—well over $1.1 billion in today's dollars—chiefly by enslaving much of its male population as laborers to tap wild rubber vines. The king's soldiers would march into village after village and hold the women hostage, in order to force the men to go deep into the rain forest for weeks at a time to gather wild rubber. Hunting, fishing, and the cultivation of crops were all disrupted, and the army seized much of what food was left. The birth rate plummeted and, weakened by hunger, people succumbed to diseases they might otherwise have survived. Demographers estimate that the Congo's population may have been slashed by as much as half, or some 10 million people.
>
> —ADAM HOCHSCHILD, "When Museums Have Ugly Pasts"

UNACCEPTABLE PARAPHRASE

In 1895, Belgium's King Leopold II was the "owner" of what he called the Congo Free State, the country that's now known as the Democratic Republic of Congo. Granting himself total power, he made a fortune by enslaving most of the male population, destroying the traditional way of life, decimating the birth rate, and leading to the death of some 10 million people.

This paraphrase fails to acknowledge the author or document the source, and borrows too much from the original syntax and wording, using some of it word for word and other parts barely changed: "In 1895, Belgium's King Leopold II," "by enslaving most of the male population." It also misrepresents the original, saying that he enslaved *most* of the male population when the original only said "much"; it is also misleading in claiming that 10 million people died; the original says that the population may have declined by that number, but also indicates a number of reasons for that decline, including that the birth rate "plummeted."

ACCEPTABLE PARAPHRASE

According to historian Adam Hochschild, Belgium's King Leopold II was once the self-proclaimed owner of the Congo Free State (now the Democratic Republic of Congo). From 1885 to 1908, he exercised total control over the Congolese people, amassing a personal fortune mostly by forcing many of the men into the rain forest to harvest wild rubber. This policy disrupted the traditional means of food production, which led to hunger, disease, and a declining birth rate. All told, that resulted in a steep decline in the Congo's population—by 10 million people, according to some estimates ("When Museums").

This paraphrase captures the main points of the passage without relying on the original wording or sentence structures. It also identifies the author and provides parenthetical documentation to the source.

SUMMARIZING

A summary captures a source's main ideas concisely, and in your own words. Unlike a paraphrase, it leaves out details. Your goal is to provide just enough information to sum up the point you are summarizing. When you're summarizing a source as part of your own writing, you'll want to make it as brief as possible—maybe only a sentence or two. As with a quotation or paraphrase, you'll need to credit the author and provide parenthetical documentation. Here's a summary of the Adam Hochschild paragraph from page 361:

> From 1885 to 1908, Belgium's King Leopold II claimed ownership and total control of today's Democratic Republic of Congo, disrupting the people's traditional way of life and giving rise to hunger, disease, and the death of millions of people (Hochschild).

REFLECT! Look at the passage on page 356 in which **Jabari Mahiri** quotes Coach LeRoy Crowe. Try your hand at paraphrasing and summarizing what Coach Crowe said. Then compare this with the direct quotation, and write a paragraph about why you think Mahiri chose to quote rather than summarize or paraphrase.

INCORPORATING SOURCE MATERIALS

Whether you quote, paraphrase, or summarize a source, you should introduce it with a SIGNAL PHRASE and explain how the information you're citing contributes to your own ideas.

> New Mexico writer and teacher Andrew Schmookler *said* he cringes when grammar rules are broken. Yet he also proposed *het, hes, hem* as a new gender-neutral pronoun, *arguing*, "Language is ours to make. (This is not France!) . . . Power to the people" (241).

Note the two signal verbs in this example: *said* to simply report what he said, but *arguing* to note something he was advocating. While you can always use a neutral verb like *say* or *think*, it's better to choose a verb that reflects the speaker's **STANCE**. For example:

> Erma Bombeck *urges* us to "Seize the moment," reminding us to "Remember all those women on the *Titanic* who waved off the dessert cart" (*Forever Erma* 56).

We could have written that Bombeck *says* to seize the moment, but we think that *urges* is more dynamic, fun—and accurate.

While signal phrases often come first in a sentence, putting them in the middle or at the end of a sentence works as well—and is a way of adding variety to our writing.

> "How about those Chiefs!" Andy Reid *shouted* from the podium after the Kansas City Chiefs won the 2020 Superbowl. "Pat Mahomes and all of his boys, our defense taking care of business. The coaches, man, a great job of keeping things right at the right time. It was a beautiful thing."

> "Knowing what you don't know is more useful than being brilliant," *advised* Berkshire Hathaway vice chair Charlie Munger (101).

SOME USEFUL SIGNAL VERBS

acknowledge	conclude	observe
add	contend	point out
advocate	declare	refute
agree	demand	report
argue	disagree	respond
assert	dispute	say
believe	imply	suggest
claim	insist	think
comment	note	urge

Verb tenses. MLA style requires the present tense (*Beyoncé asserts*) or present perfect (*Jay-Z has said*) in signal phrases that introduce source material—but the past tense (*in 2013 Pharrell urged us to "clap along"*) when you give the date when the source was written. APA recommends the past tense (*asserted*) or the present perfect (*has* or *have asserted*)—but the present tense (*asserts*) when you're citing the implications of an experiment or findings that are generally agreed on.

REFLECT! Review something you've written focusing on how you've incorporated the words or ideas of others. Whether you've quoted, paraphrased, or summarized, think about why you chose that way—and then, try it a different way. Then review your signal phrases: Are there any more accurate or interesting verbs you might use? And where have you put the signal phrases? If they're all at the beginning of a sentence, try some in the middle or at the end.

21 Giving Credit, Using Sources Ethically

There's nothing new under the sun.

—ECCLESIASTES 1:9

If I have seen further, it is by
standing on the shoulders of giants.

—SIR ISAAC NEWTON

Today, when "new" and "new and improved" scream at us from every direction, it's worth wondering whether Ecclesiastes got it wrong to say that there's nothing new under the sun. But if you stop and think about every "new" technology, every "new" idea, even every "new" story, you will soon find that they all build on earlier thinking, or earlier research. The iPhone was a new kind of phone, but it was by no means the first telephone. *Frozen* was a new film in 2013, but its story is based on "The Snow Queen," a fairy tale written by Hans Christian Andersen that was first published in 1845. And while generative AI certainly felt new when *ChatGPT* burst on the scene in late 2022, Alan Turing was working hard on machine intelligence almost 100 years ago. Just as Isaac Newton said, what's "new" is made possible only by "standing on the shoulders" of others.

Think about how this applies to your own life: Can you even begin to trace all the ways you have been influenced by the words and ideas of others? It's a good bet that you have already stood on the shoulders of a few others. The same is true of just about anything you write, especially when you write something based on research. And that's just one reason that you need to give credit to anyone—or anything, if you're using AI—whose words or ideas have informed your own. This chapter will help you know which sources you need to acknowledge, and how to use them ethically and without accidentally plagiarizing.

Who owns words and ideas, anyway?

In some cultures, words and ideas are shared, not "owned" by individuals. In others, using another person's words or ideas is viewed as a compliment, a testimony to that person's wisdom that does not need to be acknowledged explicitly. Well into the Renaissance, in fact, you could own a pig or a cow or a bed—but you couldn't own words: Shakespeare borrowed right and left from prior sources without attribution and without restraint, and indeed, that was part of his genius.

Following Great Britain's Copyright Act of 1710, however, a complex network of copyright and patent laws developed as a means of protecting the words, images, and ideas of people and businesses. These laws increasingly gave rights of ownership of both words and ideas, as long as they were "expressed" in some medium, such as in writing or speech, and these laws form the basis for the documentation systems developed by groups such as the Modern Language Association (MLA) and the American Psychological Association (APA) and used in colleges and universities today.

So what do copyright laws have to do with you? It turns out that the answer is "a lot"—and not everyone is happy about this fact of academic life. Law professor Lawrence Lessig argues that such laws act as a deterrent to innovation by making it hard for students and others today to use some words and images, especially those found on the internet. In particular, Lessig points to what he calls the "remix culture" (in which existing works are changed or combined to produce something new) as a source of great creativity that is being "choked" by existing copyright laws.

Lessig was instrumental in expanding the notion of **FAIR USE** and in creating an alternative to copyright known as Creative Commons, a non-profit organization whose motto is "When we share, everyone wins." In 2019 it launched *CC Search*, a tool that lets you search for openly licensed and public domain works that anyone—including you!—can use. Many but not all of these works are available free of charge.

Check out Creative Commons at search.creative commons.org/.

While the conventions surrounding documentation of sources will surely continue to evolve, it's still important to acknowledge and document any materials you do not create yourself.

What about sources created using AI?

Knowing what to credit can be especially tricky if you're using AI. When an article in an education journal entitled "Chatting and Cheating: Ensuring Academic Integrity in the Era of *ChatGPT*" turned out to have been produced entirely by AI, alarm bells sounded. It had been submitted by three people, who tipped off the journal editor that the article was AI-generated, but those who peer-reviewed it assumed it had been written by the scholars whose names appeared on it. So now we know that AI "wrote" the article. But more to the point, who was *responsible* for it? The answer to that question is absolutely clear: the people who used AI to create "Chatting and Cheating" are ultimately responsible for the article.

Perhaps someday texts written by people using AI will be considered to have been "co-authored" by AI. But for now most publishers stipulate that AI tools may not be listed as coauthors (since only people can be designated as authors)—and that the authors acknowledge any use of AI somewhere in their publication, and take full responsibility for all of of the content. MLA takes a slightly different tack, considering AI-generated text as a source with *no* author.

So what does this mean for you? First, it means that while AI is developing so swiftly and conventions surrounding its use are so in flux, you need to make sure you understand your instructor's policies regarding the use of AI for coursework. If you are permitted to use AI, remember that you will be responsible for what you write, and for ensuring the accuracy of the information it provides. It's no secret that AI makes mistakes, so you'll need to check any information or advice it gives you for accuracy. And finally, you'll need to acknowledge and document how it helped you.

See Ch. 30 on using AI carefully and ethically.

Why it's important to credit your sources

While we don't routinely credit others in everyday conversation, it's important to do so in academic contexts. Giving credit to others when it's due says a lot about your values, about your fairness

In everyday conversation and speeches, we don't often credit those whose ideas have influenced our own.

and trustworthiness—in other words, it demonstrates your academic integrity. Acknowledging where some of your ideas come from also shows that you've done your homework, that you know what others have said about your topic and that you understand and have considered their points of view. In short, it helps to establish your own CREDIBILITY to write on the topic. More than that, it shows you to be openhanded, crediting others for what you've gotten from them, and sharing the credit for what you yourself have written.

Remember as well to credit any collaborators. If you have worked with others on your research or writing, be sure to credit and thank them in your text. See pages 387–88 for how to format such notes MLA style and page 437 for how to do so APA style.

What sources do you need to document?

You need to DOCUMENT most ideas, texts, images, and sounds that you CITE from other sources. But there are exceptions.

Sources you do not need to document

- *Materials that you have created or collected,* such as photos you took or data you collected from a survey you conducted.

- *Common knowledge* of well-known events (the Twin Towers collapsed on 9/11), well-known facts and data (nearly 3,000 people died on 9/11), uncontroversial information (many Americans were glued to their TVs on 9/11).

- *Well-known quotations* "Yes we can." "Houston, we have a problem." "I have a dream."

- *Information that appears in many places*—so many that it is impossible to determine an original source. University definitions of "plagiarism," for instance, often use or very similar language, so documentation isn't necessary.

- *Information from public documents* such as the Bill of Rights and the US Constitution.

Sources you do need to document

- *Any materials you did not create yourself,* including charts, tables, graphs, infographics, images, and anything generated by AI. And if you've created a chart or graph using data from another source, you need to document that source.

- *Direct quotations, paraphrases, and summaries.* The only exception is famous or widely known quotations, which do not need to be documented —although you should make sure they are accurate!

- *Controversial information.* If you cite something that's debatable, document it so that readers can check out the source for themselves.

- *Anything you have a question about!* If you're in doubt about whether or not to document a source, err on the side of caution and include formal documentation.

Documenting material from AI

- *If you're following* MLA *style,* you'll need to document any AI-generated quotes, images, data, or other materials you incorporate in your text and provide a note that acknowledges the way you used AI. You'll find guidelines for creating in-text documentation on page 387 and a works-cited entry on page 417, and how to format notes on pages 387–88.

- *If you're following* APA *style,* you'll need to document any AI-generated materials you include in your text and to explain the way you used AI either in your introduction or methods section. APA also requires you to include the prompts you used. You'll find guidelines for creating in-text documentation on page 436 and a references entry on page 458.

Asking for permission

FAIR USE laws allow college students to use passages and images from copyrighted sources without getting permission from the author—as long as you are writing for "educational purposes" and provide full documentation. But here's the catch: if your writing will be posted online, where it can be seen by everyone, you need to have explicit permission from the copyright owner.

One student I know learned this lesson the hard way when an award-winning essay she wrote was posted on the award website. Within weeks, she heard from the author of a cartoon she'd included asking her to remove the essay from the web and threatening legal action if she did not comply. Another student whose essay was posted to a class website was embarrassed when his teacher received an angry email from someone saying the student had used her work in his essay and had not documented it fully.

So if in doubt, it's best to play it very safe and get permission in writing for any source material that you post online. Here is an example of a request for permission:

From: smoller@bankstreet.edu
To: lunsford@stanford.edu
Subject: Request for permission

Dear Professor Lunsford:

I am writing to request permission to quote from your essay "Teaching Writing in an Age of Misinformation and Lies." I am working on a presentation for my writing class on the proliferation of fake news and would like to use your definition to help clarify the subject. My presentation will be posted to our class website. If you are willing to grant permission, I will give full credit to you and will provide complete documentation for the journal article in which it appeared, along with the URL of the site where I first discovered your work.

Thank you very much for considering this request,

Susanna Moller

Avoiding plagiarism

Presenting someone else's words or ideas as if they were your own and without giving credit is dishonest and unethical—and is considered plagiarism. It's a masquerade, with serious consequences. Every year, students receive failing grades or are suspended from college for plagiarizing. More than that, they've given up their own agency—the chance to think through issues on their own, to create arguments that stand the test of scrutiny by others, and to learn.

Sometimes plagiarism is intentional, whether it's purchasing an essay from one of the many online "paper mills" or submitting an essay written partially or entirely by AI—but often it is unintentional. Especially if you are writing about an unfamiliar topic, it can be tricky to incorporate the words or ideas of others (your sources) fairly and to acknowledge them sufficiently. Instead, you may do some of what Professor Rebecca Moore Howard calls PATCHWRITING, using material from sources in ways that stick too closely to the original wording or structure.

In fact, I made this kind of mistake myself, when I was in junior high and writing about my hero at the time, Albert Schweitzer. With no internet to search and a very small school library, I had written to my state library asking for resources and was thrilled when a package of printed articles about Schweitzer arrived. I patched pieces of those articles into what I was writing, sometimes remembering to credit a source but often not. I felt very proud of my work. Lucky for me, I had a teacher who took the time to show me how to integrate the sources into my writing, how to use quotation marks, and how to paraphrase without copying the original author's wording or syntax. Better yet, she explained why it was important to credit my sources—and how to do so. Lesson learned!

As this example suggests, patchwriting can be a useful stage for learning how to work with sources: it certainly helped me learn a lot about Albert Schweitzer and his work. And it was a stepping stone on the path to becoming a confident researcher and to citing sources accurately and ethically.

But some instructors may well see patchwriting as plagiarism, even if it's documented. So it's something you'll want to avoid. Let's take a look at how it happens, and how you can weave the ideas of others into your own writing by using your own words and sentence structure. Imagine that you want to summarize the ideas from the following passage:

> In some professions, early decline is inescapable. No one expects an Olympic athlete to remain competitive until age 60. But in many physically nondemanding occupations, we implicitly reject the inevitability of decline before very old age. Sure, our quads and hamstrings may weaken a little as we age. But as long as we retain our marbles, our quality of work as a writer, lawyer, executive, or entrepreneur should remain high up to the very end, right? Many people think so. I recently met a man a bit older than I am who told me he planned to "push it until the wheels come off." In effect, he planned to stay at the very top of his game by any means necessary, and then keel over.
>
> But the odds are he won't be able to. The data are shockingly clear that for most people, in most fields, decline starts earlier than almost anyone thinks.
>
> According to research by Dean Keith Simonton, a professor emeritus of psychology at UC Davis and one of the world's leading experts on the trajectories of creative careers, success and productivity increase for the first 20 years after the inception of a career, on average. So if you start a career in earnest at 30, expect to do your best work around 50 and go into decline soon after that.
>
> —ARTHUR C. BROOKS, "Your Professional Decline Is Coming (Much) Sooner Than You Think: Here's How to Make the Most of It"

Suppose you wanted to make sure you remember the key information in this passage for a class discussion you are going to lead. You might be tempted to patch together a summary like this:

PATCHWRITTEN SUMMARY

Arthur C. Brooks explains that while many people believe they can stay at the top of their game well into their 60s and 70s and beyond, the odds are that these people are wrong. Brooks refers to research conducted by Dean Keith Simonton, an expert on tracking creative careers who says that success usually occurs in the first 20 years after the beginning of a career, so at age 50 people who started out at 30 are hitting the time when they will start to decline.

This summary captures the gist of Brooks's argument, but it uses far too much of Brooks's own language ("stay at the top of their game," "the odds are," "the first 20 years"). It's fine for studying, but not for writing a summary you'd submit to an instructor as your own work.

Now take a look at another summary, one that captures the main idea in the student's own words and includes a direct quotation:

ACCEPTABLE SUMMARY

While some cling to the notion that their work level will "remain high up to the very end," Arthur C. Brooks presents research that contradicts those beliefs (70). In fact, this research reveals that high-level work performance begins to decline after about 20 years into a career.

This summary relies on the writer's own language and sentence structure and uses quotation marks to enclose language taken directly from the source. It restates the main idea of the passage clearly and simply—and leaves out any details that won't be necessary for the writer's purposes. For instance, it omits information about Brooks's sources, which won't be used in the essay the student is writing on attitudes toward aging in the workplace. Finally, he documents the page where he found the original passage.

Avoiding plagiarism starts with taking meticulous notes and being very, very careful as you incorporate the words or ideas of others into your own writing. For sources you intend to use, take down all the information you'll need for a list of works cited or references, make sure that paraphrases or summaries do not use any wording or sentence structures from the original, and enclose any words you may want to include in quotation marks.

Joining the conversation ethically

Remember: your words are the ones that count the most in what you say—they are your way of getting in on the conversation about subjects you care about, sharing what you have learned with others and listening hard to learn from them. You'll be citing sources for sure, and they provide support for what you say, but those sources should play second fiddle to you and the points you are making. Nevertheless, you want to give them all the credit they deserve. That's how you become part of the larger conversation, ethically.

REFLECT! Look over something you've written that relies on outside sources. Read it carefully, paying attention to how well you've integrated words or ideas from sources into your writing, how you introduced them, what if anything you said to explain them and show how they support your point. How did you credit their authors? If you used AI, how did you acknowledge that use? How successful would you say you have been in your use of sources? What might you do differently next time?

22 MLA Style

Documentation is the means [of recording] scholarly conversations, and the specifics of those conversations matter.

—KATHLEEN FITZPATRICK, *MLA HANDBOOK*

What started out in 1951 as a 31-page style sheet for scholars submitting articles to the Modern Language Association's journal soon evolved into the *MLA Handbook*, now in its ninth edition. MLA style, recommended or required by some disciplines in the humanities, calls for brief IN-TEXT DOCUMENTATION and complete documentation in a list of WORKS CITED at the end of the text. Such documentation is important: it gives credit where credit is due, enables your readers to find sources you have used, and shows that you have done your homework. This chapter provides templates and examples to help you document the many different sources you're likely to cite.

A DIRECTORY TO MLA STYLE
In-text documentation   381

Notes   387
List of works cited   388

CORE ELEMENTS   388

AUTHORS AND OTHER CONTRIBUTORS   394

Throughout this chapter, you'll find color-coded templates and examples to help you see how writers include source information in their texts and in their lists of works cited: orange for author, editor, translator, and other contributors; yellow for titles; blue for publication information—date of publication, page number(s), DOIs, and other location information.

TITLE   AUTHOR   PUBLICATION

In-text documentation

Whenever you quote, paraphrase, or summarize a source in your writing, you need to provide brief documentation that tells readers what you took from the source and where in the source you found that information. This brief documentation also refers readers to the full entry in your works-cited list, so begin with whatever comes first there: the author, the title, or a description of the source.

You can mention the author or title either in a signal phrase— "Toni Morrison writes," "In *Beowulf*," "According to the article 'Every Patient's Nightmare'"—or in parentheses—(Morrison). If relevant, include pages or other details about where you found the information in the parenthetical reference: (Morrison 67).

Shorten any lengthy titles or descriptions in parentheses by including the first noun with any preceding adjectives and omitting any initial articles (*Norton Field Guide* for *The Norton Field Guide to Writing*). If the title doesn't start with a noun, use the first phrase or clause (*How to Be* for *How to Be an Antiracist*). Use the full title if it's short.

The first two examples below show basic in-text documentation of a work by one author. Variations on those examples follow. The examples illustrate the MLA style of using quotation marks around titles of short works and italicizing titles of long works.

1. AUTHOR NAMED IN A SIGNAL PHRASE

If you mention the author in a signal phrase, put only the page number(s) in parentheses. Do not write *page* or *p*. The first time you mention the author, use their first and last names. You can usually omit any middle initials. In subsequent references to the author, use their last name only. You can also use a pronoun (use singular "they" if you don't know the author's gender identity) or another term, like "the author."

> David McCullough describes John Adams's hands as those of someone used to manual labor (18).

2. AUTHOR NAMED IN PARENTHESES

If you do not mention the author in a signal phrase, put the author's last name in parentheses along with any page number(s). Do not use punctuation between the name and the page number(s).

> Adams is said to have had "the hands of a man accustomed to pruning his own trees, cutting his own hay, and splitting his own firewood" (McCullough 18).

Whether you use a signal phrase and parentheses or parentheses only, try to put the parenthetical documentation at the end of the sentence or as close as possible to the material you've cited—without awkwardly interrupting the sentence. When a parenthetical reference comes at the end of the sentence, the period goes at the very end.

3. TWO OR MORE WORKS BY THE SAME AUTHOR

If you cite multiple works by one author, include the title of the work you are citing either in the signal phrase or in parentheses.

> Robert Kaplan insists that understanding power in the Near East requires "Western leaders who know when to intervene, and do so without illusions" (*Eastward to Tartary* 330).

Put a comma between author and title if both are in the parentheses.

> Understanding power in the Near East requires "Western leaders who know when to intervene, and do so without illusions" (Kaplan, *Eastward to Tartary* 330).

4. AUTHORS WITH THE SAME LAST NAME

Give each author's first and last names in any signal phrase, or add the author's first initial in the parenthetical reference.

> "Imaginative" applies not only to modern literature but also to writing of all periods, whereas "magical" is often used in writing about Arthurian romances (A. Wilson 25).

5. TWO OR MORE AUTHORS

For a work with two authors, name both. If you first mention them in a signal phrase, give their first and last names.

> Lori Carlson and Cynthia Ventura's stated goal is to introduce Julio Cortázar, Marjorie Agosín, and other Latin American writers to an audience of English-speaking adolescents (v).

For a work by three or more authors that you mention in a signal phrase, you can either name them all or name the first author followed by *and others* or *and colleagues*. If you mention them in a parenthetical reference, name the first author followed by *et al.*

> Phyllis Anderson and colleagues describe British literature thematically (A54–A67).

> One survey of British literature breaks the contents into thematic groupings (Anderson et al. A54–A67).

6. ORGANIZATION OR GOVERNMENT AS AUTHOR

In a signal phrase, use the full name of the organization: American Academy of Arts and Sciences. In parentheses, use the shortest noun phrase, omitting any initial articles: American Academy.

> The US government can be direct when it wants to be. For example, it sternly warns, "If you are overpaid, we will recover any payments not due you" (Social Security Administration 12).

7. AUTHOR UNKNOWN

If you don't know the author, use the work's title in a signal phrase or in a parenthetical reference.

> A powerful editorial in *The New York Times* asserts that healthy liver donor Mike Hurewitz died because of "frightening" faulty postoperative care ("Every Patient's Nightmare").

8. LITERARY WORKS

When referring to common literary works that are available in many different editions, give the page numbers from the edition you are using, followed by information that will let readers of any edition locate the text you are citing.

NOVELS AND PROSE PLAYS. Give the page followed by a semicolon and any chapter, section, or act numbers, separated by commas.

> In *Pride and Prejudice,* Mrs. Bennet shows no warmth toward Jane when she returns from Netherfield (Austen 105; ch. 12).

VERSE PLAYS. Give act, scene, and line numbers, separated with periods.

> Shakespeare continues the vision theme when Macbeth says, "Thou hast no speculation in those eyes / Which thou dost glare with" (*Macbeth* 3.3.96–97).

POEMS. Give part and line numbers, separated by periods. If a poem has only line numbers, use *line* or *lines* only in the first reference.

> Walt Whitman sets up opposing adjectives and nouns in "Song of Myself" when he says, "I am of old and young, of the foolish as much as the wise, / . . . a child as well as a man" (16.330–32).
>
> One description of the mere in *Beowulf* is "not a pleasant place" (line 1372). Later, it is labeled "the awful place" (1378).

9. WORK IN AN ANTHOLOGY

Name the author(s) of the work, not the editor of the anthology.

> "It is the teapots that truly shock," according to Cynthia Ozick in her essay on teapots as metaphor (70).
>
> In *In Short: A Collection of Creative Nonfiction,* readers will find both an essay on Scottish tea (Hiestand) and a piece on teapots as metaphors (Ozick).

10. ENCYCLOPEDIA OR DICTIONARY

Acknowledge an entry in an encyclopedia or dictionary by giving the author's name, if available. For an entry without an author, give the entry's title.

TITLE	AUTHOR	PUBLICATION

According to *Funk and Wagnall's New World Encyclopedia*, early
in his career, most of Kubrick's income came from "hustling chess
games in Washington Square Park" ("Kubrick, Stanley").

11. LEGAL DOCUMENTS

Give whatever comes first in the works-cited entry. If you are documenting a government document in parentheses and multiple entries
in your works-cited list, start with the same government author,
with as much of the name as you need to differentiate the sources.

In 2015, for the first time, all states were required to license and
recognize the marriages of same-sex couples (United States,
Supreme Court).

12. SACRED TEXT

When citing a sacred text such as the Bible or the Qur'an for the first
time, give the title of the edition, an in parentheses give the book,
chapter, and verse (or their equivalent), separated by periods. MLA
recommends abbreviating the names of the books of the Bible in parenthetical references. Later citations from the same edition do not
have to repeat its title.

The wording from *The New English Bible* follows: "In the beginning
of creation, when God made heaven and earth, the earth was
without form and void . . ." (Gen. 1.1–2).

13. MULTIVOLUME WORK

If you cite more than one volume of a multivolume work, each time
you cite one of the volumes, give the volume *and* the page number(s)
in parentheses, separated by a colon and a space.

Sandburg concludes with the following sentence about those paying
last respects to Lincoln: "All day long and through the night the
unbroken line moved, the home town having its farewell" (4: 413).

If you cite an entire volume of a multivolume work in parentheses,
give the author's last name followed by a comma and *vol.* before the

volume number: (Sandburg, vol. 4). If your works-cited list includes only a single volume of a multivolume work, give just the page number in parentheses: (413).

14. TWO OR MORE WORKS CITED TOGETHER

If you're citing two or more works closely together, you will sometimes need to provide a parenthetical reference for each one.

> Baron (182) and Dreyer (93) describe singular *they* from slightly different perspectives.

If you are citing multiple sources for the same idea in parentheses, separate the references with a semicolon.

> Many critics have examined great works of literature from a cultural perspective (Tanner 7; Smith viii).

15. SOURCE QUOTED IN ANOTHER SOURCE

When you are quoting text that you found quoted in another source, use the abbreviation *qtd. in* in the parenthetical reference.

> Charlotte Brontë wrote to G. H. Lewes, "Why do you like Miss Austen so very much? I am puzzled on that point" (qtd. in Tanner 7).

16. WORK WITHOUT PAGE NUMBERS

For works without page or part numbers, including many online sources, no number is needed in a parenthetical reference.

> Studies show that music training helps children to be better at multitasking later in life ("Hearing the Music").

If you mention the author in a signal phrase, or if you mention the title of a work with no author, no parenthetical reference is needed.

> Arthur Brooks argues that a switch to fully remote work would have a negative effect on mental and physical health.

If the source has chapter, paragraph, or section numbers, use them with the abbreviations *ch.*, *par.*, or *sec.*: ("Hearing the Music," par. 2).

TITLE   AUTHOR   PUBLICATION

Don't count lines or paragraphs on your own if they aren't numbered in the source. For an ebook, use chapter numbers. For an audio or video recording, give the hours, minutes, and seconds (separated by colons) as shown on the player: (00:05:21–31).

17. AN ENTIRE WORK OR A ONE-PAGE ARTICLE

If you cite an entire work rather than a part of it, or if you cite a single-page article, there's no need to include page numbers.

> Throughout life, John Adams strove to succeed (McCullough).

18. GENERATIVE AI

The results of generative AI are not considered to have an author and don't have titles; instead, identify the source by using the first phrase or clause of your prompt. Use the whole prompt if it's short.

> A light bulb, also known as an incandescent bulb, works "on the principle of incandescence" ("Explain how a light bulb works")

Notes

Sometimes you may need to give information that doesn't fit into the text itself—to thank people who helped you, to acknowledge the use of AI in your writing process, to refer readers to other sources, to add comments about sources, or to provide other details. Such information can be given in a footnote (at the bottom of the page) or an endnote (on a separate page with the heading *Notes* or *Endnotes* just before your works-cited list). Put a superscript number at the appropriate point in your text, signaling to readers to look for the note with the corresponding number. If you have multiple notes, number them consecutively throughout your paper.

TEXT WITH SUPERSCRIPT
World (and Word) Building: A Gamer's Literacy[1]

NOTE
[1] I want to thank those who gave me feedback on a draft of this literacy narrative, including my teacher Vincent Yu and my classmates Karima and Luke. I also want to acknowledge the use of *ChatGPT* to brainstorm ideas early in my writing process. *ChatGPT* helped me develop the idea of sharing an anecdote about the storytelling skills I learned from playing *Dungeons & Dragons*.

List of works cited

A works-cited list provides full bibliographic information for every source cited in your text. See page 419 for guidelines on formatting this list and page 428 for a sample works-cited list.

Core Elements

MLA style provides a list of core elements for documenting sources in a works-cited list. Not all sources will include each of these elements; include as much information as is available for any title you cite. For guidance about specific sources you need to document, see the templates and examples on pages 394–417, but here are some general guidelines for how to treat each of the core elements.

CORE ELEMENTS FOR ENTRIES IN A WORKS-CITED LIST

- Author
- Title of the source
- Title of any "container," a larger work in which the source is found—an anthology, a website, a journal or magazine, a database, a streaming service like *Netflix*, or a learning management system, among others
- Editor, translator, director, or other contributors
- Version

TITLE   AUTHOR   PUBLICATION

- Number of volume and issue, episode and season
- Publisher
- Date of publication
- Location of the source: page numbers, DOI, PERMALINK, URL, etc.

The above order is the general order MLA recommends, but there will be exceptions. To document a translated essay that you found in an anthology, for instance, you'd identify the translator after the title of the essay rather than after that of the anthology. You may sometimes need additional elements as well, either at the end of an entry or somewhere in the middle—for instance, a label to indicate that your source is a map, or an original year of publication. Remember that your goal is to tell readers what sources you've consulted and where they can find them. Providing this information is one way you can engage with readers—and enable them to join in the conversation with you and your sources.

AUTHORS AND OTHER CONTRIBUTORS

- An author can be any kind of creator—a writer, a musician, an artist, and so on.
- If there is one author, put the last name first, followed by a comma and the first name: Morrison, Toni.
- If there are two authors, list the first author last name first and the second one first name first: Lunsford, Andrea, and Lisa Ede. Put their names in the order given in the work. For three or more authors, give the first author's name followed by *et al.*: Greenblatt, Stephen, et al.
- Include any middle names or initials: Toklas, Alice B.
- If the author is a group or organization, use the full name, omitting any initial article: United Nations.
- If an author uses a handle that is significantly different from their name, include the handle in square brackets after the name: Ocasio-Cortez, Alexandria [@AOC].

- If there's no known author, start the entry with the title.
- If there's an editor but no author, put the editor's name in the author position and specify their role: Guarnaschelli, Maria, editor.
- If you're citing someone in addition to an author—an editor, translator, director, or other contributors—specify their role.
- If there are multiple contributors, put the one whose work you wish to highlight before the title, and list any others you want to mention after the title. If you don't want to highlight one particular contributor, start with the title and include any contributors after the title. For contributors named before the title, specify their role after the name: Fincher, David, director. For those named after the title, specify their role first: Directed by David Fincher.

TITLES

- Include any subtitles and capitalize all the words except for articles (*a*, *an*, *the*), prepositions (*to*, *at*, *from*, and so on), and coordinating conjunctions (*and*, *but*, *for*, *or*, *nor*, *so*, *yet*)— unless they are the first or last word of a title or subtitle.
- Italicize the titles of books, periodicals, websites, and other long works: *Pride and Prejudice*, *Wired*.
- Put quotation marks around the titles of articles and other short works: "Letter from Birmingham Jail."
- To document a source that has no title, describe it without italics or quotation marks: Letter to the author, Photograph of a tree. For a short, untitled email, text message, social media post, or poem, you may want to include the text itself instead: Dickinson, Emily. "Immortal is an ample word." *American Poems*, www.americanpoems.com/poets /emilydickinson/immortal-is-an-ample-word.

TITLE   AUTHOR   PUBLICATION

VERSIONS

- If you cite a source that's available in more than one version, specify the one you consulted in your works-cited entry. Write ordinal numbers with numerals, and abbreviate *edition*: 2nd ed. Write out names of specific versions, and capitalize following a period or if the name is a proper noun: King James Version, unabridged version, director's cut.

NUMBERS

- If you cite a book that's published in multiple volumes, indicate the volume number. Abbreviate *volume*, and write the number as a numeral: vol. 2.
- Indicate volume and issue numbers of journals (if any), abbreviating both *volume* and *number*: vol. 123, no. 4.
- If you cite a TV show or podcast episode, indicate the season and episode numbers: season 1, episode 4.

PUBLISHERS

- Write publishers', studios', and networks' names in full, but omit initial articles and business words like *Inc.* or *Company*.
- For academic presses, use *U* for *University* and *P* for *Press*: Princeton UP, U of California P. Spell out *Press* if the name doesn't include *University*: MIT Press.
- Some publishers use an ampersand in their name: Simon & Schuster. MLA says to use "and" instead: Simon and Schuster.
- If the publisher is a division of an organization, list the organization and any divisions from largest to smallest: Stanford U, Center for the Study of Language and Information, Metaphysics Research Lab.

DATES

- Whether to give just the year or to include the month and day depends on the source. In general, give the full date that you find there. If the date is unknown, simply omit it.
- Abbreviate the months except for May, June, and July: Jan., Feb., Mar., Apr., Aug., Sept., Oct., Nov., Dec.
- For books, give the publication date on the copyright page. If there's more than one date, use the most recent one.
- Periodicals may be published annually, monthly, seasonally, weekly, or daily. Give the full date that you find there: 2019, Apr. 2019, 16 Apr. 2019. Do not capitalize the names of seasons: spring 2021.
- For online sources, use the copyright date or the full publication date you find there, or a date of revision. If the source does not give a date, use the date of access: Accessed 6 June 2020. Give a date of access as well for online sources you think are likely to change or for websites that have disappeared.

LOCATION

- For most print articles and other short works, give a page number or range of pages: p. 24, pp. 24–35. For articles that are not on consecutive pages, give the first page number with a plus sign: pp. 24+.
- If it's necessary to specify a section of a source, give the section name before the pages: Sunday Review sec., p. 3.
- Indicate the location of an online source by giving a DOI if one is available; if not, give a URL—and use a PERMALINK if one is available. URLs are not always reliable, so ask your instructor if you should include them. DOIs should start with *https://doi.org/*—but no need to include *https://* for a URL, unless you want the URL to be a hyperlink.

- For a geographical location, give enough information to identify it: a city (Houston), a city and state (Portland, Maine), or a city and country (Manaus, Brazil).

- For something seen in a museum, archive, or elsewhere, name the institution and its location: Maine Jewish Museum, Portland; Portland Museum of Art, Portland, Maine.

- For performances or other live presentations, name the venue and its location: Mark Taper Forum, Los Angeles.

PUNCTUATION

- Use a period after the author name(s) that start an entry (Morrison, Toni.) and the title of the source you're documenting (*Beloved*.).

- Use a comma between the author's last and first names: Ede, Lisa.

- Some URLs will not fit on one line. MLA does not specify where to break a URL, but we recommend breaking it before a punctuation mark. Do *not* add a hyphen or a space.

- Sometimes you'll need to provide information about more than one work for a single source—for instance, when you cite an article from a periodical that you access through a database. MLA refers to the periodical and database (or any other entity that holds a source) as "containers" and specifies certain punctuation. Use commas between elements within each container, and put a period at the end of each container. For example:

> Semuels, Alana. "The Future Will Be Quiet." *The Atlantic*, Apr. 2016, pp. 19–20. *ProQuest*, search.proquest.com /docview/1777443553?accountid+42654.

The guidelines that follow will help you document the kinds of sources you're likely to use. The first section shows how to acknowledge authors and other contributors and applies to all kinds of sources—

print, online, or others. Later sections show how to treat titles, publication information, location, and access information for many specific kinds of sources. In general, provide as much information as possible for each source—enough to tell readers how to find a source if they wish to access it themselves.

SOURCES NOT COVERED

These guidelines will help you document a variety of sources, but if you're citing a source that isn't covered, consult style.mla.org, or ask them a question at style.mla.org/ask-a-question.

Authors and Other Contributors

When you name authors and other contributors in your citations, you are crediting them for their work and letting readers know who's in on the conversation. The following guidelines for citing authors and contributors apply to all sources you cite: in print, online, or in some other media.

1. ONE AUTHOR

Author's Last Name, First Name. *Title*. Publisher, Date.

Anderson, Chris. *The Long Tail: Why the Future of Business Is Selling Less of More*. Hyperion, 2006.

2. TWO AUTHORS

1st Author's Last Name, First Name, and 2nd Author's First and Last Names. *Title*. Publisher, Date.

Lunsford, Andrea, and Lisa Ede. *Singular Texts/Plural Authors: Perspectives on Collaborative Writing*. Southern Illinois UP, 1990.

3. THREE OR MORE AUTHORS

1st Author's Last Name, First Name, et al. *Title*. Publisher, Date.

Sebranek, Patrick, et al. *Writers INC: A Guide to Writing, Thinking, and Learning*. Write Source, 1990.

TITLE   AUTHOR   PUBLICATION

4. TWO OR MORE WORKS BY THE SAME AUTHOR

Give the author's name in the first entry, and then use a three-em dash (or three hyphens) in the author slot for each of the subsequent works, listing them alphabetically by the first word of each title and ignoring any initial articles.

> Author's Last Name, First Name. *Title That Comes First Alphabetically*. Publisher, Date.
> ———. *Title That Comes Next Alphabetically*. Publisher, Date.
> Kaplan, Robert D. *The Coming Anarchy: Shattering the Dreams of the Post Cold War*. Random House, 2000.
> ———. *Eastward to Tartary: Travels in the Balkans, the Middle East, and the Caucasus*. Random House, 2000.

5. AUTHOR AND EDITOR OR TRANSLATOR

> Author's Last Name, First Name. *Title*. Role by First and Last Names, Publisher, Date.
> Austen, Jane. *Emma*. Edited by Stephen M. Parrish, W. W. Norton, 2000.
> Dostoevsky, Fyodor. *Crime and Punishment*. Translated by Richard Pevear and Larissa Volokhonsky, Vintage Books, 1993.

Start with the editor or translator if you are focusing on that contribution rather than the author's. If there is a translator but no author, start with the title.

> Pevear, Richard, and Larissa Volokhonsky, translators. *Crime and Punishment*. By Fyodor Dostoevsky, Vintage Books, 1993.
> *Beowulf*. Translated by Stephen Mitchell, Yale UP, 2017.

6. NO AUTHOR OR EDITOR

When there's no known author or editor, start with the title.

> *The Turner Collection in the Clore Gallery*. Tate Publications, 1987.
> "Being Invisible Closer to Reality." *The Atlanta Journal-Constitution*, 11 Aug. 2008, p. A3.

7. ORGANIZATION OR GOVERNMENT AS AUTHOR

For a government publication, give the name that is shown in the source. When a nongovernment organization is both author and publisher, start with the title and list the organization only as the publisher. If a division of an organization is listed as the author, give the division as the author and the organization as the publisher.

> Organization Name. *Title.* Publisher, Date.
> Diagram Group. *The Macmillan Visual Desk Reference.* Macmillan, 1993.
> United States, Department of Health and Human Services, National Institute of Mental Health. *Autism Spectrum Disorders.* Government Printing Office, 2004.
> *Stylebook on Religion 2000: A Reference Guide and Usage Manual.* Catholic News Service, 2002.
> Center for Workforce Studies. *2005–13: Demographics of the U.S. Psychology Workforce.* American Psychological Association, July 2015.

Articles and Other Short Works

Articles, essays, reviews, and other short works are found in journals, magazines, newspapers, other periodicals, and books—all of which you may find in print, online, or in a database. For most short works, you'll need to provide information about the author, the titles of both the short work and the longer work where it's found, any page numbers, and various kinds of publication information.

8. ARTICLE IN A JOURNAL

PRINT

> Author's Last Name, First Name. "Title of Article." *Name of Journal,* Volume, Issue, Date, Pages.
> Cooney, Brian C. "Considering *Robinson Crusoe*'s 'Liberty of Conscience' in an Age of Terror." *College English,* vol. 69, no. 3, Jan. 2007, pp. 197–215.

TITLE   AUTHOR   PUBLICATION

Documentation Map (MLA)
Article in a Print Journal

Marge Simpson, Blue-Haired Housewife: •················   TITLE OF ARTICLE
Defining Domesticity on *The Simpsons*

JESSAMYN NEUHAUS •···   AUTHOR

ORE THAN TWENTY SEASONS AFTER ITS DEBUT AS A SHORT ON *THE Tracy Ullman Show* in 1989, pundits, politicians, scholars, journalists, and critics continue to discuss and debate the meaning and relevance of *The Simpsons* to American society. For academics and educators, the show offers an especially dense pop culture text, inspiring articles and anthologies examining *The Simpsons* in light of American religious life, the representation of homosexuality in cartoons, and the use of pop culture in the classroom, among many other topics (Dennis; Frank; Henry "The Whole World's Gone Gay"; Hobbs; Kristiansen). Philosophers and literary theorists in particular are intrigued by the quintessentially postmodern self-aware form and content of *The Simpsons* and the questions about identity, spectatorship, and consumer culture it raises (Alberti; Bybee and Overbeck; Glynn; Henry "The Triumph of Popular Culture"; Herron; Hull; Irwin et al.; Ott; Parisi).

Simpsons observers frequently note that this TV show begs one of the fundamental questions in cultural studies: can pop culture ever provide a site of individual or collective resistance or must it always ultimately function in the interests of the capitalist dominant ideology? Is *The Simpsons* a brilliant satire of virtually every cherished American myth about public and private life, offering dissatisfied Americans the opportunity to critically reflect on contemporary issues (Turner 435)? Or is it simply another TV show making money for the Fox Network? Is *The Simpsons* an empty, cynical, even nihilistic view of the world, lulling its viewers into laughing hopelessly at the pointless futility of

          VOLUME

          ISSUE

          DATE

The Journal of Popular Culture, Vol. 43, No. 4, 2010, pp. 761–81 •·········
© 2010, Wiley Periodicals, Inc.

          PAGES

          NAME OF JOURNAL

Neuhaus, Jessamyn. "Marge Simpson, Blue-Haired Housewife: Defining Domesticity on *The Simpsons*." *The Journal of Popular Culture*, vol. 43, no. 4, 2010, pp. 761–81.

ONLINE

Author's Last Name, First Name. "Title of Article." *Name of Journal*, Volume, Issue, Date, DOI *or* URL.

Schmidt, Desmond. "A Model of Versions and Layers." *Digital Humanities Quarterly*, vol. 13, no. 3, 2019, www.digital humanities.org/dhq/vol/13/3/000430/000430.html.

9. ARTICLE IN A MAGAZINE

PRINT

Author's Last Name, First Name. "Title of Article." *Name of Magazine*, Volume (if any), Issue (if any), Date, Pages.

Burt, Tequia. "Legacy of Activism: Concerned Black Students' 50-Year History at Grinnell College." *Grinnell Magazine*, vol. 48, no. 4, summer 2016, pp. 32–38.

ONLINE

Author's Last Name, First Name. "Title of Article." *Name of Magazine*, Volume (if any), Issue (if any), Date, DOI *or* URL.

Brooks, Arthur C. "The Hidden Toll of Remote Work." *The Atlantic*, 1 Apr. 2021, www.theatlantic.com/family/archive/2021/04 /zoom-remote-work-loneliness-happiness/618473.

10. ARTICLE IN A NEWS PUBLICATION

PRINT

Author's Last Name, First Name. "Title of Article." *Name of Publication*, Date, Pages.

Saulny, Susan, and Jacques Steinberg. "On College Forms, a Question of Race Can Perplex." *The New York Times*, 14 June 2011, p. A1.

To document a particular edition of a newspaper, list the edition before the date. If a section name or number is needed to locate the article, put that detail after the date.

TITLE   AUTHOR   PUBLICATION

Documentation Map (MLA)
Article in an Online Magazine

Segal, Michael. "The Hit Book That Came from Mars." *Nautilus*,
8 Jan. 2015, nautil.us/issue/20/creativity/the-hit-book-that
-came-from-mars.

Burns, John F., and Miguel Helft. "Under Pressure, YouTube Withdraws Muslim Cleric's Videos." *The New York Times,* late ed., 4 Nov. 2010, sec. 1, p. 13.

ONLINE

Author's Last Name, First Name. "Title of Article." *Name of Publication,* Date, URL.

Banerjee, Neela. "Proposed Religion-Based Program for Federal Inmates Is Canceled." *The New York Times,* 28 Oct. 2006, www.nytimes.com/2006/10/28/us/28prison.html.

11. ARTICLE ACCESSED THROUGH A DATABASE

Author's Last Name, First Name. "Title of Article." *Name of Periodical,* Volume, Issue, Date, Pages. *Name of Database,* DOI *or* URL.

Stalter, Sunny. "Subway Ride and Subway System in Hart Crane's 'The Tunnel.'" *Journal of Modern Literature,* vol. 33, no. 2, Jan. 2010, pp. 70–91. *JSTOR,* https://doi.org/10.2979/jml .2010.33.2.70.

12. ENTRY IN A REFERENCE WORK

PRINT

Author's Last Name, First Name (if any). "Title of Entry." *Title of Reference Book,* edited by First and Last Names (if any), Edition number, Volume (if any), Publisher, Date, Pages.

Fritz, Jan Marie. "Clinical Sociology." *Encyclopedia of Sociology,* edited by Edgar F. Borgatta and Rhonda J. V. Montgomery, 2nd ed., vol. 1, Macmillan Reference USA, 2000, pp. 323–29.

"California." *The New Columbia Encyclopedia,* edited by William H. Harris and Judith S. Levey, 4th ed., Columbia UP, 1975, pp. 423–24.

Documentation Map (MLA)

Journal Article Accessed through a Database

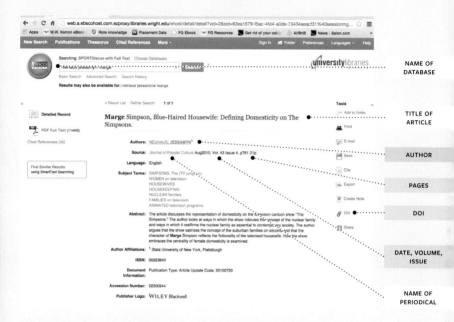

NAME OF DATABASE

TITLE OF ARTICLE

AUTHOR

PAGES

DOI

DATE, VOLUME, ISSUE

NAME OF PERIODICAL

Neuhaus, Jessamyn. "Marge Simpson, Blue-Haired Housewife:
    Defining Domesticity on *The Simpsons*." *Journal of Popular
    Culture*, vol. 43, no. 4, Aug. 2010, pp. 761–81. *EBSCOhost*,
    https://doi.org/10.1111/j.1540-5931.2010.00769.x.

ONLINE

Document online reference works the same as print ones, adding the URL after the date of publication.

"Baseball." *The Columbia Electronic Encyclopedia*, edited by
   Paul Lagassé, 6th ed., Columbia UP, 2012, www.infoplease
   .com/encyclopedia.

13. EDITORIAL OR OP-ED

EDITORIAL

Editorial Board. "Title." *Name of Periodical,* Date, Page *or* URL.
Editorial Board. "A New Look for Local News Coverage." *The
   Lakeville Journal,* 13 Feb. 2020, p. A8.
Editorial Board. "Editorial: Protect Reporters at Protest Scenes."
   Los Angeles Times, 11 Mar. 2021, www.latimes.com/opinion
   /story/2021-03-11/reporters-protest-scenes.

OP-ED

Author's Last Name, First Name. "Title." *Name of Periodical,*
   Date, Page *or* URL.
Okafor, Kingsley. "Opinion: The First Step to COVID Vaccine Equity
   Is Overall Health Equity." *The Denver Post,* 15 Apr. 2021, www
   .denverpost.com/2021/04/15/covid-vaccine-equity-kaiser.

If it's not clear that it's an op-ed, add a label at the end.

Balf, Todd. "Falling in Love with Swimming." *The New York Times,*
   17 Apr. 2021, p. A21. Op-ed.

14. LETTER TO THE EDITOR

Author's Last Name, First Name. "Title of Letter (if any)."
   Name of Periodical, Date, Page *or* URL.
Pinker, Steven. "Language Arts." *The New Yorker,* 4 June 2012,
   p. 10.

If the letter has no title, include *Letter* after the author's name.

Fleischmann, W. B. Letter. *The New York Review of Books*, 1 June
1963, www.nybooks.com/articles/1963/06/01/letter-21.

15. REVIEW

PRINT

Reviewer's Last Name, First Name. "Title of Review." *Name of
Periodical*, Date, Pages.

Frank, Jeffrey. "Body Count." *The New Yorker*, 30 July 2007,
pp. 86–87.

ONLINE

Reviewer's Last Name, First Name. "Title of Review." *Name of
Periodical*, Date, URL.

Donadio, Rachel. "Italy's Great, Mysterious Storyteller." *The New
York Review of Books*, 18 Dec. 2014, www.nybooks.com
/articles/2014/12/18/italys-great-mysterious-storyteller.

If a review has no title, include the title and author of the work
being reviewed after the reviewer's name.

Lohier, Patrick. Review of *Exhalation*, by Ted Chiang. *Harvard
Review Online*, 4 Oct. 2019, www.harvardreview.org/book
-review/exhalation.

16. COMMENT ON AN ONLINE ARTICLE

Commenter's Last Name, First Name *or* Username. Comment on
"Title of Article." *Name of Periodical*, Date posted, Time
posted, URL.

ZeikJT. Comment on "The Post-Disaster Artist." *Polygon*, 6 May
2020, 4:33 a.m., www.polygon.com/2020/5/5/21246679/josh
-trank-capone-interview-fantastic-four-chronicle.

Books and Parts of Books

For most books, you'll need to provide information about author, title, publisher, and year of publication. If you found the book in a larger volume, a database, or another work, specify that as well.

17. BASIC ENTRIES FOR A BOOK

PRINT

Author's Last Name, First Name. *Title*. Publisher, Year of
    publication.
Watson, Brad. *Miss Jane*. W. W. Norton, 2016.

EBOOK

Author's Last Name, First Name. *Title*. Ebook ed., Publisher, Year
    of publication.
Watson, Brad. *Miss Jane*. Ebook ed., W. W. Norton, 2016.

ON A WEBSITE

Author's Last Name, First Name. *Title*. Publisher, Year of
    publication, DOI *or* URL.
Ball, Cheryl E., and Drew M. Loewe, editors. *Bad Ideas about
    Writing*. West Virginia U Libraries, 2017, textbooks.lib.wvu
    .edu/badideas/badideasaboutwriting-book.pdf.

18. ANTHOLOGY OR EDITED COLLECTION

Last Name, First Name, editor. *Title*. Publisher, Year of publication.
Kitchen, Judith, and Mary Paumier Jones, editors. *In Short:
    A Collection of Brief Nonfiction*. W. W. Norton, 1996.

19. WORK IN AN ANTHOLOGY

Author's Last Name, First Name. "Title of Work." *Title of
    Anthology*, edited by First and Last Names, Publisher, Year
    of publication, Pages.
Achebe, Chinua. "Uncle Ben's Choice." *The Seagull Reader: Literature*,
    edited by Joseph Kelly, W. W. Norton, 2005, pp. 23–27.

TITLE   AUTHOR   PUBLICATION

Documentation Map (MLA)
Print Book

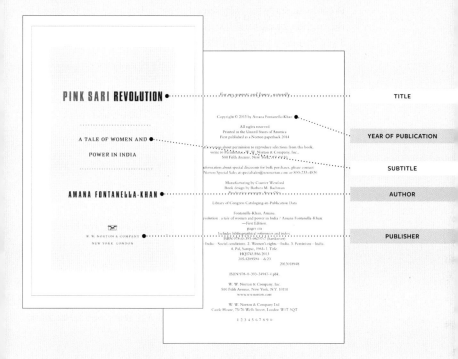

Fontanella-Khan, Amana. *Pink Sari Revolution: A Tale of Women and Power in India.* W. W. Norton, 2013.

TWO OR MORE WORKS FROM ONE ANTHOLOGY

Prepare an entry for each selection by author and title, followed by the anthology editors' last names and the pages of the selection. Then include an entry for the anthology itself (see no. 18).

Author's Last Name, First Name. "Title of Work." Anthology
  Editors' Last Names, Pages.
Hiestand, Emily. "Afternoon Tea." Kitchen and Jones, pp. 65–67.
Ozick, Cynthia. "The Shock of Teapots." Kitchen and Jones,
  pp. 68–71.

20. MULTIVOLUME WORK

ALL VOLUMES

Author's Last Name, First Name. *Title of Work.* Publisher, Year(s)
  of publication. Number of vols.
Churchill, Winston. *The Second World War*. Houghton Mifflin,
  1948–53. 6 vols.

SINGLE VOLUME

Author's Last Name, First Name. *Title of Work*. Vol. number,
  Publisher, Year of publication.
Sandburg, Carl. *Abraham Lincoln: The War Years*. Vol. 2, Harcourt,
  Brace and World, 1939.

If the volume has its own title, include it after the author's name, and indicate the volume number and series title after the year.

Caro, Robert A. *Means of Ascent*. Vintage Books, 1990. Vol. 2 of
  The Years of Lyndon Johnson.

21. BOOK IN A SERIES

Author's Last Name, First Name. *Title of Book.* Edited by First and
  Last Names, Publisher, Year of publication. Series Title.
Walker, Alice. *Everyday Use*. Edited by Barbara T. Christian, Rutgers
  UP, 1994. Women Writers: Texts and Contexts.

TITLE   AUTHOR   PUBLICATION

22. GRAPHIC NARRATIVE OR COMIC BOOK

Author's Last Name, First Name. *Title*. Publisher, Year of
   publication.
Barry, Lynda. *One! Hundred! Demons!* Drawn and Quarterly, 2005.

If the work has both an author and an illustrator, start with the one
you want to highlight, and label the role of the illustrator.

Pekar, Harvey. *Bob and Harv's Comics*. Illustrated by R. Crumb,
   Running Press, 1996.
Crumb, R., illustrator. *Bob and Harv's Comics*. By Harvey Pekar,
   Running Press, 1996.

If you want to cite several contributors, you can start with the title.

Secret Invasion. By Brian Michael Bendis, illustrated by Leinil Yu,
   inked by Mark Morales, Marvel, 2009.

23. SACRED TEXT

If you cite a specific edition of a religious text, you need to include
it in your works-cited list.

The New English Bible with the Apocrypha. Oxford UP, 1971.
The Torah: A Modern Commentary. W. Gunther Plaut, general
   editor, Union of American Hebrew Congregations, 1981.

24. EDITION OTHER THAN THE FIRST

Author's Last Name, First Name. *Title*. Edition name *or* number,
   Publisher, Year of publication.
Smart, Ninian. *The World's Religions*. 2nd ed., Cambridge UP, 1998.

25. FOREWORD, INTRODUCTION, PREFACE, OR AFTERWORD

Part Author's Last Name, First Name. Name of Part. *Title of Book*,
   by Author's First and Last Names, Publisher, Year of
   publication, Pages.
Tanner, Tony. Introduction. *Pride and Prejudice*, by Jane Austen,
   Penguin, 1972, pp. 7–46.

26. PUBLISHED LETTER

Letter Writer's Last Name, First Name. "Title of letter." Day Month Year. *Title of Book,* edited by First and Last Names, Publisher, Year of publication, Pages.

White, E. B. "To Carol Angell." 28 May 1970. *Letters of E. B. White,* edited by Dorothy Guth, Harper and Row, 1976, p. 600.

27. DISSERTATION

Author's Last Name, First Name. *Title.* Year. Institution, PhD dissertation. *Name of Database,* URL.

Simington, Maire Orav. *Chasing the American Dream Post World War II: Perspectives from Literature and Advertising.* 2003. Arizona State U, PhD dissertation. *ProQuest,* search .proquest.com/docview/305340098.

For an unpublished dissertation, end with the institution and a description of the work.

Kim, Loel. *Students Respond to Teacher Comments: A Comparison of Online Written and Voice Modalities.* 1998. Carnegie Mellon U, PhD dissertation.

Websites

Many sources are available in multiple media—for example, a print periodical that is also on the web and contained in digital databases—but some are published only on websites. A website can have an author, an editor, or neither. Some have a publisher, and some do not. Include whatever information is available. If the publisher and title of the site are the same, omit the name of the publisher.

28. ENTIRE WEBSITE

Editor's Last Name, First Name, role. *Title of Site.* Publisher, Date, URL.

Proffitt, Michael, chief editor. *The Oxford English Dictionary*.
 Oxford UP, 2021, www.oed.com.

PERSONAL WEBSITE

Author's Last Name, First Name. *Title of Site*. Date, URL.

Park, Linda Sue. *Linda Sue Park: Author and Educator*. 2021,
 lindasuepark.com.

If the site is likely to change, has no date, or no longer exists, include
a date of access.

Archive of Our Own. Organization for Transformative Works,
 archiveofourown.org. Accessed 23 Apr. 2021.

29. WORK ON A WEBSITE

Author's Last Name, First Name (if any). "Title of Work." *Title of
 Site*, Publisher (if any), Date, URL.

Cesareo, Kerry. "Moving Closer to Tackling Deforestation at Scale."
 World Wildlife Fund, 20 Oct. 2020, www.worldwildlife.org
 /blogs/sustainability-works/posts/moving-closer-to-tackling
 -deforestation-at-scale.

30. BLOG ENTRY

Author's Last Name, First Name. "Title of Blog Entry." *Title of
 Blog*, Date, URL.

Hollmichel, Stefanie. "Bring Up the Bodies." *So Many Books*,
 10 Feb. 2014, somanybooksblog.com/2014/02/10/bring-up
 -the-bodies.

31. WIKI

"Title of Entry." *Title of Wiki*, Publisher, Date, URL.

"Pi." *Wikipedia*, Wikimedia Foundation, 28 Aug. 2013, en.wikipedia
 .org/wiki/Pi.

Documentation Map (MLA)
Work on a Website

URL

TITLE OF SITE

TITLE OF WORK

DATE POSTED

AUTHORS

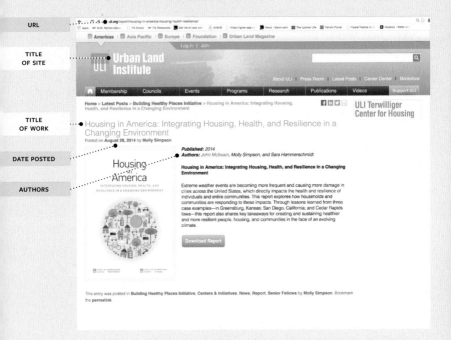

McIlwain, John, et al. "Housing in America: Integrating Housing,
Health, and Resilience in a Changing Environment." *Urban
Land Institute*, 28 Aug. 2014, uli.org/report/housing-in
-america-housing-health-resilience.

| TITLE | AUTHOR | PUBLICATION |

Personal Communication and Social Media

32. PERSONAL LETTER

Sender's Last Name, First Name. Letter to the author. Day Month
Year.

Quindlen, Anna. Letter to the author. 11 Apr. 2013.

33. EMAIL OR TEXT MESSAGE

Include the text of a short email or text message, or a concise description. If it's not clear that it's a text message or email, add a label at the end: Text message, Email. If the email or text message was sent to you, indicate that: Email to the author, Text message to the author.

Sender's Last Name, First Name. Email *or* Text Message to First
Name Last Name *or* "to the author." Day Month Year.

Smith, William. Email to Richard Bullock. 19 Nov. 2013.

Rombes, Maddy. Text message to Isaac Cohen. 4 May 2021.

O'Malley, Kit. Text message to the author. 2 June 2020.

34. POST TO *X, INSTAGRAM,* OR OTHER SOCIAL MEDIA

Author. "Title." *Title of Site,* Day Month Year, URL.

Oregon Zoo. "Winter Wildlife Wonderland." *Facebook,* 8 Feb. 2019,
www.facebook.com/80229441108/videos/2399570506799549.

If there's no title, you can use a concise description or the text of a short post.

Millman, Debbie. Photos of Roxane Gay. *Instagram,* 18 Feb. 2021,
www.instagram.com/p/CLcT_EnhnWT.

President Obama [@POTUS44]. "It's been the honor of my
life to serve you. You made me a better leader and a
better man." *X,* 20 Jan. 2017, x.com/POTUS44/status
/822445882247413761.

Audio, Visual, and Other Sources

35. ADVERTISEMENT

PRINT

Description of ad. *Name of Periodical*, Date, Page.
Advertisement for Grey Goose. *Wine Spectator*, 18 Dec. 2020, p. 22.

VIDEO

"Title." *Title of Site*, uploaded by Company, Date, URL.
"First Visitors." *YouTube*, uploaded by Snickers, 20 Aug. 2020,
    www.youtube.com/watch?v=negecoob1Lo.

36. ART

ORIGINAL

Artist's Last Name, First Name. *Title of Art*. Year created,
    Location.
Van Gogh, Vincent. *The Potato Eaters*. 1885, Van Gogh Museum,
    Amsterdam.

IN A BOOK

Artist's Last Name, First Name. *Title of Art*. Year created,
    Location. *Title of Book*, by First and Last Names, Publisher,
    Year of publication, Page.
Van Gogh, Vincent. *The Potato Eaters*. 1885, Scottish National
    Gallery. *History of Art*, by H. W. Janson, Prentice Hall /
    Harry N. Abrams, 1969, p. 508.

ONLINE

Artist's Last Name, First Name. *Title of Art*. Year created. *Title
    of Site*, URL.
Warhol, Andy. *Self-portrait*. 1979. *J. Paul Getty Museum*, www.getty
    .edu/art/collection/objects/106971/andy-warhol-self-portrait
    -american-1979.

37. CARTOON

PRINT

Author's Last Name, First Name. Cartoon *or* "Title of Cartoon."
    Name of Periodical, Date, Page.
Mankoff, Robert. Cartoon. *The New Yorker,* 3 May 1993, p. 50.

ONLINE

Author's Last Name, First Name. Cartoon *or* "Title of Cartoon."
    Title of Site, Date, URL.
Munroe, Randall. "Up Goer Five." *xkcd,* 12 Nov. 2012, xkcd
    .com/1133.

38. SUPREME COURT CASE

United States, Supreme Court. *Name of Case.* Date of
    decision. *Title of Source Site,* Publisher, URL.
United States, Supreme Court. *District of Columbia v. Heller.*
    26 June 2008. *Legal Information Institute,* Cornell Law
    School, www.law.cornell.edu/supremecourt/text/07-290.

39. FILM

Name individuals based on the focus of your project—the director, the screenwriter, or someone else. If your essay focuses on one contributor, you may put their names before the title.

Title of Film. Role by First and Last Names, Production Company,
    Date.
Breakfast at Tiffany's. Directed by Blake Edwards, Paramount, 1961.
Edwards, Blake, director. *Breakfast at Tiffany's.* Paramount, 1961.

ONLINE

Title of Film. Role by First and Last Names, Production Company, Date. *Title of Site,* URL.

Interstellar. Directed by Christopher Nolan, Paramount, 2014. *Amazon Prime Video,* www.amazon.com/Interstellar -Matthew-McConaughey/dp/B00TU9UFTS.

40. TV SHOW EPISODE

Name contributors based on the focus of your project—director, creator, actors, or others. If you don't want to highlight anyone in particular, don't include any contributors.

BROADCAST

"Title of Episode." *Title of Program,* role by First and Last Names (if any), season, episode, Production Company, Date.

"The Storm." *Avatar: The Last Airbender,* created by Michael Dante DiMartino and Bryan Konietzko, season 1, episode 12, Nickelodeon Animation Studios, 3 June 2005.

STREAMING ONLINE

"Title of Episode." *Title of Program,* role by First and Last Names (if any), season, episode, Production Company, Broadcast Date. *Title of Site,* URL.

"The Storm." *Avatar: The Last Airbender,* season 1, episode 12, Nickelodeon Animation Studios, 2005. *Netflix,* www.netflix .com.

STREAMING ON AN APP

"Title of Episode." *Title of Program,* role by First and Last Names (if any), season, episode, Production Company, Date. *Name of App.*

41. ONLINE VIDEO

"Title of Video." *Title of Site,* uploaded by Uploader's Name,
Day Month Year, URL.

"13 Severed Hands!" *YouTube,* uploaded by vlogbrothers, 30 Sept.
2009, www.youtube.com/watch?v=lDlqwbMCBg4.

42. PRESENTATION ON *ZOOM* OR OTHER VIRTUAL PLATFORM

Author's Last Name, First Name. "Title." Sponsoring Institution,
Day Month Year, online.

Budhathoki, Thir. "Cross-Cultural Perceptions of Literacies in
Student Writing." Conference on College Composition and
Communication, 9 Apr. 2021, online.

43. INTERVIEW

If it's not clear that it's an interview, add a label at the end. If you are
citing a transcript of an interview, indicate that at the end as well.

PUBLISHED

Subject's Last Name, First Name. "Title of Interview." Interview
by First Name Last Name (if given). *Title of Publication,*
Date, Pages *or* URL.

Whitehead, Colson. "Colson Whitehead: By the Book." *The New
York Times,* 15 May 2014, www.nytimes.com/2014/05/18/books
/review/colson-whitehead-by-the-book.html. Interview.

PERSONAL

Subject's Last Name, First Name. Concise description. Day Month
Year.

Bazelon, L. S. Telephone interview with the author. 4 Oct. 2020.

44. MAP

If the title doesn't make clear it's a map, add a label at the end.

Title of Map. Publisher, Date.

Brooklyn. J. B. Beers, 1874. Map.

416 RESEARCH | Find Out

45. ORAL PRESENTATION

Presenter's Last Name, First Name. "Title of Presentation."
   Sponsoring Institution, Date, Location.
Cassin, Michael. "Nature in the Raw—The Art of Landscape
   Painting." Berkshire Institute for Lifelong Learning, 24 Mar.
   2005, Clark Art Institute, Williamstown, Massachusetts.

46. PODCAST

If you accessed it on the web, give the URL; if you accessed it
through an app, indicate that instead.

"Title of Episode." *Title of Podcast*, hosted by First Name Last
   Name, season, episode, Production Company, Date, URL.
"DUSTWUN." *Serial*, hosted by Sarah Koenig, season 2, episode 1,
   WBEZ / Serial Productions, 10 Dec. 2015, serialpodcast.org
   /season-two/1/dustwun.
"DUSTWUN." *Serial*, hosted by Sarah Koenig, season 2, episode 1,
   WBEZ / Serial Productions, 10 Dec. 2015. *Spotify* app.

47. SOUND RECORDING

If you accessed it on the web, give the URL; if you accessed it
through an app, indicate that instead.

Artist's Last Name, First Name. "Title of Work." *Title of Album*,
   Label, Date, URL.
Beyoncé. "Pray You Catch Me." *Lemonade*, Parkwood
   Entertainment / Columbia Records, 2016, www.beyonce
   .com/album/lemonade-visual-album/songs.
Simone, Nina. "To Be Young, Gifted and Black." *Black Gold*,
   RCA Records, 1969. *Spotify* app.

48. VIDEO GAME

Title of Game. Version, Distributor, Date of release.
Animal Crossing: New Horizons. Version 1.1.4, Nintendo, 6 Apr.
   2020.

TITLE   AUTHOR   PUBLICATION

49. GENERATIVE AI

At the time of this printing, the MLA Style Center website gives brief advice on how to document content generated by AI tools such as ChatGPT. See style.mla.org for more information.

"Prompt fed into AI tool" prompt. *AI Tool,* version, Company, Date, URL.

"Explain how a light bulb works" prompt. *ChatGPT,* 23 Mar. version, OpenAI, 14 Apr. 2023, chat.openai.com.

If you're citing a creative work, you can use the title and a concise description instead of including the prompt. If there's no title, you can use the first few words of the text.

"New sneakers, so fresh . . ." haiku about sneakers. *ChatGPT,* 23 Mar. version, OpenAI, 24 Apr. 2023, chat.openai.com.

Formatting a research essay

Name, course, title. MLA does not require a separate title page, unless your paper is a group project. In the upper left-hand corner of your first page, include your name, your instructor's name, the course name and number, and the date. Center the title of your paper on the line after the date; capitalize it as you would a book title. If your paper is a group project, include all that information on a title page instead, listing all the authors.

Page numbers. In the upper right-hand corner of each page, one-half inch below the top of the page, include your last name and the page number. If it's a group project and all the names don't fit, include only the page number. Number pages consecutively.

Fonts, spacing, margins, and indents. Choose a font that is easy to read (such as Times New Roman) and that provides a clear contrast between regular text and italic text. Set the font size between 11 and 13 points. Double-space the entire paper, including your works-cited list and any notes. Set one-inch margins at the top, bottom, and sides of your text; do not justify your text. The first line of each paragraph should be indented one-half inch from the left margin. End punctuation should be followed by one space.

Headings. Short essays do not generally need headings, but they can be useful in longer works. Use a large, bold font for the first level of heading, and smaller fonts and italics to signal lower-level headings. MLA requires that headings all be flush with the left margin.

First-Level Heading

Second-Level Heading

Third-Level Heading

Long quotations. When quoting more than three lines of poetry or four lines of prose, or dialogue between characters in a drama, set off the quotation from the rest of your text, indenting it one-half inch (or five spaces) from the left margin. Do not use quotation marks, and put any parenthetical documentation *after* the final punctuation.

> In *Eastward to Tartary*, Robert Kaplan captures ancient and contemporary Antioch for us:
>
> > At the height of its glory in the Roman-Byzantine age, when it had an amphitheater, public baths, aqueducts, and sewage pipes, half a million people lived in Antioch. Today the population is only 125,000. With sour relations between Turkey and Syria, and unstable politics throughout the Middle East, Antioch is now a backwater—seedy and tumbledown, with relatively few tourists. I found it altogether charming. (123)

> In the first stanza of Matthew Arnold's "Dover Beach," the exclamations make clear that the speaker is addressing someone who is also present in the scene:
>
> > Come to the window, sweet is the night air!
> > Only, from the long line of spray
> > Where the sea meets the moon-blanched land,
> > Listen! You hear the grating roar
> > Of pebbles which the waves draw back, and fling. (lines 6–10)

TITLE   AUTHOR   PUBLICATION

Be careful to maintain the poet's line breaks. If a line does not fit on one line of your paper, put the extra words on the next line. Indent that line an additional quarter inch (or two spaces). If a citation doesn't fit, put it on the next line, flush with the right margin.

Tables and illustrations. Insert illustrations and tables close to the text that discusses them, and be sure to make clear how they relate to your point. For tables, provide a number (*Table 1*) and a title on separate lines above the table and a caption with source information and any notes below. Notes should be indicated with lowercase letters. For graphs, photos, and other figures, provide a figure number (*fig. 1*) and caption, with source information below the figure. If you give full source information in the caption, you don't have to include the source in your list of works cited. Punctuate as you would in the works-cited list, but don't invert the author's name: Berenice Sydney. *Fast Rhythm*. 1972, Tate Britain, London.

List of works cited. Start your list on a new page, following any notes. Center the title, Works Cited, and double-space the entire list. Begin each entry at the left margin, and indent subsequent lines one-half inch (or five spaces). Alphabetize the list by authors' last names (or by editors' or translators' names, if appropriate). Alphabetize works with no author or editor by title, disregarding *A*, *An*, and *The*. To document more than one work by a single author, list them as in no. 4 on page 395.

Student essay, MLA style

The following essay was written by Jackson Parell for a first-year writing course. It was awarded the Boothe Prize for outstanding expository and argumentative writing by first-year students at Stanford University in 2018. It's formatted according to the guidelines of the *MLA Handbook* (style.mla.org).

A STUDENT RESEARCH ESSAY, MLA STYLE

Jackson Parell

Professor Hammann

Writing and Rhetoric 1

21 May 2018

Free at Last, Free at Last:

Civil War Memory and Civil Rights Rhetoric

When Martin Luther King, Jr., addressed the huge crowd in
Washington, DC, on August 28, 1963, he did so on the steps of the
Lincoln Memorial, in Lincoln's symbolic shadow (Sundquist 146).
Using the words and legacy of the Great Emancipator, King intended
to make an appeal to the moral conscience of America to rid itself of
the vestiges of slavery and to realize Lincoln's new birth of freedom
one hundred years after it was first proposed. On this day, and
throughout the Civil War Centennial years (1961–65), African
American leaders, including King, successfully accessed the language
of the Civil War's promise of racial justice to shape a compelling
message for future progress. As historian Robert Cook writes, "The
advent of the Centennial furnished [African Americans] with powerful
leverage in their intensifying efforts to close the gap between the
promise and the reality of American community life" (96).

However, the rhetoric of the Civil War could only serve as an
appeal for racial equality if Americans commonly understood its
history in the context of social justice and equal rights. Unfortunately,
for many Americans in the 1960s, this was not the case (Blight 3).
Northerners and Southerners alike, looking to mend sectional strife
after the war, were willing to adopt a memory of reconciliation that
focused on the shared honor of battle as opposed to the racial issues
over which those battles were fought. Civil War valor, bravery, and
brotherhood shaped American wartime memory into a "shared

Title centered.

Double-spaced throughout.

Author named in signal phrase; page number in parentheses.

No signal phrase; author and page number in parentheses.

Parell   2

experience"—one that would remain a potent source of nationalism well into the civil rights era (Cook 4). "For the majority, especially of white Americans," as historian David Blight writes, "emancipation in Civil War memory was still an awkward kind of politeness at best and heresy at worst. . . . In 1963, the national temper and mythology still preferred a story of the mutual valor of the Blue and Gray to the disruptive problem of black and white" (3). Therefore, civil rights leaders, including King, attempted to remind Americans of the war's cause and enduring racial legacies. Through pen and podium, he leveraged that history in a powerful appeal for racial justice one hundred years after Lee's surrender at Appomattox.

Embeds signal phrase in the middle of the quotation.

In October 1961, President John F. Kennedy invited King to the White House for lunch. The meeting was unofficial—it was not recorded in the secretary's docket, nor was there any official business set to be discussed (Branch 27). After lunch, Kennedy led King on a tour of the residence. Hung outside the door of Lincoln's bedroom was a copy of the original Emancipation Proclamation. It gave King the opportunity to bring up, ever so gently, the issue of civil rights (27). Already, the Montgomery bus boycotts, the Greensboro sit-ins, and the Freedom Rides had brought racial tensions to the forefront of American culture. King believed he had a solution. "Mr. President," he said, "I would like to see you stand in this room and sign a [second] Emancipation Proclamation outlawing segregation 100 years after Lincoln's. You could base it on the Fourteenth Amendment" (qtd. in Sundquist 34). In the summer of 1962, King and his associates delivered the first copy of this second Proclamation to the White House, bound in leather. This document serves as an important example of the ways in which King reshaped the memory of the Civil War and leveraged its rhetoric to advance claims for equality in civil rights. The proclamation directly engages in the battle between white reconciliationist memory and the memory of racial justice. In it, King pushes back on

Brackets indicate the quotation has been altered for clarity.

1″

traditional narratives of mutual valor and bravery by instead placing emphasis on the guarantees of equality embodied in Civil War documents. But before King could make the revisions to Civil War history necessary to frame his plea for racial justice, he needed to provide Kennedy with a compelling reason for doing so. By 1962, racial tensions in the United States had come to a head. Politicians, including Kennedy, wished to deescalate the problem as fast as possible (Branch 52), so in his preamble, King cites increasing racial tensions as well as the Centennial of the Civil War as impetus to dive into the "wellsprings of history" from which the civil rights movement began ("Appeal" 3):

> Mr. President, sometimes there occur moments in the history of our nation when it becomes necessary to pause and reflect upon the heritage of the past in order to determine the most meaningful course for the present and the future. America today in the field of race relations is such a moment. We believe the Centennial of the Emancipation Proclamation is a particularly important time for all our citizens to rededicate themselves to those early precepts and principles of equality before the law. ("Appeal" 1)

With his first words, therefore, King encourages the president to think about Civil War history as a tool for addressing modern issues.

After establishing the importance of looking to the past to resolve the racial tensions of the present, King proposes the version of Civil War history upon which he believes Kennedy should reflect. It is a version that promotes the war's promises of racial equality over the valor and bravery of its veterans. He references the Gettysburg Address and the Emancipation Proclamation as the war's defining documents, both of which place the issue of slavery as the central cause of the Civil War and uphold concepts of equal justice for all

Parell 4

("Appeal" 1–2). King engages here with a larger historical movement to remind Americans of the documents and narratives from their past that support claims for racial equality. In the 1960s, historians and researchers alike looked to rewrite Civil War memory in a way that neither disregarded the importance of slavery as the agent of conflict in the Civil War nor portrayed African Americans as naturally inferior—a people without agency in the struggle for their own freedom (Snyder 1–2, 36). By reshaping the narratives of the past to reflect a nuanced version of the Civil War, these historians attempted to break down the justifications for the racial hierarchy that structured the white status quo.

> Includes short title because there's more than 1 source from that author.

By reshaping Civil War memory to focus on its promises of equality, King develops a strong appeal for change on the grounds that those promises had not yet been fulfilled. He draws compelling parallels between the past and present, which framed the Civil War as a battle unfinished, one fought today by the civil rights movement:

> Paragraphs indent ½ inch or 5 spaces.

> The struggle for freedom, Mr. President, of which our Civil War was but a bloody chapter, continues throughout our land today. The courage and heroism of Negro citizens . . . is only further effort to affirm the democratic heritage so painfully won, in part, upon the grassy battlefields of Antietam, Lookout Mountain, and Gettysburg. ("Appeal" 3)

The metaphor of a modern Civil War presents Kennedy with the moral imperative to follow in the footsteps of Lincoln, his forebearer, and to help finally end the battle for equality begun one hundred years before. "The time has come, Mr. President, to let those dawn-like rays of freedom, first glimpsed in 1863, fill the heavens with noonday sunlight of complete human decency" ("Appeal" 4). King believed that the present situation demanded more than legislative

Parell 5

action—it demanded from Kennedy an executive order that appealed to the "moral conscience of America" ("Appeal" 4).

But Kennedy never responded, and King found his ambivalence very disheartening. Without Kennedy, King felt that the civil rights movement would stall. He needed to re-create the conditions under which a document like the first Emancipation Proclamation came about—to foster the same tensions that brought to light the deep moral flaws of racism and propelled them to a national stage (Ward and Badger 141). Time was running out. The eyes of the world were focused on the civil rights movement, and King intended to capitalize. At midnight on June 1, he called his aides with an urgent message: in August, the civil rights movement would descend on the capital (Branch 53).

If King could not convince the president to change the moral conscience of America, he would attempt to do it himself. Two months later, King began to outline the speech that would conclude the ceremonies of the March on Washington. In essence, it reflected the same historical appeal he had made to the president in the Second Emancipation Proclamation. He intended to shift predominant public memory from one that highlighted the mutual sacrifice of the Blue and Gray to one that focused on the Civil War's guarantees of equality. These guarantees served as the grounds on which King would build his argument for modern civil rights progress. Evoking the language of past Republican leaders, including Lincoln, he appealed to the American public to adopt a policy of inclusion, one with a vision for the future that was, in many ways, shaped in stark contrast to America's oppressive past.

On the morning of August 28, the turnout was slim, estimated at 25,000. Soon, however, protesters began arriving in swarms. At Union Station, trains pulled in first from Baltimore, then Georgia, the Carolinas, Maryland, and further north (Hansen 33–35). By the time King took the podium, he spoke before a crowd of nearly 250,000.

Names both authors in a work with 2 authors.

Includes page range because the information cited spans multiple pages.

Parell   6

"Five score years ago," King began, "a great American in whose symbolic shadow we stand today signed the Emancipation Proclamation" ("Dream" 1). This first sentence of King's "Dream" speech refers both to Lincoln's Gettysburg Address and to the Emancipation Proclamation, placing both documents at the forefront of America's Civil War consciousness (Sundquist 145). As in the Second Emancipation Proclamation, King intended to divert the predominant reconciliationist memory of the Civil War to one that memorialized the guarantees of racial justice embodied in the war's documents. Although his remarks on those documents were brief, the broader, more inclusive historical narratives toward which they gesture—those in which slavery is accepted as the cause of the Civil War and African Americans are acknowledged for their strategic contributions to military efforts— gave further justification to uphold the guarantees of equality memorialized in the documents themselves.

Uses past tense ("began") to describe the scene—and present tense ("refers") to describe the text.

These guarantees served as the moral structure of King's national appeal for racial justice. If, as King argues, equality was a right ensured by the course of American history, then segregation was simply a breach of contract between the American government and its African American constituents. He employs the metaphor of a "bad check" to explain the chasm between historical promises of racial equality and the realities faced in 1960s culture:

> In a sense we've come to our nation's capital to cash a check. . . . This note was a promise that all men—yes, black men as well as white men—would be guaranteed the unalienable rights of life, liberty and the pursuit of happiness. It is obvious today that America has defaulted on this promissory note insofar as her citizens of color are concerned. ("Dream" 1)

Ellipses indicate that some words are left out.

For a nation that claimed to uphold basic precepts of justice, the "bad check" metaphor was particularly compelling. Americans were posed with a moral imperative to rid themselves of the modern vestiges of slavery or else risk contradicting the principles of equality upon which the nation was founded.

King's powerful appeal to the moral conscience of America was only made possible by shaping a new narrative in Civil War memory that upheld equality as a basic right for all: "Many of our white brothers . . . have come to realize that their freedom is inextricably bound to our freedom ("Dream" 3). King begins here the process of linking the fulfillment of the civil rights cause to the betterment of the nation as a whole, a process necessary to garner the support of white moderates, partial to their own self-interest and thus indifferent to historical appeals for racial justice.

The incentive for civil rights progress was only strengthened by King's final moments at the podium, from which his speech gains its name. The appeal of King's utopian dream serves as a powerful motive to pursue civil rights equality. He dreams that "sons of former slaves and the sons of former slave-owners will be able to sit down together at the table of brotherhood" ("Dream" 4). He dreams that freedom will ring from "Stone Mountains of Georgia"—where the faces of Confederate generals are etched in rock—to "Lookout Mountain of Tennessee," the site of one of the Civil War's most famous battles (6). In essence, King's dream is that America will finally live up to the principles of freedom espoused at the time of its origin and live out "the true meaning of its creed" (4). Only then, King believes, will the battle for freedom begun at Fort Sumter finally reach its conclusion. King's direct references to the issue of slavery and to the battlegrounds on which the Civil War was fought serve as anchors in history that shape a clearer vision of future progress for all Americans. The moral imperative that King presents to white individuals in order to tender the check of racial justice is thus only made more pressing by the

Parell   8

collective will to realize King's dream—a dream rooted in the rhetoric of the Civil War.

Ultimately, therefore, King's "Dream" speech promoted a memory that prioritized the war's promises of equality as opposed to the honor of its many battles. Historian David Blight explains:

> As Lincoln implied in that brief address at Gettysburg, the
> Civil War necessitated a redefinition of the United States,
> rooted somehow in the destruction of slavery and the . . .
> principle of human equality. In the "Dream" speech, King
> argued the same for his own era: the civil rights movement
> heralded yet another re-founding in the same principle, one
> hundred . . . years after Lincoln's promise. (2)

Throughout the Centennial years, civil rights leaders, including King, waged war not only over modern policies and ideals, but over historical truth as well. African American activists pushed back on the predominant Civil War memory of the 1960s, promoting the war's guarantees of equality over those of reconciliation. Such guarantees became the grounds on which King and others shaped a compelling appeal for civil rights progress in the modern era. "Just as abolitionists had sought to exploit the promises enshrined in the Declaration of Independence," historian Robert Cook writes, "their intellectual successors had used the events of the Centennial to raise the conscience of the American public in the 1960s" (qtd. in Ward and Badger 144). Ultimately, therefore, civil rights leaders molded the rhetoric of the Civil War to inspire a nation to throw off its shackles of oppression and to breathe new life into the old slave hymn: "Free at last, Free at last, Great God a-mighty, We are free at last" (King, "Dream" 6).

Source quoted in
another source.

1"

Works Cited

Blight, David W. *American Oracle: The Civil War in the Civil Rights Era.*
Belknap Press of Harvard UP, 2013.

Branch, Taylor. "A Second Emancipation." *Washington Monthly*,
Jan.–Feb. 2013, pp. 27–52.

Cook, Robert. *Troubled Commemoration: The American Civil War
Centennial, 1961–1965.* Louisiana State UP, 2011.

Hansen, Drew. *The Dream: Martin Luther King, Jr., and the Speech
That Inspired a Nation.* HarperCollins, 2003.

King, Martin Luther, Jr. "An Appeal to the Honorable John F.
Kennedy President of the United States." 17 May 1962.
Civil Rights Movement Archive, www.crmvet.org/info/eman
cip2.pdf.

———. "I Have a Dream . . . Speech by the Rev. Martin Luther King
Jr. at the 'March on Washington.'" 28 Aug. 1963. *National
Archives*, www.archives.gov/files/press/exhibits/dream-speech
.pdf. Accessed 14 May 2019.

Snyder, Jeffrey Aaron. *Making Black History: The Color Line, Culture,
and Race in the Age of Jim Crow.* U of Georgia P, 2018.

Sundquist, Eric. *King's Dream.* Yale UP, 2009.

Ward, Brian, and Tony Badger. *The Making of Martin Luther King and
the Civil Rights Movement.* Macmillan, 1996.

Heading centered.

The list is alphabetized
by authors' last names.

Double-spaced.

Each entry begins
at the left margin;
subsequent lines are
indented ½ inch or
5 spaces.

Multiple works by
a single author are
listed alphabetically
by title. After first
entry, the author's
name is replaced with
a 3-em dash (or
three hyphens).

Every source used is in
the Works Cited.

23 APA Style

Write with clarity, precision, and inclusion.

*—PUBLICATION MANUAL OF THE
AMERICAN PSYCHOLOGICAL
ASSOCIATION*

I n 1929, a group of anthropologists and psychologists and business writers got together to come up with guidelines that would standardize the way scholars documented sources, assuming that such standards would make articles easier to read and understand. That short guide expanded into the *Publication Manual of the American Psychological Association*, published in its 7th edition in 2020. Almost all the disciplines in the social sciences now recommend following this style. This chapter provides guidelines for formatting and documenting an essay in APA style, along with an essay written by a college student that demonstrates that style.

A DIRECTORY TO APA STYLE
In-text documentation   432

Notes   437
Reference list   437

TITLE	AUTHOR	PUBLICATION

This chapter provides models and examples that are color-coded to help you see how to include source information in a text: orange for author or editor, yellow for title, blue for publication information—publisher, date of publication, page number(s), DOI or URL, and so on.

In-text documentation

Brief documentation in your text makes clear to your reader precisely what you took from a source. If you are quoting, provide the page number(s) or other text that will help readers find the quotation in the source. You're not required to give the page number(s) with a paraphrase or summary, but you may want to do so if you are citing a long or complex work.

PARAPHRASES and SUMMARIES are more common than QUOTATIONS in APA projects. As you cite each source, you will need to decide whether to name the author in a signal phrase—"as Duffy (2020) wrote"—or in parentheses—"(Duffy, 2020)." Note that APA requires the past tense when there's a date or present perfect tense when there's no date in SIGNAL PHRASES: "Moss (2019) argued," "Moss has argued."

1. AUTHOR NAMED IN A SIGNAL PHRASE

Put the date in parentheses after the author's last name, unless the year is mentioned in the sentence. Put any page number(s) you're including in parentheses after the quotation, paraphrase, or summary. Parenthetical documentation should come *before* the period at the end of the sentence and *after* any quotation marks.

> McCullough (2020) described John Adams as having "the hands of a man accustomed to pruning his own trees, cutting his own hay, and splitting his own firewood" (p. 18).

> In 2020, McCullough noted that John Adams's hands were those of a laborer (p. 18).

If the author is named after a quotation, put the page number(s) after the date.

> John Adams had "the hands of a man accustomed to pruning his own trees," according to McCullough (2020, p. 18).

2. AUTHOR NAMED IN PARENTHESES

If you do not mention an author in a signal phrase, put the name, the year of publication, and any page numbers in parentheses at the end of the sentence or right after the quotation, paraphrase, or summary.

> John Adams had "the hands of a man accustomed to pruning his own trees, cutting his own hay, and splitting his own firewood" (McCullough, 2020, p. 18).

3. AUTHORS WITH THE SAME LAST NAME

If your reference list includes more than one first author with the same last name, include initials to distinguish the authors from one another.

> Eclecticism is common in modern criticism (J. M. Smith, 1992, p. vii).

4. TWO AUTHORS

Always mention both authors. Use *and* in a signal phrase, but use an ampersand (&) in parentheses.

> Carlson and Ventura (1990) wanted to introduce Julio Cortázar, Marjorie Agosín, and other Latin American writers to an audience of English-speaking adolescents (p. v).

> According to the Peter Principle, "In a hierarchy, every employee tends to rise to his level of incompetence" (Peter & Hull, 1969, p. 26).

5. THREE OR MORE AUTHORS

When you refer to a work by three or more contributors, name only the first author followed by *et al.*, Latin for "and others."

> Peilen et al. (1990) supported their claims about corporate corruption with startling anecdotal evidence (p. 75).

6. ORGANIZATION OR GOVERNMENT AS AUTHOR

If an organization name has a familiar abbreviation, give the full name and the abbreviation in brackets the first time you cite the source. In subsequent references, use only the abbreviation. If the organization does not have a familiar abbreviation, always use its full name.

FIRST REFERENCE

(American Psychological Association [APA], 2020)

SUBSEQUENT REFERENCES

(APA, 2020)

7. AUTHOR UNKNOWN

Use the complete title if it's short; if it's long, use the first few words of the title under which the work appears in the reference list. Italicize the title if it's italicized in the reference list; if it isn't italicized there, enclose the title in quotation marks.

TITLE   AUTHOR   PUBLICATION

According to *Feeding Habits of Rams* (2000), a ram's diet often changes from one season to the next (p. 29).

The article noted that one healthy liver donor died because of "frightening" postoperative care ("Every Patient's Nightmare," 2007).

8. TWO OR MORE WORKS TOGETHER

If you document multiple works in the same parentheses, place the source information in alphabetical order, separated by semicolons.

Many researchers have argued that what counts as "literacy" is not necessarily learned at school (Heath, 1983; Moss, 2003).

9. TWO OR MORE WORKS BY ONE AUTHOR IN THE SAME YEAR

If your list of references includes more than one work by the same author published in the same year, order them alphabetically by title, adding lowercase letters (*a*, *b*, and so on) to the year.

Kaplan (2000a) described orderly shantytowns in Turkey that did not resemble the other slums he visited.

10. SOURCE QUOTED IN ANOTHER SOURCE

When you cite a source that was quoted in another source, add the words *as cited in*.

Thus, Modern Standard Arabic was expected to serve as the "moral glue" holding the Arab world together (Choueri, 2000, as cited in Walters, 2019, p. 475).

11. WORK WITHOUT PAGE NUMBERS

Instead of page numbers, some works have paragraph numbers, which you should include (preceded by the abbreviation *para.*) if you are referring to a specific part of such a source.

Russell's dismissals from Trinity College at Cambridge and from City College in New York City have been seen as examples of the controversy that marked his life (Irvine, 2006, para. 2).

In sources with neither page nor paragraph numbers, refer readers to a particular part of the source if possible, perhaps indicating a heading: (Brody, 2020, Introduction, para. 2).

12. AN ENTIRE WORK

You do not need to give a page number if you are directing readers' attention to an entire work.

> Kaplan (2000) considered Turkey and Central Asia explosive.

When you're citing an entire website, give the URL in the text. You do not need to include the website in your reference list. To document a webpage, see number 18 on page 446.

> Beyond providing diagnostic information, the website for the Alzheimer's Association (https://www.alz.org) includes a variety of resources for the families of patients.

13. PERSONAL COMMUNICATION

Document emails, telephone conversations, interviews, personal letters, messages from nonarchived online discussion sources, and other personal texts as *personal communication*, along with the person's initial(s), last name, and the date. You do not need to include such personal communications in your reference list.

> L. Strauss (personal communication, December 6, 2013) told about visiting Yogi Berra when they both lived in Montclair, New Jersey.

14. GENERATIVE AI

The author is the name of the company that created the generative AI tool.

> AI models can be used for predictive modeling, helping researchers anticipate trends, behaviors, or outcomes based on historical data (OpenAI, 2023).

Notes

You may need to use footnotes to give an explanation or information that doesn't fit into your text or to acknowledge the use of AI in your writing process. To signal a content footnote, place a superscript numeral at the appropriate point in your text. Include this information as a footnote, either at the bottom of that page or on a separate page with the heading **Footnotes** centered and in bold, after your reference list. If you have multiple notes, number them consecutively throughout your text. Here is an example from *In Search of Solutions: A New Direction in Psychotherapy* (2003).

TEXT WITH SUPERSCRIPT

An important part of working with teams and one-way mirrors is taking the consultation break, as at Milan, BFTC, and MRI.[1]

FOOTNOTE

[1]It is crucial to note here that while working with a team is fun, stimulating, and revitalizing, it is not necessary for successful outcomes. Solution-oriented therapy works equally well solo.

Here's an example acknowledging and explaining the use of AI.

TEXT WITH SUPERSCRIPT

This essay argues that teacher looping in middle-school grades has multiple benefits for students.[1]

FOOTNOTE

[1]I acknowledge the use of *ChatGPT* in researching my topic and then in writing about it. It helped me get an overview of the concept of belonging in college before starting my research. And then it helped me create an outline for writing my essay. I've included my initial prompts and the full conversation with *ChatGPT* in an appendix.

Reference list

A reference list provides full bibliographic information for every source cited in your text with the exception of entire websites, common computer software and mobile apps, and personal communications. See page 460 for guidelines on preparing such a list; for a sample reference list, see page 474.

Key Elements for Documenting Sources

To document a source in APA style, you need to provide information about the author, the date, the title of the work you're citing, and the source itself (who published it; volume, issue, and page numbers; any DOI or URL). The following guidelines explain how to handle each of these elements generally, but there will be exceptions. For that reason, you'll want to consult the entries for the specific kinds of sources you're documenting; these entries provide templates showing which details you need to include. Be aware, though, that sometimes the templates will show elements that your source doesn't have; if that's the case, just omit those elements.

AUTHORS

Most entries begin with the author's last name, followed by the first and any middle initials: Smith, Z. for Zadie Smith; Kinder, D. R. for Donald R. Kinder.

- If the author is a group or organization, use its full name: Black Lives Matter, American Historical Association.
- If there is no author, put the title of the work first, followed by the date.
- If the author uses a screen name, first give their real name, followed by the screen name in brackets: Scott, B. [@BostonScott2]. If only the screen name is known, leave off the brackets: AvalonGirl1990.

DATES

Include the date of publication, in parentheses right after the author. Some sources require only the year; others require the year, month, and day; and still others require something else. Consult the entry in this chapter for the specific source you're documenting.

TITLE   AUTHOR   PUBLICATION

- For a book, use the copyright year, which you'll find on the copyright page. If more than one year is given, use the most recent one.
- For most magazine or newspaper articles, use the full date that appears on the work, usually the year followed by the month and day.
- For a journal article, use the year of the volume.
- Give the volume and issue for journals and magazines that include that information. No need to give that information for newspapers.
- For a work you found on a website, use the date when the work was last updated. If that information is not available, use the date when the work was published.
- If a work has no date, use *n.d.* for "no date."
- For online content that is likely to change, include the month, day, and year when you retrieved it. No need to do so for materials that are unlikely to change.

TITLES

Capitalize only the first word and any PROPER NOUNS and adjectives in the title and subtitle of the work you're citing. But sometimes you'll also need to provide the title of a periodical or website where a source was found, and those are done differently: capitalize all the principal words (excluding articles and prepositions).

- ***For books, reports, webpages, podcasts***, and other works that stand on their own, italicize the title—*Provocations of virtue*, *Radiolab*. Do not italicize the titles of the sources where you found them, however: NPR, ProQuest.
- ***For journal articles, book chapters, TV series episodes***, and other works that are part of a larger work, do not italicize the title: The snowball effect, Not your average Joe. But do italicize the title of the larger work: *The Atlantic*, *Game of thrones*.

- ***If a work has no title***, include a description in square brackets after the date: [Painting of sheep on a hill].
- ***If the title includes another title***, italicize it: *Frog and Toad and the self*. If the title you're documenting is itself in italics, do not italicize the title within it: *Stay, illusion!* The Hamlet *doctrine*.
- ***For untitled social media posts*** or comments, include the first twenty words as the title, in italics and followed by a bracketed description: *TIL pigeons can fly up to 700 miles in one day* [Post].

SOURCE INFORMATION

This indicates where the work can be found (in a database or on a website, for example) and includes information about the publisher; any volume, issue, and page numbers; and, for some sources, a DOI or URL. For books, films, and other works that stand on their own, the source might be a publisher, a database, or a website. For articles, essays, and works that are part of larger works, the source might be a magazine, an anthology, or a TV series.

DOIS OR URLS

Include a DOI (digital object identifier, a string of letters and numbers that identifies an online document) for any work that has one, whether you accessed the source in print or online. For an online work with no DOI, include a URL unless the work is from an academic database. You can use a short DOI (which you can find at shortdoi.org) or a short URL (using tinyURL.com or another URL shortener) as long as it leads to the right source. *Please note that almost all the documentation templates include a DOI or URL; if the work you are documenting does not have one, just leave it off.*

TITLE   AUTHOR   PUBLICATION

Authors and Other Contributors

Most entries begin with authors—one author, two authors, or twenty-five. And some include editors, translators, or others who've contributed. The following nine templates show you how to document the various kinds of authors and other contributors.

1. ONE AUTHOR

Author's Last Name, Initials. (Year of publication). *Title*. Publisher. DOI *or* URL

Lewis, M. (2003). *Moneyball: The art of winning an unfair game*. W. W. Norton.

2. TWO AUTHORS

First Author's Last Name, Initials, & Second Author's Last Name, Initials. (Year of publication). *Title*. Publisher. DOI *or* URL

Montefiore, S., & Montefiore, S. S. (2016). *The royal rabbits of London*. Aladdin.

3. THREE OR MORE AUTHORS

For three to twenty authors, include all names.

First Author's Last Name, Initials, Next Author's Last Name, Initials, & Final Author's Last Name, Initials. (Year of publication). *Title*. Publisher. DOI *or* URL

Greig, A., Taylor, J., & MacKay, T. (2013). *Doing research with children: A practical guide*. (3rd ed.). Sage.

For a work by twenty-one or more authors, name the first nineteen, followed by three ellipsis points, and end with the final author.

4. TWO OR MORE WORKS BY THE SAME AUTHOR

List works published in different years chronologically.

Lewis, B. (1995). *The Middle East: A brief history of the last 2,000 years*. Scribner.

Lewis, B. (2003). *The crisis of Islam: Holy war and unholy terror*. Modern Library.

If the works were published in the same year, list them alphabetically by title, adding *a*, *b*, and so on to the year.

> Kaplan, R. D. (2000a). *The coming anarchy: Shattering the dreams of the post Cold War*. Random House.
> Kaplan, R. D. (2000b). *Eastward to Tartary: Travels in the Balkans, the Middle East, and the Caucasus*. Random House.

5. AUTHOR AND EDITOR

If a book has an author and an editor who is credited on the cover, include the editor in parentheses after the title.

> Author's Last Name, Initials. (Year of publication). *Title*. (Editor's Initials Last Name, Ed.). Publisher. DOI *or* URL (Original work published Year)
> Dick, P. F. (2008). *Five novels of the 1960s and 70s*. (J. Lethem, Ed.). Library of America. (Original works published 1964–1977)

6. AUTHOR AND TRANSLATOR

> Author's Last Name, Initials. (Year of publication). *Title* (Translator's Initials Last Name, Trans.). Publisher. DOI *or* URL (Original work published Year)
> Hugo, V. (2008). *Les misérables* (J. Rose, Trans.). Modern Library. (Original work published 1862)

7. EDITOR

> Editor's Last Name, Initials (Ed.). (Year of publication). *Title*. Publisher. DOI *or* URL
> Jones, D. (Ed.). (2007). *Modern love: 50 true and extraordinary tales of desire, deceit, and devotion*. Three Rivers Press.

8. UNKNOWN OR NO AUTHOR OR EDITOR

> *Title*. (Year of publication). Publisher. DOI *or* URL
> *Feeding habits of rams*. (2000). Land's Point Press.

Clues in salmonella outbreak. (2008, June 21). *The New York Times*, A13.

If the author is listed as Anonymous, use that as the author's name.

9. ORGANIZATION OR GOVERNMENT AS AUTHOR

Sometimes an organization or a government agency is both author and publisher. If so, omit the publisher.

Organization Name *or* Government Agency. (Year of publication). *Title*. DOI *or* URL

Catholic News Service. (2002). *Stylebook on religion 2000: A reference guide*.

National Institute of Mental Health. (2004). *Autism spectrum disorders*.

Articles and Other Short Works

Articles, essays, reviews, and other short works are found in periodicals and books—in print, online, or in a database. For most short works, provide information about the author, the date, the titles of both the short work and the longer work, plus any volume and issue numbers, page numbers, and DOI or URL if there is one.

10. ARTICLE IN A JOURNAL

Author's Last Name, Initials. (Year). Title of article. *Title of Journal, volume*(issue), page(s). DOI *or* URL

Gremer, J. R., Sala, A., & Crone, E. E. (2010). Disappearing plants: Why they hide and how they return. *Ecology, 91*(11), 3407–3413. https://doi.org/10.1890/09-1864.1

11. ARTICLE IN A MAGAZINE

If a magazine is published weekly, include the year, month, and day. Put any volume number and issue number after the title.

Author's Last Name, Initials. (Year, Month Day). Title of article. *Title of Magazine, volume*(issue), page(s). DOI *or* URL

Klump, B. (2019, November 22). Of crows and tools. *Science, 366*(6468), 965. https://doi.org/10.1126/science.aaz7775

12. ARTICLE IN A NEWSPAPER

If page numbers are consecutive, separate them with an en dash. If not, separate them with a comma.

> Author's Last Name, Initials. (Year, Month Day). Title of article. *Title of Newspaper,* page(s). URL

> Spencer, A. (2021, February 15). Backlash for film about autism. *The New York Times,* C1–C2.

> Schneider, G. (2005, March 13). Fashion sense on wheels. *The Washington Post,* F1, F6.

13. ARTICLE ON A NEWS WEBSITE

Italicize the titles of articles on *CNN, HuffPost, Salon, Vox,* and other news websites. Do not italicize the name of the website.

> Author's Last Name, Initials. (Year, Month Day). *Title of article.* Name of Site. URL

> Travers, C. (2019, December 3). *Here's why you keep waking up at the same time every night.* HuffPost. https://bit.ly/3drSwAR

14. JOURNAL ARTICLE FROM A DATABASE

> Author's Last Name, Initials. (Year). Title of article. *Title of Journal, volume*(issue), pages. DOI

> Simpson, M. (1972). Authoritarianism and education: A comparative approach. *Sociometry, 35*(2), 223–234. https://doi.org/10.2307/2786619

15. EDITORIAL

Editorials can appear in journals, magazines, and newspapers. If the editorial is unsigned, put the title in the author position.

> Author's Last Name, Initials. (Year, Month Day). Title of editorial [Editorial]. *Title of Periodical.* DOI *or* URL

> *The Guardian* view on local theatres: The shows must go on [Editorial]. (2019, December 6). *The Guardian.* https://bit.ly/2VZHIUg

Documentation Map (APA)
Article in a Journal with a DOI

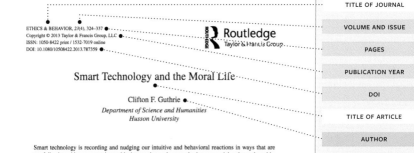

TITLE OF JOURNAL

VOLUME AND ISSUE

PAGES

PUBLICATION YEAR

DOI

TITLE OF ARTICLE

AUTHOR

ETHICS & BEHAVIOR, 23(4), 324–337
Copyright © 2013 Taylor & Francis Group, LLC
ISSN: 1050-8422 print / 1532-7019 online
DOI: 10.1080/10508422.2013.787359

Routledge
Taylor & Francis Group

Smart Technology and the Moral Life

Clifton F. Guthrie
*Department of Science and Humanities
Husson University*

Smart technology is recording and nudging our intuitive and behavioral reactions in ways that are not fully shaped by our conscious ethical reasoning and so are altering our social and moral worlds. Beyond reasons to worry, there are also reasons to embrace this technology for nudging human behavior toward prosocial activity. This article inquires about four ways that smart technology is shaping the individual moral life: the persuasive effect of promptware, our newly evolving experiences of embodiment, our negotiations with privacy, and our experiences of risk and serendipity.

Keywords: persuasive technology, morality, ethics, virtue

PERSUASIVE TECHNOLOGY

For some time, cars have worked to shape our behaviors, beeping to warn us when a door is unlocked or a seat belt unfastened, or giving us fuel efficiency feedback. These straightforward but persuasive sensor systems nudge us toward a repertoire of safe driving behaviors, and we often cannot override them even if we want to. Newer cars include an increasing number of smart technologies that interact with us more intelligently. Some detect the presence of electronic keys and make it impossible for drivers to lock themselves out. Others use sensors to monitor approaching obstacles or lane boundaries and give warnings or even apply the brakes. We are seeing the emergence of street intersections that communicate directly with cars and cars that can communicate with one another (Dean, Fletcher, Porges, & Ulrich, 2012). These are so-called smart technologies because they draw data from the environment and from us, and often make decisions on our behalf. A leading researcher in automated driving noted, "The driver is still in control. But if the driver is not doing the right thing, the technology takes over" (Markoff & Sengupta, 2013).

As cars become smarter they are helping to lead us into what technologists describe as a pervasive, ambient, or calm computing environment. In 1991, Mark Weiser of the Palo Alto Research Center presciently called it "ubiquitous computing" or "ubicomp" in a much-quoted article from *Scientific American*, in which he outlined what has come to be accepted as a standard interpretation of the history of human interaction with computers. This is the age in which computers are increasingly liberated from manual input devices like laptops and cell phones to become an invisible, interactive, computational sensorium. Early examples include motion sensors, smart

Correspondence should be addressed to Clifton F. Guthrie, Department of Science and Humanities, Husson University, 1 College Circle, Bangor, ME 04401. E-mail: cfguthrie@gmail.com

Guthrie, C. F. (2013). Smart technology and the moral life. *Ethics & Behavior*, 23(4), 324–337. https://doi.org/10.1080/10508422.2013.787359

16. REVIEW

Reviewer's Last Name, Initials. (Year, Month Day). Title of review [Review of the work *Title*, by Author's Initials Last Name]. *Name of Periodical* or *Blog*. DOI *or* URL

Johnson, S. (2017, December 15). Mysteries unfold in a land of minarets and magic carpets [Review of the book *The city of brass,* by S. A. Chakraborty]. *The New York Times.* https://nyti.ms/2kvwHFP

17. COMMENT ON AN ONLINE PERIODICAL ARTICLE OR BLOG POST

Writer's Last Name, Initials. [username]. (Year, Month Day). Text of comment up to 20 words [Comment on the work "Title of work"]. *Title of Publication.* DOI *or* URL

PhyllisSpecial. (2020, May 10). How about we go all the way again? It's about time . . . [Comment on the article "2020 Eagles schedule: Picking wins and losses for all 16 games"]. *The Philadelphia Inquirer.* https://rb.gy/iduabz

If the author of the comment does not provide a real name, use the username without brackets.

Simon. (2019, August 28). I've never read him, maybe I should? [Comment on the blog post "H. P. Lovecraft. What am I doing wrong?"]. *Reader Witch.* https://readerwitch.com/2019/08/26/lovecraft/

18. WEBPAGE

Author's Last Name, Initials. (Year, Month Day). *Title of work.* Title of Site. URL

Pleasant, B. (n.d.). *Annual bluegrass.* The National Gardening Association. https://garden.org/learn/articles/view/2936/

If the author and the website name are the same, use the website name as the author. If the content of the webpage is likely to change and no archived version exists, use *n.d.* as the date and include a retrieval date.

> Centers for Disease Control and Prevention. (2019, December 2). *When and how to wash your hands*. https://www.cdc.gov/handwashing/when-how-handwashing.html
>
> Worldometer. (n.d.). *World population*. Retrieved February 2, 2020, from https://www.worldometers.info/world-population/

Books, parts of books, and reports

19. BASIC ENTRY FOR A BOOK

Author's Last Name, Initials. (Year of publication). *Title*. Publisher. DOI *or* URL

PRINT BOOK

Penny, L. (2008). *A rule against murder*. Minotaur Books.

EBOOK

Jemisin, N. K. (2017). *The stone sky*. Orbit. https://amzn.com/B01N7EQOFA

AUDIOBOOK

Obama, M. (2018). *Becoming* (M. Obama, Narr.) [Audiobook]. Random House Audio. http://amzn.com/B07B3JQZCL

Include the word *Audiobook* in brackets and the name of the narrator only if you've mentioned the format and the narrator in what you've written.

20. EDITION OTHER THAN THE FIRST

Author's Last Name, Initials. (Year). *Title* (Name *or* number ed.). Publisher. DOI *or* URL

Rowling, J. K. (2015). *Harry Potter and the sorcerer's stone* (Illustrated ed.). Arthur A. Levine Books.

Burch, D. (2008). *Emergency navigation: Find your position and shape your course at sea even if your instruments fail* (2nd ed.). International Marine/McGraw-Hill.

Documentation Map (APA)
Webpage

URL

TITLE OF SITE

TITLE OF WORK

DATE OF PUBLICATION

AUTHOR

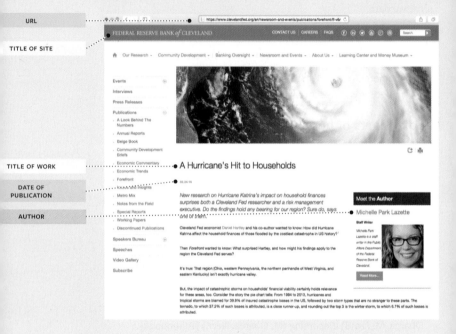

Lazette, M. P. (2015, February 24). *A hurricane's hit to households.*
Federal Reserve Bank of Cleveland. https://www.cleveland
fed .org/en/newsroom-and-events/publications/forefront/
ff-v6no1/ff-20150224-v6no107-a-hurricanes-hit-to-
households.aspx

Documentation Map (APA)
Book

YEAR OF PUBLICATION

TITLE

SUBTITLE

AUTHOR

PUBLISHER

Stiglitz, J. E. (2015). *The great divide: Unequal societies and what we can do about them.* W. W. Norton.

21. EDITED COLLECTION OR ANTHOLOGY

Editor's Last Name, Initials (Ed.). (Year). *Title* (Name or
   number ed., Vol. number). Publisher. DOI or URL
Gilbert, S. M., & Gubar, S. (Eds.). (2003). *The Norton anthology
   of literature by women: The traditions in English* (3rd ed.,
   Vol. 2). W. W. Norton.

22. WORK IN AN EDITED COLLECTION OR ANTHOLOGY

Author's Last Name, Initials. (Year of edited edition). Title of
   work. In Editor's Initials Last Name (Ed.), *Title of collection*
   (Name or number ed., Vol. number, pp. pages). Publisher.
   DOI or URL (Original work published Year)
Choi, Y. (2018). The art of losing. In H. Pitlor & R. Gay (Eds.),
   The best American short stories 2018 (pp. 38–61).
   Houghton Mifflin. (Original work published 2017)
Baldwin, J. (2018). Notes of a native son. In M. Puchner, S. Akbari,
   W. Denecke, B. Fuchs, C. Levine, P. Lewis, & E. Wilson (Eds.),
   The Norton anthology of world literature (4th ed., Vol. F,
   pp. 728–743). W. W. Norton. (Original work published 1955)

23. CHAPTER IN AN EDITED BOOK

Author's Last Name, Initials. (Year). Title of chapter. In Editor's
   Initials Last Name (Ed.), *Title of book* (pp. pages). Publisher.
   DOI or URL
Amarnick, S. (2009). Trollope at fuller length: Lord Silverbridge
   and the manuscript of *The duke's children*. In M. Markwick,
   D. Denenholz Morse, & R. Gagnier (Eds.), *The politics of
   gender in Anthony Trollope's novels: New readings for the
   twenty-first century* (pp. 193–206). Routledge.

24. ENTRY IN A REFERENCE WORK

If the entry has no author, use the name of the publisher as the author.
If the reference work has an editor, include their name after the

title of the entry. If the entry is archived or is not likely to change, use the publication date and do not include a retrieval date.

Author's Last Name, Initials. (Year). Title of entry. In Editor's
    Initials Last Name (Ed.), *Title of reference work* (Name or
    number ed., Vol. number, pp. pages). Publisher. URL
Merriam-Webster. (n.d.). Epoxy. In *Merriam-Webster.com
    dictionary*. Retrieved January 29, 2020, from https://www.
    merriam-webster.com/dictionary/epoxy

25. BOOK IN A LANGUAGE OTHER THAN ENGLISH

Author's Last Name, Initials. (Year). *Title of book* [English
    translation of title]. Publisher. DOI *or* URL
Ferrante, E. (2011). *L'amica geniale* [My brilliant friend].
    Edizione E/O.

26. ONE VOLUME OF A MULTIVOLUME WORK

Author's Last Name, Initials. (Year). *Title of entire work*
    (Vol. number). Publisher. DOI *or* URL
Spiegelman, A. (1986). *Maus* (Vol. 1). Random House.

If the volume has a separate title, include the volume number and title in italics after the main title.

27. RELIGIOUS WORK

If the date of the original publication is known, include it at the end.

Title. (Year of publication). Publisher. URL (Original work
    published Year)
New American Bible. (2002). United States Conference of
    Catholic Bishops. http://www.vatican.va/archive/ENG0839/
    _INDEX.HTM (Original work published 1970)

28. REPORT BY AN ORGANIZATION OR GOVERNMENT AGENCY

Author's Last Name, Initials. (Year). *Title* (Report No. number if
there is one). Publisher. DOI *or* URL

Centers for Disease Control and Prevention. (2009). *Fourth
national report on human exposure to environmental
chemicals.* US Department of Health and Human Services.
https://www.cdc.gov/exposurereport/pdf/fourthreport.pdf

Include the year, month, and day if the report you're documenting
includes that information. If more than one government department
is listed as the publisher, list the most specific department as the
author and the larger department as the publisher.

29. DISSERTATION

Author's Last Name, Initials. (Year). *Title* (Publication No.
number if there is one) [Doctoral dissertation, Name
of School]. Database or Archive Name. URL

Martin-Brualla, R. (2016). *Exploring the world's visual history*
[Doctoral dissertation, University of Washington]. Research
Works. https://digital.lib.washington.edu/researchworks/
handle/1773/37075

If the dissertation is in a database, do not include a URL.

Solomon, M. (2016). *Social media and self-examination:
The examination of social media use on identity, social
comparison, and self-esteem in young female adults*
(Publication No. 10188962) [Doctoral dissertation, William
James College]. ProQuest Dissertations & Theses Global.

30. PAPER OR POSTER PRESENTED AT A CONFERENCE

Presenter's Last Name, Initials. (Year, Month First Day–Last Day).
Title [Paper *or* Poster presentation]. Name of Conference,
City, State, Country. URL

Dolatian, H., & Heinz, J. (2018, May 25–27). *Reduplication and finite-state technology* [Paper presentation]. The 53rd Annual Meeting of the Chicago Linguistic Society, Chicago, United States. http://chicagolinguisticsociety.org/public/CLS53 _Booklet.pdf

Audio, Visual, and Other Sources

If you are citing an entire website, do not include it in your reference list; simply mention the website's name in the body of your paper and include the URL in parentheses. Email and other unarchived discussions also do not need to be included in your list of references.

31. *WIKIPEDIA* ENTRY

Wikipedia archives its pages so give the date when you accessed the page and the URL of the version you're citing.

Title of entry. (Year, Month Day). In *Wikipedia*. URL

List of sheep breeds. (2019, September 9). In *Wikipedia*. https://en.wikipedia .org/w/index.php?title=List_of_sheep _breeds&oldid=914884262

32. ONLINE FORUM POST

Author's Last Name, Initials [username]. (Year, Month Day). *Content of the post up to 20 words* [Online forum post]. Name of Site. URL

Hanzus, D. [DanHanzus]. (2019, October 23). *GETCHA DAN HANZUS. ASK ME ANYTHING!* [Online forum post]. Reddit. https://bit.ly/38WgmSF

33. BLOG POST

Author's Last Name, Initials [username]. (Year, Month Day). Title of post. Name of Blog. URL

gcrepps. (2017, March 28). Shania Sanders. *Women@NASA*. https:// blogs.nasa.gov/womenatnasa/2017/03/28/shania-sanders/

If only the username is known, use it without brackets.

34. ONLINE STREAMING VIDEO

Uploader's Last Name, Initials [username]. (Year, Month Day). *Title* [Video]. Name of Video Platform. URL

CinemaSins. (2014, August 21). *Everything wrong with National Treasure in 13 minutes or less* [Video]. YouTube. https://www.youtube.com/watch?v=1ul-_ZWvXTs

Whoever uploaded the video is considered the author, even if someone else created the content. If only a username is known, use it without brackets.

35. PODCAST

Host's Last Name, Initials (Host). (First Year–Last Year). *Podcast name* [Audio podcast]. Production Company. URL

Poor, N., Woods, E., & Thomas, R. (Hosts). (2017–present). *Ear hustle* [Audio podcast]. PRX. https://www.earhustlesq.com/

36. PODCAST EPISODE

Host's Last Name, Initials (Host). (Year, Month Day). Episode title (No. episode number if any) [Audio podcast episode]. In *Podcast name*. Production Company. URL

Tamposi, E., & Samocki, E. (Hosts). (2020, January 8). The year of the broads [Audio podcast episode]. In *The broadcast podcast*. Podcast One. https://podcastone.com/episode/the-year-of-the-broads

37. FILM

Director's Last Name, Initials (Director). (Year). *Title* [Film]. Production Company. URL

Cuarón, A. (Director). (2016). *Harry Potter and the prisoner of Azkaban* [Film; two-disc special ed. on DVD]. Warner Brothers.

Jenkins, B. (Director). (2016). *Moonlight* [Film]. A24; Plan B; PASTEL.

TITLE   AUTHOR   PUBLICATION

Indicate how you watched the film only if the format is relevant to what you've written.

38. TELEVISION SERIES

Executive Producer's Last Name, Initials (Executive Producer). (First Year–Last Year). *Title of series* [TV series]. Production Company. URL

Iungerich, L., Gonzalez, E., & Haft, J. (Executive Producers). (2018–present). *On my block* [TV series]. Crazy Cat Lady Productions.

Indicate how you watched the TV series (2-disc DVD set, for example) only if the format is relevant to what you've written.

39. TELEVISION SERIES EPISODE

Last Name, Initials (Writer), & Last Name, Initials (Director). (Year, Month Day). Title of episode (Season number, Episode number) [TV series episode]. In Initials Last Name (Executive Producer), *Title of series*. Production Company. URL

Siegal, J. (Writer), Morgan, D. (Writer), & Sackett, M. (Director). (2018, December 6). Janet(s) (Season 3, Episode 10) [TV series episode]. In M. Schur, D. Miner, M. Sackett, & D. Goddard (Executive Producers), *The good place*. Fremulon; 3 Arts Entertainment; Universal Television.

40. MUSIC ALBUM

Artist's Last Name, Initials. (Year). *Title of album* [Album]. Label.

Lennox, A. (1995). *Medusa* [Album]. Arista.

41. SONG

Artist's Last Name, Initials. (Year). Name of song [Song]. On *Title of album*. Label.

Giddens, R. (2015). Shake sugaree [Song]. On *Tomorrow is my turn*. Nonesuch.

42. POWERPOINT SLIDES

Author's Last Name, Initials. (Year, Month Day). *Title of presentation* [PowerPoint slides]. Publisher. URL

Pavliscak, P. (2016, February 21). *Finding our happy place in the internet of things* [PowerPoint slides]. Slideshare. https://bit.ly/3aOcfs7

43. RECORDING OF A SPEECH OR WEBINAR

Author's Last Name, Initials. (Year, Month Day *or* Year). *Title* [Speech audio recording *or* Webinar]. Publisher. URL

Kennedy, J. F. (1961, January 20). *Inaugural address* [Speech audio recording]. American Rhetoric. https://bit.ly/339Gc3e

For a webinar, include only the year.

Rodrigo, S. (2020). *Keep calm (and compassionate) & move everything online* [Webinar]. W. W. Norton. https://seagull.wwnorton.com/CompositionTeachingOnline

44. MAP

Mapmaker's Last Name, Initials. (Year). *Title of map* [Map]. Publisher. URL

Daniels, M. (2018). *Human terrain: Visualizing the world's population, in 3D* [Map]. The Pudding. https://pudding.cool/2018/10/city_3d/

45. SOCIAL MEDIA POSTS

If only the username or organization is known, provide it without brackets. List any attachments (e.g., videos, images, or links) in brackets. Replicate any emoji or include a bracketed description. Do not change spelling or capitalization in a social media reference, even if it looks wrong.

Author's Last Name, Initials [@username]. (Year, Month Day).
    Content of post up to 20 words [Description of any
    attachments] [Type of post]. Platform. URL

X POST

Baron, D. [@DrGrammar]. (2019, November 11). *Gender conceal:*
    Did you know that pronouns can also hide someone's
    gender? [Thumbnail with link attached] [Post]. X. https://bit.
    ly/2vaCcDc

INSTAGRAM PHOTOGRAPH OR VIDEO

Jamil, J. [@jameelajamilofficial]. (2018, July 18). *Happy Birthday*
    to our leader. I steal all my acting faces from you.
    @kristenanniebell [Face with smile and sunglasses emoji]
    [Photograph]. Instagram. https://www.instagram.com/
    p/BlYX5F9FuGL/

FACEBOOK POST

Black Lives Matter. (2015, October 23). *Rise and grind! Did*
    you sign this petition yet? We now have a sign on for
    ORGANIZATIONS to lend their [Image attached]. Facebook.
    www.facebook.com/BlackLivesMatter/photos/a.29480720
    4023865.1073741829.180212755483311/504711973033386/
    ?type=3&theater

46. DATA SET

Author's Last Name, Initials. (Year). *Title of data set* (Version
    number if there is one) [Data set]. Publisher. DOI *or* URL
Pew Research Center. (2019). *Core trends survey* [Data set].
    https://www.pewresearch.org/internet/dataset/core-trends-
    survey/

If the publisher is the author, no need to list it twice.

47. SUPREME COURT CASE

Name of Case, volume U.S. pages (year). URL
Plessy v. Ferguson, 163 U.S. 537 (1896). https://www.oyez.org/
cases/1850-1900/163us537
Obergefell v. Hodges, 576 U.S. ___ (2015). https://www.oyez.org/
cases/2014/14-556

The source for most Supreme Court cases is United States Reports, which is abbreviated *U.S.* in the reference list entry. If the case does not yet have a page number, use three underscores instead. Italicize the name of the court case in any in-text citations, but do not italicize it in the reference list entry.

48. GENERATIVE AI

The author is the name of the company that created the generative AI tool.

Author. (Date). *Name of tool* (Version of tool) [Description]. URL
OpenAI. (2023). *ChatGPT* (Mar 14 version) [Large language
model]. https://chat.openai.com/chat

Sources Not Covered by APA

To document a source for which APA does not provide guidelines, look at models similar to the source you have cited. Give any information readers will need in order to find the source themselves—author; date of publication; title; and information about the source itself (including who published it; volume, issue, and page numbers; and a DOI or URL). You might want to check your reference note to be sure it will lead others to your source.

Formatting a research essay

Title page. APA generally requires a title page. The page number should go in the upper right-hand corner. Center the full title of the paper in bold in the top half of the page. Center your name, the name of your department and school, the course number and name, the instructor's name, and the due date on separate lines below the title. Leave one line between the title and your name.

Page numbers. Place the page number in the upper right-hand corner. Number pages consecutively throughout.

Fonts, spacing, margins, and indents. Use a legible font that will be accessible to everyone, either a serif font (such as Times New Roman or Bookman) or a sans serif font (such as Calibri or Verdana). Use a sans serif font within figure images. Double-space the entire paper, including any notes and your list of references; the only exception is footnotes at the bottom of a page, which should be single-spaced, and tables and images, where the spacing will vary. Leave one-inch margins at the top, bottom, and sides of your text; do not justify the text. The first line of each paragraph should be indented one-half inch (or five to seven spaces) from the left margin. APA recommends using one space after end-of-sentence punctuation.

Headings. Though they are not required in APA style, headings can help readers follow your text. The first level of heading should be bold and centered; the second level should be bold and flush with the left margin; the third level should be bold, italicized, and flush left. Capitalize the first word and all other important words; do not capitalize *a, an, the,* or PREPOSITIONS.

First Level Heading

Second Level Heading

Third Level Heading.

Abstract. An abstract is a concise summary of your paper that introduces readers to your topic and main points. Most scholarly journals require an abstract; an abstract is not typically required for student papers, so check your instructor's preference. Put your abstract on the second page, with the word *Abstract* centered and in bold at the top. Unless your instructor specifies a length, limit your abstract to 250 words or fewer.

Long quotations. Indent quotations of forty or more words one-half inch (or five to seven spaces) from the left margin. Do not use quotation marks, and in-text documentation in parentheses *after* the end punctuation. If there are multiple paragraphs in the quotation, indent the first line of each subsequent paragraph another one-half inch.

> Kaplan (2000) captured ancient and contemporary Antioch:
>> At the height of its glory in the Roman-Byzantine age, when it had an amphitheater, public baths, aqueducts, and sewage pipes, half a million people lived in Antioch. Today the population is only 125,000. With sour relations between Turkey and Syria, and unstable politics throughout the Middle East, Antioch is now a backwater—seedy and tumbledown, with relatively few tourists. (p. 123)
>
> Antioch's decline serves as a reminder that the fortunes of cities can change drastically over time.

List of references. Start your list on a new page after the text but before any endnotes. Title the page *References*, centered and in bold, and double-space the entire list. Each entry should begin at the left margin, and subsequent lines should be indented one-half inch (or five to seven spaces). Alphabetize the list by authors' last names (or by editors' names, if appropriate). Alphabetize works that have no author or editor by title, disregarding *a*, *an*, and *the*. Be sure every source listed is cited in the text; do not include sources that you consulted but did not cite.

Tables and figures. Above each table or figure (charts, diagrams, graphs, photos, and so on), write *Table* or *Figure* and a number, flush left and in bold (e.g., **Table 1**). On the following line, give a descriptive title, flush left and italicized. Below the table or figure, include a note with any necessary explanation and source information. Number tables and figures separately, and be sure to discuss them in your text so that readers know how they relate.

TITLE   AUTHOR   PUBLICATION

Table 1

Hours of Instruction Delivered per Week

	American classrooms	Japanese classrooms	Chinese classrooms
First grade			
Language arts	10.5	8.7	10.4
Mathematics	2.7	5.8	4.0
Fifth grade			
Language arts	7.9	8.0	11.1
Mathematics	3.4	7.8	11.7

Note. Adapted from *Peeking Out from Under the Blinders: Some Factors We Shouldn't Forget in Studying Writing*, by J. R. Hayes, 1991, National Center for the Study of Writing and Literacy (https://archive.nwp.org/cs/public/print/resource/720).

Student research essay, APA style

Eli Vale was a kinesiology major at Texas A & M University, San Antonio, when he wrote this essay. He wrote it for his Composition 2 course, in which students spent the entire term researching and writing about a topic of their choice. Vale wrote about the challenges that nurses in San Antonio face—and he then revised the essay for this book in order to address how a situation that did not exist when he first wrote it affected those nurses: the coronavirus pandemic. In addition to being a full-time student, Vale worked as a rehab aide at a hospital in San Antonio, so his essay is based in part on his own firsthand observations and interviews.

A STUDENT RESEARCH ESSAY, APA STYLE

1

Page number appears
in upper right corner.

The Causes of Burnout in San Antonio Nurses—
And Some Possible Solutions

Title is bold
and centered.

Eli Nicholas Vale

Department of Language, Literature, and Arts

Texas A&M University, San Antonio

English 1302: Composition 2

Professor Sarah Dwyer

May 22, 2020

Name is centered
below the title, with
1 double-spaced line
in between.

2

Abstract

The COVID-19 pandemic has led to widespread recognition of the heroic actions that nurses take every day. It has also shed light on the many stressors that nurses face even under the best circumstances— stressors that can lead to burnout. Nurses experience burnout due to problematic nurse-to-patient ratios, intense physical and mental demands, and a lack of necessary breaks. This paper explores these causes of burnout in nurses and suggests solutions based on leading research in the field. The demands of caring for many patients at one time affects the physical and emotional health of nurses, long shifts with few breaks even to sit and eat can cause other physical strain including musculoskeletal disorders, and the nature of the medical field can leave nurses in complicated and stressful legal situations without clear legal protection. Burnout can appear as exhaustion, depersonalization, and frequent illness. Once burnout is recognized and acknowledged, a crucial first step, hospitals can start to consider solutions. These solutions include mandatory breaks from work, better staffing regulation, discounted therapy, and an increase in physical and legal protection. A damaged healthcare system has created the burnout experienced routinely by nurses, which is harmful to the nurses themselves and to their patients, and contributes to high turnover rates. Implementing solutions to nurse burnout is key in providing the best possible care for both patients and hospital employees.

Abstract begins a new page. Heading is bold and centered.

Abstract text does not need a paragraph indent.

3

The Causes of Burnout in San Antonio Nurses—
And Some Possible Solutions

Title is bold and centered.

Hospitals today are facing challenges never seen prior to the COVID-19 outbreak. Of all medical personnel, nurses are at the forefront of the battle against this virus. Consider the experiences, for example, of one nurse working in the coronavirus unit at Methodist Hospital in San Antonio, Texas. Here's how this nurse (who wished to remain anonymous and will be referred to as "Nurse A") described her work with COVID-19 patients: "As a COVID nurse, you become everything the patient could possibly need. You are the phlebotomist, physical therapist, respiratory therapist, patient care tech, and housekeeper. But most importantly, you become their family in this time of need" (personal communication, May 12, 2020). This is because family members are not allowed to visit loved ones who are in isolation, even if they are dying; as a result, a nurse is their last comforter, holding their hand as they pass away. Such experiences take a large emotional toll on COVID nurses.

Personal communication is documented in the text but not in the reference list.

In fact, Nurse A (personal communication, May 12, 2020) said that the mental stress is greater than the physical stress. Even the process of gowning up and making sure all personal protective equipment (PPE) is clean and worn securely can be nerve wracking. Changing out of her clothes and then putting on the gown, mask, face shield, and gloves takes time and mental energy, even before she enters the patient's room. And when she leaves the room, she has to make sure all PPE are taken off in a way that does not contaminate other surfaces. And then she must repeat this process each time she enters and exits a patient's room.

Because of the increased responsibilities and stressful conditions, however, Nurse A (personal communication, May 12, 2020) reported that the nurses in her unit are being treated better than they were before

1″

4

the pandemic. COVID nurses have meals provided throughout the day and have ready access to bathrooms, both hard to come by in regular shifts. She pointed out that it took a global pandemic to recognize the need for safer nurse-to-patient ratios, lunch breaks, and bathroom breaks—and to finally recognize the heroic work being done by nurses, work they have always done every single day.

These improved conditions have diminished since the virus surged, and in later communication Nurse A (personal communication, August 4, 2020) said the situation in the COVID unit was vastly different than it had been prior to the surge, with nurses responsible for as many as five patients at a time. A single nurse caring for so many patients in serious condition creates a dangerous amount of stress. However, stress is something these nurses are familiar with: they have dealt with exhaustion for a long time.

1″

1″

In fact, while nurses are finally being recognized as heroes during this pandemic, they have always played an essential though often unappreciated role in the Bexar County healthcare system. According to the Texas Board of Nursing (2018), there are 11,161 registered nurses employed at inpatient and outpatient facilities in Bexar County. Nurses who work in hospital settings are likely to deal with many more daily stressors than nurses at other facilities. Many of these nurses are employed at some of the most well-known healthcare systems in San Antonio, including Methodist Hospital, Baptist Medical Center, University Hospital, and Christus Santa Rosa Medical Center (Hernandez, 2018). Unfortunately, in spite of some improvements like those described by Nurse A, the working conditions at these well-known hospitals continue to undermine their nurses' ability to provide optimal care to patients.

In-text documentation that includes only the date goes right after the author.

In San Antonio, a damaged healthcare system has created an epidemic of dangerous nursing conditions. In many cases, the ratio of

5

nurses to patients is problematic, and nurses have to take on more patients than they should. This can affect patient care, and the demands of caring for too many patients at one time can also impact nurses' own physical, emotional, and mental health. Together, these conditions put nurses at risk of experiencing burnout. Signs of such burnout include exhaustion, a lack of interest in personal interaction with others, and frequent illness (Nursing.org, n.d.). In sum, problematic nurse-to-patient ratios, intense physical demands, insufficient breaks, and mental health issues create dangerous stress, which can lead to burnout. The city of San Antonio needs to recognize these issues and come up with solutions to prevent them. Potential solutions include a permanently lowered nurse-to-patient ratio, mandatory lunch breaks, increased security, and discounted physical and mental health therapy for nurses.

For a closer look at how damaging such burnout can be, Nursing.org (n.d.) provided a succinct description of its signs and symptoms:

> Nurse burnout is caused by many different work-related issues. Nurses deal with death on a regular basis, and the emotional strain of losing patients and assisting grieving family members may become overwhelming. In addition, long shifts of 12 or more hours often lead to exhaustion and stress. ("Causes of Nursing Burnout")

Nursing.org (n.d.) went on to suggest the need to recognize those symptoms:

> The most important thing is to recognize symptoms as early as possible before they become overwhelming. No matter how minute warning signs may seem at the time, it's crucial to listen to your body and mind. All healthcare professionals should be familiar with potential burnout symptoms and should be

Signal phrases are in past tense.

No extra space added between long quotations and the rest of the text.

1″

6

prepared to deal with them as quickly as possible. ("Warning Signs and Symptoms of Nursing Burnout")

Parenthetical documentation follows the punctuation in a block quote.

The first step toward solving the issue of nurse burnout, as Nursing .org (n.d.) pointed out, is to recognize the signs of burnout and start to combat their causes in the workplace. As Reineck and Furino (2005) concluded in a study on nursing careers: "Not only does workload take a toll on the nurse, but also affects the quality of care" (p. 30). Recognizing and reducing nurse burnout is crucial for the well-being of both the nurses and their patients.

Year follows author names, page number follows quotes.

Insufficient Staffing

Insufficient staffing is one of the primary causes of burnout, including shortages of registered nurses on overnight shifts and of supporting staff such as certified nursing assistants and patient care assistants in all shifts (Reineck & Furino, 2005). To provide some context for the situation in San Antonio, consider how many nurses there are (20,972) relative to the overall population (1,988,364). Keep in mind that the entire population of nurses—20,972—is not employed at hospitals. This total includes nurses who work in schools, home health agencies, and other settings that are less strenuous than hospitals. Table 1 compares the nurse-to-patient ratio in Bexar County (all of it in San Antonio) with that in another county in Texas and calculates how many nurses there are per 100,000 people.

2 authors in parenthetical documentation are linked with ampersand.

Table 1 shows that nurses in Bexar County have to care for many more patients than those in Bastrop County. In other words, Bastrop County is more equipped to give patients the care they need; if 100,000 people were to become ill in Bastrop County, each nurse would need to care for 2.369% of those patients. On the other hand, if 100,000 people were to fall ill in Bexar County (San Antonio), each nurse would have to care for 10.54% of them, creating a dangerous ratio of nurses to population in San Antonio.

Table 1

Ratio of Nurses to Population in Bastrop and Bexar Counties

	2018 Population	2018 RN Total	Ratio of RNs to 100,000 Population
Bastrop	94,545 citizens	224 nurses	224 nurses caring for 94,545 citizens

$$\frac{224 \text{ nurses}}{94,545 \text{ citizens}} = \frac{236.9 \text{ nurses}}{100,000 \text{ citizens}} = 2.369\%$$

Bastrop Ratio   Comparison Ratio

Based on the number of nurses in Bastrop County, each nurse would have to care for 2.369% of a population of 100,000.

The higher the percentage, the more patients each nurse needs to care for. Therefore, as the percentage increases, there is a lower number of nurses available to sufficiently care for the population.

	2018 Population	2018 RN Total	Ratio of RNs to 100,000 Population
Bexar	1,988,364 citizens	20,972 nurses	20,972 nurses caring for 1,988,364 citizens

$$\frac{20,972 \text{ nurses}}{1,988,364 \text{ citizens}} = \frac{1,054 \text{ nurses}}{100,000 \text{ citizens}} = 10.54\%$$

Bexar Ratio   Comparison Ratio

Based on the number of nurses in Bastrop County, each nurse would have to care for 10.54% of a population of 100,000.

These statistics indicate that Bexar County, which San Antonio encompasses, faces dangerous nurse-to-patient ratios due to a high population and a proportionately low number of nurses.

Note. Data from the Texas Department of State Health Services (2018).

8

Potential staffing solutions could include a set nurse-to-patient ratio of 1:3. Hospitals could also have a staff of on-call nurses, which would help maintain the nurse-to-patient ratio even when patient admissions increase.

When presented with evidence of insufficient staffing, people outside the nursing profession might argue that measuring the nursing population relative to the general population is misleading, given that not every person in Bexar County seeks treatment at the same time. Others might note that most nurses chose to pursue a career in a fast-paced work environment despite the risks and challenges. The shortage of nurses in San Antonio could also be attributed to factors outside of a hospital administration's control, such as a lack of younger nurses to take the place of the many older nurses in San Antonio who regularly go into retirement (Pelayo, 2013).

We might address the need for more young nurses by encouraging students to go into hospital nursing as a way to gain hands-on experience, rather than going straight into non-clinical nursing roles. But many potential nurses may look at the job description and feel that the paycheck is not worth the intense work demands. And increasing the base pay might then impact the number of nurses hired, as the hospital would have to distribute costs.

Another option is to promote bridge programs, in which student nurses take classes at a community college or university while completing their clinical work at an affiliated hospital, which then hires the nurses upon graduation. This would offer young nurses guaranteed employment once they graduate while also helping to solve the hospital's staffing shortage.

Notes what others might think.

9

Intense Physical and Mental Demands

Another major cause of burnout is the intense physical and mental demands of nursing. A significant part of a nurse's everyday regimen includes standing for prolonged periods, lifting patients, and pushing wheelchairs and gurneys, all of which can harm a nurse's physical health. The most common nursing injury is a strained back, but other physical stress points include sore shoulders from pushing wheelchairs and gurneys and injuries from falling while they work (Fohn, 2014). Nurses typically stand for most of their shift, leading to foot and knee complications and foot pain. Regardless of their fitness level, they are required to lift and transport immobile patients. As a result of this continuous lifting and bending, nurses are at a high risk of developing musculoskeletal disorders (Fohn, 2014).

While hospitals cannot eliminate the heavy physical demands of the job, they can help nurses manage such complications by providing discounted physical therapy sessions. A physical therapist can treat the aches, strains, and injuries that accumulate over long shifts, helping alleviate the fatigue and pain and other physical symptoms of burnout. Providing this kind of help would increase nurses' productivity.

Mental health issues also contribute to burnout. While many nurses in San Antonio are passionate about the care they provide to patients, that care sometimes presents life-and-death choices. As a result, nurses can become excessively worried and anxious about their work. Across the country, the nursing profession has been shown to be incredibly taxing on the mental well-being of employees. In a study conducted on 332 hospital nurses in Colorado, 86% showed symptoms of burnout (Mealer et al., 2009). And burnout was not the only mental health concern found; other psychological conditions included PTSD, depression, and anxiety (Mealer et al., 2009).

Headings help organize the essay.

Past tense is used to discuss the results of a study.

10

Hospital administrators also need to respond to the psychological effects this profession can have. To ensure the mental health of nursing staff, hospitals should offer a healthcare-worker hotline. Nurses struggling with the death of a patient would be able to call this hotline for support. As with physical therapy, nurses should be offered discounted psychiatric therapy sessions. Helping nurses take care of their mental health would help prevent psychological symptoms of burnout such as irritability, dissociation, or depression.

Some of the most stressful situations are when patients become violent. And nurses who are threatened or assaulted by a patient cannot engage in self-defense without risk of losing their licenses. It wasn't until 2013 that a nurse assaulted by a patient could expect any legal defense at all. In that year, Governor Rick Perry signed a bill stating that assaulting a nurse will result in punishment ranging from a Class A misdemeanor to a third-degree felony (Emergency Nurses Association, 2013)—a welcome, if somewhat late, protection for nurses.

Parenthetical documentation goes right after the information cited, so it is not always at the end of a sentence.

Especially when life-and-death choices are on the line, emotions take over, leading to a patient confronting the caregiver or the patient's family expressing anger toward hospital staff. Some of those observing such confrontations may point out that it is reasonable for people to become aggressive when there are serious choices to be made. Families might feel worried or scared for their loved one. Or the patient might be very frightened and exhausted from treatment. However, not every such confrontation is fueled by legitimate emotions, and sometimes nurses are confronted by irrational verbal and even physical violence.

Preventing such dangerous confrontations calls for increased security in hospital units, which should be based on patient capacity. Using the same strategy as for nurse-to-patient ratios to maintain optimum patient care, hospitals should adopt a reasonable security-to-patient ratio in each hospital unit of 1:50. Having one officer present for every 50 patients in a hospital unit would provide nurses with increased safety in the event of an assault. Additional officers should also be present in any unit housing hostile patients. For example, once any patients have threatened to harm themselves or others, an officer should remain in their rooms so that nurses can continue providing care without risking their own safety. Hospitals also need to regulate visitors. First, patients must approve all visitors. This requirement will help prevent abusive family members from assaulting patients or staff. In addition, no one with a record of violence, assault, or abuse should be allowed to visit. Not admitting visitors who have a history of confrontation and aggression will help decrease the frequency of violence in hospitals. Nurses in San Antonio will then be able to trust that they are safe and can put all their focus on patient care.

Skipping Necessary Breaks

Skipping meals and even bathroom breaks is a third cause of burnout among nurses. To alleviate the stress of long shifts, hospitals should require nurses to take a lunch break. An uninterrupted lunch break would not only enable nurses to take care of their own basic needs, but would also help prevent fatigue and low blood sugar levels by allowing them to rehydrate. Depending on the patient load, a nurse should have a minimum break of 30 minutes and a maximum of one hour. Nurses working 12-hour shifts should have an hour break. Unfortunately, nurses in Texas are not legally entitled to take lunch breaks (Texas Workforce Commission, n.d.). Medical employers take advantage of the fine print, which is why many nurses go without any breaks at all and administrators face few if any penalties.

We all know that in this time of pandemic, COVID nurses in San Antonio (and everywhere) are working heroically in unbelievably

12

stressful conditions. But all nurses, even those working in non-COVID units, are experiencing burnout due to problematic nurse-to-patient ratios, intense physical and mental demands, and the lack of necessary breaks. To help prevent nurse burnout, hospital administrators need to consider more staffing, discounted therapy sessions, and mandatory lunch breaks. San Antonio's nurses are taking on more patients than they can handle, which affects the quality of care they can provide. In order to deliver the best care to patients in the Bexar County area, we need to deliver the best care to those who look after them—remembering that they are our lifelines, the heroes we cannot do without.

References

Emergency Nurses Association. (2013). *Emergency Nurses Association applauds Texas legislation that raises assaults against emergency department personnel to third degree felony*. https://prnewswire. com/news-releases/emergency-nurses-association-applauds-texas-legislation-that-raises-assaults-against-emergency-department-personnel-to-third-degree-felony-212198351.html

Fohn, R. (2014, December 4). Stress test: Researchers studying soaring stress levels among nurses. *Mission*. uthscsa.edu/mission/stress-test-researchers-studying-soaring-stress-levels-among-nurses/

Hernandez, K. (2018, July 27). Largest San Antonio hospitals by beds. *San Antonio Business Journal*. https://www.bizjournals.com/sanantonio/subscriber-only/2018/07/27/hospitals-by-beds.html

Mealer, M., Burnham, E. L., Goode, C. J., Rothbaum, B., & Moss, M. (2009). The prevalence and impact of post traumatic stress disorder and burnout syndrome in nurses. *Depression & Anxiety, 26*(12), 1118–1126. http://doi.org.10.1002/da.20631

Nursing.org. (n.d.). *Nurse burnout*. Retrieved April 18, 2019, from https://www.nursing.org/resources/nurse-burnout/

Pelayo, L. W. (2013). Responding to the nursing shortage: Collaborations in an innovative paradigm for nursing education. *Nursing Education Perspectives, 34*(5), 351–352.

Reineck, C., & Furino, A. (2005, January–February). Nursing career fulfillment: Statistics and statements from registered nurses. *Nursing Economic$, 23*(1).

Texas Board of Nursing. (2018). *Practice—Peer review: Incident-based or safe harbor*. Retrieved January 24, 2019, from https://www.bon.texas.gov/practice_peer_review.asp

List of references begins a new page.

Entries are arranged alphabetically by author's last name.

Entries flush left; subsequent lines indent ½" or 5 spaces.

DOI is provided when one is available.

Retrieval date is included when the content of an online source may change.

14

Texas Department of State Health Services. (2018, November 29). *Registered nurses, 2018*. Texas Health and Human Services. https://www.dshs.texas.gov/chs/hprc/tables/2018/RN18.aspx

Texas Workforce Commission. (n.d.). *Fair Labor Standards Act—What it does and does not do*. Retrieved April 18, 2019, from https://twc. texas.gov/news/efte/flsa_does_and_doesnt_do.html

PART FIVE

LANGUAGE & STYLE

GET ATTENTION

24 Getting & Keeping Attention

Good writing is . . . still one of the best tools we have to get and capture people's attention.

—ROBIN SLOAN

Once upon a time—and for a very long time, too—style in writing meant ornamentation, "dressing up" your language the way you might dress up if you were walking down the red carpet at the Academy Awards. In fact, ancient images often show rhetoric as a woman, Dame Rhetorica, in a glittery, flowing gown covered with figures of speech—metaphors, similes, alliteration, hyperbole, and so on: her "stylish" ornaments. This view eventually led many writers to a view of style as "mere decoration" like the verbal icing on the cake of thought.

But not today. Not in a time of instantaneous communication, of being inundated with messages

Dame Rhetorica, from Gregor Reisch's *Margarita Philosophica* (1504).

of all kinds—news, posts, notifications, ads—all of them coming at us with the force of a fire hose. In such a time, how can we get others to pay attention to what we say or write? One good answer to this question is by attending carefully to our use of language and style. And by style I mean *how* a message is presented, not simply what it says. In this view, style isn't just the use of pretty "dressed up" language. Rather, it is a crucial element in making a message effective, memorable, compelling—and heard.

Today, then, style and substance are inseparable, and style is more important than ever before for getting and holding an audience's attention. Rhetorician Richard Lanham argues that the most important task facing writers and speakers today is not learning as much as possible about a subject or presenting the most convincing evidence to support a claim about that subject. Rather, the most important task today is *getting the attention of those we want to address!* For a dramatic example, think of CLICKBAIT, those provocative headlines or subject lines that are intended solely to grab readers' attention and pull them into an article, regardless of whether they are accurate or not:

> "Man tries to hug mountain lion: guess what happens next!"
> "Once a huge star, today he lives alone. What happened?"
> "Was Amelia Earhart eaten by coconut crabs?"

These headlines fairly shout "click on me!" Marketers tell us that shocking readers is an effective way of getting their attention, though perhaps not always in holding it. And these days, getting and holding attention is sometimes a pretty desperate business. Lady Gaga recalls a time, before she was well known, when she was singing in jazz bars in New York. One evening she faced a crowd of loud college students who would not be quiet; she just couldn't seem to get their attention. What did she do? She undressed down to her underwear, singing all the time—and getting, in short order, a very attentive audience. Later she said that night marked a kind of turning point for her, when she learned the importance of being able to "command attention."

Commanding attention is definitely a challenge in a time when we are so frequently drowning in information. This chapter provides some time-tested strategies for doing so—without taking your clothes off!

GETTING ATTENTION

In ancient Rome, orators spoke without the aid of microphones or visual aids, often in large outdoor amphitheaters. The technology they used was the human voice, which they trained to perfection so that they could project and be heard by thousands of people.

Researchers are still trying to figure out how they did it, but we can assume that these speakers commanded attention through stylish elements such as the sounds and rhythms of their voices as well as of the words they chose to use. But it's important to remember that these words count: getting attention will usually backfire if you don't have anything important, meaningful, or entertaining to say. Fortunately, speakers and writers today have many more tools available for drawing an audience's attention. Here are some that you may want to take advantage of.

Attention-getting titles

While you'll want to avoid the kind of exaggerated titles that are not followed up with substance, choosing provocative and memorable titles is a good way to command attention. One student writing about the architecture of her hometown began with a title that was less than inspired: "A Brief Look at Chicago's Architecture." That title was certainly clear, but it didn't do much to attract attention. After some thought and response from friends, she came up with a revision: "Sweet Home Chicago: Preserving the Past and Protecting the Future of the Windy City." This title refers to the blues song "Sweet Home Chicago," as well as to the well-known saying "home, sweet home." The subtitle then fills in details of what the essay will be about.

See pp. 117–18 for more examples of effective titles.

Here are several other ways that titles can get an audience's attention:

- *A puzzling statement* can interest readers in finding out what it means. A science student writing about the need for additional research on Lyme disease chose "The Mystery of Post-Lyme Disease Syndrome," thinking that readers might be attracted to the mysterious aspect of her topic.
- *A provocative question* can call out to readers. One student writing about clubs at her university chose "Minority Clubs: Integration or Segregation?" Here the title states the subject, while the subtitle poses an unexpected question.

- *An intriguing allusion* can make readers want to read on. The title of an article in *Wired* caught my attention with an allusion: "Dr. Elon and Mr. Musk" recalls "Dr. Jekyll and Mr. Hyde" and made me want to find out how the author would connect the two.

Start strong, get readers interested

The OPENING sentences in your writing carry big responsibilities when it comes to drawing your readers in by arousing their interest and curiosity. Whether what you're writing is a college essay or a business report, the way it begins has a lot to do with whether your audience will stay with you. Georgina Kleege opens the introduction to a collection of essays entitled *Sight Unseen* with this enigmatic and arresting statement: "Writing this book made me blind." Readers immediately want to ask "why?" Kleege goes on to explain that while she is "just as blind" as she was before writing these essays, the process of composing them brought her to accept the label "blind." Since she began these essays, she says, "I have learned to use braille and started to carry a white cane."

The way you begin an essay can grab an audience's attention, or not. Here are some ways of making them interested in what you've got to say, and wanting to read on.

WITH A DECEPTIVELY SIMPLE STATEMENT
Lois Carson always wanted to find a new way to fold a tortilla.

—ANTONIA HITCHENS, "The Crunch Bunch:
How Taco Bell Fired the First Shot in the Stunt-food Wars"

WITH A PROVOCATIVE QUESTION
Have you ever thought about whether to have a child?

—PETER SINGER, "Should This Be the Last Generation?"

WITH A SURPRISING STATEMENT
I was transported recently to a place that is as enchanting to me as any winter wonderland: my local post office.

—ZEYNEP TUFEKCI, "Why the Post Office Makes America Great"

WITH AN AMUSING IMAGE

The seven deadly sins—avarice, sloth, envy, lust, gluttony, pride, and wrath—were all committed Sunday during the twice-annual bake sale at St. Mary's of the Immaculate Conception Church.

—*THE ONION*, "All Seven Deadly Sins Committed at Church Bake Sale"

Each of these sentences is startling, prompting us to read on in order to find out more. And each is brief, leaving us waiting for what is to come. And of course they all make powerful statements, ones that get readers' attention.

It usually takes more than a single sentence to open an essay. Consider, for example, this opening paragraph of an essay on animal rights:

The first time I opened Peter Singer's *Animal Liberation*, I was dining alone at the Palm, trying to enjoy a rib-eye steak cooked medium-rare. If this sounds like a good recipe for cognitive dissonance (if not indigestion), that was sort of the idea. Preposterous as it might seem to supporters of animal rights, what I was doing was tantamount to reading *Uncle Tom's Cabin* on a plantation in the Deep South in 1852.

—MICHAEL POLLAN, "An Animal's Place"

The first sentence presents an incongruous image that holds our attention: he's eating a steak while reading about animal liberation. Then the rest of the paragraph makes this incongruity even more pronounced, comparing the situation to reading an antislavery novel while on a slave-owning plantation. It's an opening that makes us want to read on.

Since the title and opening lines are the first things your audience will see or hear, it's well worth the effort to make sure they'll draw readers in. And it might be good to keep in mind the admonition of one reader who doesn't have a lot of patience: "I give the

For more on opening sentences, see pp. 116 and 482–84.

writer one paragraph, maybe two; if I'm not hooked by then, I stop reading." Your goal is to write openings so compelling that even impatient readers will want to keep going.

KEEPING ATTENTION

Once you've gotten your audience's attention, you need to think about how you can keep them with you. Fortunately, there are a number of strategies and techniques that will help you to do so. Take a look at how writers use some of these techniques.

Tell a story

Just as a story or **ANECDOTE** can draw an audience in, it can enliven much of what you write and keep them with you. Surgeon and author Atul Gawande is well known for his use of stories in the articles and books he has written about how to improve medical care in this country. In speaking about his special interest in improving end-of-life care in order to match it more closely to what patients really want, instead of following "keep alive at all cost" policies and procedures, Gawande paused to tell a story about one particular patient who, when asked his preferences for end-of-life care, said that he "wanted to stay alive as long as he could enjoy chocolate ice cream and watch football on television." This brief narrative brought home the point Gawande was making in concrete, human terms—and kept his audience interested in what he was saying.

See pp. 56–57 for more on using narrative to support a point.

Offer good examples

"A single good example is often worth a dozen lengthy explanations," says English professor Thomas Cooley. That's for sure: there's no better way to support a generalization or to bring an abstraction to life. It's also a good way to help readers understand and be interested in what you're saying. In discussing Emma

Emma Stone as a child-woman in *Poor Things*.

Stone's Oscar-winning performance as Bella Baxter, a woman with the brain of a child, in *Poor Things*, Jackson McHenry offers an example of the technical precision he and many others so admired in Stone's performance:

> As Bella's brain ages inside her adult body, her gait changes from stilted lumbering to a posture of confidence and control. Her face, which she can spread open with wonder, scrambles with confusion and interest at new ideas and experiences.
>
> —JACKSON McHENRY, "The Evolutions of Emma Stone: A Master at Playing Characters Who Are Only Halfway Out of the Cocoon"

The descriptive language in this passage ("stilted lumbering," a face "spread open with wonder") and its use of repeated sounds ("confidence and control") makes it a persuasive example that holds our attention just as Stone's performance held the attention of this film critic.

See p. 55 for more on examples.

Use an analogy

You can use **ANALOGIES** to help explain an unfamiliar subject by comparing it to a more familiar one. Analogies are one more way to make abstract ideas more concrete, and to help an audience visualize what you're saying. They're an especially good way to hold readers' attention when you're writing about something abstract or complicated. See how investor Warren Buffett uses the analogy of not being able to see the forest for the trees, in his annual letter to stockholders, to frame the point he is making:

> Investors who evaluate Berkshire sometimes obsess on the details of our many and diverse businesses—our economic "trees," so to speak. Analysis of that type can be mind-numbing, given that we own a vast array of specimens, from twigs to redwoods. A few of our trees are diseased and unlikely to be around a decade from now. Many others, though, are destined to grow in size and beauty. Fortunately, it's not necessary to evaluate each tree individually to make a rough estimate of Berkshire's intrinsic business value. That's because our forest contains five "groves" of major importance, each of which can be appraised, with reasonable accuracy, in its entirety. Four of these groves are differentiated clusters of businesses and financial assets that are easy to understand. The fifth—our huge and diverse insurance operation—delivers great value to Berkshire in a less obvious manner, one I will explain later in this letter.
>
> —WARREN BUFFETT, Letter to Stockholders

Here Buffett uses a simple analogy between a forest and his very large company, introducing readers to the "groves" and individual "trees" that make it up. The analogy helps readers visualize the company in a concrete way and paves the way for data that will support Buffett's claim that the fifth "grove" delivers "great value to Berkshire."

Appeal to emotion

Appealing to an audience's emotions can be a very effective way to both get and keep attention. After the University of South Carolina claimed the 2024 Women's NCAA championship, coach Dawn Staley, in tears, praised her team, and their opponent, in a moving speech that was widely circulated and admired. Saying she was "so proud, so proud" of her players, Staley continued:

> It doesn't always end like you want it to end, much like last year. But my freshies are at the top of my heart. . . . And I hope we can erase whatever pain they had last year, experiencing not being able to finish it here. So I'm just super proud of where I work. I'm super proud of our fans. It's awesome! It's unbelievable! . . .

And then, shortly after finishing the interview, Staley returned to the mike, saying she wanted to say one more thing:

> I have to congratulate Iowa on an incredible season. Also . . . I want to personally thank Caitlin Clark for lifting up our sport. She carried a heavy load for our sport. And it just is not going to stop here on a collegiate tour—but when she is the number one pick in the WNBA draft, she's gonna lift that league up as well. So Caitlin Clark, if you're out there, you are one of the GOATs of our game.

> —DAWN STALEY, 2024 interview after the NCAA victory

Dawn Staley celebrates South Carolina's NCAA victory.

Staley's emotions were clearly on display in these remarks, and they were contagious. Cameras focused on the crowd showed fans weeping along with her, in joy. Staley celebrates the trip her team had taken from defeat to victory, and then, knowing full well what it is like to lose, turns to speak glowingly of the star of the losing team on this day: Iowa's Caitlin Clark, thus appealing to the emotions and holding the attention of both winners and losers, and their fans.

Use a startling contrast

Contrasts, especially sharp or startling ones, can create images in readers' minds that capture and hold attention. Consider how columnist Frank Bruni uses such a contrast in a headline—"She Went Blind. Then She Danced."—and then builds on that contrast as he introduces readers to Marion Sheppard:

> She pitied herself. . . . She raged. . . . She trembled. . . . She spent months wrestling with those emotions, until she realized that they had pinned her in place. Time was marching on and she wasn't moving at all. Her choice was clear: She could surrender to the darkness, or she could dance. She danced.
>
> —FRANK BRUNI, "She Went Blind. Then She Danced."

Use reiteration

A kind of repetition, reiteration provides emphasis: like a drumbeat, the repetition of a keyword, phrase, or image can help drive home a point. And it's a good way to command attention. REITERATION is especially powerful in spoken texts—think "I Have a Dream" and "Yes we can!" At the March for Our Lives rally in Washington, DC, following the killing of students and staff members at a Florida high school, student X González provided a powerful example of how reiteration can command an audience's attention, telling their audience that among the students and staff at school that day, "no one understood" what had happened, "no one could comprehend

Marion Sheppard may be blind, but she can dance!

the devastating aftermath," or where it would go. Note the chillingly effective use of repetition as González spoke:

> Six minutes and 20 seconds with an AR-15, and my friend Carmen would never complain to me about piano practice. Aaron Feis would never call Kyra "miss sunshine" . . . Alyssa Alhadeff would never, Jamie Guttenberg would never, Meadow Pollack would never.
>
> —X GONZÁLEZ, March for Our Lives

Consider the power of silence

Sometimes silence can be extremely powerful, startling an audience and helping them focus on you and your lack of words. X González provides an example of the power of silence. Once their riveting repetitions of "would never" came to a halt, they stood there, silently, for six minutes and twenty seconds: the amount of time it had taken a killer to take the lives of seventeen innocent people. That silence held the crowd captivated, stunned, and very, very attentive.

LEAVE YOUR AUDIENCE THINKING

Your CONCLUSION is a chance to leave your audience thinking about what you've said. You might simply restate your main point, but here are some other ways to conclude:

WITH A WITTY STATEMENT THAT MAKES YOUR POINT

Anyone who believes emoji are having even the slightest effect on English syntax is an utter 😃.

—GEOFFREY PULLUM,
"Emoji Are Ruining English, Says Dumbest Story of the Week"

WITH A STARTLING IMAGE

The next time we go to war, we should truly understand the sacrifices that our service members will have to make. Which is why, when my colleagues start beating the drums of war, I want to be there, standing on my artificial legs under the great Capitol dome, to remind them what the true costs of war are.

—TAMMY DUCKWORTH, "What I Learned at War"

WITH A STATEMENT THAT SHOWS WHY THEY SHOULD CARE

The closer we get to mass incarceration and extreme levels of punishment, the more I believe it is necessary to recognize that we all need mercy, we all need justice, and—perhaps—we all need some measure of unmerited grace.

—BRYAN STEVENSON, *Just Mercy*

WITH A CALL FOR ACTION

It's time, it's past time, to pay our Black citizens what they are owed.

—JANE SEARLE, "On Reparations"

The bottom line for this chapter: it's high time to start exercising your attention-getting muscles! We surely don't see any let-up in the oceans of information and data washing over us 24/7. In such an atmosphere, those who can command attention are the ones whose words will count.

See pp. 117 and 490 for more ways of concluding.

REFLECT! Think about something you've read or seen recently that really held your attention: a book you couldn't put down, an op-ed piece you're still thinking about, something you saw on *Facebook* or *YouTube*. Study it now to see if you can figure out how it did that, and then write a short paragraph about how you can do something similar in your own writing.

25 Writing Great Sentences

A student once asked me, "How can I make my sentences sing?" Making sentences "sing" might not be something you've ever thought about—but I'm willing to bet that you know something about how important sentences are. Anyone who has ever tried to craft the perfect social media post or, better yet, write the perfect love letter knows about choosing just the right words for each and every sentence—and about the power of the three-word sentence "I love you."

In his book *How to Write a Sentence*, English professor Stanley Fish declares himself to be a "connoisseur of sentences" and offers some particularly noteworthy examples. Here's one, written by a fourth grader in response to an assignment to write something about a mysterious large box that had been delivered to a school:

I was already on the second floor when I heard about the box.

This sentence reminded me of a favorite sentence of my own, this one the beginning of a story written by a third grader:

Today, the monster goes where no monster has gone before: Cincinnati.

Here the student manages to allude to the famous line from *Star Trek*—"to boldly go where no man has gone before"—while suggesting that Cincinnati is the most exotic place on earth—and even using a colon effectively. It's quite a sentence.

Finally, here are two sentences, one that opens a chapter from a PhD dissertation on literacy among young people today and another that opens a study of the rise and fall of America's public monuments:

Hazel Hernandez struck me as an honest thief.

The king's head lay on a table near the sofa.

Such sentences are memorable: They startle us a bit and demand attention. They make us want to read more. Who's Hazel Hernandez? What's an honest thief, and what makes her one? Which king? What happened here?

As these examples suggest, you don't have to be a famous author to write a great sentence. In fact, crafting effective and memorable sentences is a skill everyone can master with careful attention and practice. Sometimes a brilliant sentence comes to you like a bolt of lightning, and all you have to do is type it out. More often, though, the perfect sentence is a result of tweaking and tinkering during your revision stages. Either way, crafting good sentences is worth the effort it may take. You may not come up with a zinger like the famous sentence John Updike wrote about Ted Williams's fabled home run in his last at bat at Fenway Park—"It was in the books while it was still in the sky."—but you can come close.

Just as special effects in film—music, close-ups—enhance the story, a well-crafted sentence can bring power to your writing. So think about the kind of effect you want to create in what you're writing, and then look for the type of sentence that will fit the bill. Though much of the power of the examples above comes from being short and simple, remember that some rhetorical situations call for longer, complex sentences. The kind of sentence you write also depends on its context, such as whether it's opening an essay, summing up what's already been said, or providing an example. This chapter looks at some common English sentence patterns and provides some good examples for producing them in your own work.

FOUR COMMON SENTENCE PATTERNS

We make sentences with words, and we arrange those words into patterns. If a sentence is defined as a group of words that expresses a complete thought, then we can identify four basic sentence structures: a SIMPLE SENTENCE (expressing one idea); a COMPOUND SENTENCE (expressing more than one idea, with the ideas being of equal importance); a COMPLEX SENTENCE (expressing more than one idea, with one of the ideas more important than the others); and a COMPOUND-COMPLEX SENTENCE (with two or more ideas of equal importance and at least one idea of less importance).

Simple sentences: one main idea

Let's take a look at some simple sentences:

- Resist!

- Consumers revolted.

- Angry consumers revolted against new debit-card fees.

- Protests from angry consumers forced banks to rescind the new fees.

- The internet's capacity to mobilize people all over the world has done everything from forcing companies to rescind debit-card fees in the United States to bringing down governments in the Middle East.

Each of these, whether one word or many, is a simple sentence, because it contains a single main idea or thought; in grammatical terms, each contains one and only one MAIN CLAUSE. As the name suggests, a simple sentence is often the simplest, most direct way of saying what you want to say—but not always. And often you want a sentence to include more than one idea. In that case, you need to use a compound sentence, a complex sentence, or a compound-complex sentence.

Compound sentences: joining ideas that are equally important

Sometimes you'll want to write a sentence that joins two or more ideas that are equally important, like this one attributed to former president Bill Clinton:

> You can put wings on a pig, but you don't make it an eagle.

In grammatical terms, this is a compound sentence with two MAIN CLAUSES, each of which expresses one of two independent and equally important ideas. In this case, the ideas are joined with a comma and the COORDINATING CONJUNCTION *but*. But there are several other options for joining these ideas. Here it is with only a semicolon:

> You can put wings on a pig; you don't make it an eagle.

And here it is with a semicolon, a TRANSITION like *however*, and a comma:

> You can put wings on a pig; however, you don't make it an eagle.

All of these compound sentences are perfectly acceptable—but which one is most effective? In this case, I think the one attributed to Clinton is: it is clear and very direct; and if you read it aloud you'll hear that the words on each side of *but* have the same number of syllables, creating a pleasing, balanced rhythm—and one that balances the two equally important ideas. It also makes the logical relationship between the two ideas explicit: *but* indicates a contrast. The version with only a semicolon, by contrast, indicates that the ideas are somehow related but doesn't show how.

Using *and, but,* and other coordinating conjunctions

In writing a compound sentence, keep in mind that different coordinating conjunctions carry meanings that signal different logical relationships between the main ideas in the sentence. There are only seven coordinating conjunctions.

> **COORDINATING CONJUNCTIONS**
>
> | and | for | or | yet |
> |-----|-----|-----|-----|
> | but | nor | so | |
>
> China's one-child policy slowed population growth, *but* it helped create a serious gender imbalance in the country's population.
>
> Most of us bike to the office, *so* many of us stop at the gym to shower before work.
>
> The first two batters struck out, *yet* the Cubs went on to win the game on back-to-back homers.

See how the following sentences express different meanings depending on which coordinating conjunction is used:

> You could apply to college, *or* you could start looking for a job.
>
> You could apply to college, *and* you could start looking for a job.

Using a semicolon

Joining clauses with a semicolon only is a way of signaling that they are closely related without specifying how. Often the second clause will expand on an idea expressed in the first clause. Note that while the compound sentences below could be written as two simple sentences, joining them with a semicolon makes their relationship clearer and also creates a smoother rhythm.

My first year of college was a little bumpy; it took me a few months to get comfortable at a large university far from home.

The Wassaic Project is an arts organization in Dutchess County, New York; artists go there to engage in "art, music, and everything else."

Adding a TRANSITION can make the logical relationship between the ideas more explicit:

My first year of college was a little bumpy; *indeed*, it took me a few months to get comfortable at a large university far from home.

Note that the transition in this sentence, *indeed*, cannot join the two main clauses on its own—it requires a semicolon before it. If you use a transition between two clauses with only a comma before it, you've made a mistake called a COMMA SPLICE.

SOME COMMON TRANSITIONS

also	indeed	otherwise
certainly	likewise	similarly
furthermore	nevertheless	therefore
however	next	thus

REFLECT! Look over something you've written to see if there are any compound sentences joined by *and*. If so, does *and* express the relationship between the two parts of the sentence that you intend? Would *but, or, so, nor,* or *yet* work better?

Complex sentences: when one idea gets more emphasis than another

Many of the sentences you write will contain two or more ideas, with one that you want to emphasize more than the other(s). You can do so by putting the idea you wish to emphasize in the MAIN CLAUSE, and those that are less important in SUBORDINATE CLAUSES.

Although she worried constantly, Yazmin passed her exams easily.

She decided to celebrate *while she had time to do so.*

Her final projects, *which are due in three weeks,* will demand all her time and attention.

As these examples show, the ideas in the subordinate clauses (italicized here) usually don't stand alone as sentences: when we read "although she worried constantly" or "which are due in three weeks," we know that something's missing. Subordinate clauses begin with words such as *if* or *because*, SUBORDINATING WORDS that signal the logical relationship between the subordinate clause and the rest of the sentence.

SOME SUBORDINATING WORDS

after	even though	until
although	if	when
as	since	where
because	that	while
before	though	who

Notice that a subordinate clause can come at the beginning of a sentence, in the middle, or at the end. When it comes at the beginning, it is usually followed by a comma, as in the first example. If the opening clause in that sentence were moved to the end, a comma would not be necessary: "Yazmin passed her exams with flying colors although she worried constantly."

Grammatically, each of the three examples above is a complex sentence, with one main idea and one other idea of less importance. In writing you will often have to decide whether to combine ideas in a compound sentence, which gives the ideas equal importance, or in a complex sentence, which makes one idea more important than the other(s). Looking once more at our sentence about the pig and the eagle, for example, Bill Clinton could also have made it a complex sentence:

Even though you can put wings on a pig, you don't make it an eagle.

Looking at this sentence, though, I think Clinton made a good choice in giving the two ideas equal weight because doing so balances the sentence perfectly—and tells us that both parts get the same emphasis. In fact, neither part of this sentence is very interesting in itself: it's the balancing and the contrast that make it memorable.

Compound-complex sentences: multiple ideas—some more important, some less

When you are expressing three or more ideas in a single sentence, you'll sometimes want to use a compound-complex sentence, which gives some of the ideas more prominence and others less. Grammatically, such sentences have at least two MAIN CLAUSES and one SUBORDINATE CLAUSE.

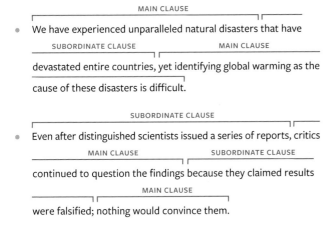

- MAIN CLAUSE
  We have experienced unparalleled natural disasters that have
  SUBORDINATE CLAUSE — MAIN CLAUSE
  devastated entire countries, yet identifying global warming as the
  cause of these disasters is difficult.

- SUBORDINATE CLAUSE
  Even after distinguished scientists issued a series of reports, critics
  MAIN CLAUSE — SUBORDINATE CLAUSE
  continued to question the findings because they claimed results
  MAIN CLAUSE
  were falsified; nothing would convince them.

As these examples show, English sentence structure is flexible, allowing you to combine groups of words in different ways in order to get your ideas across to your audience most appropriately and effectively. These four basic patterns can be stretched or squeezed to match your goals. After all, there's never only one way to write a sentence to get an idea across: as the author, you must decide which way works best for your RHETORICAL SITUATION.

WAYS OF EMPHASIZING THE MAIN IDEA

Sometimes you will want to lead off a sentence with the main point; at other times you might want to hold it in reserve until the end. CUMULATIVE SENTENCES start with a main clause and then add on to it, "accumulating" details. PERIODIC SENTENCES start with a series of phrases or subordinate clauses, saving the main clause for last.

Cumulative sentences: starting with the main point

Cumulative sentences, which start off with a MAIN CLAUSE and then add details in phrases and SUBORDINATE CLAUSES, can be useful for describing a place or an event. They operate almost like a camera panning across a room or a landscape. The sentences below create such an effect:

> The San Bernardino Valley lies only an hour east of Los Angeles by the San Bernardino Freeway but is in certain ways an alien place: not the coastal California of the subtropical twilights and the soft west-erlies off the Pacific but a harsher California, haunted by the Mojave just beyond the mountains, devastated by the hot dry Santa Ana wind that comes down through the passes at 100 miles an hour and whines through the eucalyptus windbreaks and works on the nerves.
>
> —JOAN DIDION, "Some Dreamers of the Golden Dream"

> Public transportation in Cebu City was provided by jeepneys: refurbished military jeeps with metal roofs for shade, decorated with horns and mirrors and fenders and flaps; painted with names, dedications, quotations, religious icons, logos—and much, much more.

> She hit the brakes, swearing fiercely, as the deer leapt over the hood and crashed into the dark woods beyond.

> The celebrated Russian pianist gave his hands a shake, a quick shake, fingers pointed down at his sides, before taking his seat and lifting them imperiously above the keys.

These cumulative sentences add details in a way that makes each sentence more emphatic. Keep this principle in mind as you write. And then when you revise, see if there are sentences you might modify to add emphasis in the same way. Take a look at the following sentences, for instance:

> In 1979, China initiated free-market reforms that transformed its economy from a struggling one to an industrial powerhouse. As a result, it became the world's fastest-growing major economy. Its annual growth rates averaged almost 10 percent over the next four decades.

These three sentences are clearly related, with each one adding detail about the growth of China's economy. Now look what happens when the writer eliminates a little bit of repetition, adds a memorable metaphor, and combines them as a cumulative—and more emphatic—sentence:

> China's free-market reforms led to almost 10 percent average annual growth from 1979 to 2018, transforming it from a paper tiger to an industrial dragon that is still one of the world's fastest-growing major economies.

Periodic sentences: delaying the main point until the end

In contrast to sentences that open with the main idea, periodic sentences delay the main idea until the very end. Withholding the main point until the end is a way of adding emphasis. It can also create suspense or build up to a surprise or inspirational ending, especially when the sentence is long.

> In spite of everything, in spite of the dark and twisting path he saw stretching ahead for himself, in spite of the final meeting with

Voldemort he knew must come, whether in a month, in a year, or in ten, he felt his heart lift at the thought that there was still one last golden day of peace left to enjoy with Ron and Hermione.

—J. K. ROWLING, *Harry Potter and the Half-Blood Prince*

Unprovided with original learning, unformed in the habits of thinking, unskilled in the arts of composition, I resolved to write a book.

—EDWARD GIBBON, *Memoirs of My Life*

Whether stringing together multiple polysyllabic rhymes, or endless assonance and alliteration, or creating compound internal rhymes, or back-to-back chain rhymes, or multiple mosaic rhymes, or building bridge rhymes, Hip Hop poets/MC's offer a vast body of poetic and linguistic data.

—H. SAMY ALIM, *Roc the Mic Right*

Here are three periodic sentences in a row about Whitney Houston, each of which withholds the main point until the end:

When her smiling brown face, complete with a close-cropped Afro, appeared on the cover of *Seventeen* in 1981, she was one of the first African-Americans to grace the cover, and the industry took notice. When she belted out a chilling and soulful version of the "Star-Spangled Banner" at the 1991 Super Bowl, the world sat back in awe of her poise and calm. And in an era when African-American actresses are often given film roles portraying them as destitute, unloving, unlovable, or just "the help," Houston played the love interest of Kevin Costner, a white Hollywood superstar.

—ALLISON SAMUELS, "A Hard Climb for the Girl Next Door"

These three periodic sentences create a drumlike effect that builds in intensity as they move through the stages in Houston's career; in all, they suggest that Houston was, even more than Kevin Costner, a "superstar."

Samuels takes a chance when she uses three sentences in a row that withhold the main point until the end: readers may get tired of waiting for that point. And readers may also find the use of too many such sentences to be, well, too much. But as the example above shows, when used carefully, a sentence that puts off the main idea just long enough can keep readers' interest, making them want to reach the ending with its payoff.

You may find in your own work that periodic sentences can make your writing more emphatic. Take a look at the following sentence from an essay on the use of animals in circuses:

> The big cat took him down with one swat, just as the trainer, dressed in khakis and boots, his whip raised and his other arm extended in welcome to the cheering crowd, stepped into the ring.

This sentence paints a vivid picture, but it gives away the main action in the first six words. By withholding that action until the end, the writer builds anticipation and adds emphasis:

> Just as the trainer stepped into the ring, dressed in khakis and boots, his whip raised and his other arm extended in welcome to the cheering crowd, the big cat took him down with one swat.

VARYING YOUR SENTENCES

Read a paragraph or two of your writing out loud, and listen for its rhythm. Is it quick and abrupt? slow and leisurely? singsong? stately? rolling? Whatever it is, does the rhythm you hear match what you had in mind when you were writing? And does it put the emphasis where you want it?

One way to establish the emphasis you intend and a rhythm that will keep readers reading is by varying the length of your sentences and the way those sentences flow from one to the other. A string of sentences that are too much alike is almost certain to be boring.

While you can create effective rhythms in many ways, one of the simplest and most effective is by breaking up a series of long sentences with a shorter one that gives your readers a chance to pause and absorb what you've written. Take a look at the following passage, from an article in the *Atlantic* about the finale of the *Oprah Winfrey Show*. See how the author uses a mix of long and short sentences to describe one of the tributes to Oprah, this one highlighting her support of Black men:

> Oprah's friend Tyler Perry announced that some of the "Morehouse Men," each a beneficiary of the $12 million endowment she has established at their university, had come to honor her for the scholarships she gave them. The lights were lowered, a Broadway star began singing an inspirational song, and a dozen or so black men began to walk slowly to the front of the stage. Then more came, and soon there were a score, then 100, then the huge stage was filled with men, 300 of them. They stood there, solemnly, in a tableau stage-managed in such a way that it might have robbed them of their dignity—the person serenading them (or, rather, serenading Oprah on their behalf) was Kristin Chenoweth, tiniest and whitest of all tiny white women; the song was from *Wicked*, most feminine of all musicals; and each man carried a white candle, an emblem that lent them the aspect of Norman Rockwell Christmas carolers. But they were not robbed of their dignity. They looked, all together, like a miracle. A video shown before the procession revealed that some of these men had been in gangs before going to Morehouse, some had fathers in prison, many had been living in poverty. Now they were doctors, lawyers, bankers, a Rhodes Scholar—and philanthropists, establishing their own Morehouse endowment.
>
> —CAITLIN FLANAGAN, "The Glory of Oprah"

The passage begins with three medium-length sentences—and then one very long one (seventy-two words!) that points up the strong contrast between the 300 Black men filling the stage and the "whitest of white" singer performing a song from the "most feminine" of musicals. Then come two little sentences (the first one eight words long and the second one, seven) that give readers a chance to pause and absorb what has been said while also making an important point: that the men "looked, all together, like a

Morehouse Men surprise Oprah.

miracle." The remainder of the passage moves back toward longer sentences, each of which explains just what this "miracle" is. Try reading this passage aloud, and listen for how the variation in sentences creates both emphasis and a pleasing and effective rhythm.

In addition to varying the lengths of your sentences, you can also improve your writing by making sure that they don't all use the same structure or begin in the same way. You can be pretty sure that a passage in which every sentence is a simple sentence that opens with the subject will not read smoothly at all but rather will move along awkwardly. Take a look at this passage, for example:

> The sunset was especially beautiful today. I was on top of Table Mountain in Cape Town. I looked down and saw the sun touch the sea and sink into it. The evening shadows crept up the mountain. I got my backpack and walked over to the rest of my group. We started on the long hike down the mountain and back to the city.

There's nothing wrong with these sentences. Each one is grammatically correct. But if you read the passage aloud, you'll hear how it moves abruptly from sentence to sentence, lurching along rather than flowing smoothly. The problem is that the sentences are all the same: each one is a simple sentence that begins with the subject of a main clause (*sunset, I, I, evening shadows, I, We*). In addition, the use of personal pronouns at the beginning of the sentences (three *I*'s in only six sentences!) makes for dull reading. Finally, these are all fairly short sentences, and the sameness of the sentence length adds to the abrupt rhythm of the passage—and doesn't keep readers reading. Now look at how this passage can be revised by working on sentence variation:

> From the top of Cape Town's Table Mountain, the sunset was especially beautiful. I looked down just as the fiery orb touched and then sank into the sea; shadows began to creep slowly up the mountain. Picking up my backpack, I joined the rest of my group, and we started the long hike down the mountain.

This revision reduces the number of sentences in the passage from six to three (the first simple, the second compound-complex, the third compound) and varies their length. Equally important, the revision eliminates all but one of the subject openings. The first sentence now begins with the prepositional phrase ("From the top"); the second with the subject of a main clause ("I"); and the third with a participial phrase ("Picking up my backpack"). Finally, the revision varies the diction a bit, replacing the repeated word "sun" with a vivid image ("fiery orb"). Read the revised passage aloud, and you'll hear how varying the sentences creates a stronger rhythm that makes it easier to read.

ARTFUL SENTENCES

So far, we have been looking at the basic building blocks of sentences in English and, more specifically, in the standardized variety of English used in most schools and businesses. Even in these settings, as we've seen, sentences are pretty flexible, allowing for a good deal of variation. And writers today are being more inventive and perhaps more playful than ever before. Let's take a look now at some sentences that can help us think more creatively about what we can do with the sentences we write.

Sentences with inverted word order. A little bit of this technique will go a long way, but you might consider surprising readers by rejecting the expected word order of a sentence to gain attention or add some emphasis, as in this famous example from J. R. R. Tolkien, the first sentence in *The Hobbit*:

> In a hole in the ground there lived a hobbit.

Instead of just saying "A hobbit lived in a hole in the ground," putting the two prepositional phrases up front leads readers, slowly, to the central character of this book.

Sentence fragments. A well-timed fragment can make a big impression. When Hitler told Winston Churchill that in just a few weeks he would wring England's neck like a chicken, Churchill retorted with two fragments: "Some chicken. Some neck." These words rallied his country and lifted the spirits of his troops. Much more recently, here is Samara Bay, with a couple of potent fragments used to conclude the anecdote with which her book opens:

> At my local indie bookstore . . . I got to chatting with the cashier. She asked what I was going to call the book I was writing, and when I told her, the man behind me in the queue . . . piped up with a guffaw: "Permission to speak? That's not something I've ever waited for!"
>
> The cashier and I shared delicious looks. *Precisely, sir. Precisely.*
>
> —SAMARA BAY, *Permission to Speak*

And now see how professor of botany Robin Kimmerer creates special emphasis in an essay about strawberries by following a very long sentence with two fragments and one very short sentence:

> Even now, after more than fifty Strawberry Moons, finding a patch of wild strawberries still touches me with a sensation of surprise, a feeling of unworthiness and gratitude for the generosity and kindness

that comes with an unexpected gift all wrapped in red and green. "Really? For me? Oh, you shouldn't have."

—ROBIN KIMMERER, "The Gift of Strawberries"

Repetition, rhyme, and rhythm. The Reverend Martin Luther King Jr. was a master of repetition and rhythm, as well as of what linguist and rhetorician Geneva Smitherman describes as "lyrical balance, cadence, and melodious voice rhythm." She goes on to quote one of her favorite King sentences as an example:

> Lord, we ain what we ought to be, and we ain what we want to be, and we ain what we gon be, but thank God, we ain what we was.
>
> —MARTIN LUTHER KING JR.

If you have heard some of Dr. King's speeches or sermons, you will be able to hear his "melodious voice rhythm" at work here, as the repetition creates its own rhythm. And here is another sentence, this one by Indigenous author Tommy Orange:

> We made powwows because we needed a place to be together. Something intertribal, something old, something to make us money, something we could work toward, for our jewelry, our songs, our dances, our drum.
>
> –TOMMY ORANGE, *There There*

Note that Orange puts a period after the first two clauses and sets off the rest of the sentence as a fragment. By creating a pause, the period adds emphasis to both parts of the sentence, along with repetition and rhythm, moving from solemn statement to a cumulative explanation of the opening statement.

Finally, here is poet and educator Jimmy Santiago Baca, who taught himself to read and write while in solitary confinement and who says, "Suddenly, through language, through writing, my grief and joy could be shared with anyone who would listen. . . . Through language I was free." The following sentence concludes one of Baca's best-known poems.

It's all I have to give,
and all anyone needs to live,
and to go on living inside,
when the world outside
no longer cares if you live or die;
remember,

I love you.

—JIMMY SANTIAGO BACA, "I Am Offering This Poem"

The rhymes of "give" and "live," of "inside" and "outside" and the repetition of "live" create the rhythm of the sentence, leading up to a semicolon marking an attention-getting pause—followed by the injunction to "remember" that "I love you." Read the sentence once more, and think about how it might feel to receive such an "offering."

Sentences that imitate what they describe. Writing a sentence that enacts what it is saying presents challenges, for certain, but also offers a great opportunity for experimentation. Here's a sentence Tom Wolfe wrote about Junior Johnson, a twentieth-century race car driver who ran bootlegged whiskey and was famous for evading law officials. And then, one night . . .

they had Junior trapped on the road up toward the bridge around Millersville, there's no way out of there, they had the barricades up and they could hear this souped-up car roaring around the bend, and here it comes—but suddenly they can hear a siren and see a red light flashing in the grille, so they think it's another agent, and boy, they run out like ants and pull those barrels and boards and sawhorses out of the way, and then—Ggghhzzzzzzzhhhhhgggggzzzzzzzeeeeong!—gawdam! there he goes again, it was him, Junior Johnson, with a gaw-dam agent's si-reen and a red light in his grille!

—TOM WOLFE, "The Last American Hero Is Junior Johnson"

Wolfe's very long sentence revs up just like Junior's car, building momentum, careening around curves, and thundering right past the agents. Foiled again. Note as well that Wolfe's sprawling run-on sentence includes a made-up word—to capture the sound of the squealing tires?—and the use of colloquialisms as well as a word, "si-reen," spelled and punctuated to match the dialect of that area of North Carolina in the 1960s.

And finally, here is a sentence that concludes a memoir reflecting on the death of a sister. The passage begins with the author saying "And now I lay me down to roll" and then doing so—in words:

> I push off and roll once, twice, more, bumping clumsily, laughing, disoriented, eyes open, eyes closed, getting a rhythm, arching now, whipping down, fish flopping down, rolling, rolling, rolling down, and when I stop the whole world spins, I am dizzy, I am sick, I am breathing, I am smiling, I am holding on until the streaking world slows, rights itself, shows me again this grass, these trees, these stones, these roads I know so well.
>
> —ELLEN ASHDOWN, *Living by the Dead*

The repetitive rolling rhythm of this sentence takes us along, introducing us to the landscape that the author knows so well.

This brief chapter has barely scratched the surface of what we might say about sentence style and about how it can practically leap off the page, grab us by the collar, and say "hey, look at me!" But I hope it says enough to show how good sentences can be better than your best digital assistant, helping you get your ideas out there to connect with audiences as successfully as possible. And that writing such sentences can be a whole lot of fun!

REFLECT! Read aloud an essay you've written, listening for rhythm and emphasis. If you find a passage that doesn't read well or doesn't have the emphasis you want, analyze its sentences for length (count the words) and emphasis (how does each sentence begin?). Revise them using the strategies discussed in this chapter.

26 Using Languages & Dialects Rhetorically

Language is power . . .
the instrument of domination *and* liberation.

—ANGELA CARTER

A language is a dialect with an army and navy.

—MAX WEINREICH

How many languages do you know well enough to speak or write? Which languages would you like to know? Today the US Census Bureau estimates that some 20 percent of Americans speak two or more languages, and that roughly 70 million of us speak a language other than English at home—Spanish, Chinese, and Tagalog are the three most common, and American Sign Language is probably number four. So the United States is a country of many languages. It is also a nation of multiple dialects, varieties of language spoken by people in particular regions, ethnic groups, or social classes,

511

Notice all the languages and dialects you encounter in a day—on signs, in conversations, and elsewhere.

like the English spoken in Appalachia, the Chicano English spoken primarily by Mexican Americans in the US Southwest, the Cajun English spoken in southern Louisiana, or the New England dialect spoken by Boston Brahmins.

Using Englishes

No matter how many languages you speak, you probably use a number of different DIALECTS of English, including "standardized English," the variety used in writing for school, business, and other institutional purposes. Proponents of the standardized dialect argue that it has some real benefits: it allows for stability, efficiency, and ease of communication across differences. In the abstract, these justifications make some sense. But the very name "standard" implies that anything else is *not* standard or even that it's substandard, leading to privileging the "standard" over all other dialects. As Angela Carter points out, language can lead to domination. But as she also notes, it can lead the way to liberation.

This debate over the advantages and disadvantages of standardized languages is ongoing. And you can bet that it will continue to be an issue as generative AI programs develop. Since they are trained on vast databases of text largely written in standardized English, these programs at present reinforce linguistic hierarchies.

And yet. Languages and dialects have their own ways of evolving, and people have their own ways of resisting standardization. We can see such evolution at work in the many words from Spanish and Arabic and Hindi and many other languages that have entered the English vocabulary. To take just one recent example, linguist John McWhorter writes about the "new Miami English," a living, breathing dialect blending Spanish and English, in which each language borrows from the other. And there's plenty of other borrowing and mixing going on, even in academic genres of writing. As the linguists Geneva Smitherman and H. Samy Alim note, "it is a decided benefit for American citizens to be able to speak in more than one tongue." And, we would add, to *write* in more than one tongue too.

This chapter provides some pretty intriguing examples of writing and speaking that reach beyond standardized English. Here you'll meet a number of writers deploying multiple languages and dialects in ways that not only resist standardization but create powerful ways of communicating—from Jay-Z combining standardized English with street talk in a narrative about how he first encountered hip-hop, to Sandra Cisneros using both English and Spanish in stories that will be read by speakers of both languages.

In short, this chapter aims to demonstrate that "English" is way more than just one thing: as Walt Whitman famously once said of himself, language is "large" and it "contains multitudes." And to that I would add, there's way more than just English for us to use. So get ready to see how these and other writers make good, and very different, use of multiple languages and dialects—and to think about how you might do the same!

Using languages and dialects

Some who are bilingual (or multilingual) mix languages or dialects routinely, especially when they're engaging with others who speak the same languages. But even those of us who are not bilingual will use one or more dialects on occasion. Sometimes it can help us connect with an audience, or simply get their attention. It can also be a way of illustrating a point or evoking a particular person, place, or community. Following are some good examples demonstrating how to use different varieties of language for these purposes.

To evoke a person, place, or community

Using the language of a specific person, place, or community is a good way to help readers understand what makes them tick. In the following passage, Jay-Z (Shawn Carter) is describing the neighborhood he grew up in, "full of concrete corners to turn, dark hallways to explore . . . and grassy patches that passed for a park." He's describing a scene from 1978 when he was nine, and he opens this autobiographical account with an arresting sentence: "I saw the circle before I saw the kid in the middle." Jay-Z is about to be introduced to hip-hop, and in writing about that he uses both street language and standardized English to evoke a particular community:

> His name was Slate, and he was a kid I used to see around the neighborhood, an older kid who barely made an impression. In the circle, though, he was transformed, like the church ladies touched by the spirit, and everyone was mesmerized. He was rhyming, throwing out couplet after couplet . . . thirty minutes straight off the top of his head, never losing the beat, riding the handclaps. He rhymed about nothing—the sidewalk, the benches—or he'd go in on the kids who were standing around listening to him, call out someone's leaning sneakers or dirty Lee jeans. And then he'd go in on how clean he was, how nice he was with the ball, how all our girls loved him. Then he'd just start rhyming about the rhymes themselves, how good they were, how much better they were than yours, how he was the best that ever did it. . . . He never stopped moving, not dancing, just rotating in the center of the circle, looking for his next target. . . . All he had were his eyes, taking in everything, and the words inside him. I was dazzled. *That's some cool shit* was the first thing I thought. Then: *I could do that.*
>
> —JAY-Z, *Decoded*

Jay-Z at 10, 1979—and performing in his Magna Carta World Tour, 2013.

Notice that this passage is written mostly in fairly standardized English—but it's got a beat: we can almost hear Slate "rhyming, throwing out couplet after couplet . . . never losing the beat, riding the handclaps." And while it includes some street talk ("leaning sneakers," "he'd go in on the kids," "that's some cool shit"), it also includes a simile ("like the church ladies touched by the spirit"). In short, it's a great example of writing that mixes different dialects of English.

To take another example, here's Lee Tonouchi, the author of *Living Pidgin: Contemplations on Pidgin Culture*, using both English and Hawaiian's Pidgin, now one of Hawaii's official languages, responding to a question about his work:

> [This book is] about finding humor in tragedy. It's about da relationship between one son and his uncommunicative faddah in da wake of da maddah's early passing. An den, it's also about da son's relationship with his grandmas as he discovers what it means for be Okinawan in Hawaii.
>
> —LEE TONOUCHI

Notice that Tonouchi uses both academic English and Hawaiian Pidgin to evoke family relationships in his community, and that he uses them both within sentences and not just between them, bringing the two into even closer contact.

When using the language of a community you don't belong to yourself, be very careful to do so with respect. When possible, ask someone who does speak the language to look over what you've drafted to ensure that it's accurate and respectful.

To connect with an audience

As speakers and writers, we all need to connect with our audiences, and that's especially true with audiences that speak more than one language.

Sandra Cisneros, a Mexican American writer who's fluent in both English and Spanish, makes exactly this rhetorical choice in a collection of short stories inspired by her experience growing up in the United States surrounded by Mexican culture. See how she uses both languages to connect to an audience that's likely to include both English and Spanish speakers:

> "¡Ay!" The true test of a native Spanish speaker. ¡Ay! To make love in Spanish, in a manner as intricate and devout as la Alhambra. To have a lover sigh mi vida, mi preciosa, mi chiquitita, and whisper things in that language crooned to babies, that language murmured by grandmothers, those words that smelled like your house, like flour tortillas.
>
> —SANDRA CISNEROS, "Bien Pretty"

Kenyan rapper Bamboo makes similar choices in a remix of the song "Mama Africa," first written and sung by Jamaican reggae artist Peter Tosh. Bamboo connects to his international audience of hip-hop fans by moving back and forth between Swahili and English.

> tunaishi vizuri
> check out the way we be livin
> na tunakula vizuri
> we always eating the best
> poteza yako kwa nini
> why should you settle for less
> TV haiwezi kuambia
> they never show on your screen

kwa hivyo mi ntawaambia
so you can see what I mean
Africa maridadi
Africa's beautiful baby

—BAMBOO, "Mama Africa"

Bamboo uses hip-hop rhythms and dialects to connect with the audiences he wants to reach. By using both Swahili and English, he reaches more people than if he'd used just one language—and exposes those who speak just one of these languages to the other.

And here's Denise Lajimodiere, the North Dakota Poet Laureate and a member of the Turtle Mountain Band of Pembina Chippewa, opening her 2023 commencement address to the graduates of the University of North Dakota using two languages, Ojibwe and English, acknowledging her whole audience:

Boozhoo! Aaniin! Good morning!

And she does the same in her conclusion, thus making sure to acknowledge and connect with the Native as well as non-Native graduates:

Congratulations UND Class of '23!
It's time to celebrate!
Native graduates, Lets Soodis! Skooden! Lelelele!

—DENISE LAJIMODIERE, University of North Dakota
commencement address

For one more example, remember that mixing varieties of language can include different genres as well. In a eulogy for the Reverend and Senator Clementa Pinckney, who was killed with eight other worshippers in the Emanuel AME Church in Charleston, Barack Obama adopted biblical language and African American preaching rhythms throughout. But what seemed on that day to connect most viscerally to his audience was his shift from speech to song. As he meditated on the grace surrounding Pinckney and his fellow

Barack Obama giving the eulogy for Clementa Pinckney, then shifting into song. Charleston SC, 2015

worshippers, Obama quietly slipped into song, singing the words of "Amazing Grace." If you take a look at the eulogy on *YouTube*, you'll see that at this shift into song, the congregation rises to their feet and joins in: the connection is clear, and very powerful.

As writers and speakers, we have to think carefully about when using different varieties of language (or media!) will help us connect with our audiences—and when it won't. In most cases, writers have a kind of informal contract with readers: while readers may need to work some to understand what a writer is saying, the writer in turn promises to consider the audience's expectations and abilities. The end goal is usually accessibility: Will your message be understood by those you are trying to reach? If some members of your audience aren't likely to understand, should you provide a translation? At times you may choose not to translate so that your readers experience what it's like *not* to understand, you'll usually want to be sure they understand what you've written.

To illustrate a point

Sometimes you'll want to use words from different varieties of language to illustrate a point. Professor Geneva Smitherman illustrates the point she is making perfectly in the last sentence of the following passage. Writing in the 1970s, Smitherman noted that in recent years Black English had become a "very hot controversy":

and there have been articles on Black dialect in the national press as well as in the educational research literature. We have had pronouncements on Black speech from the NAACP and the Black Panthers, from highly publicized scholars of the Arthur Jensen–William Shockley bent, from executives of national corporations such as Greyhound, and from housewives and community folk. I mean, really, it seem like everybody and they momma done had something to say on the subject!

—GENEVA SMITHERMAN,
Talkin and Testifyin: The Language of Black America

Smitherman's purposefully abrupt shift from standardized English to Black English gets our attention—almost as if she had reached out and given our shoulders a shake and said "listen up!"—and underscores her point that Black English is garnering a whole lot of attention from a whole lot of people.

And here is Buthainah, a Saudi Arabian student writing a literacy narrative for an education class at an American college:

ومن يتهيّب صعود الجبال   ~~~   يعش ابد الدّهر بين الحفر

"I don't want to" was my response to my parents' request of enrolling me in a nearby preschool. I did not like school. I feared it. I feared the aspect of departing my comfort zone, my home, to an unknown and unpredictable zone. . . . To encourage me, they recited a poetic line that I did not comprehend as a child but live by it as an adult. They said, "Who fears climbing the mountains ~~~ Lives forever between the holes." As I grew up, knowledge became my key to freedom; freedom of thought, freedom of doing, and freedom of beliefs.

—BUTHAINAH, "Who Fears Climbing the Mountains
Lives Forever between the Holes"

The inclusion of an Arabic proverb (which also serves as the title of her essay) draws readers' attention and illustrates the importance of Arabic in her journey to become the writer she is, while also letting non-Arabic speakers feel a bit of what it's like to encounter a foreign language they don't understand. At the same time, she makes a point of translating the proverb for her readers as the essay progresses—"They said, 'Who fears climbing the mountains ~~~ Lives forever between the holes.'" Buthainah's essay illustrates how using more than one language can grab attention and show—rather than tell—your audience something that's important to you.

Quoting people directly and respectfully

If you're writing about people you've interviewed, you will want to let them speak for themselves. From 1927 to 1931, Zora Neale Hurston, the famed Black anthropologist, interviewed Cudjo Lewis, one of the last living slaves to have made the journey across the Atlantic. Lewis's story, told from Hurston's perspective, appears in *Barracoon: The Story of the Last "Black Cargo."* See how Hurston takes care to let him speak his mind, and in his own words. She begins by telling us, "I hailed him by his African name," Oluale Kossula, which she had learned from prior research. In the next paragraph, Lewis speaks:

> Oh Lor', I kno it you call my name. Nobody don't callee me my name from cross de water but you. You always callee me Kossula, jus' lak I in de Affica soil!
>
> —ZORA NEALE HURSTON, *Barracoon: The Story of the Last "Black Cargo"*

Notice how Hurston alternates between standardized English ("I hailed him by his African name") and the actual speech of the person whose words she quotes. Quoting him helps establish her credibility as a careful researcher. Finally, the use of quotations appeals to her audience's emotions; we can hear Lewis's surprise and delight. Readers familiar with the dialect Lewis speaks might sense kinship with him, while those of us who are not will be reminded that Hurston is writing about a context different from our own experience.

When you're quoting others, let them speak for themselves—not only in their own words but also in their own language. And whenever possible, ask your subjects to review any quotations you use to ensure that they're accurate.

Providing translation

One way to stay true to a language or dialect you identify with while still reaching readers who may not understand is to provide a translation. Bamboo's example, which invites English speakers to think about Africa's rich culture in part by including Swahili, demonstrates how translation helps when you're mixing languages.

When translating, you will usually want to introduce the word or words in their original language, followed by the translation, as is done on the poster on page 522 announcing a conference taking place in the Navajo Nation. Note that the Navajo title comes first, and in slightly larger and bolder text, to underscore the importance of the Navajo language at this conference.

See how linguist Guadalupe Valdés uses translation in an ethnographic study of a family of Mexican origin.

> During his kindergarten year, . . . winning was important to Saúl. Of all the cousins who played together, it was he who ran the fastest and pushed the hardest. *"Yo gané, yo gané"* (I won, I won), he would say enthusiastically. . . . Saúl's mother, Velma, wished that he would win just a bit more quietly. . . . *"No seas peleonero"* (Don't be so quarrelsome), she would say. *"Es importante llevarse bien con todos"* (It's important to get along with everyone).
>
> —GUADALUPE VALDÉS, *"Con Respeto*: Bridging the Distances between Culturally Diverse Families and Schools"

Note especially that Valdés always puts the Spanish words first, as they were spoken, and only then gives the English translation. She could have chosen to put the translation first, or to write only in English, but giving the Spanish first puts the spotlight on her subjects' voices and their own words. By including the English translation, Valdés acknowledges readers who don't speak Spanish and makes sure they can understand what she's written.

Notice too that Valdés italicizes words that are in a language other than English, which is a common academic convention when mixing languages.

Conference poster announcing in both Navajo and English a gathering of writers in Window Rock, the capital of the Navajo Nation.

Thinking about your rhetorical situation

Whether you're using standardized English with another language or dialect, shifting from formal language to informal, or something else, you need to think about how doing so suits your purpose and audience and the rest of your rhetorical situation.

Purpose. What do you want to accomplish: to bring attention to something you're saying? to let someone you're writing about speak for themselves? to illustrate an important point?

Audience. Will using different dialects or languages help you connect with your audience? If you weave in a language they don't understand, will you need to translate? How likely are they to find your language choices engaging? Is anything at risk, like clarity?

Stance. How do you want to come across to your audience, and how will using various dialects or languages affect that? How would it affect your credibility?

Genre. If you're writing a NARRATIVE, quoting someone in their own dialect will let readers hear that person's voice; if you're making an ARGUMENT, using various dialects or languages can help to emphasize what you're saying. If you're making a serious PROPOSAL, however, will doing so detract from your goals?

Context. If you're writing in response to an assignment, will it be appropriate to mix languages or dialects? Do you have the knowledge to do so accurately and respectfully? Are you addressing members of a field that is likely to welcome this kind of language use?

Medium. Shifting to another dialect or language can sometimes help to get an audience's attention in a spoken presentation—provided that fits well with the occasion and the audience.

REFLECT! Have you ever used language in any of the ways this chapter demonstrates? If not, find something you've written, think about its intended audience, and see if mixing dialects or languages would help to get their attention or connect with them in some way. Try it!

PART SIX

DESIGN

STRATEGIES

MAKE AN IMPRESSION

27 Designing What You Write

Fonts, colors, contrast, capitalization, spacing . . .
all these affect whether or not people read your words.

—JOHN SAITO, "HOW TO DESIGN WORDS"

Design is all about storytelling. . . . about communicating
with an audience through images and language
and color and type and scale and nuance. . . .

—STEPHEN DOYLE

Once upon a time student writers had little control over the way their texts were designed: black type on white paper was pretty much it. But that was then. Today you can choose from hundreds of fonts, use color, add images of all kinds. So you need to know something about design. Whether you're drafting an essay, creating slides for a presentation, or writing up a lab report, you'll need to think about how you can use design to help readers follow, understand, and remember what you say. What fonts should you choose? Do you need headings? Is there anything you want to highlight? This chapter is here to help.

THINKING RHETORICALLY ABOUT DESIGN

The way you design a text plays a big role in how well you reach your audience and whether your text achieves its purpose. And the fact that you *can* design what you write gives you a lot of control over how effectively you present your message. In short, you have more than black ink and white paper at your disposal.

> The test of design is how well it assists the understanding of the content.
>
> EDWARD TUFTE

Let's take a look at two McDonald's images to see the difference that design can make. The one on the left is an ad run in the United States in the 1950s; the one on the right is a sign seen recently in the Czech Republic. The ad provides information that might make someone think of McDonald's when they're looking for a quick meal: 15 cents, "speedee" service, over 100 million sold. The focus is on the words, especially the largest one: HAMBURGERS. But nowadays the McDonald's brand is so well known that the recent sign consists simply of the famous golden arches with two words: *Máš hlad*—in English, "Are you hungry?"—and an arrow pointing the way. The colors, image, and two-word message work to conjure up the brand.

Of course, the designers' rhetorical situations were drastically different. Those designing the ad were probably limited to black and white and could assume an audience of readers, whereas those who designed the sign could use colors—and were able to be much more playful, knowing that the golden arches would be familiar to anyone passing by.

You may not be called on to design a McDonald's ad, but you too will need to think carefully about how to design the texts you write so that they capture your audience's attention and deliver your message effectively. In short, you'll need to think *rhetorically* about how to design what you write.

Think about your rhetorical situation

Purpose. What are you trying to do—provide information? persuade readers to do something? tell a story?—and what design elements will help you to do that? If you're writing a narrative about a soccer match, you might include photos or a short video clip. But if you're creating a poster to publicize a concert, you'll need to make the name of the group large enough to be seen from a distance and make sure the time and place are in one place on the poster.

Audience. Are there any design elements they are likely to need, or expect? If you're writing a market analysis for a business class, will it include data that readers will expect to see in a graph or chart?

Stance. How do you want to come across to readers: as objective? authoritative? outraged? What fonts or colors might help establish such a stance? Bright red words might signal outrage on a poster for a protest, but that would not be appropriate on a business résumé.

Genre. Does your genre have any design requirements? A lengthy REPORT, for instance, may require headings to label its parts.

Context. Does your assignment specify any design requirements? And when is it due? Do you have time to find or create visuals?

Language. Are there any words you want to highlight? If you'll be including unfamiliar words in a language other than English, MLA recommends italicizing single words but not full sentences.

What do you want readers to focus on, and how can design help?

Your message may start with words, but it doesn't end there. Whether you write out your words by hand or put them in a certain font, whether you arrange them on a page or a screen, the way you design your text focuses your message in a certain way and gives it a certain look. It also affects how easy your message is to read—and sometimes whether it gets read at all.

Design brings content into focus.

JENNIFER MORLA

So give some thought to what you want readers to focus on, and how you can design your text to help them do that. What do you want them to look at first? What do you want them to look at next? And after that? Is there anything you want to highlight? How do you want readers to move through the text—and how can you help them to do so? And what goes with what? Following are some principles from graphic designer Robin Williams that can help you design your texts so that they're easy to read and navigate.

FOUR BASIC PRINCIPLES OF DESIGN

Contrast draws our eyes to certain parts of a page or screen. A contrasting color, a **bold font**, a larger type size: these are all ways of getting readers to focus on something. The first letter of each chapter in this book, for example, is gigantic, as if to say "start here!" The bold heading on this page does the same: it's larger and bolder than most of the words on this page, so it gets your attention. And later in this chapter you'll find a **Reflect!** prompt, with a pale blue background to make it easy to spot.

Repetition of keywords, images, fonts, and colors can help readers move through a text—as the bold italics do on this page.

Alignment refers to where text and images are positioned on a page. Most of the text in this book is aligned flush with the left-hand margin; the examples and bulleted lists, however, are indented, making them easier to spot on the page.

Proximity involves putting ideas, images, or text that are related close, or "proximate," to one another. Images need to be near to where they're discussed in the text, and captions need to be next to the images they label. And of course closely related ideas need to be connected visually, as the four basic design principles are here.

DESIGN ELEMENTS
Fonts

Words have meaning. Type has spirit.
PAULA SCHER

The fonts you use affect how easy your text is to read—and they also contribute to the look of what you write. You'll want to choose fonts that suit your genre and purpose, and that reflect your stance: academic, playful, businesslike, informal, whatever.

There are two basic kinds of fonts: *serif* fonts such as Times New Roman, Garamond, and Century Schoolbook, which have short cross lines at the ends of letters; and *sans serif* fonts such as Calibri, Helvetica, and Futura, which do not have such cross lines. This book is set in three different fonts: what you're reading here is set in Freight Text Book, the examples in the book are set in Freight Sans, and the blue headings are set in Clarendon.

Most fonts have **bold**, *italic*, and underlined versions. You might use bold for headings in an academic text or for getting attention on posters or other texts that will be read from a distance, and italic to emphasize or highlight certain words. Italics are also used for titles of books, magazines, movies, and other full-length works (*Don Quixote, The Atlantic, Mamma Mia!*).

She feels in *italics* and thinks in CAPITALS.
HENRY JAMES, *Daisy Miller*

You may be required or expected to use certain fonts. MLA specifies only that you use a font that's easy to read, whereas APA recommends several specific fonts: Calibri, Arial, Times New Roman, and others.

Whatever fonts you decide to use, make sure that they are legible: depending on the font, anything smaller than 11 or 12 point will be difficult to read. And, in general, resist the temptation to use really ornate or fancy fonts or a lot of different fonts: too much of a good thing is . . . too much.

Color and white space

Color can help highlight certain words or design elements and guide your readers. You might use one color for all the headings, for example, which would make them easy for readers to spot. In digital texts, you might use color to signal that certain words are hyperlinks. Notice the use of color in this book, for instance: the parts of the book are color-coded (note the gold band at the top of this page), the main headings are blue and the secondary ones are **black**, and key terms are **red**—all designed that way for the purpose of helping you find your way through the book.

Choose colors that are easy to see, and remember that contrast is key. Dark type on a light background—or light type on a dark background—will provide contrast that makes text easy to read and that can highlight something you want to emphasize. Note, however, that some people may not be able to distinguish between certain colors (between green and red, for example) so it's best not to use these colors together. Yellow can be hard to see on a light background, so avoid that combo as well.

If you use more than one color in a text, be careful to choose colors that complement one another. Take a look at the color wheel below,

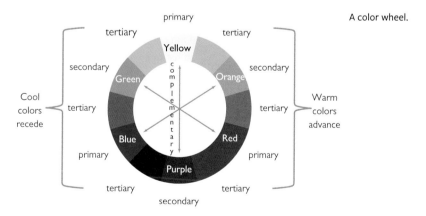

A color wheel.

which shows colors that work well together. But remember that too many colors jousting for the reader's attention can be a distraction. And be sure as well that any color you use has a purpose, and is not there as mere decoration.

Finally, don't forget white space. Leave a one-inch margin around your text, and add some space above headings, above and below lists, and around any visuals.

Layout

No matter how many different elements a text has, they all have to be arranged in some way—and elements that are related need to be near to one another.

Paragraphs, lists, graphs, and charts. If you're writing a print text that's organized in paragraphs, you'll generally want to double-space the text and indent each paragraph five spaces. Online, however, you should single-space your text, skip a line between paragraphs, and begin each paragraph flush left, without indenting. If there's anything that you want to set off as a list, use bullets to make it easy to see—or numbers if you want to put items in a certain sequence. If you're including numerical data, would it be easier for readers to understand if you presented it in a graph or chart? Remember, too, that AI can help you with formatting: it can, for instance, put text into a bulleted list or a chart or graph.

For more on creating graphs and charts, see Ch. 28.

Headings can help guide readers through a written text, especially one that is long or complex, and can also be useful on slides with an oral presentation. Make sure that your headings are parallel in structure. They might be noun phrases: **The Dangers of E-cigarettes.** They could also be gerund phrases: **Assessing the Dangers of E-cigarettes.** Or even questions: **Why Have E-cigarettes Hooked So Many Teens?** But whatever form you choose, use it consistently: all noun phrases, all gerunds, and so on.

If you have both headings and subheadings, you can distinguish them by using bold, italics, underlining, or all caps. For example:

FIRST-LEVEL HEADING

Second-Level Heading

Third-Level Heading

If you're following a particular documentation style, check to see if it has any requirements about headings. Both MLA and APA require that you use the same font for headings that you do in the rest of the text, and APA requires that headings be boldface.

Visuals should be placed carefully. Putting them at the top or bottom of a print page will make it easy to lay out pages. If your text is online, however, you'll have more flexibility. For online text, be careful that image files are not large; save them as JPEGs or TIFFs, compressed files that readers will be able to download.

See Ch. 28 for more on creating visual texts.

REFLECT! Look over this book's use of fonts, color, and headings. Do they help you follow the text? Now look at something you've written that's fairly lengthy. Have you used those same elements? If not, how do you think doing so might help readers follow your text more easily?

DESIGNING VISUAL TEXTS

The basic design principles of contrast, repetition, alignment, and proximity apply to all kinds of texts, visual ones included. Take a look at the two posters that follow on pages 534–35, and consider how these principles are put to good use—and how they help us read each one.

In this poster, the subtle color contrast draws our eyes to the large, all-caps word VOTE, which ripples beneath the water's surface. At the same time, the rippling draws our eyes down to where the color smooths out to match the darker blue of "VOTE" and then further down, from cause (voting) to effect: "Cause an effect." This phrase, presented in sharply contrasting white letters in the classic Century Schoolbook font, also plays on the familiar phrase "cause and effect" in ways that make readers stop and pay attention to the difference between a familiar three-word phrase and a somewhat unexpected three-word command. This poster was created by award-winning designer **Stephen Doyle** for the American Institute of Graphic Arts, a professional design association, so we can assume it had two purposes: to persuade viewers to vote, and to demonstrate design at its very best. How well do you think he succeeded?

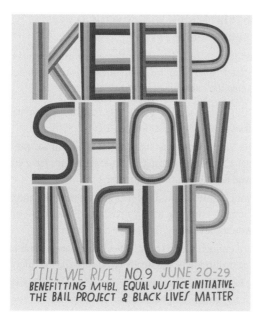

Created by **Lisa Congdon**, an award-winning artist and author of books about drawing and art, this poster also urges viewers to "cause an effect." The design choices, however, are very different from Stephen Doyle's. Here the large, sharply contrasting candy-stripe letters in all caps leap out at us. Colors are repeated—primarily red, blue, red, blue—as our eyes are drawn down the poster, focusing on the central message: we need to show up. At first glance you may focus on the imperative—SHOW UP—since "SHOW" is in the middle, and "ING" is on the next line. Clustered at the bottom of the poster is the pertinent information inviting viewers to show up at a particular fundraising event (No. 9) sponsored by Still We Rise supporting the work of four specific groups. The quirky, hand-drawn font also gets our attention, suggesting that this is something out of the box and important, something viewers will want to show up for.

Look at your design with a critical eye, get response—and revise

It's a good idea to test-drive your design by asking a classmate or friend to react to it. Here are some questions that will help you or someone else look at your design with a critical eye.

- Does the overall look suit your RHETORICAL SITUATION— and does it reflect your STANCE?

- Are the fonts you've used appropriate for your GENRE and PURPOSE? If you're writing for an assignment, have you followed any design requirements?

- Will your AUDIENCE find the text easy to navigate and read? If it's long or complex, have you included headings—and if not, would they help?

- Is there enough white space? Check the margins and any spacing around lists and heads to be sure they're adequate.

- If you've used color, does it suit your purpose, and have you used it to provide emphasis where it's needed?

- Is there any information that would be easier to understand if it were set off in a list?

- If you've included any statistics or other data, should it be presented in a chart or graph?

- If your text includes any VISUALS, what do they contribute to your point? Have you explained how they relate to the topic? If they are mostly decorative, consider deleting them.

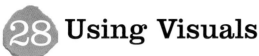

28 Using Visuals

Use a picture. It's worth a thousand words.
—ARTHUR BRISBANE

Photography helps people to see.
—BERENICE ABBOTT

Many of the texts we write include visuals of various kinds—photos, maps, tables, charts and graphs, still or moving images—all of which can help draw readers in and support what we have to say. In some cases, visuals make information much easier to understand than it would be with words alone. You'll likely have reason to include visuals in some of your academic writing: paintings or drawings in an art history essay, bar graphs or pie charts in a business proposal, historical documents and maps in a history presentation. Whatever visuals you include, make sure that they support what you're saying—and that you use them ethically.

KINDS OF VISUALS

Photos can help readers visualize what you are describing or explaining. Imagine describing with words alone this scene from *Akhnaten*, an opera by Philip Glass, in which jugglers visually represent the rhythms of Glass's music. You could do it—but the photo lets readers *see* what you're describing.

Maps can help orient readers to a place you refer to in your text. The map here is one you might include in a literary analysis of J. R. R. Tolkien's *The Return of the King*, showing Gondor, where much of the story takes place.

Table 1

US College Degrees by Males and Females, 2020

Degrees	Class of 2020		
	Percentage		Female per 100 Males
	Male	Female	
Associate's	39.1%	60.9%	**156**
Bachelor's	42.6%	57.4%	**135**
Master's	40.1%	59.9%	**149**
Doctor's	46.2%	53.8%	**116**
All Degrees	41.4%	58.6%	**142**

Source: US Department of Education

Tables are a way of presenting data in columns, which makes it easier to see than it would be in a paragraph—and are especially useful for comparing data. The table here compares degrees earned by men and women as a percentage of the total number of degrees earned at US colleges in 2020. See page 419 on setting up tables MLA style, and pages 460–61 for APA style.

Bar graphs are useful for comparing quantitative data. In this example, the bars make it easy to see at a glance what a sample of US adults thought about the widespread use of driverless cars expected to operate on their own.

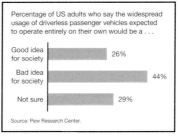

Percentage of US adults who say the widespread usage of driverless passenger vehicles expected to operate entirely on their own would be a . . .

Good idea for society	26%
Bad idea for society	44%
Not sure	29%

Source: Pew Research Center.

Line graphs are useful for showing changes in data that occur over time. One data set can be shown with a single line, as in the example here. Two or more data sets, each represented by its own line, can easily be compared over time using a single line graph.

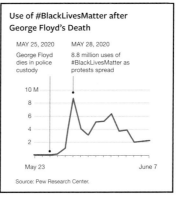

Use of #BlackLivesMatter after George Floyd's Death

MAY 25, 2020
George Floyd dies in police custody

MAY 28, 2020
8.8 million uses of #BlackLivesMatter as protests spread

May 23 — June 7

Source: Pew Research Center.

Pie charts provide a broad overview of how parts of a whole relate to one another—for example, how much of a family's earnings go for food, housing, transportation, savings, charity, and so on. Each part needs to be clearly labeled, and it's best to have no more than six or seven parts, because if the slices are too small, they can be hard to see or interpret.

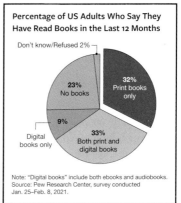

Percentage of US Adults Who Say They Have Read Books in the Last 12 Months

Don't know/Refused 2%
32% Print books only
23% No books
9% Digital books only
33% Both print and digital books

Note: "Digital books" include both ebooks and audiobooks.
Source: Pew Research Center, survey conducted Jan. 25–Feb. 8, 2021.

USING VISUALS ETHICALLY

"What you see is what you get." "A picture is worth a thousand words." Maybe so. But maybe not. These familiar sayings rest on the assumption that what we see with our own eyes is real and true, unmediated, while words somehow come between us and reality, shaping and altering it, for better or worse.

It's true that our brains process images much faster than words: in fact, our eyes will recognize a familiar image in 100 milliseconds, 60 times faster than they can process the words for that image. Perhaps it's the sheer speed with which images enter our consciousness that makes them seem more trustworthy: "Seeing is believing," as the saying goes. But speed doesn't equal accuracy, much less truth or fairness. And as contemporary generative AI technology has made painfully clear, pictures, even photographs, are just as constructed as sentences or paragraphs. Not only constructed: they can be manipulated, even completely falsified.

Be aware of doctored photos

You can find links to these two covers at letstalklibrary.com.

In June 1994, *Time* and *Newsweek* featured the same photo of O. J. Simpson on their covers. Sharp-eyed readers were quick to point out, however, that Simpson's skin color was decidedly darker on the *Time* cover. When questioned, the photo artist for *Time* admitted to having darkened the image, saying that he simply wanted to "give the image a dramatic tone" and that no deception or racial implication was intended. Maybe so, maybe not, but the altered image caused a huge public outcry against such practices.

Over two decades ago, environmentalist Kenneth Brower raised an alarm in an essay titled "Photography in the Age of Falsification," in which he pointed out that even well-established magazines like *National Geographic* had been known to "doctor" photographs to make them more appealing. Noting that while the wildlife images we see in movies and magazines are often "stunning," they may well be "fake, enhanced, or manufactured by . . . digital technologies that have transformed—some say contaminated—the photography landscape." In Brower's view, such alterations raise serious ethical questions.

Faking a sunset or moving animals around in a photo is decep-tive, but some altered images, videos, and sounds go beyond deception and cause harm or embarrassment. This happened to President Biden in early 2024 when thousands of people in New Hampshire got a call from a supposed Joe Biden. The voice sounded like Biden—in fact, Biden himself was taken aback by its believabil-ity. But it wasn't Biden's voice but rather a voice created by AI.

A leopard can't change his spots, but the modern photographer can easily do it for him.
KENNETH BROWER

Photographers have always been able to alter images on film; *Photoshop* makes it possible to alter them digitally—and now with AI, anyone can alter images instantly, so the warning Kenneth Brower sounded long ago is more pertinent than ever. You can heed that warning by looking very carefully at digital images, searching for inconsistencies or anomalies (a shadow in the wrong place, for example). You can also use *Google Images* to do a reverse image search to find the original version and use it for comparison. And there are fake image detector apps, such as *Mirage*, that can help as well.

See pp. 105–7 for tips on detecting altered images.

As you no doubt already know, AI is remarkably good at faking images of real people—so much so that politicians are fearful that such fake images could create confusion and even turn the tide of elections to come. To further muddy the waters, research shows that we are often unable to distinguish AI-generated "people" from the real ones!

One photo is real, and one's been digitally altered to change its message. Easy to do, hard to know what to trust.

Think before taking and sharing photos

The easy manipulation of images has led to a new field of study, visual ethics, that explores the way in which images, even unaltered ones, always reflect a particular point of view and hence have ethical dimensions. Think for a moment of the highly unflattering photos of politicians used in ads against them—or of ones that have been enhanced to make them look flawless: Are those photos fair?

And think of your own experience: Has a photo ever represented you in ways you felt were unfair, especially if it was taken without your knowledge? That's what leads scholars of visual ethics to argue that both "the production and reception of images always have ethical dimensions," and to ask us to consider when it is morally acceptable to photograph people who may be highly vulnerable.

Take the case of an image of a dying pregnant Ukrainian woman being evacuated from a hospital that had been hit by Russian air strikes. The Associated Press won a Pulitzer Prize for this and other graphic photos that captured the horrors unfolding in Ukraine, surely in part because it helped raise awareness of the inhumane treatment of civilians targeted by Russian forces. Others, however, found such photos intrusive, insensitive, and disrespectful of those suffering such trauma—in short, ethically questionable. What's your take?

Certainly, photojournalist Paul Martin Lester wished he had thought more carefully when as a young reporter he was sent to an airport on assignment to photograph the reunion of two brothers who'd been separated for forty years. A ho-hum assignment, he thought, but as he waited for the brothers to emerge, Faye Dunaway, a very big star back then, exited the plane—and when she saw Lester and all his cameras, she screamed and turned her face toward a wall. Lester was frozen in place for a moment, realizing that he hadn't been sent there to photograph her. But when she pulled herself together enough to walk toward him, he automatically took a photo. He later said that this was the most unethical photo he'd ever taken, so much so that he decided to begin every photography class he taught with this story and his realization that he had acted in a selfish, intrusive, and unethical way. In short, he made a bad choice he didn't want his students to replicate!

You may never have such challenging decisions to make, but even so, you need to be aware of the issues involved in taking and sharing photos, and to think critically and carefully before you post or repost images, regardless of who took the photos. Consider this advice from one professional photographer:

> If you are taking a photograph, ask yourself why you are doing it. Try to imagine yourself on the other side of the camera. Would you want that picture taken, maybe published in blogs or magazines? Would you want this particular [image to represent you] or your community? If you can answer with an informed yes, then you are good to go.
>
> —GRAHAM MacINDOE

Get permission, credit sources

It's likely that you will use photos and other visuals from other sources. In such cases, remember that the legal doctrine of fair use allows you to use images in your college writing without explicit permission—*if* that writing is not going to be published. Today, some online works may be published under a CREATIVE COMMONS license, which grants permission to use the work as long as you credit the person who created the work. In such cases, you'll need to send an email asking for permission, explaining why you want to use the image, saying where it will appear, and saying that full credit will be given and documented. If it is for educational use and will not be for sale, you may receive permission.

Remember, too, that for now in the United States, text (including images) generated by AI can be copyrighted only if created by humans. This means you do not need permission to use AI-generated material; however, you do need to document it, using the company or software creator as "author."

Consider the need for alt text

ALT TEXT is a way of describing images in digital texts for readers who are visually impaired or when computers do not load images. The goal is to describe the image in enough detail that readers who cannot see the image will be able to understand what it shows. That said, it needs to be succinct, generally no more than 125 characters.

What detail you provide depends on your own RHETORICAL SITUATION. If readers need to know only what or who is in the image, your description might be just what you'd see at a glance: "Susanna and Jeremy holding their dog Gus." If, however, you were writing about the gentrification of neighborhoods in Brooklyn, New York, you might describe the same photo differently: "A young white couple in front of a modest wooden house in Brooklyn. She holds a little dog; he's holding boxes from Amazon." And some very familiar images do not need to be described, only named: McDonald's golden arches, for instance, or the Nike swoosh.

The way you provide alt text will depend on where the text will be read. *Word* has a built-in tool for inserting alt text, but any text that will be read on the internet needs to be embedded using HTML. Some social media programs allow you to include alt text with any images that you post. On *X*, for example, you can add descriptions of up to 1,000 characters when posting a photo by clicking the "alt" button. *Instagram* uses object recognition technology to provide alt text for images posted there—and lets you write your own alt text if you prefer.

Think about your own use of visuals

- Consider whether any visuals you use will speak to your AUDIENCE. Will they understand any charts or graphs you want to use?

- Be sure that any photos you take or use represent your subjects accurately and fairly. Avoid stereotyping; be aware of your own biases, and don't let them influence images you take or use.

- Provide any necessary visual CONTEXT. Editing out any essential contextual detail can make a photo misleading or hard to understand.

- Treat everything and everyone you photograph with RESPECT. Give special consideration to vulnerable subjects.

- Be sure to include a CAPTION with every visual you include.

- Remember that visuals do not speak for themselves; introduce every visual before it appears in your text, and explain how it supports your point ("as the following pie chart demonstrates . . .").

- DOCUMENT any visuals you don't create yourself.

- In academic writing, provide a number (Figure 1, Table 1) and a descriptive title above each visual, and an explanatory caption and source note below.

See Ch. 22 on **MLA** style and Ch. 23 on **APA** style for advice on documenting sources and setting up figures and tables.

REFLECT! Choose an essay or something else you've written for a class, and read it over with an eye for how visuals might help support your point. Is there something you describe where a photo would help? Do you include any numerical data that would be easier to understand in a line or bar graph? If so, try creating or locating a visual to include. Ask a friend to read the before and after and tell you which version is more persuasive.

PART SEVEN

SPEAKING

WITH OTHERS

29 The Need for Conversation— & Collaboration

Conversation, in its ideal form, involves no audience, just partners; no fixed agenda, just process. Perhaps it's in long, wandering discussions that we learn how to be human.

—HUA HSU

Listen, listen, listen, listen, and if you do, people will talk.

—STUDS TERKEL

In a small town in Colorado, it's old-timers against newcomers in a fight to the finish over the town's future. Deep in the heart of Texas, another small town is seriously divided as well—over *beer*. Meanwhile, students on dozens of college campuses have set up tents to protest the suffering of the Palestinian people while others protest, equally vehemently, against antisemitism. And still today students at more than one campus are shouting down guest speakers whose views differ from their own. If ever there was a need for conversation—instead of hostile attacks and counterattacks—this is the time.

When the citizens of that "small town in Colorado"—Silverton, to be exact, found themselves so divided that they were threatening one another's lives, it seemed to many that the wounds would never heal. The debate hit fever pitch after the sheriff advised the young mayor to stay out of town for a while: threats against him were credible, and frightening. The trouble had been brewing for a couple of years. As one person put it,

> Less educated workers and "old-timers"—baby boomers with links to the mining past—felt left behind, manipulated and even persecuted by the new liberal, educated millennial professionals imprinting their ideas on Silverton with little or no consultation, according to their critics.
>
> —JONATHAN WEISMAN, "Divided by Politics, a Colorado Town Mends Its Broken Bones"

Now things had gotten out of hand; finding a way forward seemed impossible—that is, until a Colorado group called Community Builders, who had been retained to help out with a new town plan, quietly went into action. They met resistance, for sure, but they kept at it, and little by little, barriers begin to come down ever so slightly. Community Builders kept it up, and somewhat to their own surprise, the town started to come back together: "Through painstaking conversations," they said, "the temperature began to drop, the groups grew larger, and common ground was reestablished." In short, conversations—*taking time to speak and time to listen*—helped the people of Silverton remember what it means to be human.

At the heart of Silverton's finding common ground to stand on together was *conversation,* a word we use all the time but maybe haven't given the attention and credit it deserves. Stop and think for a bit about conversations you have had that still stick with you after years, conversations with a friend that led you to see something in a new way, or to an important insight. Or perhaps you remember conversations that turned into hotheaded debates, with everyone talking (or shouting) and no one listening; or a classroom conversation with a couple of classmates, where you started out with widely divergent views but found a bit of common ground that helped you come together to solve a problem or make a decision. This chapter asks you to think hard about what conversation can mean and aims to guide you in joining conversations and collaborating with others in ways that can make a difference in your life, both in and out of school.

WHY DO WE NEED CONVERSATION?

Especially today, when so many people, both online and in person, are shouting accusations, and when deep division, intolerance, and ill will seem to be the new normal, it's not surprising that many of us choose to avoid conversations, especially those that seem partisan or likely to lead to confrontation. Or that many people feel that their voices don't count, that they can't possibly make a difference. Or that many students say they have spent so much time on *Zoom* and social media that they've gotten out of the habit of joining in on conversations, preferring to remain more or less anonymous. So why are we suggesting that entering conversations, even the most difficult ones, is actually very important to your development as a speaker, writer, and thinker? Why are we talking about a *need* for conversation? Stick with us while we count the ways.

To talk through ideas with someone else. You may think of conversation as a casual, everyday activity—no big deal. And you'd be right to do so. But those casual everyday conversations can carry some pretty big payoffs. In fact, educational researchers point to conversation as a key element of "deep learning," the kind of learning that takes you up a level or two. In interviews during a five-year study of student writing and learning, students reported "really learning" something when they were able to talk through ideas with someone else, sometimes a teacher but often a friend or even a family member. These conversations, they said, helped them understand things "at a deeper level." As philosopher Michael Oakeshott puts it, what counts most in conversation and what makes it so valuable for learning is that it is open-ended, which makes space for exploration and for entertaining a wide range of ideas and perspectives in a safe, low-stakes environment that leads to understanding and to empathy for others.

To make sure your voice is heard. Conversation is also a way to get *your* perspective out there, to share your ideas, and to test them out with others. Joining a conversation doesn't guarantee that your ideas will be accepted or agreed to, but there's a good possibility that they will be understood.

To deal positively with people who think differently than you do. Conversations can also help you to engage with those whose beliefs differ from yours. That's surely what happened to Steve Deline, a gay activist who was shocked when, in 2008, voters in his home state of California voted to ban same-sex marriage. He was outraged and deeply frustrated; how could he possibly move forward?

Deline answered this question by joining a project talking one-on-one with people who voted for the proposition against same-sex marriage, in an effort to understand why they did so. As Deline put it, he felt like he "had no other choice but to try to talk to the people I didn't think I could talk to." To his surprise, as he engaged in such conversations, he felt less desperate and more hopeful: these one-on-one conversations made room for sharing vulnerabilities and for listening, removed from any national debates or ideological agendas—and led the people talking together to begin to see one another as people, not as positions.

To learn how others see the world. In a book about the power of conversation to solve problems and build understanding, journalist Charles Duhigg calls those who are able to talk with people they don't agree with "supercommunicators." Such talks, he says, will help us to learn how other people see the world and, in turn, help them understand our perspectives.

> Seek first to understand, then to be understood.
> STEPHEN COVEY

Every meaningful conversation is made up of countless small choices. There are fleeting moments when the right question, or a vulnerable admission, or an empathetic word can completely change a dialogue. A silent laugh, a barely audible sigh, a friendly smile during a tense moment: Some people have learned to spot these opportunities to understand what others really want. They have learned how to hear what's unsaid and speak so others want to listen. . . . Because the right conversation, at the right moment, can change everything.

—CHARLES DUHIGG, *Supercommunicators: How to Unlock the Secret Language of Connection*

We'll come back to some of the specific tips for really connecting with others. But first, one other question.

Who gets to speak?

When Kansas City Chiefs kicker Harrison Butker rose to address the graduates of Benedictine College, he spoke directly and passionately about his Catholic faith and about the role that it played in his life. Saying that the "Church of Nice" won't work in today's world, he criticized priests, saying they are not the leaders they

Harrison Butker speaking at Benedictine College.

should be, condemned President Biden for "pretending that you can be Catholic and pro-choice," admonished the women graduates to realize that being a homemaker is their highest calling, and railed against "abortion, IVF, surrogacy," and "dangerous gender ideologies." Butker received a standing ovation along with a few boos—and then, predictably, culture warriors on all sides went at him, and at each other.

But not everyone. Some, including Butker's teammates Travis Kelce and Patrick Mahomes, resisted any knee-jerk taking of sides. Instead, both men defended Butker's right to speak his mind. Kelce said that while he didn't agree with most of what Butker said "or just about any of it," he "cherishes" him as a teammate. Quarterback Patrick Mahomes said that he too valued Butker as a "good person," though he did not necessarily agree with his commencement comments. And here's how Andy Reid, their coach, responded to questions at a press conference: "He's got his opinions and we all respect that. Just like some of you have opinions that I don't like."

Mahomes and others who spoke warmly of Butker as a teammate and person chose not to "cancel" him just because they don't agree with some of his views: they recognize his right to speak. But does everyone "get" to speak? It is important to note that some voices speak louder than others, and that some are not heard at all.

Who doesn't get to speak?

In the United States, women were once discouraged from speaking in public. Maria W. Stewart became one of the first women of any race (she was African American) to speak in public in 1832 when she delivered an address advocating for education for African American women. Although Stewart's speech attracted some followers, it also drew a lot of predictably hostile response.

Even in colleges and universities in the nineteenth century, women were expected to keep quiet. At Oberlin College, where the top student traditionally gave an address during commencement, all went well—until the top student happened to be a woman. So overwhelmed was the college at the thought of a woman rising to deliver the address that it simply abandoned the tradition entirely!

We could go on. And on. Enslaved persons were not to be taught to read or write—and they

Maria W. Stewart

were expected for the most part to remain silent. And think of religious groups that have been silenced or are being silenced right now. Think of other groups—incarcerated people, for example—who often have very few ways of getting their voices heard. What other people or groups can you think of that are either overtly or subtly ignored or silenced? Has someone who was invited to speak on your campus been shouted down or kept from speaking because the message was unacceptable to protesters? On your own campus, is the speech of some groups protected—and others not so much? Think about it. Hard.

REFLECT! Take some time to talk with elderly women in your family or community, and ask them about their experiences of being kept silent or not listened to. Ask your mother or aunts about their experiences and what they remember about their opportunities to speak in public, and to be listened to. Then think about your own experiences: Have there been times when you felt you were not given a chance to speak, or were not listened to when you did try to speak? How did you react to that experience, and what do you think of it now?

Getting—and giving—permission to speak

Samara Bay, a speech coach and workshop leader, has thought a lot about who gets to speak, and why—or why not. Out of her experience and research came her book *Permission to Speak: How to Change What Power Sounds Like, Starting with You.* When she was a graduate student in an acting program, she lost her voice—not good for someone trying to be an actor. It turns out that she had developed nodules on her vocal cords caused by her attempt to speak in a lower register than was natural for her, attempting to sound pleasing to others. The road to recovery, to claiming her voice and giving herself "permission to speak," led Bay to work with other women who felt they had no such permission, and eventually with business and political leaders as well as actors, all in an attempt to support "a new, diverse sound of power." Power, she argues, does not have to sound "white" or "masculine" or "sophisticated" or any of the other "attributes" long associated with powerful speech. She challenges all of us to find our own true voices, to insist on our own permission to speak—and in turn to give that permission to others.

This woman looks like she too is tired of being interrupted.

Conversation as a process

Conversation means talking *with* someone, not talking *at* them. It is an occasion for both speaking and listening. The best conversations may be heading somewhere specific, but they build as they go: rather than aiming for one "right" answer, you'll be working with others to explore or understand or decide something important. In short, the *process* of speaking and listening is as important as the destination (maybe even more so). Here are some guidelines for participating in conversations, whether in person or online.

- *Think* before you speak (or post).
- *Everyone* needs to have a chance to speak—and to be heard. Don't interrupt!
- *Listen* with genuine interest and an open mind—and with the goal of understanding. Try to see things from the other person's perspective.
- *If you're not sure you understand* what someone says, try summarizing it in your own words and then asking if you got it right. ("So you're saying X? Do I have that right?")
- *If you disagree,* do so respectfully. ("I understand where you're coming from, but what about X?")
- *Respond* with curiosity rather than judgment. ("That's a good point; tell me more"; "Maybe so, but have you considered X?")

- **Ask questions** that are open-ended, and that invite others to say what they think. ("What do you think we should do?" rather than "Don't you think we should do this?")
- **Pay attention to body language and tone of voice**—yours and theirs. Compliment others when it's appropriate, and to demonstrate empathy.

Hard conversations

Now is the time to have the difficult conversations we've been avoiding . . . to listen for the sake of learning, instead of waiting for our turn to speak.

SHANNON MULLEN

It's no secret that we live in a deeply divided world, one where we struggle to communicate with people whose ideas differ from ours. That makes for some hard conversations, especially ones about issues that are controversial and fraught with emotion—reproductive rights, gun ownership, immigration policies, race relations, and more.

Conservative columnist David Brooks says it's taken him years to listen with genuine curiosity to people he doesn't agree with. Research for his book *How to Get to Know a Person: The Art of Seeing Others Deeply and Being Deeply Seen* led him to identify two layers in any conversation. The first layer is the subject, what we are literally talking about. The second layer, he says, is the "ebb and flow of underlying emotions that get transmitted as we talk." This second layer is important: Is it making the speakers feel safe, or less so? Listened to and respected, or not?

Contentious conversations often have more to do with that emotional dimension than with the topic. Paying attention to the emotional dimensions led Brooks to ask different questions: not "What do you think about X?" but "What led you to think that?" And to keep opening doors by saying "Tell me more. What am I missing? Tell me more."

Rarely if ever are conversations easy between people whose views differ. Here's a lesson from Lee C. Camp, Christian commentator and host of the *No Small Endeavor* podcast. Saying he has been trying to teach himself as he encounters people with views that differ radically from his own, Camp reflects on growing up in a Southern "culture of politeness." He was used to avoiding conflict while bottling up his anger, which left him frustrated and feeling he wasn't being true to himself. So he worked hard to learn how to be straightforward and honest about his convictions—but with charity, kindness, and curiosity. In short, he says, he learned how to "be forthright without being an ass about it." Enough said!

Fostering conversations on campus

Conversations take place all across campus, in dorms, in lecture halls, in dining halls, on the quad or other places where students gather. At Ohio State, the Oval is one place where such conversations take place, from the solitary religious recruiter who sets up a table every spring and engages small groups of students in conversations sometimes aimed at converting them to his beliefs, to large political protests aimed at changing university policies. Think for a moment about where such gatherings take place on your campus and what kinds of conversations (or protests) have taken place there recently. Which ones, if any, have you participated in, and why?

The 2024 campus protests over the war in Gaza led in some cases to violence and to leaving many students on all sides of the conflict feeling harassed, threatened, and fearful. Part of the chaos seemed to be due to campus policies on freedom of speech, which were often vague or even contradictory. This situation led many to agree with Alex Morley, a First Amendment lawyer who argued that speech on all sides of this or any issue is protected unless there is "a serious intent to commit unlawful violence." Rather than taking sides, then, protecting the speech of some while not protecting that of others, Morley believes that colleges and universities should focus on keeping all students safe—and on helping to foster open and honest dialogue.

> Protest should not be seen as synonymous with violence, but with dialogue.
> LEENA HOFFMAN

That is precisely what some students at the University of Texas at Austin wanted—a safe space for students of different backgrounds and beliefs to come together and "simply talk, to understand." Arguing that students should step up, since "the adults have kind of effed up the situation," Elijah Kahlenberg founded Atidna

From left,
Elijah Kahlenberg
and Jadd Hashem.

(the name is a combination of "future" in Hebrew and the suffix "our" in Arabic), an organization that aims to find connections and develop understanding between Jewish and Arab students. Soon Kahlenberg, who is Jewish, was joined by Palestinian sophomore Jadd Hashem, and together they began to organize open, honest, and respectful conversations.

The only rules are to discuss their viewpoints civilly and to remain open to hearing the views of others. "Through these conversations," Kahlenberg says, "we begin to understand the 'other.'" Not that such conversations are easy: after the October 7 attacks, some left the organization in anger and despair. But the group held on, in spite of the many obstacles they faced. And as this book goes to press, Hashem and Kahlenberg are meeting with students at fifteen other colleges and have so far established six additional Atidna chapters at universities across the country aimed at achieving understanding and, eventually—dare they hope—peace.

Here are some guidelines for navigating hard conversations—ones about controversial issues, and with people whose ideas strongly differ from yours:

Be a serious listener. Listen with the goal of understanding what others say. And show that you're listening, that you have heard them, and that you want to see things from their perspective. The best way to do so is by summarizing in your own words what you think they said, and then asking, "Did I get that right?"

Even if you disagree with what someone says, keep an open mind and remember that they just might be right. Say what you think clearly and respectfully, but don't vilify someone you deeply disagree with. And no matter how strongly you disagree, remember that shouting them down gets no one anywhere!

Look for common ground, anything, even something very small, you can agree on. Asking questions and trying to see things from their perspective can help you discover common ground. You may be surprised by the common beliefs, hopes, and fears that you share with someone whose background and perspective differ from yours. Be willing to compromise, and even to change your mind.

Demonstrate respect Even if you don't agree with what someone says, show that you are interested in their opinions, and that you respect their right to be heard. And if you say something that you regret, apologize! We all make mistakes.

Conversations about controversial issues can be especially problematical online. During the war in Gaza, a student at Boston University posted an essay in its newspaper arguing that in order to move beyond the vitriolic and even violent instances of antisemitism and Islamophobia and other kinds of hate speech then rampant on campus, students needed to "take the conversation offline" and strive for "in-depth, informed, and empathetic interactions beyond the screen."

> While online discussions have their merits, nothing replaces the value of face-to-face interactions, as difficult as those interactions might be. Campuses should be epicenters of these genuine conversations. . . . To genuinely understand and address sensitive topics

> Listening means letting someone else tell their story and then, even if you disagree with them, trying to understand why they feel that way.
> BRITTANY WALKER PETTIGREW

like the Israel-Hamas war, we must strive for in-depth, informed, and empathetic interactions beyond the screen. After all, conversations flow better if you have more than 280 characters to speak.

—HAILEY MOON, "When It Comes to Talking about Israel and Hamas, We Need to Take the Conversation Offline"

Moon acknowledges that such conversations will be hard, and that they will not always succeed. But in-person conversations are more likely to succeed than vicious online exchanges, where accountability is usually lacking. And if such conversations are conducted honestly and respectfully, they can lead to some real learning. You may not end up changing your mind (or anyone else's), but you will almost certainly have thought more deeply about the subject and about just how you came to take a stand on it, and why.

REFLECT! Take a few minutes to make a list of conversations you have had in the last week. Cast a wide net, thinking of talks you have had online and off, in class and out, with friends and family as well as people you don't agree with. Choose the conversation that seems most important and impactful to you and then, after glancing back through this chapter, describe the conversation, recalling the substance of what was said as well as what **David Brooks** calls the "ebb and flow" of emotions going back and forth during the conversation. Finally, make some notes to yourself about how the conversation might have been improved, or changed in some way.

THE NEED FOR COLLABORATION

As the examples above suggest, the kinds of conversations this chapter describes are deeply collaborative. They also exemplify one of the great benefits of collaboration: working with people who have different backgrounds, interests, skills, and ideas inevitably helps us to think in new, more creative and expansive ways. And research shows that such collaborations lead to better results, partly because the group has considered alternative positions and viewpoints and worked through knotty issues together in pursuit of a common goal.

Such collaborations are at the heart of most of the work that gets done in the world today. Think about how many people need to work well together to produce a film, a video game, or a podcast.

And collaboration is a guiding principle in business, as headlines like "Collaboration Gets You More in 2024" or "Shift from Competition to Collaboration!" proliferate online. Beyond the worlds of entertainment and business, some historians argue that the crucial problems facing the world today—climate change, immigration, ongoing wars, human rights—are so complex that they can only be addressed successfully through collaboration—and the conversations that inevitably enable it.

And how about you? Try tracking the kinds of collaborations you are routinely involved in, from playing a group sport or a video game, to developing a group project for an engineering class, meeting with a writing center tutor, contributing to a shared *Google* doc, joining in a rally asking for a reduction in tuition fees, or creating a cooking podcast to interview friends about their favorite foods. All collaborations that call for cooperative, exploratory conversation.

> For excellence, the presence of others is always required.
>
> HANNAH ARENDT

Kinds of collaboration

As the examples above suggest, not all collaborations are alike, though all feature a group, from a twosome like Elijah Kahlenberg and Jadd Hashem of Atidna to a multinational group of 1,200 scientists; and all aim at achieving a shared goal.

In a study on collaboration among people in seven different professional organizations in the United States, Lisa Ede and I found that a very large percentage of the writing done in these groups was collaborative and that two kinds of collaboration predominated.

The kind of collaboration most often practiced we called *hierarchical*, in that the collaborative group had a leader who organized the project along with others, each of whom took on specific tasks. You probably have done group projects in one of your classes that followed this model: one person took responsibility for gathering the group and managing logistics, and you then divided up the work so that everyone contributed to the final project. This kind of collaboration can be very efficient and is especially useful when deadlines loom.

A second kind of collaboration we saw at work we called *dialogic*: in this model, leadership is shared throughout the group, and the members, together, make decisions about how most effectively to get the work done. Actor Richard Thomas links this kind of collaboration to an open and fruitful discussion when he says "If people work together in an open way with porous boundaries . . . and listen to each other and really talk to each other, then they are bound to trade ideas and be influenced by each other. That open system of working creates collaboration." As you can imagine, dialogic collaboration, while open, transparent, and democratic, can be time consuming and even messy. Yet, as our research showed, it often yields surprising and outside-the-box insights.

Nobel Prize–winning psychologist and economist Daniel Kahneman identified a third kind of collaboration, one that he practiced throughout his long career. Kahneman was known for enthusiastically collaborating with his intellectual opponents, a model he called *adversarial collaboration*. In this form, rather than fighting it out, people who disagree come together to pursue a common goal, in spite of their disagreements: they want to find the truth.

Here's an example: Professor Kahneman and colleague Angus Deaton published a study showing that people who have higher incomes are generally happier, up to the point of about $100,000. Some years later, another researcher, Matthew Killingsworth, found the opposite, that people making more money were happier . . . period. Kahneman and Deaton could have attacked Killingsworth and his study, arguing that their results were better and more accurate. But that would be participating in what Kahneman calls "angry science," a "nasty world of critiques, replies, and rejoinders" that attempts to destroy the position. (Does this kind of argument sound familiar today?)

Kahneman rejected angry science and instead invited Killingsworth to collaborate. Together they looked closely at the data in both studies and eventually found Killingsworth had accidently missed a data point that explained the discrepancy. Together, through a series of long conversations, they made the correction. That's adversarial collaboration—and conversation—at work.

Of course, adversarial collaboration can work only if all parties agree to it and to pursuing a common goal. Still, it seems like a much more useful way to make progress than the accusatory, angry shouting matches that groups so often engage in.

Some tips for collaborating productively

Chances are, you will have the opportunity to practice all these kinds of collaboration during your college years, and in your work life, on projects that range from a short-term, low-stakes assignment to write a collaborative response to a campus lecture, to a four-week group project that will count for a third of your grade, to a project a group you belong to initiates to raise money for a campus food pantry. While we can't offer advice on how to approach every collaboration you will encounter, we can offer some tips that should help you make your collaborative work effective, equitable, and productive.

- *Set out guidelines everyone in the group agrees to follow.* The group will work much more smoothly if all members agree on logistics: when, where, and how often to meet; how tasks will get assigned or chosen; what timeline the group needs to follow, and so on. It's worth taking time in your first meeting to work these guidelines up and to talk about how each person is going to contribute.

- *Agree on overall goals and a work plan to achieve them.*
  Here's another task for your first meeting: articulating your goals, from satisfying an assignment to appealing to your audience and sketching out a plan of work. These can be revised if necessary as your work continues.

- *Aim for inclusivity and openness—and listen, listen, listen.*
  Make sure that every group member has a chance to speak and contribute. Effective collaborators "take the pulse" of every member periodically, asking if they feel they are being listened to and heard.

- *Develop a group "persona."* If at all possible, allow some time to get to know one another, sharing stories about yourselves and information about what's important to you and what you hope to get out of this experience. Share cookies or other snacks as well! And whenever possible, allow for some brainstorming that can lead to ideas and build trust. (Some groups give themselves nicknames as a way of building a common bond: "the VCC groupies," "the rhetorical questioners," and so on.)

- *Work out a problem-solving process—and use it!*
  If and when disagreements arise, make sure everyone gets a say and is listened to with respect. Use questions rather than commands ("What would happen if we did X?" rather than "Ditch this; it's not working.") and don't forget that a little humor can help defuse tense situations.

- *Build in plans for contingencies and surprises.*
  Remember the old saying, "Anything that can go wrong will go wrong." Build in a little extra time here and there to help out when something "goes wrong." Also make an effort to foresee problems that might occur (a person you want to interview turns you down, a source you need is not available), and have fallback options ready to go.

- *Schedule at least a couple of debriefings* where you talk about the progress you are making (or not), the fairness of workloads, and any problems you are facing, along with plans to address them.
- *When the project is complete,* take a bow, and then take time to celebrate—together!

REFLECT! Take some time to think about a collaborative effort you have been involved in—for one of your classes, perhaps, or with a campus group you belong to. Make some notes about what you can recall: Did your collaboration fit one of the three models described above? Who took the lead, and why? How were tasks assigned and carried out? What problems did you encounter, and how did you try to solve them? Were there any personality conflicts, and if so, how were they resolved? What did you like best (and least) about the experience? What was the goal of the collaboration, and was it achieved? Then write a memo to yourself explaining how you would change the way you work on future collaborative projects.

Let's Chat: Using AI Carefully & Ethically

Just as calculators did not replace
the need for learning math,
AI will not replace the need for learning
to write and think critically.

—ETHAN MOLLICK

I magine you were able to compose a sonata and write rap lyrics. Win at *Jeopardy* and defeat world-class chess players. Score in the 98th percentile of both the ACT and TOEFL exams, and pass the qualifying exam to become a neurosurgeon. Predict hurricanes. Paint a realistic picture of something you've never even seen. Score more three-pointers than Steph Curry.

Except for beating Steph, AI can do all of those things—and can help you do them too. Many say that's a good thing: pick up almost any account of AI and you will see commentators raving about the ways in which it can be incredibly helpful to us humans. But others warn of potential dangers if it is left unregulated.

Some instructors are among those sounding an alarm, warning that having AI help with your writing is no way to learn how to write well yourself. Ethan Mollick, an AI expert and professor at Wharton, the business school of the University of Pennsylvania, believes otherwise: that AI will in no way eliminate the need to learn to write.

As with other new technologies, time will tell. But AI is here now, and it's not likely going away. This chapter provides an overview of some ways you might use it. We say "might" because you will need to find out what *your* instructor's policy is about using AI for help with class assignments. If you're permitted to do so, this chapter is here to help you get started.

So what exactly is AI—and what is a chatbot?

AI is short for artificial intelligence, software that is programmed to seem as though it can think, learn, and make decisions like humans. That's what makes it intelligent. Siri and Alexa, *Google* search, and the recommendations you get from *Netflix* all use AI to make predictions, answer questions, and give recommendations: Chinese restaurants near you, winners of the Nobel Peace Prize, movies you might like. GENERATIVE AI has the ability to do all that, and also to understand and generate language, images, code, and more.

Chat is a kind of talk, and a bot is a software application programmed to perform certain tasks. CHATBOTS are designed to respond to requests from humans—us!—for information or help of various kinds. A key word here is "chat," because that's what drives the bot, what gets us whatever help we need. And *we* are the ones who initiate the chat, by writing prompts, questions that ask for and specify exactly what we need. In other words, it's up to us—humans—to tell the chatbot what to do.

And now there's *ChatGPT, Copilot,* and other similar chatbots trained on massive amounts of data (whole websites, *Wikipedia,* books, articles, software, and more) that can follow instructions in a prompt and generate detailed responses. These chatbots are a new kind of communication, and a new way of getting information.

If only they came with a user's manual, or even an index. Alas, they do not. So when Professor Mollick says that he can find better instruction on how to use his garden hose than he can for "the immensely powerful AI tools being released by the world's largest companies," he's not kidding. That means we need to figure out ourselves how to tell a chatbot what we need—and how to use AI tools carefully and ethically. So let's chat!

What kinds of help can AI provide?

AI can do a lot. But let's focus here on how it can help you with the kinds of writing and research you're expected to do in college. Still a lot! It can explain complex concepts. Explore ideas. Find facts. Provide examples. Summarize and paraphrase. Analyze. Synthesize. Answer questions of all kinds. And more. Here are some things that you might find most useful.

Brainstorming. AI can be especially helpful as a brainstorming tool, especially when you're first getting started. Ask what's been said or written about your topic, who is talking or writing about it. What are some of the angles you might consider?

Research. *ChatGPT* has been trained on *Wikipedia,* so it can give an overview on your topic: who you should research, the various perspectives and schools of thought, key words to research. It might help you narrow a research question. Some AI platforms might suggest kinds of sources while others may provide specific forces. In either case, you'll want to find and verify any sources AI suggests.

Finding evidence. When you're looking for help supporting or expanding on a point, AI can help. Whether you're looking for a definition or an analogy, facts and statistics or expert testimony, examples or comparisons, see what it suggests. One thing it cannot do, however, is to provide any evidence from your own personal experience—in your own voice.

Anticipating counterarguments. Whatever your position, there are bound to be others as well, which AI can help identify.

Getting response. If your instructor permits it, AI can even serve as a kind of peer reviewer, responding to your drafts. You'll want to give it some guidance about what to look for, perhaps by uploading a rubric with information about your rhetorical situation: your genre, purpose, audience, and any requirements. If you're writing in one of the genres taught in this book, you could try using the guidelines for getting response and revising in that chapter.

Editing and proofreading. AI can also help you edit, but again you'll need to tell it what kinds of help you're looking for: Does each paragraph contribute to your point? Do you need to add transitions? Are there any unnecessary words? Again, you could use the guidelines for editing on pages 120–22 and for proofreading on page 123.

Formatting. This is something where AI shines. Is there something in your text that would be best presented as a bulleted or numbered list? or in a pie chart or a line graph? AI can help! But again, you need to do some work first, to think about whether there's anything you want to highlight in a certain way and then to tell the AI what you'd like it to try.

Those are all things that generative AI can help you with. But while it also has the ability to write, there's a reason it is not included in the above list. For it's one thing to get AI to *help* you as you write, but another thing entirely for AI to do your writing for you. *ChatGPT* is a tool that can help—but the thinking, the ideas, and the words on the page or screen need to be yours.

Is there anything AI does not do well?

Yes! No one's perfect and AI is no exception. Here are some of the problems you'll need to look out for:

- *Bias.* AI learns from human data, the good and the bad— and this data reflects the biases and stereotypes that exist in our world.

- *Accuracy.* AI always has an answer, but what it says is not always accurate. That's called *hallucinating* in AI-speak, but whatever it's called, it's a problem.

- **It can't sound like you.**

How can you use AI carefully and ethically?

If you can't completely trust what AI says, then you need to check everything and verify it's accurate before it informs what you say—and to be sure to document anything you cite that comes from AI.

Check for bias and stereotyping. Because AI is trained on real-world data, it reflects the biases of the real world. This is compounded by the fact that many of the chatbots based on AI are fine-tuned at firms that tend to be dominated by male computer scientists. Consider a 2023 study by Leonardo Nicoletti and Dina Bass, "Human Beings Are Biased, Generative AI Is Even Worse," which showed that when one text-to-image AI was asked to show an image of a judge, it generated a picture of a man 97 percent of the time, even though 34 percent of US judges are women.

And when we asked *ChatGPT* to name ten important poets from the eighteenth century, it pulled up a list of nine from the United Kingdom and one, Phillis Wheatley, from the United States. No poets of note anywhere else in the world? Hmmmm. Turns out we would need to keep prompting to get AI to look beyond the UK and North America.

AI companies are working to address this kind of bias, with some success—but still you need to be on the lookout for bias and stereotyping in anything you get from AI. And if you find it, stop and think about what might have led to it—and trust your common sense. If it looks suspicious, it may well be. And if so, be careful not to include it in anything you write or say.

Do your own writing—and remember that you are responsible for what you write. AI is only a tool—one that can help you, not do your writing for you. Do not ask AI to write a thesis statement, or an introduction to an essay, or something else you may need help with. Above all, don't assume that AI is going to write better than you do. It will almost always write "correctly," but it cannot produce writing in your own voice or with your personality.

If you use AI, acknowledge doing so. Most important, you need to be transparent about using AI: submitting AI-generated work as if it is your own is plagiarism. Be sure to take careful notes so that you can explain, clearly and explicitly, how you've used AI and why. Check with your instructor to see if there's a specific way you need to acknowledge use of AI in your written work.

And if you quote, paraphrase, or summarize something from AI in your writing, you need to provide documentation. You'll find documentation guidelines on pages 417 (**MLA**) and 458 (**APA**).

ChatGPT can make mistakes. Consider checking important information.
ChatGPT

Check for accuracy. *ChatGPT* and other AI tools may be able to pass the bar exam with ease, but they still generate false information. As Oren Etzioni, the founding CEO of the Allen Institute for Artificial Intelligence, puts it, "It's going to be a long time before you want any GPT to run your nuclear power plant." You may not be running a nuclear power plant, but you're responsible for what you write and for making sure that any facts you cite are correct. You cannot assume that anything AI says is correct; and so you'll need to check everything it says to be sure it's true.

It might help to know what causes this problem. The AI that chatbots use is trained to predict the most likely next words in a text—so while it may be "intelligent," it doesn't actually know what it is saying, and it bases its answers on the probability of certain words following other words. And if it doesn't have enough information to answer a question, it will likely answer it anyway, almost always in a way that sounds plausible. That's why you need to **FACT-CHECK** everything AI says and verify it's correct before it informs what you say. **READING LATERALLY** will help, but keep in mind that you can only check the content of what it says, since there is no

See Chs. 7 and 17 for tips on checking facts and reading laterally.

author and no source to check. The way to check is to verify that sources that have been created by humans make similar claims. Remember, however, that wherever you get your information, *you* are responsible for anything that you say or write.

Distrust and verify.
SIMON WILLISON

How to chat with a bot

Experts tell us that the more we work and experiment with AI, the better we will get at using it—and the more helpful it will be. Some even say we should just ask for what we need and see where it takes us. In any case, you should assume that you'll need to do more than ask a question and get an answer—that it will likely take some back and forth for you to get the information you need. That's why it's called a chat. But you have to start somewhere, so here's some information that will help the AI give you the assistance you want:

- *Role.* Tell the AI what role you want it to play—a first-year college student, for example, or a college writing instructor, and so on.

- *Task.* Tell the AI what you want it to do (explain quantum mechanics? define artificial intelligence? compare two poems?).

- *Purpose.* Make sure to say what *you* need to do (get started on some research? narrow a topic? find multiple perspectives on an issue?).

- *Audience.* Tell the AI who your audience is (first-year college students? followers on *TikTok*? ninth graders?). It can also help to specify the appropriate amount of detail (a brief paragraph? a list of three main points?) or kind of language (avoid jargon? in conversational language? so that a first-year college student will understand the response?).

- *Any requirements.* Be sure to specify what needs to be included (examples? references to a particular source? a list of key points?) and what else you want or need.

- ***Clear instructions***. Sometimes giving step-by-step instructions will help get you exactly the information that you need, for example: *first*, read and summarize this article; *next*, identify its main points in a list; *then*, suggest key words to use in researching the topic. You can also ask the AI to "explain its answer step by step," telling it both what you want and asking it to show the steps it used to get to that answer.

- ***Format.*** You can ask the AI to respond in a specific format (in a brief paragraph? as a bulleted list? in a pie chart?).

You won't likely want to include all of this information in a single prompt, but chances are that you'll use most of it along the way. Remember that when you ask a question of AI, you are starting a conversation, and that it will almost certainly take several prompts to get you what you need. Be patient!

And keep in mind that *you* are the one driving the bus. AI can get you the help you need, but you need to tell it where to go and what to do. In short, AI depends on human help—and that's you. Turn to pages 576–77 to see an example chat with *ChatGPT* looking for help at the start of a research project.

As you will see, the more you chat with AI, the better you'll understand what it can and cannot do to help you.

Have some fun with AI!

When *ChatGPT* first burst onto the scene in late 2022, a couple of students on one college campus challenged each other to come up with the worst fake love poem imaginable, using AI. The challenge soon spread across campus, with some pretty hilarious results. So that's one more thing you can do with AI: use it to have a little fun! A friend and I decided to play around with it too, so we asked our buddy *ChatGPT* to write an advertising blurb about this chapter, in two sentences, for an audience of college writing teachers, and to make it "kind of fun." See what we got on the facing page.

> Embark on an exhilarating journey into the realm of artificial intelligence with this dynamic chapter, where students can uncover the secrets to harnessing AI's power responsibly and ingeniously in their academic pursuits. Bursting with practical insights, ethical musings, and engaging reflections, this chapter serves as a compass, guiding students through the thrilling landscape of AI integration with flair and finesse.

When we could stop chuckling at AI's over-the-top language and its idea of "fun," we asked it to revise the blurb for a different audience: members of a college fraternity.

> Get ready to dive deep into this epic chapter, packed with all the juicy deets on how to rock your academic game with artificial intelligence! From slick tips on chatting with bots to deep thoughts on keeping it ethical, this chapter's got your back as you navigate the wild world of AI in college. So grab your buddies, crack open this chapter, and get ready to slay those research papers like a boss!

Really? What member of a fraternity do you know who sounds like this? See any stereotypes at work here? Finally, we asked it to revise for a different medium: as a slogan for a t-shirt.

> AI: Your College Game Changer. Chat, Learn, Slay!

Not bad! Do you think *ChatGPT* had the 2010 hit movie *Eat Pray Love* in its database? Can you think of a better slogan?

REFLECT! If you've used AI, what tasks has it helped you with, and how helpful has it been? What's been the most helpful information or advice it's provided? Has any of it been confusing, or not useful? How have you found the process of working with AI—easy? fun? challenging? something else? Has any information it provided been inaccurate—and if so, how did you determine that? How much time have you spent fact-checking information from AI? What is your overall impression of working with AI? Have you found it helpful overall, and do you want to use it again? If not, why not?

A SAMPLE CHAT

Prompt specifies role, purpose, and topic.

You

You're an English teacher. Please help me get started on a research project about pop culture. Define pop culture in a paragraph.

AI's response is totally abstract.

ChatGPT

Pop culture refers to the ideas, perspectives, images, and phenomena within mainstream society. It encompasses various aspects of everyday life, including music, fashion, film, tv, slang, and consumer goods. . . .

Prompt asks for a definition for a younger audience.

You

Please revise this definition so a 14-year-old understands it.

ChatGPT

Pop culture is basically all the stuff that's super popular and trendy in our everyday lives, like the music we listen to, the movies and TV shows we watch, the clothes we wear, the latest apps and gadgets we use, and even the slang we use. It's always changing because it's influenced by what's happening, what's cool, and what people are into. It's like a snapshot of what we're all about as a culture.

AI's response is more concrete—gives a better sense of pop culture.

You

Thank you! Now provide specific examples of pop culture that show what's "going on" in US society now.

Prompt asks for examples.

ChatGPT

Certainly! Here are 4 pop culture trends in the United States:

1. **Streaming:** Netflix, Hulu, and Disney+ have transformed how we consume entertainment. . . .

AI gives examples; need to check other sources to see if these represent what's "going on" in the US.

2. **Social Media:** Influencers on Instagram, TikTok, and YouTube have immense sway over consumer behavior and trends. . . .

3. **Music:** TikTok is now a major influencer in the music industry. . . .

4. **Fashion:** Brands like Supreme, Off-White, and Yeezy dominate fashion trends. . . .

You

Now please focus on one TV show: Abbott Elementary. Please summarize it in a brief paragraph.

Prompt narrows focus of topic.

ChatGPT

"Abbott Elementary" is a comedy TV series set in a struggling Philadelphia public school, following a group of dedicated teachers as they navigate the challenges of education with humor and heart. With a diverse cast of characters and witty writing, "Abbott Elementary" offers both laughs and poignant moments as it tackles issues of race, class, and the pursuit of excellence in education.

AI responds with a credible paragraph about the topic.

You

Please write 3 questions to help me think about how this show addresses issues in US society now.

Prompt asks for questions for brainstorming.

ChatGPT

Certainly! Here are 3 questions:

1. How does "Abbott Elementary" portray the challenges facing public education?

2. In what ways does the show incorporate current cultural trends into its storytelling and character development?

3. How do the reactions among critics reflect societal attitudes and concerns about public education?

AI provides questions that suggest 3 approaches our research might take.

You

Thank you! You've helped me find some angles to research. What's your name, by the way?

ChatGPT

You're welcome! You can call me ChatGPT! Good luck with your research project!

31 Presentations & Podcasts

Before the rise of print texts, the spoken word ruled: orators worked long and hard to make their words unforgettable and their voices audible, even to very large crowds—and with no amplification. Then came the rise of writing, and of print texts, which, ironically, seemed to drown out speech: we began to say we wanted to "see it in writing" before accepting a message; written documentation became paramount in legal proceedings; and writing was considered more authoritative than "just talk."

Today, however, the spoken word is again of major importance in delivering information: from town halls devoted to speeches and discussion, to public lectures, to rap and spoken-word poetry, to TED Talks, to televised newscasts, to countless podcasts, live human voices speak to us around the clock.

Writing and speaking are both major ways to communicate, to deliver messages, and they are similar in some ways: both use language, both convey information, both address audiences. But there are significant differences too. In general, written texts are more precise, stable, and permanent than spoken texts; they are also often more formal. In addition, readers can exert some control over how they engage with written texts, re-reading, for instance, or going at a slower or faster pace.

Spoken texts are considerably more dynamic, allowing for more immediacy and more interaction; they are often able to engage audiences more personally and quickly. Moreover, speakers can make use of many kinds of nonverbal communication: tone of voice and volume, pacing and inflection, gestures, movement, and more. But unless what is spoken is also recorded, listeners can't go back and check on something they hear, or slow it down. As speakers, then, we need to pay very careful attention to our audiences, and be on the lookout for cues that will tell us whether the audience is following along (or not). In other words, we need to learn to "read" an audience if we can, to be aware of puzzled looks, nods, smiles, and eye contact. And if we can't actually see the audience, we need to anticipate their reactions as much as possible and try hard to connect to them.

> Designing a presentation without an audience in mind is like . . . addressing a love letter "to whom it may concern."
>
> KEN HAEMER

You will surely have opportunities to give oral presentations and work with other spoken texts during your college years. Outside of class, you might participate in spoken word events, or take part in a Poetry Out Loud program. Almost certainly, you will make oral presentations in some of your classes or for groups you belong to, and you may well have a chance to create or participate in a podcast. In any case, you will want to make your words count. And while it's impossible to provide detailed guidelines in this small book, this chapter offers some tips that can help.

Oral presentations

Many oral presentations follow one common structure, beginning by describing "what is" and then suggesting "what could (or should) be." Then in the middle of the speech, the presenter moves back and forth between discussing that status quo and contrasting that with what it could or should be. The conclusion evokes what could be and calls for some kind of action. In fact, this is a classic storytelling technique, setting up a conflict that needs to be resolved. And presenting your main point as a story works well in a spoken presentation because stories are easy to follow and to remember. As you'll see, this is the way Trey Connelly structured his presentation about modes of instruction in video games. You can see the script of his presentation on pages 584–89 and watch the video on letstalklibrary.com.

Podcasts

Podcasts are digital audio or video series that can be streamed over the internet. Some focus on the news, others tell stories, still others feature people in conversation or exploring a topic. You may be familiar with some of the most popular podcasts—*Radiolab, Joe Rogan, The Daily, Stuff You Should Know*—or some of the political ones—*Pod Save America, Everything's Going to Be All Right*. Some colleges now produce podcasts, from Longwood University's *Day after Graduation* to the Stanford engineering school's *The Future of Everything*. Podcasts are a good way to stay informed about what's going on in the world, and to learn about things you know little or nothing about.

And if you have a smartphone and a computer and a quiet place to record, you can create a podcast too. That's not to say it's simple, and it's beyond the scope of this little book to teach you how. But let's look at some basic features of podcasts. They usually have a host, who introduces the topic and might interview guests or lead the discussion. Some podcasts are scripted in advance, but some are organized more like a Q & A, with questions prepared in advance that guests answer. Any questions should be open-ended, eliciting more than a yes or no. Most podcasts strike an informal, conversational tone.

Most of all, the best podcasts are both informative and entertaining. The best podcasters know their subject thoroughly and are at ease talking about it. And the more articulate and relatable the guests, the better the podcast. In short, doing a podcast calls on you to come up with a topic that matters, to research your topic, to find knowledgeable, engaging guests—and to think hard about how you can make the discussion one that will interest *and engage* others. On pages 590–93, you'll find the transcript of a podcast produced at Ohio State, "On Being First-Gen Students." Note that in this podcast, after the host introduces himself and his two guests, he turns the microphone over to them and, instead of using a question-and-answer interview format, lets them tell their stories without interruption.

Some tips for developing a spoken text

- *Think about your* AUDIENCE. What will they expect to hear from you, and how can you engage their interest? What will they know about your topic and what will they need to know to follow your thoughts? Whenever possible, make eye contact with them—in person or on video by looking directly into the camera.

- *What's your* PURPOSE? Are you expected to provide some kind of information? to persuade? to entertain? something else?

- *What's the* CONTEXT? Will you be presenting in person? on *Zoom?* in an audio recording? Whatever it is, make sure you have the technology you'll need, and be sure to test it before it's showtime.

- *What* TONE *do you want to convey*—formal and serious? conversational and informal? humorous? something else?

- *Work hard on your* OPENING, and think about how you can get and keep your audience's attention. See Chapter 24 for ideas about how to begin a presentation.

- *Use vivid language,* but keep in mind Mark Twain's advice: "Don't use a five-dollar word when a fifty-cent word will do." And think about how you can use languages and dialects rhetorically, to connect with your audience and emphasize key points.

- *Add signpost language*, words (*first, next*) and phrases (*in addition, in the same way*) to help your audience follow you.

- *Narrative is a tried-and-true way to engage listeners.* A good ANECDOTE can support a point memorably—and presenting your main point as a narrative, perhaps starting with "what is" and moving on to "what could or should be," works well in a presentation because stories are easy for an audience to follow and remember.

- *Pay special attention to your* CONCLUSION. This is your chance to leave your audience thinking about what you've said, and why it matters. See Chapter 24 for ideas about how to conclude memorably.

- *Less is often more in a spoken text.* As has often been noted, one mistake inexperienced speakers make is trying to say too much. Keep it simple, and clear. Rely on relatively brief sentences whenever you can.

- *If you're preparing a presentation,* you'll need to draft a script, an outline, or note cards, all marked up for pauses and emphasis, **and think about how you can use gestures and your voice to create emphasis.** *If you're preparing a podcast*, you'll need to draft some questions if you're the host—or some answers if you're a guest.

- *Will you need to include visuals*—graphs or charts? maps? photos or videos? Make sure that any visual you include illustrates a point you're making, and that you tell your audience what they show. And design any slides carefully. Make sure that any fonts are large enough to be legible; use a light background if your text is dark, and a dark background if your text is light.

- **Think about accessibility.** Can you provide real-time captioning? audio description for any videos? alt text for any images? Do you need to arrange for an ASL interpreter?

- **Practice makes perfect.** Practice until you are completely comfortable with your message—and with how you'll be delivering it. Practice your delivery—your pacing, and where you'll need to pause—and think about whether you'll need a microphone.

REFLECT! If you have given a presentation or participated in a podcast recently, now might be a very good time to step back and reflect on how it went. Revisit any research you did; any outlines, notes, or scripts you prepared; and any audio or video recordings. Review them carefully, and write up a brief assessment of your presentations: in retrospect, how effective does it seem to you, and what makes it so? What is most memorable, and why? If you were going to revise the presentation, what advice would you give yourself?

An Oral Presentation

A Podcast

AN ORAL PRESENTATION

Sign and Design: Modes of Instruction in Digital Games

Trey Connelly gave this oral presentation for his sophomore writing class, one that focused on the theme of "How We Got Schooled: The Rhetoric of Literacy and Education." He was a computer science major and was especially interested in the study of gaming. In the following pages, you will see the script that Connelly worked from in making this presentation, along with eight of the 158 slides he prepared to accompany it.

Opening engages audience directly, including them with use of we.

Hi, I'm Trey Connelly, and I'm here to talk about games.

Games are fun! We all know that. But what's not fun is not knowing how to play.

Everyday language ("gonna be") sets informal tone.

Scrabble, baseball, karate, all of these activities can be very fun. But if you don't know how to play—if you don't know the rules—then you're just gonna be confused and frustrated, and not have a good time.

Now normally, though, this isn't much of a problem, because these are all social activities, so there's bound to be someone around who can show you the ropes.

Describes "what is"— the current state of gaming.

Except when we get to video games. Video games are unique in that they're primarily solo activities, so the job of teaching the player falls not on another person but rather on the game itself. Combine that with the fact that games, systems, and controls have gotten more, and more, and more, complicated over time, and you'll see that the job of the game designer is not an easy one.

Introduces his research project.

So my research project was about Sign and Design: Modes of Instruction in Digital Games, and what that can tell us about instruction in other contexts.

Simple, uncluttered
slide announces
the topic.

For this presentation, we'll be stepping into the role of the game designer in order to answer one question: How do you teach players how to play your game?

Now you might think, why not just tell them how to play? What else *would* you do? Well let's see how this works out with a case study, of *Final Fantasy X*, one of the most popular game franchises of all time. So it's gotta be good, right? And by the time you get to the tenth in the series, most fans are gonna buy it no matter what. But it introduces a few new mechanics, like this thing called a sphere grid.

Use of questions
helps keep audience's
attention.

So let's see how the game teaches players how to use the sphere grid system: First, you select "Sphere Grid" from the main menu. The cursor appears at the selected character's current position. Use the d-pad to move the cursor. So far so good. Information on the upgrades is displayed at the top of the screen... defense upgrades... learn an ability... nodes... press X... <yawn, click through slides>

Explains how "just
telling how to play"
currently works.

Slide shows how
one game explains
how it works.

How are you all doing? Oh! Hey, we're done. Did you get all that? Because the game isn't gonna tell you that information ever again. Not great.

Use of short direct sentences to show failure of explicit instruction.

So the problem with explicit instructions is that when someone who wants to play a game instead encounters a wall of text, they're not likely to pay attention. And even if they do, the chances they'd actually retain all that information by the time they get into the *game* part where it matters are essentially zero. <pause>

A note reminds the speaker to pause here.

And this has been verified by cognitive science. Learning theorist James Gee of Arizona State explains that "Human beings are quite poor at using verbal information when given lots of it out of context and before they can see how it applies in actual situations." If this sounds like too much verbal information out of context for you, let me restate that: When it comes to games, words are bad. Or better yet, <slide>

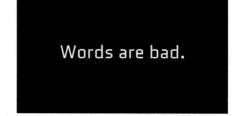

Slide underscores his main point with 3 words that will grab his audience's attention.

All that is to say, it seems like just telling players how to play is not the way to go.

Uses an analogy to make his point.

So what if we just . . . *don't* tell them how to play? I mean, think about it. There's tons of things we do all the time without being explicitly told how to do so. Think of a toaster, for example. Sure, it comes with an instruction manual, but has anyone ever read it? We can just figure it out.

Describes one alternative of what "could be."

So maybe that's what we should do with games too. One game that does this is *Dwarf Fortress*. It's a bit of a cult classic, but you may know it was the inspiration behind *Minecraft*. Here's a little taste of *my* first hour trying to figure out how to play *Dwarf Fortress*:

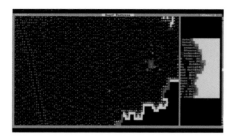

Points out that this alternative is no better than explicit instruction.

Um. Huh. Am I in a field? Is that blue thing a river? What do all these symbols mean? What should I do here? Maybe I'll just press these buttons? Oh no, am I in a cave? Is it night? I have no idea.

Yeah. In fact, *Dwarf Fortress* is so hard to understand that people have written entire books on how to *get started*, which brings us right back where we started with that same verbal information out of context that Professor Gee warned us against.

So going back to our main question, it seems like we can't just tell players how to play, but we can't *not* tell them either. But there's actually a third option. Think back to toasters. Yes, we can easily figure out how to use it—and that's no accident. It's by design. Here's what a toaster *really* looks like.

Returns to toaster analogy.

If this was your toaster, you might need an instruction manual to figure out what to do with it. But the toaster we see hides all the stuff that we don't need to see in order to understand, and leaves us with this sleek model with two visual elements: slots at the top that are just the size and shape of a slice of bread, and a lever on the side that almost screams "push me down."

Toaster analogy shows the importance of intentional design to instruction.

This use of intentional design to convey information without words is what game designers Anna Anthropy and Naomi Clark call a "communicative visual vocabulary." And it can be incredibly effective.

Proposes a better alternative to explicit instruction: implicit instruction.

In games as in toasters, Anthropy and Clark argue that we shouldn't tell the player explicitly how to play using words they won't read or remember, but nor should we abandon them to their own devices in a way that makes things incredibly hard to figure out. Instead, they say, the best way to teach a player *is* to tell them how to play, but do so *implicitly*, using visual vocabulary and intentional design that make it easy for them to figure out what to do.

Use of vivid description language evokes the experience of the game.

Points out intentional design—as easy as using a toaster!

To see what I'm talking about here, let's look at one more game: *The Witness*, my personal favorite. Here's the opening segment of the game. The player starts off in a long, dark hallway that's got a brightly lit door at the other end that clearly indicates that they should move forward to get to it. Once there, there's a door with an orange panel. And actually... it kind of looks familiar. If we just... and then . . . yeah! It looks a little like a toaster! It's got the same knob and track.

So let's see if this visual vocabulary matches what actually happens in the game: the player comes up to the door, grabs the knob, slides it across the track, lets go—and pop, the door opens!

Returns to what explicit verbal instruction would look like.

The designers of *The Witness* could have put a big block of instruction text next to the door saying, "When you approach an orange panel, click the circle and navigate your mouse to the end of the track."

Or they could have just thrown you right into one of the later puzzles like this one, and let you struggle to figure it out. But instead they went the way of the toaster, making it visually clear what to do without needing to be told. And the game is much better for it.

Transition signals that the presentation is coming to a close.

Now, as we wrap up here, you might be wondering, *Who cares? We're just talking about video games*. But really, we're talking about more than just games. The principles of instruction we've seen here are relevant in pretty much any instructional context.

Notes the implications of intentional design beyond video games.

No matter the situation, one of the best ways to teach someone is not just to tell them what to do or what to know, but rather to let them figure it out for themselves in an environment designed to make that easy.

Sums up his argument.

Hmm. Makes you wonder, then, why so much of the instruction we get in school is still so tied to textbooks. That's a question for another time, but for now I want to leave you thinking like a game designer. So today, try to notice something in your life that uses a visual vocabulary to tell you what to do without *telling* you what to do. Appreciate the toasters in your life. Thank you.

Poses a provocative question.

Closes by asking his audience to take action.

Works Cited

Go to letstalk library.com to watch a video of this presentation. Notice how he ad-libbed as he spoke, adapting on the spot to connect with his audience.

A PODCAST

On Being First-Gen Students

The podcast that follows was produced by Jack Long as part of his work with The Lantern, *Ohio State's student newspaper. The podcast here features two interviews with OSU students about their experiences as first-generation students. Jack Long graduated from Ohio State majoring in journalism and now works at* Fortune *magazine as a newsletter production editor.*

Host introduces himself, the topic of this podcast, and his 2 guests.

Jack Long: This week, you're going to hear a few stories from first-generation students. In fact, they're first-generation students who are in their first semester. I'm Jack Long, and you're listening to *The Third Chair*.

First guest gives background information.

Colin Flanagan: So I grew up in this suburb on the east side of Toledo called Oregon. Just, you know, a typical American residential suburb. Really not a whole lot to do unless you cross the river into the actual city of Toledo. We have this state park, Maumee Bay—it has a nice lodge if you're looking to stay there for, you know, a wedding or something, but other than that, you know, metro parks, but really you have to cross into Toledo. I'm Colin Flanagan, I'm a first-generation student at The Ohio State University studying political science, economics, and public policy.

Colloquial language ("yeah") reflects an informal tone.

Yeah, so my family.... I live in a typical 1950s American household. It's me, my mom, my dad, and my younger brother, who is currently a sophomore in high school where I went to school, named Chase. My dad is . . . he was an auto mechanic for 23 years and now he works for the city of Oregon as a street department employee, so he, you know, he'll crack seal or fix potholes in the roads, he'll plow snow or cut the grass in public areas. And right now my mom is a waitress.

My family raised me to go to college, so I would say, yeah, it was expected of me to go to college. I know that various extended family members from, say, more rural areas didn't really care if I went to college, and they warned me about the debt that I was going to endure and encouraged me to go to trade school, but I didn't think twice about going to college. I feel like college provides the most opportunity to me. I want to go into politics and hopefully attend law school before doing that and I really wasn't going to do that unless I went to college, so that's why I'm here now.

Host does not interrupt, giving the guest time and space to speak.

I come from a lower-middle-class family, maybe you could have guessed that from my parents' occupations. The government seems to think [*laughter*] that we can fork out a lot of money to pay for my education and, well, I'm not getting any of that. My expected family contribution is upward of $8,000, so I knew we really couldn't afford that. My parents' interaction with me was, I think, not all that common, although it could be. They told me from the get-go, even before senior year of high school started—start looking for scholarships, start looking for scholarships.

A touch of humor regarding college costs helps connect with his audience.

Being a first-generation student is just . . . a lot of the time, people are going to tell you that you don't know what to do . . . and you know, maybe you don't have a really good direction about where you're going. But I think that people who aren't first-generation students fall into this category of certainty when they go away to school, go away to college or university, that they know exactly what's going to happen. And I think in some ways first-generation students have an advantage because they don't fall into that track, they don't fall into that. I think you run the line of, you really get to find things out for yourself and learn on your own. You know, you don't learn things unless you do it on your own. Like when you're a little kid and they say—cliché example—when you're a little kid and they say don't touch the stove, and you touch the stove. Well you're really not going to touch it after you do that.

Points out one advantage of being a first-gen student.

Uses an analogy to underscore doing things "on your own."

Brandon Hernandez: I believe my dad was fifteen when he first came to the United States, but he stayed in California and that's where he, you know, did the typical work, he worked on farms and stuff like that. He told me how he used to pick lettuce. My name's Brandon Hernandez. I'm studying political science and economics here at The Ohio State University.

My dad works for the city of Hamilton, he works in waste-water treatment, and my mom is a quality control specialist at a Tyson food factory. Both of my parents never finished high school, but they've always strongly emphasized and pushed for education because they believe education is kind of like a tool for success and it opens up so many doors and gives you so many opportunities that it's just necessary to have in today's day and age.

You know, I usually don't get like stressed out over things, but the whole aspect of the finances has taken a little bit of its toll, because I know at the end of the day it's an investment, like you're investing in your future. And as long as you find the career path that you know you'll make money, I mean it'll be worth it. But just seeing all those big numbers... I would say I went through a mini panic attack. If it wasn't for one of my high school teachers, whose name was Mr. Stebbins, he really helped me out throughout the process because I was really worried once I saw, you know, I didn't get a full ride.

And you know, growing up and things like that, you're predicting your path and you're like, "All right, I'm going to do this, this and that, and it's just all going to work out." And then adulthood and reality hits you and you're just like, "Well, okay, that didn't work out... how am I going to go about this and solve it?" And I was really worried for a time in my senior year, like that was like the main thing occupying my mind, and I would say I kind of lost sleep sometimes about it, just thinking about it.

But Mr. Stebbins reassured me, you know: "Don't worry about it *too* much. If you let it consume you, you're going to start slacking

Host chooses to have second guest introduce himself directly to audience.

Tells something about his background and upbringing.

Subject of college costs comes up again, something on the minds of many students.

Shift to second-person ("And you know") helps connect with his audience.

Advice helps him get beyond "lost sleep."

on your sleep, which will impact your grades, which will impact all that." And he just said, "It's going to be a domino effect. It's going to affect you that way, so what you need to do is, you need to relax, don't be afraid too much about loans and the huge sums that there are, just, you go out there, you prove to them through your effort and your grades and all that that you belong here, and eventually you'll be able to pay it off."

Colin Flanagan: One more thing I want to add: I think a lot of people come in being a first-generation student and they're really afraid because they don't know what to expect. But there's a certain comfortableness in the chaos of it. Because it's just . . . you don't know what to expect. And so, with that, there's no expectations. And I think that's a lot better than having expectations not being met.

First guest sums up the message he wants to leave listeners with.

Jack Long: *The Third Chair* is produced and written by *Lantern* reporters and myself. We're published by *The Lantern* at The Ohio State University. Special thanks to Brandon Hernandez and Colin Flanagan. You can find other great podcasts from *The Lantern* on thelantern.com.

Host returns to close the session, thank his guests, and note the podcast website.

You can listen to the full podcast at letstalklibrary.com.

Credits

Photographs

CHAPTER 28: **P. 538 (TOP):** Marilyn Moller; **(CENTER):** Photo 12/Alamy Stock Photo; **P. 541:** D'Action Images/Shutterstock.

CHAPTER 29: **P. 553:** public domain; **P. 555:** beej christie karpen; **P. 558:** Courtesy of Elijah Kahlenberg.

CHAPTER 30: **P. 567:** Barry Blitt from February 19, 2024, *New Yorker*. A.I. Einstein.

CHAPTER 31: **PP. 584–87:** Courtesy of Trey Connelly; **P. 587 (BOTTOM):** HollyHarry/Shutterstock; **P. 588:** AlexLMX/Shutterstock; **P. 589:** Trey Connelly; **P. 590 (TOP):** Courtesy of Jack Long; **(BOTTOM):** Courtesy of Colin Flanagan; **P. 592:** Courtesy of Brandon Hernandez.

Text and illustrations

FRONTMATTER AND PART OPENERS: All collages of *Birdsong* by Stephen Doyle.

CHAPTER 9: **GABRIELA MORO:** "Minority Students Clubs: Segregation or Integration?" Originally published in *Fresh Writing: An Interactive Archive of Exemplary First-Year Writing Projects*, Vol. 16. Reprinted by permission of the University of Notre Dame College of Arts and Letters. **GAIL O. MELLOW:** Excerpt from "The Biggest Misconception about Today's College Students." From *The New York Times*, August 28, 2017. © 2017 The New York Times Company. All rights reserved. Used under license. **JUNE JORDAN:** "Nobody Mean More to Me Than You and the Future Life of Willie Jordan" from *On Call: Political Essays*, South End Press, 1985. Copyright 2017, 2022 June Jordan Literary Estate. Reprinted with the permission of the June M. Jordan Literary Estate. www. junejordan.com.

CHAPTER 11: **RAINESFORD STAUFFER:** "I Learned in College That Admission Has Always Been for Sale." From *The New York Times*, March 13, 2019. © 2019 The New York Times Company. All rights reserved. Used under license. **JULIA LATRICE JOHNSON:** "Can Money Buy Almost Anything?" by Julia Latrice Johnson. Reprinted with permission of the author. **TAYLOR JORDAN:** Summary of "I Learned in College that Admission Has Always Been for Sale" by Taylor Jordan. Reprinted with permission of the author.

CHAPTER 12: **SAM FORMAN:** Excerpts from "The Future of Food Production." Originally published in Andrea Lunsford, *Everyone's an Author,* First Edition (W. W. Norton, 2011). Reused with permission of the author. **RESHMA SAUJANI:** Excerpt from *Girls Who Code 2017 Annual Report.* Used by permission of Girls Who Code. **MAJA PAWINSKA SIMS:** Excerpts from "2019 Trust Barometer: Employers Emerge as Most Trusted Institution," *Holmes Report*, January 21, 2019. Used by permission of PRovoke Media. **JEAN M. TWENGE:** Adapted from iGEN by Jean M. Twenge, Ph.D. Copyright © 2017 by Jean M. Twenge, Ph.D. Reprinted with the permission of Atria Books, a division of Simon & Schuster, Inc. All rights reserved.

CHAPTER 13: MELISSA HICKS: Excerpts from "The High Price of Butter." Used by permission of the author. **LYNDA BARRY:** "The Sanctuary of School" and "I'm Home!" written and illustrated by Lynda Barry. Originally published in *The New York Times*, January 5, 1992. Copyright © 1992 by Lynda Barry. All rights reserved. Used courtesy of Darhansoff & Verrill Literary Agents. **YAZMIN CARBAJAL:** "Living the Narrative" by Yazmin Carbajal. Reprinted by permission.

CHAPTER 14: AUDREY ASHDOWN: "There's a New Girl in Town—and She's Still Here!" by Audrey Ashdown. Reprinted by permission of the author.

CHAPTER 19: BEN HEALY: Republished with permission of The Atlantic Monthly Group, LLC, from "Hell Is Other People's Vacations," Ben Healy, *The Atlantic Monthly*, June 2019; © 2019 The Atlantic Monthly Group, LLC; permission conveyed through Copyright Clearance Center. Courtesy of Atlantic Media.

CHAPTER 23: ELI VALE: "The Causes of Burnout in San Antonio Nurses—and Some Possible Solutions" by Eli Vale. Reprinted with permission of the author.

CHAPTER 25: JIMMY SANTIAGO BACA: "I Am Offering This Poem" by Jimmy Santiago Baca, from *Immigrants in Our Own Land*, copyright ©1979 by Jimmy Santiago Baca. Reprinted by permission of New Directions Publishing Corp. **CAITLIN FLANAGAN:** Republished with permission of The Atlantic Monthly Group, LLC, from "The Glory of Oprah," Caitlin Flanagan, *The Atlantic Monthly*, October 2011; © 2011 The Atlantic Monthly Group, LLC; permission conveyed through Copyright Clearance Center. Courtesy of Atlantic Media.

CHAPTER 26: BAMBOO: Lyrics reprinted by permission of Bamboo from "Mama Africa Remix."

CHAPTER 28: BAR GRAPH: From "AI and Human Enhancement: Americans' Openness Is Tempered by a Range of Concerns." Pew Research Center, Washington, D.C. (2021). www.pewresearch.org/internet/2022/03/17/ai-and-human-enhancement-americans-openness-is-tempered-by-a-range-of-concerns/ps_2022-03-17_ai-he_00-01/. **LINE GRAPH:** From "#BlackLivesMatter Surges on Twitter after George Floyd's Death," Fact Tank, Pew Research Center, Washington, D. C. (June 10, 2020). https://www.pewresearch.org/fact-tank/2020/06/10/blacklivesmatter-surges-on-twitter-after-george-floyds-death/. **PIE CHART:** From "One-in-Five Americans Now Listen to Audiobooks," Fact Tank, Pew Research Center, Washington, D. C. (September 25, 2019). https://www.pewresearch.org/fact-tank/2019/09/25/one-in-five-americans-now-listen-to-audiobooks/. **TABLE:** US College Degrees by Gender. Used by permission of Mark J. Perry.

CHAPTER 31: TREY CONNELLY: "Sign and Design: Modes of Instruction in Digital Games" by Trey Connelly. Reprinted by permission of the author. **JACK LONG, COLIN FLANAGAN & BRANDON HERNANDEZ:** Excerpts from Episode 4: "First Generations," *The Third Chair*, *The Lantern*, October 22, 2018. Reprinted by permission of the contributors.

Submitting Papers for Publication
by W. W. Norton & Company

We are interested in receiving writing from college students to consider including in our textbooks as examples of student writing. Please send this form with the work that you would like us to consider to Elizabeth Pieslor, Student Writing, W. W. Norton & Company, 500 Fifth Avenue, New York, NY 10110. For questions, or to submit electronically, email us at composition@wwnorton.com.

Text Submission Form

Student's name_____

School_____

Address_____

Department_____

Course_____

Writing assignment the text responds to_____

_____

_____

_____

_____

_____

Instructor's name_____

Please write a few sentences about what your primary purposes were for writing this text. Also, if you wish, tell us what you learned about writing from the experience of writing it.

_____

_____

_____

_____

_____

_____

_____

_____

CONTACT INFORMATION

Please provide the information below so that we can contact you if your work is selected for publication.

Name_____

Permanent address_____

Email_____

Phone_____

Author/Title Index

The title of this book, *Let's Talk*, assumes that communication is a two-way street: if someone is talking, somebody else is listening, and responding. It's an assumption that goes far beyond the title, however, and this is a book of many voices—and many, many perspectives. And that turns out to be a lot of folks, of widely varying backgrounds and convictions and from widely varying places around the country and beyond. In essays and epigraphs, examples and prompts for reflection, these voices provide information, inspiration, intriguing examples, and instructive viewpoints that enliven and enrich the book before you now. Here they are—collaborators and contributors all.

Glossary/Index

This glossary/index defines key terms and concepts and directs you to pages in the book where you can find specific information on these and other topics. Please note the words set in SMALL CAPITAL LETTERS are themselves defined in the glossary/index.

A

ABSTRACT, 459 A GENRE of writing that summarizes a book, an article, or a paper, usually in 100–200 words. An *informative abstract* summarizes a complete report; a briefer *descriptive abstract* works more as a teaser; a stand-alone *proposal abstract* (also called a PROJECT PROPOSAL) requests permission to conduct research, write on a topic, or present a report at a scholarly conference. Key Features: a SUMMARY of basic information • an objective description • brevity

ACADEMIC HABITS OF MIND, 70–78 Practices that are essential for success in college: being curious, creative, flexible, persistent, and open to new ideas; collaborating; taking responsibility and engaging with your work; reflecting on what you're learning; and not being afraid to fail.

Academic Search Complete, 325

acknowledging multiple viewpoints,
    20, 116–17
    in arguments, 141–43
    in reports, 209
acknowledging sources, 20, 366–76

ACTIVE VOICE When a VERB is in the active voice, the subject performs the action: *Gus tripped Bodie. See also* PASSIVE VOICE

***AD HOMINEM* ARGUMENT, 66** A logical FALLACY that attacks someone's character rather than addresses the issues. (*Ad hominem* is Latin for "to the man.")

AGRIS, 326
AI. *See* ARTIFICIAL INTELLIGENCE;
    GENERATIVE AI
AllSides.com, 34, 104

ALLUSION, 482 An indirect reference to something. Telling a friend that they look like they're carrying the weight of the world on their shoulders alludes to the Greek god Atlas, whom Zeus punished by making him support the heavens on his shoulders.

ALT TEXT, 544 A way of describing images in digital texts for readers who are visually impaired or whose computers do not display images.

ANALOGY, 486 A **STRATEGY** for **COMPARISON** by explaining something unfamiliar in terms of something that is more familiar. *See also* **FALSE ANALOGY**

ANALYSIS, 156–83 A **GENRE** of writing in which you look at what a text says and how it says it. Key Features: a **SUMMARY** of a text or other subject • attention to **CONTEXT** • a clear **INTERPRETATION** or judgment • reasonable support for your conclusions

ANECDOTE, 116, 270, 484 A brief **NARRATIVE** used to illustrate a point.

ANNOTATED BIBLIOGRAPHY, 341–45 A **GENRE** of writing that gives an overview of published research and scholarship on a topic. Each entry includes complete publication information for a source and a **SUMMARY**. A *descriptive annotation* summarizes the content of a source without commenting on its value; an *evaluative annotation* gives an opinion about the source along with a description of it. Key Features: complete bibliographic information • a brief **SUMMARY** or **DESCRIPTION** of the work • evaluative comments (for an evaluative bibliography) • some indication of how the source will inform your **RESEARCH**

ANNOTATING, 72, 84–87 The process of taking notes, underlining key information, and marking aspects of a text that strikes you as important while reading.

ANTECEDENT The **NOUN** or **PRONOUN** to which a pronoun refers: *Maya lost her wallet.*

APA STYLE, 429–75 A system of **DOCUMENTATION** used in the social sciences. APA stands for the American Psychological Association.

APPENDIX A section at the end of a written work for supplementary material that would be distracting in the main part of the text.

ARGUMENT, 43–69, 125–55 Any text that makes a **CLAIM** supported by **REASONS** and **EVIDENCE**. Also a **GENRE**. Key Features: an explicit **POSITION** • a response to what others have said • appropriate background information • a clear indication of why the topic matters • good **REASONS** and **EVIDENCE** • attention to more than one **POINT OF VIEW** • an authoritative **TONE** • an appeal to readers' values. *See also* **EVIDENCE; LOGICAL APPEALS**

ARTIFICIAL INTELLIGENCE (AI), 566–77 Software that is programmed to seem as though it can think, learn, and make decisions like humans. *See also* **CHATBOT, GENERATIVE AI**

ASSUMPTION, 134 A belief that is not stated explicitly which supports a **CLAIM**. If you claim that voting by mail increases voter turnout, the unstated assumption is that making it easier to vote encourages more people to do so.

ATTRIBUTION BIAS, 101 The tendency to think that our motivations for believing what we believe are objectively good while thinking that those who we disagree with have objectively wrong motivations.

AUDIENCE, 25–26 Those to whom a text is directed—the people who read, listen to, or view the text. Audience is a key part of any **RHETORICAL SITUATION**.

AUTHORITY, 85, 137–38 A person or text that is cited as support for an **ARGUMENT**. A structural engineer may be quoted as an authority on bridge construction, for example. Authority also refers to a quality conveyed by writers who are knowledgeable about their subjects.

B

BANDWAGON APPEAL, 66 A logical **FALLACY** that argues for thinking or acting in a certain way just because others do.

BEGGING THE QUESTION, 66 A logical **FALLACY** that argues in a circle, assuming as a given what the writer is trying to prove.

BLOCK QUOTATION, 356, 357 In a written work, long **QUOTATIONS** are indented and set without quotation marks: in **MLA STYLE**, set off text of more than four typed lines, indented five spaces (or one-half inch) from the left margin; in **APA STYLE**, set off quotes of forty or more words, indented five spaces (or one-half inch) from the left margin. *See also* **QUOTE**

proceeds in the other direction, from the end to the beginning.

CITATION, 353–65 In a text, the act of giving information from a source, for example, by **QUOTING, PARAPHRASING,** or **SUMMARIZING.** A citation and its corresponding parenthetical **DOCUMENTATION,** footnote, or endnote provide minimal information about the source; complete information appears in a list of **WORKS CITED** or **REFERENCES** at the end of the text.

CLAIM, 47–50, 115, 129–31 A statement of a belief or **POSITION.** In an **ARGUMENT,** a claim needs to be stated in a **THESIS** or clearly implied, and requires support by **REASONS** and **EVIDENCE.**

CLASSICAL ARGUMENT A system of **ARGUMENT** developed in Greece and Rome during the classical period. Key Features: an introduction that states the **CLAIM;** a body that includes background information, good **REASONS** and **EVIDENCE,** and attention to **COUNTERARGUMENTS;** and a **CONCLUSION.**

CLASSIFICATION, 52, 220–21 A **STRATEGY** that groups a number of items by their similarities (classifying cereal, bread, and rice as carbohydrates, for instance). Classification can serve as the organizing principle for a paragraph or whole text.

CLAUSE, 495–500 A group of words that consists of at least a **SUBJECT** and a **VERB;** a clause may be either **MAIN** or **SUBORDINATE.**

CLICKBAIT, 480 On the internet, headlines or links designed to get readers to read something or to increase page views.

CLUSTERING A process for **GENERATING IDEAS AND TEXT,** in which a writer visually connects thoughts by jotting them down and drawing lines between related items.

COLLABORATION, 42, 75, 560–65 From *co* ("with") + *labor*, collaboration most simply means to work (or labor) together to accomplish a task or goal. It's a method that allows most of the world's work to get done, and it works best through cooperation, mutual support, and respect.
adversarial, 562
dialogic, 562
hierarchical, 562
tips for collaborating, 563–65

COMMA SPLICE, 497 Two or more **MAIN CLAUSES** joined with only a comma: *I came, I saw, I conquered.*

COMMON GROUND, 9, 37–41, 141–43 Shared values. Writers build common ground with **AUDIENCES** by acknowledging their **POINTS**

D

DATA ANALYSIS A kind of **ANALYSIS** that looks for patterns in numbers or other data, sometimes in order to answer a stated or implied question.

DATABASES, 325–26 Digital collections of articles from journals, newspapers, and other periodicals. General databases cover a range of disciplines and topics; subject-specific databases focus on a single topic. Some databases are open-access; those that require a subscription and can usually be accessed through your campus library website.

DEFINITION, 53 A **STRATEGY** that says what something is. *Formal definitions* identify the category that something belongs to and tell what distinguishes it from other things in that category: A worm is an invertebrate (a category) with a long, rounded body and no appendages (distinguishing features). *Extended definitions* go into more detail: a paragraph or even an essay explaining why a character in a story is tragic. *Stipulative definitions* give a writer's own use of a term, one not

found in a dictionary. Definitions can serve as the organizing principle for a paragraph or whole text.

DESCRIPTION, 54 A **STRATEGY** that tells how something looks, sounds, smells, feels, or tastes. Effective description creates a clear **DOMINANT IMPRESSION** built from specific details. Description can be *objective, subjective,* or both. Description can serve as the organizing principle for a paragraph or whole text.

DESIGN, 526–36 The way a text is arranged and presented visually. Elements of design include **FONTS**, colors, visuals, **LAYOUT**, and white space.

DIALECTS, 513–20 Varieties of language that are spoken by people in a particular region, social class, or ethnic group.

DICTION, 506 Word choice.

DOCUMENTATION, 381–417, 432–58 Publication information about the sources cited in a text. **IN-TEXT DOCUMENTATION** usually appears in parentheses at the point where it's cited or in an endnote or a footnote. Complete documentation usually appears as a list of **WORKS CITED** or **REFERENCES** at the end of the text. Documentation styles vary by discipline. *See also* **APA STYLE; MLA STYLE**

DOI, 440 A digital object identifier, a stable number identifying the location of a source accessed through a database.

DOMINANT IMPRESSION, 54 The overall effect created by specific details in a **DESCRIPTION**.

DRAFTING, 115–17 The process of putting words on paper or screen. Writers often write several drafts, **REVISING** each until they achieve their goal or reach a deadline.

E

echo chambers, 31

EDITED ACADEMIC ENGLISH The conventions of spelling, grammar, and punctuation that have traditionally been expected in academic discourse, which tends to be more formal than conversational English. These conventions vary from country to country and change over time. *Edited* refers to the care writers are expected to take in reviewing formal written work.

EDITING, 120–22 The process of fine-tuning a text—examining each word, phrase, sentence, and paragraph—to be sure that the text is correct and precise and says exactly what the writer intends. *See also* **DRAFTING; PROOFREADING; REVISING**

effect. *See* **CAUSE AND EFFECT**

EITHER-OR ARGUMENT, 66 A logical **FALLACY**, also known as a false dilemma, that oversimplifies to suggest that only two possible **POSITIONS** exist on a complex issue.

ELLIPSES, 358 Three spaced dots (. . .) that indicate an omission or a pause.

EMOTIONAL APPEALS, 58–59, 140–41, 486–88 Ways of appealing to an **AUDIENCE**'s emotions, values, and beliefs by arousing specific feelings—compassion, sympathy, anger, and so on. *See also* **ETHICAL APPEALS; LOGICAL APPEALS**

EMPATHY, 9, 34–35 The ability to be aware of and understand what someone else is feeling.

endings. *See* **CONCLUSION**
endnotes, 387, 460
engaging with others, 29–42
    demonstrate respect, 35–37
    find common ground, 37–41
    invite response, 41–42
    meet people different from you, 31–34
    practice empathy, 34–35
    say what you think as a response to what others say, 11
engaging with ideas, 72
Englishes, 512–13
ERIC, 326

ETHICAL APPEALS, 59–60, 137–38 Ways that authors establish **CREDIBILITY** and **AUTHORITY** to persuade an **AUDIENCE** to trust their **ARGUMENTS**—by showing that they know what they're talking about (by citing **TRUSTWORTHY SOURCES**), demonstrating that they're fair (by representing opposing views accurately and even-handedly), and establishing **COMMON GROUND**. *See*

also **EMOTIONAL APPEALS; LOGICAL APPEALS**

ETHICS, 14–15 Principles that guide our conduct and choices in life.
    using sources ethically, 366–76
    using visuals ethically, 540–45

ETHOS From the Greek word for "character," ethos reflects the values and ideals of a person or culture. *See* **ETHICAL APPEALS**

evaluating sources, 331–40
    reading critically, 338–39
    for reliability, 334–38
    for usefulness, 332–34

EVALUATION A **GENRE** of writing that makes a judgment about something—a source, poem, film, restaurant, whatever—based on certain **CRITERIA**. Key Features: a description of the subject • clearly defined **CRITERIA** • knowledgeable discussion of the subject • a balanced and fair assessment
    evaluating sources, 331–34

EVIDENCE, 51–58, 133–37 The data you present to support a **CLAIM**. Such data may include statistics, calculations, **EXAMPLES, ANECDOTES, QUOTATIONS**, case studies, or anything else that will convince your readers that your reasons are compelling. Evidence should be *sufficient* (enough to show that the reasons have merit) and *relevant* (appropriate to the argument you're making).

EXAMPLES, 55, 484–85 Specific things that illustrate and support a point. An essay on the best films directed by Spike Lee would cite specific examples from his work that support the **ARGUMENT** that they are indeed the "best."

EXPLETIVES Words such as *it* and *there* used to introduce information provided later in a sentence: *It was difficult to drive on the icy road. There is plenty of food in the refrigerator.*

F

Facebook

FACT-CHECKING, 102–5, 334–35 The process of verifying the accuracy of **FACTS** and **CLAIMS** presented in a piece of writing, a speech, or elsewhere—by **READING LATERALLY, TRIANGULATING,** or consulting fact-checking sites.

FactCheck.org,

FACTS, 61–62, 99–100 Information that can be backed up and verified by reliable evidence.

FAIR USE, 368, 372, 543 A legal principle permitting the use of copyrighted material without permission for specific educational, scholarly, or research purposes.

FAKE NEWS, 98–100, 318 False or misleading information designed and written to look like authentic news. *See also* **MISINFORMATION**

FALLACY Faulty reasoning that can mislead an **AUDIENCE**. Fallacies include **AD HOMINEM, BANDWAGON APPEAL, BEGGING THE QUESTION, EITHER-OR ARGUMENT, FALSE ANALOGY, FAULTY CAUSALITY** (also called *post hoc, ergo propter hoc*), **HASTY GENERALIZATION,** and **SLIPPERY SLOPE.**

FALSE ANALOGY A **FALLACY** comparing things that resemble each other but are not alike in the most important respects.

FAULTY CAUSALITY, 66–67 A **FALLACY,** also called *post hoc, ergo propter hoc* (Latin for "after this, therefore because of this"), that mistakenly assumes the first of two events causes the second.

FIELD RESEARCH, 326–30 Collecting first-hand data through observation, interviews, conversation, and surveys.

    conversations, 327–28
    interviews, 327
    observations, 328–29
    surveys, 329–30

first person. *See* **POINT OF VIEW**

FLASHBACK, 250 In **NARRATIVE,** an interruption of the main story in order to show an incident that occurred at an earlier time.

FLASH-FORWARD In **NARRATIVE,** an interruption of the main story in order to show an incident that will occur in the future.

flexibility, 73–74

FONTS, 530 Typefaces: Calibri, Times Roman, **Comic Sans,** etc.
    APA style, 459
    MLA style, 417

FORMAL WRITING Writing intended to be evaluated by someone such as an instructor or read by an audience expecting academic or businesslike argument and presentation. Formal writing should be carefully revised, edited, and proofread. *See also* **INFORMAL WRITING**

FRAGMENT A group of words that is capitalized and punctuated as a sentence but is not one, either because it lacks a subject, a **VERB,** or both, or because it begins with a word that makes it a **SUBORDINATE CLAUSE.**

FREEWRITING, 113 A process for **GENERATING IDEAS AND TEXT** by writing continuously for several minutes without pausing to read what has been written.

FUSED SENTENCE Two or more **MAIN CLAUSES** with no punctuation between them: *I came I saw I conquered.*

G

gender-neutral pronouns, 122, 358, 363–64. *See also* **SINGULAR *THEY***

GENERATING IDEAS AND TEXT, 112–13 Activities for exploring and developing a topic by **BRAINSTORMING, CLUSTERING, FREEWRITING, LOOPING, OUTLINING,** and **QUESTIONING.**

GENERATIVE AI, 570–71 A kind of artificial intelligence that can generate text, images, video, audio, and code based on patterns learned from vast amounts of existing data. *See also* **ARTIFICIAL INTELLIGENCE, CHATBOT**
    documenting APA style, 436, 458
    documenting MLA style, 387, 417

GENERATIVE AI, 570–71 A kind of artificial intelligence that can generate text, images, video, audio, and code based on patterns learned from vast amounts of existing data. *See also* **ARTIFICIAL INTELLIGENCE, CHATBOT**

GENRE, 26, 112, 309 A way of classifying things. The genres this book is concerned with are kinds of writing that writers can use to accomplish a certain goal and to reach a particular **AUDIENCE.** As such, they have well-established features that help guide writers, but they are flexible and change over time, and can be adapted by writers to address their own **RHETORICAL SITUATIONS.** Genres covered in this book include **ANALYSES, ANNOTATED BIBLIOGRAPHIES, ARGUMENTS, NARRATIVES, REPORTS, SUMMARY/RESPONSE** essays, and **VISUAL ANALYSES.**

GERUND A **VERB** form ending in -*ing* that functions as a **NOUN:** *Swimming improves muscle tone and circulation.*

getting and keeping attention, 478–91
    analogies, 486
    conclusions, 117, 490
    contrast, 488
    emotional appeals, 486–88
    examples, 484–85
    opening sentences, 116, 119, 482–84
    reiteration, 488–89
    silence, 489
    stories, 484
    titles, 481–82
getting to know people different from you, 31–34
Google News, 321
Google Scholar, 319
government sites, 320

GRAPH, 539 A diagram showing a relationship between two or more things. *Bar graphs* are useful for comparing quantitative data; *line graphs* are useful for showing changes in data over time.

H

HASHTAG A metadata tag created by placing a number sign (#) in front of a word or unspaced phrase (for example,

#BlackLivesMatter), used in social media to mark posts by **KEYWORD** or theme and make them searchable by these tags. Also used to add commentary in **SOCIAL MEDIA**.

HASTY GENERALIZATION, 67 The **FALLACY** that reaches a conclusion based on insufficient or inappropriately qualified **EVIDENCE**.

HYPOTHESIS, 312 A supposition that's a starting point for exploration and investigation.

I

I / WE Personal pronouns that we all use frequently. Be aware, though, that they can send signals: sometimes using *I* suggests a focus on yourself, perhaps to the exclusion of others, whereas using *we* can send the opposite message, that you're one of many—or that you're including your **AUDIENCE** in what you say.

IMRAD, 221 A **GENRE** of writing scientific reports organized in four parts: an introduction (asks a question), methods (tells about experiments), results (states findings), and discussion (tries to make sense of findings in light of what was already known).

INDEFINITE PRONOUN Words such as *all, anyone, anything, everyone, everything, few, many, nobody, nothing, one, some*, and *something* that do not refer to a specific person or thing.

INFINITIVE *To* plus the base form of the **VERB**: *to come, to go*. An infinitive can function as a **NOUN** (*He likes to run first thing in the morning*); an adjective (*She needs a campaign to run*); or an adverb (*He registered to run in the marathon*).

INFORMAL WRITING Writing not intended to be evaluated, sometimes not even to be read by others. Informal writing is produced primarily to explore ideas or to communicate casually with friends and acquaintances. *See also* **FORMAL WRITING**

A process for investigating a topic by posing questions, searching for multiple answers, and keeping an open mind.

INTERPRETATION An explanation or the process of making sense of something or explaining what you think it means. Interpretation is one goal of writing a **LITERARY ANALYSIS** or rhetorical analysis.

IN-TEXT DOCUMENTATION Brief **DOCUMENTATION** in a text that tells readers what the writer has taken from a source and where in the source they found that information.

introductions. *See* **OPENING**

INVITATIONAL ARGUMENT A system of **ARGUMENT** that aims for understanding and shared goals by listening carefully to everyone concerned. Invitational arguments introduce the issue, present all **PERSPECTIVES** on it fairly, identify any commonalities among the **PERSPECTIVES**, and conclude by seeking a resolution that is agreeable to all.

IRONY The use of words and phrases that convey a message that is opposite the literal meaning of the words, often for humorous effect, as in calling cafeteria food "delicious" when it is actually almost inedible.

J

journals, for reflecting, 75–76
JSTOR, 326

K

KAIROS An ancient Greek term meaning "the opportune moment"—for example, to look for just the right moment to make a particular **ARGU-MENT**, appeal to a particular **AUDI-ENCE**, and so on.

KEYWORD, 113, 319, 325 A term that a researcher inputs when searching for information in library catalogs, databases, and elsewhere on the internet.
    about current issues, 113
    in the library catalog, 325
    on the web, 319–20

L

LAB REPORT A **GENRE** of writing that covers the process of conducting an experiment. Key Features: **TITLE** • **ABSTRACT** • **PURPOSE** • methods • results and discussion • **REFERENCES** • **APPENDIX** • appropriate format

languages and dialects, using
    rhetorically, 511–23
    Englishes, 512–13
    providing translation, 521–22

quoting directly, 520
standardized English, 512
thinking about rhetorically,
    523

LATERAL READING, 336–37 A process for evaluating a source by checking what others say about it. *See also* **VERTI-CAL READING**

LAYOUT, 531–33 The way text is arranged on a page or screen—for example, in paragraphs, in lists, on charts, with headings, and so on.

Lexis/Nexis Academic, 326
libraries
    databases, 325–26
    library catalogs, 325
    using your college library, 324–26
Library of Congress Subject Headings, 325
lies, 98–100
line graphs, 221, 539
Listen First Project, 10–11
listening, 4–11
    to multiple views, 10–11, 29–31
    rhetorical listening, 7–9
    tips on being a good listener, 9
    and writing, 11

LITERACY NARRATIVE, 237–39 A **GENRE** of writing that tells about a writer's experience learning to read or write or do something else. Key Features: a well-told story • a first-hand account • an indication of the narrative's significance

LITERARY ANALYSIS A **GENRE** of writing that examines a literary text and argues for a particular i**NTERPRE-TATION** of the text. Key Features: arguable **THESIS** • careful attention to the text's language • attention to patterns or themes • a clear **INTERPRETATION** • **MLA STYLE**

LITERATURE REVIEW, 255 A **GENRE** of writing that surveys and synthesizes the prior research on a topic. In the sciences, a literature review is a required part of the introduction to an **IMRAD** report. Key Features: a survey of relevant research on the topic • an objective summary of the literature • an evaluation of the literature • an organization appropriate to your assignment and **PURPOSE** • **DOCUMENTATION**

LIVE CAPTIONS The real-time transcription of speech in a live video, displayed on a screen.

Living Room Conversations, 33

LOGICAL APPEALS, 60–65, 133–37 Ways of using **REASONS** and **EVIDENCE** to persuade an audience to accept a **CLAIM**. *See also* **EMOTIONAL APPEALS; ETHICAL APPEALS**

    experiments, 64
    facts, statistics, 61
    interviews, conversations, 62

    observations, 62
    personal experience, 65
    surveys, questionnaires 61
    testimony, 62–23
    visuals, 64–5

logos. *See* **LOGICAL APPEALS**

LOOPING A process for **GENERAT-ING IDEAS AND TEXT** by writing about a topic quickly for several minutes and then writing a one-sentence summary of the most important or interesting idea, which becomes the beginning of another round of writing and summarizing—and repeating this process until you find a tentative topic for writing.

M

MAIN CLAUSE, 495, 497–501 A **CLAUSE**, containing a subject and a **VERB**, that can stand alone as a sentence: *She sang. The world-famous soprano sang several arias.*

maps, 163, 215, 538
    documenting APA style, 456
    documenting MLA style, 415

means of persuasion, 58–65

MEDIA, 26–27, 187, 240, 280–81 The means of delivering messages—for example, digital, oral, print, and social. The singular of *media* is "medium."

NOUN A word that refers to a person, place, animal, thing, or idea (*a justice, Ruth Bader Ginsburg, a forest, Mexico, a tree frog, a notebook, democracy*).

O

OP-ED A short opinion piece in a newspaper written by a writer who is not a member of that paper's editorial board. Traditionally op-eds have been printed on the page opposite a newspaper's official editorial page, hence the name op-ed.

OPENING, 116, 482–84 How a text begins. Some ways of beginning an essay: with a dramatic or deceptively simple statement, with something others have said about your topic, with a provocative question or a startling **CLAIM**, or with an **ANECDOTE**.

OUTLINING, 243 A process for **GEN-ERATING IDEAS AND TEXT** or for examining a text. An *informal outline* simply lists ideas and then numbers them in the order that they will appear; a *working outline* distinguishes support from main ideas by indenting the former; a *formal outline* is arranged as a series of headings and indented subheadings, each on a separate line, with letters and numbers indicating relative levels of importance.

P

PARALLELISM Writing technique that puts similar items into the same grammatical structure. For example, every item on a to-do list might begin with a command: *clean, wash, iron*; or a discussion of favorite hobbies might name each as a **GERUND**: *running, playing basketball, writing poetry.*

PARAPHRASE, 361–62 To reword a text in about the same number of words but without using the word order or sentence structure of the original. Paraphrasing is generally called for when you want to include the details of a passage but do not need to **QUOTE** it word for word. Paraphrasing a source in academic writing requires **DOCU-MENTATION**. *See also* **PATCHWRITING**

parenthetical documentation. *See* **IN-TEXT DOCUMENTATION**

PASSIVE VOICE When a **VERB** is in the passive voice, the subject is acted upon: *Bodi was tripped by Gus*. *See also* **ACTIVE VOICE**

PATCHWRITING, 373–75 **PARA-PHRASES** that lean too heavily on the words or sentence structure of the original, adding or deleting some words, replacing words with **SYNONYMS**, altering the syntax slightly—in other words, not restating the passage in fresh language and structure.

pathos. *See* **EMOTIONAL APPEALS**

PERIODIC SENTENCE, 501–3 A sentence that delays the main idea, expressed in a **MAIN CLAUSE**, until after details given in phrases and

PREPOSITION A word or group of words that tells about the relationship of a **NOUN** or a **PRONOUN** to another word in the sentence. Some common prepositions are *after, at, before, behind, between, by, for, from, in, of, on, to, under, until, with,* and *without.*

PRIMARY SOURCE, 315 A source such as a literary work, historical document, work of art, or performance that a researcher examines first-hand. Primary sources also include experiments and **FIELD RESEARCH**. In writing about the Revolutionary War, a researcher would probably consider the Declaration of Independence a primary source, whereas a textbook's analysis of the document would be a **SECONDARY SOURCE**.

PROBLEM/SOLUTION A **STRATEGY** for supporting an **ARGUMENT** by framing it as a way of solving a problem, or of introducing a change of some kind. If you can first convince readers that there's a problem (and that it matters), they'll be more likely to read on to hear about how it can be solved. This is also a classic storytelling technique: setting up a conflict that needs to be resolved is a good way of getting and keeping an **AUDIENCE**'s attention.

PROCESS ANALYSIS A kind of **ANALYSIS** that closely examines the steps of a process.

PROFILE A **REPORT** about people, places, events, institutions, or other things. Key Features: a first-hand account • detailed information about the subject • an interesting angle

PROJECT PROPOSAL A **GENRE** of writing that describes the **PURPOSE** of a research project, the steps of the project, and its goal. Key Features: a discussion of the topic • an indication of a specific focus • the reason you're interested in the topic • a research plan • a schedule

PRONOUN A word that takes the place of a **NOUN** or functions the way a **NOUN** does.

PRONOUN REFERENCE The way in which a **PRONOUN** indicates its **ANTECEDENT**. Pronoun reference must be clear and unambiguous in order to avoid confusing readers.

PROOFREADING, 123 The process that follows **REVISING** for checking surface issues: spelling, punctuation, **TRANSITIONS**, headings, **FONTS**. *See also* **EDITING; REVISING**

PROPER NOUN A **NOUN** that names a specific person, place, or thing (*Steph Curry, Brazil, Google*).

PROPOSAL A **GENRE** that argues for a solution to a problem or suggests some kind of action. Key Features: a precise description of the problem • a clear and compelling solution • **EVIDENCE** that your solution will address the problem • acknowledgment of other possible solutions • a statement of what your proposal will accomplish. *See also* **PROJECT PROPOSAL**

ProQuest Central, 326
PsychINFO, 326
punctuating quotations, 358–60

PURPOSE, 24–25 In writing, your goal: to explore a topic, to express an opinion, to entertain, to report information, to persuade, and so on. Purpose is one element of the **RHETORICAL SITUATION**.

Q

QUALIFY, 115, 130 To limit a **CLAIM**—saying, for example, that most people like cake rather than people like cake. Words like *frequently, often, generally,* or *sometimes* can help you qualify what you claim—and make it something you'll be able to support.

QUALITATIVE DATA, 157 Data that describes something in unquantifiable terms—for example, with **DESCRIPTION, ANECDOTES,** and other nonquantitative information, including that found through **FIELD RESEARCH**.

QUANTITATIVE DATA, 96, 157, 539 Data that can be presented in concrete, measurable ways, such as with statistics or measurements.

QUESTIONING, 113 A process of **GENERATING IDEAS AND TEXT** about a topic—asking, for example, What? Who? When? Where? How? and Why?
    for generating ideas, 113
    interviewing, 327
    as a reading strategy, 87–88, 90
    with a research question, 311–12
    starting with questions, 111,
        307–12

questionnaires, 61

QUOTE, 355–60 To cite someone else's words exactly as they were said or written. Quotation is most effective when the wording is worth repeating or makes a point so well that no rewording will do it justice or when you want to cite someone's exact words. Quotations in academic writing need to be acknowledged with **DOCUMENTATION**.

R

REASONS, 133–34 Support for a **CLAIM** or a **POSITION**. A reason, in turn, requires its own support.

REFERENCES, 437–58 The list of sources at the end of a text prepared in **APA STYLE**.

REFERENCE WORKS, 324–25 Encyclopedias, handbooks, atlases, biographical dictionaries, almanacs, and other such sources that provide overviews of a topic.

REFLECT, 75–76, 123–24 To explore a topic thoughtfully. Reflections are a **GENRE** of writing. Key Features: a topic that you think about • specific details • a speculative **TONE**

REGISTER, 186, 284 Ways that language is used in particular situations, like the *informal register* we speak with friends, the *technical register* used by engineers, or the language used in certain sports (think *pick-and-roll* and *layup* in basketball).

For sentences with more than a single MAIN CLAUSE, *see* COMPOUND SENTENCE; COMPOUND-COMPLEX SENTENCE; COMPLEX SENTENCE.

SINGULAR *THEY* The use of *they*, *them*, and *their* to refer to a person whose gender is unknown or not relevant to the context. *Everyone locks their bikes.* It is also used to refer to a person who is nonbinary, trans, or gender-nonconforming: *Jess asked for skim milk in their latte.*

SLIPPERY SLOPE, 67 A FALLACY that asserts, without EVIDENCE, that one event will lead to a series of other events that will end in disaster.

SPATIAL ORGANIZATION A way of ordering a text that mirrors the physical arrangement of the subject—for instance, from top to bottom, left to right, outside to inside.

STANCE, 17–18, 26, 138–40 A writer's attitude toward the subject—for example, reasonable, neutral, angry, curious. Stance is conveyed through TONE and word choice.

STANDARDIZED ENGLISH, 512 The variety of English taught in schools and generally expected in most academic and professional contexts. There is now a growing recognition in the United States of the validity of other, broader ways of speaking and writing.

STASIS THEORY, 50–51 A simple system for identifying the crux of an ARGUMENT—what's at stake in it—by asking four questions: (1) What are the facts? (2) How can the issue be defined? (3) How much does it matter, and why? (4) What actions should be taken as a result?

ASSUMPTIONS that aren't explicitly stated but that also support the claim; further evidence or backing for those underlying assumptions; and a **CONCLUSION**.

TRANSITIONS, 497 Words that help to connect sentences and paragraphs and to guide readers through a text. Transitions can signal **COMPARISONS** (*also, similarly, likewise, in the same way*); **CONTRASTS** (*but, instead, although, however, nonetheless*); **EXAMPLES** (*for instance, in fact, such as*); place or position (*above, beyond, near, elsewhere*); sequence (*finally, next, again, also*); **SUMMARIES** or **CONCLUSIONS** (*on the whole, as we have seen, in brief*); time (*at first, meanwhile, so far, later*); and more.

in multimodal presentations, 289–90

translating, 521–23

TRIANGULATE, 102–3, 337–38 To confirm the accuracy of **CLAIMS** or data by consulting three sources.

TROLL, 105 On the internet, someone who says something provocative or disruptive.

TRUSTWORTHY, 138–40 Reliable, dependable.

Twitter. See X

V

VANTAGE POINT The physical position from which a writer describes something—a stationary vantage point, describing the object from one angle only; or a moving vantage point, describing it from various points.

VERB A word that expresses an action (*dance, talk*) or a state of being (*be, seem*). A verb is an essential element of a sentence or a **CLAUSE**. Verbs have four forms: base form (*smile*), past tense (*smiled*), past participle (*smiled*), and present participle (*smiling*). *See also* **ACTIVE VOICE; PASSIVE VOICE**

signal verbs, 364

VERTICAL READING, 336 A way of **EVALUATING** a text's reliability by focusing on the text itself and how well it supports its **ARGUMENT**. *See also* **LATERAL READING**

videos, 321
documenting APA style, 454
documenting MLA style, 412–16
fact-checking, 105–7

VISUAL ANALYSIS, 93–95, 164–65 A **GENRE** of writing that examines an image, video, or some other visual text and how it communicates its message to an **AUDIENCE**. Key Features: a description of the visual • some contextual

personal communication and
social media, 411
websites, 408–10
writing in multiple modes. *See*
MULTIMODAL WRITING

WRITING PROCESSES, 110–24
Activities that writers engage in
when producing a text: considering
our **RHETORICAL SITUATION**, **GEN-
ERATING IDEAS AND TEXT** and doing
RESEARCH, coming up with a **THESIS**
and **EVIDENCE**, considering multiple
PERSPECTIVES, **DRAFTING**, getting
response and revising, thinking about
DESIGN, **EDITING**, and **PROOFREADING**.

X

X [formerly *Twitter*]
with alt text, 544
documenting APA style, 457
documenting MLA style, 411
as a source, 321

MLA DOCUMENTATION DIRECTORY